NO QUARTER

KILL ALL MASTERS

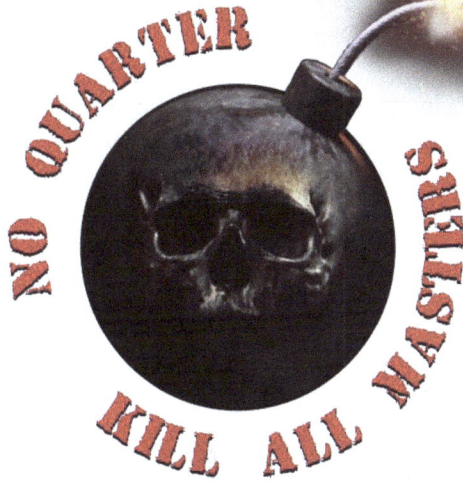

BY ETHAN DETTENMAIER

VENGER I-III-MMI

First edition. January 2021

SPECIAL THANKS to my friend Derek Mazer, who worked around the clock to turn this 600+ page adventure into a workable format for publication. Without him, it wouldn't have happened!

Art Design / Layout: Derek Mazer
Logo Design: Ray Ollaway,
Logo / Art File Work: Martina Matteucci

Get into the action and get the audio book
noquarterkillallmasters.com
@noquarter_killallmasters

DEDICATION

For my family, my mother Robin, my wife Lota, and my daughter Shawn, who remain…the REAL adventure.

And for revolutionaries everywhere.

ON THE BOOK...

"Highly atmospheric and frightening...the perfect combination of almost too frightening to read and yet, compelling enough to make you read on."

-Director Stephen Surjik
(The Witcher, The Umbrella Academy, The Punisher)

"The writing is extraordinary! The action sequences are particularly vivid...as if recalled from memory or his REAL experiences!"

-Former Warner Bros Studios Senior Vice President Bill Daly
(Batman, Harry Potter and Lethal Weapon)

"Sinister, hugely compelling... a mesmerizing and captivating tale well told, this book is above and beyond the genre. Read it."

-Oscar nominated FX Ace Harrison Ellenshaw (Star Wars, Tron, The Empire Strikes Back, Ghost)

"Thought provoking, clearly a metaphor for today's society and gives the reader a lot to think about!"

-Shawn D. (Tales From The Script)

"No Quarter is an adventure that instantly grabs you and never let's go... makes you feel like you're taken along on a life and death journey from another era."

-Writer/Producer Mark Amato
(SNL, Mutant X, Tripping The Rift)

"Ethan Dettenmaier is a force of nature ... at once dramatic, expansive, witty, and one hell of a storyteller. He will surprise and delight you. It's a great ride."

-Lou Waters, CNN Alumnus

"Epic! My kind of book! Saved from a cannibal cooking pot by pirates, taken aboard a three decked, fighting ship flying the skull and cross bones, oh yeah...I'm in for this!

-Oscar Nominated, BAFTA Award winning Production
Designer William Sandell (Hocus Pocus, Robocop)

"Masterful...Mystery, adventure, horror and suspense ALL have a new name – Ethan Dettenmaier! Be forewarned as this heart-in-your-throat story unfolds: Mr. Dettenmaier truly gives the reader 'no quarter."

-Mark Marshall
(Post-Production Supervisor on Harry Potter, Assassins)

" Radio host, showbiz empresario, relentless caregiver for the less fortunate. And now he roars out of the gate as a novelist with No Quarter! Kill All Masters! The day Ethan decides to become a TV writer, I'm cooked."

-Writer/Producer Dan Truly (Law and Order SVU)

"No Quarter was great fun to listen to. If you are a pop culture fan, you'll love this audio book with great narration and sound effects that transports you to a mystical, magical world filled with cannibals, pirates and action."

-Adrian Paul (Highlander, Arrow, Dark Shadows)

Reader Beware!
Hold tight, weapons ready and let God be your agent…

…for all hell is about to break loose!!!

…There's no going back now!'

COMBAT-ACTION-REPORTS/SURVIVAL STORIES

I.
LUCIFER AND THE MEN WITH PAINTED FACES
'New Orleans attacked, shadows emerge from the bayou swamps to kill, and a prisoner with a Bengal scar on his face, escapes…'

II.
THE HAMMER OF DOOM
'A shipwreck with survivors trapped inside, cannibals in war-paint and the skull and crossbones…'

III.
WORLD ON THE EDGE OF THE HORIZON
'Privateers, the gun tigers and weapons of war!'

IV.
THE WITCH'S DEN
'The death card, refined killers, an act of fate…'

V.
UNDER THE BLACK FLAG
'The Articles of war, Lucifer's skull, samurai soldiers in the fog…and the battle of Japan!'

VI.
LET GOD BE YOUR AGENT
'Storming the decks, killing slave traders, the plank, plague doctors in the shadows and… the battle of Black Thorn Prison!'

VII.
THE ISLE OF THE DEAD
'Zombies, the Dark Coast, Christmas and…Jesus the Killer!

VIII.
THE STEEL MACHINE WILL EAT YOU
'Invasion, the sacking of Panama, battle in the graveyard and the Jesuits.'

'They come out of darkness….

Sometimes with thunder, sometimes with lightning….

Their presence means…death!'

--Survivor's statement.
Raven Point Asylum 1738

NO QUARTER! KILL ALL MASTERS!

I.

LUCIFER....AND THE MEN WITH PAINTED FACES!

NEW ORLEANS. HURRICANE SEASON….

Lightning struck the bayou horizon, behind the hangman's noose, where death was waiting. Darkness gripped the town. The streets had been cleared, only the shadows moved in the wind, when the lightning flashed – making the place feel eerie and alive, creating a strange sense of dread.

The prison stocks were empty…

The graves, on the edge of the parade ground were open and waiting for their tenants…

The Grim Reaper was close --and the noose, this symbol of death that slowly rocked in the wind, waiting to snap the neck of its next victim was a wicked reminder of the work that was done here. The French marines, armed and in battle dress, stood guard under the lantern light –one, rolling a cigarette as his eyes cautiously shifted on the skyline around him.

On the edge of town, a proclamation read:

BEWARE

BE INSIDE BEFORE DARK

AND

BOLT YOUR DOORS

The town square was vacant, with nothing more than dust blowing through it as the odd shutter banged in the wind. Even the local tavern, the surrounding structures and cottages were dark with only the occasional lantern –or candle--to mark the window or signpost....

Jack-Karr waited in the shadows of his dark prison cell, locked in shackles.

--The Prison Master was afraid of him.

--The guards…were afraid of him.

--THE TOWN…was afraid of him.

Even the blacksmith was afraid to pass by his cell and yet there he waited, concealed in darkness until the occasional flash of lightning lit up his cell to remind them all of his presence.

--The 'claw mark' scar from a Bengal attack in Siam that had carved up the right side of his face, twisted with his sinister smile as he looked up at the lightning, marking him with the visual pattern of extreme wickedness and violence.

He remained defiant –the idea of asking for mercy was offensive. He just waited –and waited-- in his dark cell for 'the horseman of death' in silence, until the church bells struck midnight, that was the signal --the day of his execution had arrived.

There was the sound of bending steel as the massive cell door was opened up and the French marines came –in platoon strength--to collect him. They looked into that dark corner of the cell and ordered him to stand.

--There was no movement. No sign of life in the shadows.

They asked again and then looked to each other to see which one had the guts to approach him and drag him to his feet. Then, suddenly, with another flash of lightning, he moved --quick –sudden, and with force that made the French marines move back and then, like the devil moving out of the shadows to collect a debt, he slowly stepped into the lantern light…

A hammer slammed down and removed the hundred-pound prison ball from his ankle and then he was grabbed and forced outside as if the guards wanted to get this lynching over with, quick.

There he stood in the damp air, surrounded by a low-lying fog. He could see the gallows ahead of him. The others who had been hanged throughout the previous day, still marked their place at the end of a rope —Barclay, Claws, Tax-Lassiter, and the Mohawk native, Tier, with his faded warpaint on his face and shoulders, their bodies decaying in the wind and labeled with crude signs around the neck that marked them --PIRATE!

Jack-Karr was pushed forward for his turn, keeping his eyes fixed on the hangman's platform, the executioner, and the dead bodies that rocked in the wind, as he moved closer, closer, and closer to this instrument of his death.

The executioner swallowed in nervous fashion. There was something about this he didn't like.

"Your neck won't snap right away," said a marine whose fear of this man had built up into bitter resentment. "Your death will be a long one."

ON THE EDGE OF TOWN…

Something started moving through the darkness, closing in on the town --like monsters that would slowly emerge from the shadows…

These 'shadows' rose up from the swamps and the bayou. Some of these shadows came out of the tide or through the graveyard on the edge of town. They moved with a stealth like rhythm and a hint of violence, the moonlight reflecting off the steel of their weapons –the axe, the blade, and the gun.

Some of them wore black armor and weapons from Japan, some carried the weapons and the mark of the Aztec. Others wore colorful war paint on their faces like the scalp-happy natives of the Americas –and some were scarred –by the saber and the whip-- with dark skin and white skulls painted

on their faces –which was the only thing that was visible in this darkness –
except, when the lightning flashed, revealing the shoulders and size of
these walking 'shadows' to be massive.

--Death had arrived!

This evil element started to move out of the swamps and forward into
the town, from shadow to shadow, through the headstones and crypts of the
old cemetery, past the old windmill and up the dark streets…

It was the blind beggar tapping his stick on the bricks as he moved up
Royal Street, who was suddenly gripped with a sense of impending doom.
He could feel something closing in on him and went into a near panic as he
spit out his warning "The Venger! The Venger is here!" He exhaled; arms
extended as if to grab for help in the dark. "My God! They're coming!
Death…" He shivered, "Death is coming!"

As the 'shadows' moved forward, picking up speed and tempo, the
sense of dread seemed to mount. One man –a night watchman--stepped
around the corner and suddenly stopped as a shadow slowly rolled over
him. There was the sudden sound of steel cutting through the air, striking
bone --as this man fell into the dirt in two pieces.

At the guard house, a suspicious sentry, feeling evil closing in around
him, raised a lantern. His hand trembled with a touch of fear "Who-who
goes th-there?" As he moved his lantern for a better look, the wind moved
the landscape around him, and the shadows seemed to shift —as if
something alive was out there. Then, out of the darkness, there was a
'whoooomp' and a 'craaaaaaaccccccck' as a tomahawk was planted into the
crown of his skull. He gasped, held his balance, and blinked in silence with
blood dripping down his temple as if he didn't realize yet that he was now
–DEAD! Then there was the quick sound of sawing and he collapsed in the
dirt with the top of his head –his scalp—removed.

–Bolas cut through the darkness and quickly wrapped the neck of a
second sentry –snapping his neck—and dropping him to his knees. A third
civic guard was pulled back into the darkness as steel came down on him

–lantern light reflected off a massive, curved Arabian blade as it removed his shoulder and almost cut this man in two. The bolas were removed from the dead sentry's neck as the 'shadows' moved up and over him....

Suddenly, light illuminated the street! A curious little girl cracked her front door, "Mama, what's out there?" she said peering out into the darkness with curiosity. In a panic, the mother jumped in front of her and slammed the door closed –bringing back the darkness-- as she blew out her candle in the windowsill. She slapped her hand over her daughter's mouth, shivering in fear --hoping to keep her absolutely silent. There was only the whisper-- "Don't move!" followed by a quiet prayer as she begged God to protect her in the hope that these shadows would not come through the walls and doors and kill them....

The rest of the townspeople remained inside and out of sight. Doors bolted! Lights out!

The marine at the edge of the parade ground turned, just as something closed in on him cutting his vision to black...

AT THE GALLOWS....

With a flash of lightning the noose was placed around Jack-Karr's neck. The Commandant looked at his victim "It's five
minutes past midnight...and I'm going to enjoy watching your bones snap!" He smiled and dropped the blindfold, unwilling to even allow this simple courtesy...

"Rest easy." Karr said slowly in a low tone, "You're in the final thirty seconds of your life." The Commandant suddenly took an uneasy step back as the lightning illuminated some of Karr's more sinister features, making his eyes appear lifeless --and-- solid black. "Lucifer is coming for you!'

Then –as if on cue-- the crickets stopped, and things went silent. A strange sort of unnatural silence. A forced silence and a silence that in its own, evil way, seemed unnerving.

Suddenly, out of the darkness a black helmet and the metal face of a monster, closed in and a samurai blade swung up in the lightning, struck out of the shadows and then disappeared again as the last sentry fell to the ground --his head rolled a few meters up the dirt road.

The Commandant turned as he was suddenly surrounded, jumped, and pulled back into the darkness --the sound of steel closed in on him, like a cyclone of metal working its way through bone, quickly taking him apart!

--His screams could he heard as they echoed through every dark corner of town....

Moments later, the cellblock, prison barracks and guard house were put to the torch. The flames being the only signature left as these shadows withdrew back into the darkness...

At dawn, the next day, as the smoke cleared, what was left of the commandant was found hanging from his own gallows, his damaged body gently blowing in the wind –the town buildings, still burning all around him and a sign around his neck that read....

'KILL ALL MASTERS!'

The Devil now owned New Orleans.

II

THE HAMMER OF DOOM!

I was nothing more than a schoolteacher, of mathematics, in route to the Americas when the storm overtook our ship and tipped my world on its axis…

Waves rolled over our decks --Men were washed overboard into the darkness.

There was a wicked --satanic—monster-like sound from the hull as it was crushed. A hole was suddenly ripped into our super-structure as a wall of water came up from below, trapping passengers –and crew--in the darkness of the lower decks and forcing the ship off-balance….

I made it to the top deck as lightning struck the stern. Waves hit me and forced me across the planks, and I slammed into the railing where I 'splashed over' the side and suddenly dropped into the ocean below….

--It was dark and silent as I was dragged down into the depts.

Suddenly, with the force of the tide I splashed to the surface, gasping. I looked to see the ship as she capsized –LOST! She spent the next several hours upside down, rolling on the ocean in darkness, hull to the sky. I could hear faint screaming from passengers trapped inside with no way out….

This dark part of the ocean was to be my grave –I lost my strength to tread water—and my world went black…

I woke up in the tide at dawn and found that I --and few passengers-- were washed up on the beach of an unknown, tropical land….

I was hurt, exhausted and broken but I was also alive. The heat was stifling, the air thick and wet and the sounds of the wilderness –tropical birds as such—were constant, close and all around.

The first few days on this island were spent making inventory of what supplies had made it through the storm with us and washed ashore --and trying to find a source of fresh water. Heat and exposure began to take its toll with the sun beating down on us day after day in crushing fashion but, something far more dangerous and wicked surrounded us --and I was unaware that our camp was encircled by death.

It wasn't long before some of our survivors went missing in the night. The cause was at first a mystery. Why would someone wander off or disappear and not come back? And why would different people disappear at different times? This was a far more sinister situation than we came to suspect and one night we bolted awake to the sound of panicked screaming. Hysteria had raised the alarm in our camp…

We cleared out of our fabricated shelters and surroundings and saw nothing in the darkness but… our ship's Quartermaster was now gone! Something terrible had taken him! There was a sudden scream, and I turned with my torch just as two other members of our crew were dragged into the jungle wilderness…

-Cannibals!

And they viewed us from the edge of the jungle with a keen eye.

One by one, even though we moved the camp, more of my fellow survivors began to disappear over the next few nights. If we posted a guard, he was taken. Those who tried to move up the beach and relocate were never heard from again and soon….it was just me.

I made an effort to find a quiet place to hide but, an island is, just that, an island and my options were to become more and more limited. The beach was now out of the question and as days passed, I moved from place to place and eventually found what I believed to be safe refuge, under a waterfall but one morning when I went to drink, I was suddenly grabbed by my scalp and overwhelmed by painted natives. I was forced to a wooden spit and carried into the jungle by runners....

--I slammed into trees and bounced through the wilderness as they moved and was only able to see the ground. Human bones –former survivors like myself-- mapped the trail...

I was brought to a clearing enclosed by some huts built on stilts and lit by torches with a sharp bamboo fence, decorated with painted human skulls around it...

--Native drums beat a tempo that mixed with some wicked chanting in the crowd. Here, I was to meet my end, tied to a stake post with a fire being built at my feet....

I, of course, was no hero so I began the only rational course of action and started to beg for my life! I had read at university about some island natives and how they hoped to absorb the qualities of their victims through consumption. Bravery was not a quality of mine –panic and cowardice were much more natural, and these became the character traits I offered up...

Through their grey war paint, they only smiled at my performance and seemed to laugh as they brought the torches forward. "I'm a cursed individual!" I shouted, "You should reconsider this? I'm a coward! I promise you; I WILL taste terrible! You'll hate the way I taste! I'll make you sick! Save yourself the trouble!" Sheer terror turned my rant into a scream as they loaded me over their cooking pit. "I recommend a balanced diet of fruit and veeeeeeeeegtables." I screamed and tried to blow the torches out as they passed by me to ignite the kindling....

It got hot fast, this barbeque was well underway when the natives suddenly became still, very still almost frozen in place --and suspicious of something. It became dead silent, and no one moved. They looked almost nervous as they peered into the edge of the jungle. Something seemed to frighten them...

Then –without warning—the jungle seemed to open up and be pushed apart as men emerged from the wilderness...

These men appeared fierce, large, and strong, tan and weathered as if they had spent many a week outside in the tropical sun. Their eyes were fixed and still. They were armed with fighting blades and pistols. One, at the front appeared to resemble the natives of North America, his face painted with a sinister black across the eyes and a black handprint on his shoulder. He carried a large gun but was outfitted with an axe and knife in his sash.   Others were covered – like Moors—armed with large swords that curved. Another man wore a Chinese hat –like that of bamboo or straw --that covered his whole face with shade and made his features mysterious. His swords were on his back and of a type I had never seen. Many were of a European look, with tan, white faces, although the fashion of their clothes and weapons escaped me…

Upon facing off with the natives, these men remained still, their movement limited to that of drawing breath...

-What was to happen next? I feared for sudden violence but my position, on a spit, with a growing fire below me, made my future bleak in any event.

Suddenly one of these men stepped forward and spoke in their native language. His voice had scratch and directness to it. He also used a set of hand signals to add to his message and then, he waited for a reply…

After a moment of silence, he was met with words from one of my captors to which all the other natives laughed...

An imposing man, decked with a scar down his cheek moved towards me. His voice low, his speech deliberate and his words unknown to me but my hosts understood him all too well, as their expressions changed and many of them became fixed with a smile.   For these men were all acquainted and although I did not know the terms of their relationship, it was clear, they spoke from a position of mutual respect.

This man continued to move forward, motioned to me again and the natives cut me from the spit and removed me from this funeral pyre and not a moment too soon for my clothes were smoking. I fell to the ground – saved!

The other men then parted and supplies, in barrels and crates were marched up and turned over to my captors. Crates were opened to reveal muskets, tools and bottles marked by the St. Jacques Rum Company…

Another one of these strangers stepped forward to me. He pulled my head up by my scalp and checked my eyes. My vision had cleared, and he gave a nod back to the more senior man on the team and then helped me to my feet. "You're alive son." He suddenly said…

I managed to overcome my surprise to speak "You-you speak English?"

He gave me a cunning smile and slowly said, "I do lad!" He identified himself as a Mister Rush, pulled a large knife and began to cut my bonds.

"Are-are they going to kill me?" I asked.

"Not if we have anything to say about it. We just included you in the bargain."

"Bargain?"

He smiled again, "We traded for ya."

"The supplies" I looked to the weapons, "Is that all I'm worth?'

I was given a very direct reply, "Today…. Yes." he stood back up, "Tomorrow, maybe more, if you prove yourself." He turned and was pitched a jug which he in turn gave to me. It was water. Thank God.

The man at the jungle's edge who opened up the conversation proved to be the master and commander of this expedition and he continued to speak with a mixture of signs and this 'island tongue' and moments later my cannibal hosts and my rescuers forced me on a walk-through the jungle trees to a lagoon….

Once there, these men began digging. The digging continued for many hours until the shovel blades struck iron. Giant iron boxes were then unearthed and heaved from the sand –and there were many of them. The locks were opened to have their inventories checked, –GOLD, the likes of which I had never seen. Spanish and French coins! Jewelry! Gold plates! Even a crown and I had come to realize the compact that was in place here. These iron crates which contained items useless to the island's cannibal inhabitants were buried here for them to safeguard with their 'dining habits' in exchange for the supply and inventory just delivered. Guns, powder, food stuffs, canvas. And it was my good fortune to be part of the bargain.

The natives gave aid, and this cargo was hauled to the beach as the sun began to set and under the glow of torches and lantern light, it was loaded on to several long boats.

I was told to 'climb aboard' with a forceful push in my back. So, I did. I moved through the tide and with some assistance and laughter, was pulled onboard the launch. I was rescued…but….by who?

The ship in the bay got larger, much larger as the rhythm of the rowing pulled us closer. It was a very imposing ship, marked with the word VENGER across the back. I was unaware of the class system applied to ships but would come to know this one as a man-o-war. It was painted in dark colors, had three-gun decks, and looked like she had been under repair from previous battle damage….

Then, my fears became confirmed, and I suddenly became gripped with a new wave of tension for there, under the glow the deck torches waved a massive black flag marked with a SKULL AND CROSS BONES!

"Pirates!" I swallowed. What was to become of me now?

I could hear deck commands from above as our long boat pulled aside. Cargo nets, ropes and pulleys raised the chests to the decks as we made the climb up… and I managed –in my damaged, nervous state—to work the ropes and ladder enough to get to the top deck. This was a place of industry; every man struck a formidable character and clearly had both job and intentions before him.

I was given a hand and pulled over the railing by a massive man with dark skin and what appeared to be African paint on his face and shoulders in the pattern of a human skull. This made him appear fearsome and even taller than he was. He immediately pushed me aside and began to help the next man up….

From here, I looked around and made my observation of men of mixed cultures working in common purpose. There were men in armor from the Japans, equipped with swords known only in that region and others with the look of The Orient. There were Europeans, men scarred –some badly—

and a man with dented chest armor marked with the code of arms of the King of Spain and those who spoke in Portuguese.

There were natives from the Americas in the north and south –I could recognize from books. Some from New Spain, called Az-tec-as marked with tattoos…

I heard some French spoken on deck and a word or two of Spanish but the commands were given in English and, without question, obeyed.

A man stood on the top deck by the steering --awash with shadows and moving orange lantern light, his arms crossed and eyes fixed. He observed the work and said not a word….

This man –it would become known-- was Captain Essex. The master and commander of The Venger.

The chests of gold were lowered through a large opening in the top deck by cargo nets to the decks below along with supplies of coconuts, tropical birds, and barrels of what appeared to be fresh water also taken from this native island and brought aboard by what was called a foraging party.

From there a hand reached out in the confusion, gripped my shoulder and turned me 'round "Who might you be?'

"My-my name is Donovan Reed sir."

"Donovan Reed….an Irishmen?"

"On my mother's side."

"I see." He hissed, "Well…. nobody's perfect!" He yelled to man on the deck behind him, "Mister Archer, take this man to the sick bay. Let's see if Mister Donovan Reed here can survive the night."

"Yes sir." Under the observation of Mister Archer, and with the assistance of lantern light, I climbed below deck, banged my head on the low cross beam and was directed to keep moving forward. I walked past the cannon, housed in place, and stamped with names like 'Sudden Death' or 'Inferno' and 'Storm of Steel' to the sick bay or what is known as an infirmary or hospital.

"Doctor Johannis?" Archer called out ahead as we walked under a medical sign, "We have a new tenant for ya'."

There, the doctor turned and asked me to sit. He held a candle close to my eyes to see if I could focus and I was asked a series of questions. "Are you unbalanced? Dizzy?"

I shook my head no...

"Do you have fluctuation of temperature?" He checked me for fever, I was also checked for malaria, scurvy, and yellow fever --which would be a death warrant.

My answers proved that I was fit to be aboard and as my evaluation continued, I could see another man, in English clothes but with some native attire around the wrists and neck, like 'tiger teeth' of Africa. He also wore face paint which resembled the wilds of Africa –or so my books would have me believe. This man was assisting this doctor in the mixing of herbs and medicines...

My eyes became fixed on the animal teeth, fashioned into the necklace around his neck and his other curious beads and charms.

"That is Mister Jega Jopo, from the prairies of West Africa," the doctor said, "Since I can see you're curious." He checked my wounds and cuts and prepared to stich it up the gash on my temple.

"I am. I know very little of Africa or, medicine for that matter."

"Mister Jopo is a doctor in his homeland, unique in design and master of untraditional medicines and medicinal means." He looked back upon him and then to me, "He is what the frontier troops refer to as a 'witch doctor' but, I assure you, he is quite qualified." He began to work the stitches through my skin....

"And your name, sir?"

"Doctor Johannis at your service," he continued stitching, "I spent a decade suppressing the natives of that region. And although quite prejudice to Mister Jopo's ways at first, I soon came to realize that not everything that can help a man is to be found in books."

Mister Jopo handed Doctor Johannis a steaming mug who in turn handed it to me. "You may rest here for now," he pointed to a hammock, "Until you get your strength back!" He turned, "Mister Gordon..."

"Yes Doctor?" A voice rang back from down the deck.

"Bread and bacon for our guest here, if you please...."

"Yes sir."

"How-how can I thank you?"

"You'll earn your keep until we make port. From there, your life will be your own."

"You mean, I'd be free to go my own way?"

"Of course ---we're not white slavers here, son." He motioned to the mug, "Drink up!"

I did as commanded but struggled not to expel it from my mouth for it was not tea, but a medicinal drink made from plants and herbs that tasted like water from a pig trough but before too much suffering, my world then went dark....

III

WORLD ON THE EDGE OF THE HORIZON

The next morning, I woke up and as my eyes slowly began to focus and I tried to place my surroundings. I felt the wind blow off the waves and in through the infirmary window. I heard deck commands in the distance and then the good doctor's voice from behind me….

"Congratulations."

"Sir?"

"You survived the night." The doctor said as he came around and checked my eyes again, "How do you feel?"

"Better."

"You need more water in your system but, I can assign you some light duty."

The kindness I had received made me question what I had witnessed the night before when coming aboard --that being the black flag. So, I summoned my courage to make an inquiry, "If-if I ma-may ask, what manner of his ship is this?"

"You're a guest aboard The Venger sir."

"Of that I am aware, but-but my curiosity begs the question, what…manner…of ship….is this?"

He stopped his actions and looked at me. "Why, we're privateers, son."

My fears were confirmed, "Pirates!" I exhaled through my now chattering teeth.

The doctor snapped-- "Silence man!" He fixed his eyes on me. "A word of advice, lad, do not, EVER, use that word again in the presence of myself or these men here" He motioned to the ship and his surroundings.

"Sir?"

"It's bad language!" He saw my confusion, "It's an insult sir, a slur. Like thief or beggar and we are none of these things! We are our own commercial enterprise and thus deserving of respect. Call a man here pirate and you're likely to find yourself skinned alive."

"I'm sorry sir, I meant no offense."

He eased his tone and added a touch of understanding for my ignorance, "Of course you didn't lad." He paused and looked out the open window to the ocean, then back to me. "You're a victim of the English newspapers." He exhaled, "They print terrible stories 'bout us –some of them true by God-- but I can assure you, here, aboard The Venger, a strict code of conduct applies." He turned to me, "Understand?"

I gave a nod. Not that I fully understood but I knew to keep my place.

"Now, report to Mister Harrow on deck... off you go."

I passed by the 'witch doctor' grinding plants and herbs and made my exit of the sick bay where I banged my head yet again on a low cross beam. I moved forward, there were two or three blue and yellow tropical birds, flying from rafter to rafter on this deck and I passed the working men and gun crews to the steps aloft for my climb up to the top deck...

Once on deck, I stopped a man, a former French Marine named Abel, "Excuse me sir, can you direct me to Mister Harrow?"

He pointed to a man giving commands towards the front of the ship and I made my way forward. His name, I would come to know was actually 'Arrow' but, many of the nationalities onboard would pronounce the A with an H, hence the name 'Harrow' applied...

He stood at the prow –or the forward most part of the ship's bow-- supervising the repair of the ship's figurehead, a massive wooden sculpture of a wicked Grim Reaper, complete with a skull, black hood, and scythe. Very ominous in its look. It was apparently damaged in an engagement – or battle-- before my arrival here, the carpenters had chiseled it back together and a man was being lowered in a rope harness, over the side to apply new black paint....

"Mister Harrow, sir?"

He turned to face me…

"I was told to report to you for light duty sir."

He was a weathered man, weathered and scared by the elements -like the sun and what appeared to be a life of combat. He appeared to size me up and although I wasn't embraced, I felt nothing negative in his glance either. He gave a nod "Mister Arson…"

The shadow of Mister Arson rolled over me. A man with broad shoulders and a saber scar down the right side of his face from the forehead—over his eye—and down his cheek. His original dark features had been lightened by the sun. He was a deck officer or bosun of sorts with a commanding presence….

Harrow continued his command in a mild yet direct tone. "Teach this man 'the trade' if you please."

"Aye." and Arson put me to work. I had limited education in seamanship, none in fact, so my duties pertained to some rudimentary tasks. I swabbed the decks all day and as I did, I watched the carpenters work and the iron workers work with fire. I watched the various ranks – like armorers-- apply their trade. My trade was to be the bucket and brush –under the hot sun--for many days to come. But I remained grateful for my life and began my education with observance of the talk and method around me….

I had heard that before my arrival aboard this ship, The Venger ran a French blockade, was damaged, then stormed New Orleans and escaped after a twelve-hour cannon fight and bombardment exchange. They had used the island of my hosts to hide their 'wealth' for safe keeping among the cannibals, then set sail into a firestorm where combat and weather favored the ship with an eventual victory. They then came back, to fetch their treasure –and myself, fortunate for me.

At sunset, a bell rang out and the action on deck began to shift. I was told to stand up and ordered below deck to the galley with the others to que up for what was an evening meal….

In the galley, wild boar hung from the rafters to be carved. In an open pen next to the kitchen boar and other animals, like ox, were kept alive until the day of their purpose was at hand. There were stoves baking bread, a distillery for water, coconuts, and other island-based food stuffs such as bananas and mangos. I was encouraged by Mister Hobby --who ran the galley-- to take pieces of lime -for I was told it would help fight scurvy....

The meal was served on a square plate; hence the term 'square meal' and I was grateful for what I was given. I took a seat at a table, a table not braced by the floor but fashioned with iron and chains to hang from the ceiling. This allowed the table to move with the ship and sea providing minimal disruption to our meal –and I would learn that they could be raised and pinned to the ceiling during a fight, so the gun crews could operate without interference.

I looked around this deck, under the lantern light and I could see ronin soldiers from the Japans, cut and scared –above them were rope nets with Japanese armor and weapons—there were also tattooed natives from the Americas and the Pacific Islands who mixed in conversation with the European crew members as if there was little difference between them....

Just as I took my place at a table, a line of Moors, in tight head wraps and carrying giant, curved swords walked past me on their way to evening prayer....

--This was a very curious place.

Although new to my surroundings, I was not alienated by the other men though, conversation was not, at first, forthcoming. At my table were men from the African Coast, Mister Calixto a former police constable from Lisbon, Mister Blythe, and Mister Duncan-Howe, two former members of the Royal Navy who were kind enough to assist me in interpretation and understanding. A man named Lo Tan –Mister Lo-- who wore robes, a bamboo hat of the orient and carried a weapon on his back fashioned from three equal sized metal rods, each roughly a meter and a half in length and each attached to the other by chain. It was a weapon of his design made not by the metal workers here on the ship but back in his home province of Shanghai. Details like this, I was not to learn until much later in our voyage, at this time, he was nothing more than a man from Asia with a unique killing machine on his back.

We were also joined by a man from the Highlands of Scotland – evidenced by his kilt-- named Blackwood, a Mister Wicks, Kannon Saint James, a Mister Irons –a former cavalry officer and another called Rajiv, a gunner with tan skin, a Sikh headdress, and a baldric across each shoulder, like and 'X' across his body, who hailed from an island off India called Ceylon. He needed more room than the rest of us because of his big shoulders. Men on the gun decks seemed to grow stronger than other members of the crew perhaps because the art of iron and cannon required the development of great strength.

"What do we call you?" Mister Blythe asked….

"Reed, Donovan Reed."

"Red?" Rajiv said with a look of curiosity.

The gent across from me, Wicks, shook his head no, "R-e-e-d."

"Red." Rajiv now believed he got my name right even though it was still just as wrong as the first time.

"I'm Blythe," he motioned to the man at his left, "This is Mister Duncan-Howe, formerly of his majesty's navy."

I gave a nod, hello.

"Mister Calixto from Portugal," he pointed to the next table, in close proximity with our own, "Mister Jupiter, Mister Obal and Dakar, all from The Africas. Rajiv, Therrinfall, Ward, Dutch because he's well --Dutch, Mister Foxx, Merciless, there sharpening his cutlass, Mister Cage, Jack-Karr, Whitney, Mister Fury, Dax-Varro asleep there in his hammock and" he pointed, "That's Mister Lo, with the metal pipes at his back."

I tried to remember and apply my manners with a hello to each one of the men. Lo didn't look away from his meal. Rajiv seemed more curious for some reason.

At that point, a giant mass of a man walked by, shaved at the head but part of his skull was covered in metal plating screwed into the bone. It was a horrifying sight to me.

"Same award-winning service is waiting for you lad, should you require it." Blythe smiled as he caught my curiosity….

"I'm sorry I don't understand."

"Take a musket ball to the head like Cheval there, and with any luck, Doctor Johannis can carve it out of your skull and patch you up with a little help from our metal workers."

"He survived a musket shot to the head?"

"He did."

"Don't acquire the practice son," Wicks added, "He's the only man I've ever seen survive something like that."

"He did, in fact, survive," continued Blythe "Though he cannot remember his name most days or, tell you where he is but..." he added almost as an afterthought. "Still good in a fight though, I suppose."

Rajiv mumbled a few words in his native language of Tamil and mixed in some broken English "Your trade?"

Mister Blyth leaned forward to me, "He wants to know your trade. Fencing? Gunnery?"

I confessed my profession to be a teacher. There was some slight amusement and Blythe laughed but no real disdain and –as it would turn out—there was some appreciation for intelligence with these men.

"A teacher? Teach! You teach sounds?" Rajiv asked.

My mind quickly worked towards an understanding of his question, "Yes. I can write and read sounds. Also...numbers, language and, scripture."

"Scripture?" Mister Jupiter, one of the African asked.

"Christian teachings, like Sunday services."

"Sunday? Serv--" Rajiv stopped. He had a deep rumbling laugh and his English, though serviceable, was stifled by accent. "I am not Christian, I am Sikh. We have the same God, Christian but, Sikh make better use of our Sundays!" The men chuckled and I tried to let out a smile as if to agree – for now.

"I'd be happy to have you take part in our Sunday service Mister Reed." Mister Rush, the de facto minister –who also served as a cook during the morning watch-- walked by with a pitcher of grog checking on the crew as he often did at this time. "Despite what Mister Rajiv –and these heathens here think…" he said with a touch of comedy, "Sundays are best spent in the company of the almighty wouldn't you agree?"

I gave a nod.

"And Mister Jaffar and our Moor brothers, there" He pointed to a group of Moors down in the shadows of the far deck, "--will be happy to cover your duties until such time as the service has ended."

I was grateful to hear this and eager to attend for I needed something holy in my life at this time and I did owe Mister Rush in part for my salvation from the cannibals....

"Unless cannon balls start to slam into our side," said Mister Blythe, "In which case, church is cancelled, and we immediately get down to the business of killin'!"

I forced a nervous swallow. The prospect of a sudden cannon ball attack made me insecure, a thought I obviously betrayed to my new comrades here....

"You have nothing to fear here Mister Reed," said Mister Lynch, smoking his long-stemmed pipe from the table next to us. A sophisticated man by appearance, he was an African gentleman, with tattoos on his cheeks, who spoke with a refined British accent and wore proper, clean European clothes by design. He looked up from a book of illustrations he was drawing. "Do as you are told, do it to the best of your ability and you'll be home, safe and sound in no time at all." It was strange to see an African man speak with a fine British accent but here he was, commanding my attention with his presence. "Above all…" he continued, "Listen –and learn."

And this I agreed to do….

The crew's kindness towards me was not sympathy, I would come to learn that on this ship, trade and the success of these men was better if all men, including myself were given aid and put into a position to succeed. This is not how it was back home in school. There, I found myself put down by my colleagues who looked for favoritism and rewards for themselves. Here --as I would come to know-- the culture was different. Here, the better these men did collectively, the better they did financially. I was not to be degraded. I was to be built up into a man worth having around and these were the men that would do it.

After our food, pipes and tobacco were passed around and we climbed the deck to find ourselves under the stars. Coffee and rum were passed between us although some of our Asian compatriots preferred tea or a drink, they made themselves in barrels below deck called sake. It was like wine but, they cooked it on a small deck fire and drank it warm –Kannon Saint James stood with them, drinking it and they seemed to talk in a mix of English and the samurai language.

I was also surprised by sudden music, a melody provided by my shipmates who until now had hid this talent. A cello in the hands of Mister Sterling, some violins and something called a sitar from India in the hands of Mister Adai-Rajal applied the harmony along with some percussion instruments from Africa that mixed in to create a mood upon deck that was quite lively....

I had to almost check my surroundings. I looked to the sky to realize that this was the same moon above me that shined over London. What were they doing back home? School? Dinner parties? The opera? But I was now a world away, down from this same moon, on the decks of this ship --a different world all together...

In days to come, my skin became dark like the other men from the long hours working on deck. My hair was also cooked to a gold color –like many of us-- and although I was sore, and my muscles worn out I could feel myself getting stronger....

I learned the task of the 'powder monkey' hauling barrels of gun powder from below deck to the guns. This ship was of such scope and size that it had three-gun decks –all had to be supplied and it was the job of the 'least among us' to get it done. Powder supplies were to be stocked each day in anticipation of a fight or sudden gunnery practice. Merciless told me that one 'powder monkey' blew himself up doing this daily chore, a few weeks back so, I was most careful in this task –and-- I must admit, I did find the work and science of the gun crews fascinating. They had a language all their own and applied a good use of arithmetic and mathematical calculation. These men, many from East India --called The Bengals or, The Gun Tigers-- all had an ordnance manual of sorts memorized in their head for the handling of these weapons, fuses and more. I watched Mister Kipling, Mister Saxon, Mister Tane –from the South Pacific-- and a man called 'Java' captain their guns --and gun crews— shouting commands, under the watchful eye of Mister Rajiv--and they put precision and speed into their gunnery practice…

They also had a variety of both cannon and shot. Some shot was designed to ignite enemy shipping like a fire ball. Some just to shatter, blast and turn the deck to lethal splinters. Some shot was a chain to cut the masts of a target or, metal nails. They even had a shell known as a 'smoker' which omitted a chemical smoke when fired but it was considered 'none too useful' for it made raiding an enemy deck most unpleasant and even induced sickness on the boarding party….

On deck these men manned mortars and rail guns. They were often part of the boarding party when the need presented itself and were skilled in the use of grenades –a metal ball with five scoops of gunpower in it and a five second wick fuse, to explode and blow shrapnel into its victims.

I continued to meet men of many nations, the crew being as large as it was. At home, this mix of cultures would be met with disdain. Most men with dark skin would not be allowed in my local public house but here – that nonsense didn't apply. I was now being educated in the ways and means of men of this nature. For example, when I betrayed a look of curiosity at some of the painted Africans working on board, I was told by Mister Blythe, "Kick the animosity from your head boy."

"No animosity, I was just curious--"

He did not stop in his work but continued, "Of what?"

"Men of different cultures, I doubt the King of Spain would dine with his subjects from Panama." I looked across the deck at American natives and former conquistadors working a like, "Yet, here they all are, working together."

"The King may not find it proper but, out here, what would you rather be? Alive and wealthy? Or proper amongst your own class and kind?" He worked closer to me, "Give me the best men, any day in a fight, when my life is at stake... save your class system, we have no use for that nonsense here!" And like that, he was down the deck, attending to his other tasks.

I admit, as a man interested in education, and curious of the wonders of the world, I found the culture here fascinating....

The natives from Spanish America or the Southern Americas –that served on the crew-- were of a smaller stature but very quick in their movement and they never seemed to get tired. Known onboard as the jaguars, this was the one contingent un-interested in gold, their allotment – or service-- was exchanged for weapons, gun powder and various food stuffs, much of which they would run home to their native tribes. Gold to them made no sense and they laughed at many of us who fancied it. They also preferred to work –and fight –without shoes. Many of them had tattoos like the hide –and print—of the Jaguar across their shoulders and chest. Some wore rings in their noses and ears with long hair. Some had shaved down the middle of their scalp, different from our samurai friends onboard, who tied their hair back or our 'Hu-ron' allies who also wore their hair long but some in their ranks shaved the sides of their scalp and applied war paint to their faces....

These men from Spanish America were fierce fighters but preferred the use of their own weapons –with the exception of the gun –which all aboard admired and used. Often, after their muskets were discharged, they would use axes or spears of their own making in battle. Some even had a hollow wooden pole –called a blow gun-- and they would blow a poisonous dart through it, deadly although it was seldom used. These native types –the Aztecs-- were friendly but preferred meals together as a group huddled on the floor, unlike the rest of us who took the meal with whatever company may be present.

At this time, I became aware that many of these men onboard had been prisoners. Some, like Mister Obal, were rescued from the water when The Venger was running down a slave ship and the master of that ship, tried to reduce the weight and increase speed, by throwing its cargo –the slaves-- overboard. The ploy didn't work. The slaves were picked up from the water by long boat, the ship overtaken with the remaining cargo liberated. Oddly enough, according to the story, none of the crew of that particular slave ship seemed to survive the raid. Apparently, they 'fought to the death' I was told with a smile, though that part of the story seems ripe with wit and sarcasm. Never-the-less, this was my introduction to the fighting term NO QUARTER. Meaning…No one will be allowed to live!

Other crewmen like Mister Kipling were taken off of the rowing decks of Spanish galleons or stockades ashore. All seeking a better life than that of a dungeon. Many men joined for even different, yet similar reasons and in some respects the Royal Navy was its own form of ownership and –dare I suggest– slavery. Sailors often lived and served in horrid conditions for little or no wage. They were governed by the whip or what was called the cat o' nine tails, because it was essentially nine whips wound into one handle. Many of these men were victims of an English press gang –a practice that I felt should not be legal. The press gang was the art of raiding taverns, brothels, and seaside inns, taking men, even British citizens by force and making them go aboard and join the navy so they could keep 'enlistments' up. How many men, left families at home –for years –as prisoners on one of his majesty's ships? How many children were left to wonder where their fathers were?

--It was a thought I could not bear, and it seemed to make the proposition of privateering a more inviting one for many of these characters….

This was also part of the reason that the whip and the flogging practices of the Royal Navy were not tolerated onboard this ship. Our crew men who were former slaves –for obvious reasons-- despised it….

In addition, some of the men on board just signed up for adventure, work or…because they were not good at anything else but this. In all, the promise of life aboard The Venger seemed a much better prospect for many of them….

IV

THE WITCH'S DEN

The next day at dawn, our black flag flew in the wind and moving fog as the night watch moved below deck for breakfast and sleep. The day watch surfaced, and men climbed the rigging through the early morning mist, aloft and took to their stations. I began my duties under the watch of Mister Newcastle, Mister Arson and Mister Teague, a hardened man who commanded the deck with determination.

Newcastle applied example. Unafraid of hard work, Mister Newcastle would show me what my duties were and how to carry them out in exact fashion.

With Teague, there was something different. There was a sinister edge to this man, and it became known to me that Mister Teague was a former Royal Marine who fought in Queen Anne's War with the Spanish. He had fought in the French township of Mobile on the Gulf Coast and in Spanish Florida where rumor had it that he had put Spanish missions to the torch.

--They also said he had taken the head of a judge!

--A thought I preferred to keep from my mind. Teague did have an unforgiving nature about him as if he could do a job most other men could not, and he never wasted his words. Everything was a direct command. No small talk.

Mister Harrow, the second in command, was also on deck and he also made sure I kept on task but seemed more sympathetic, sometimes even taking a moment or two to show me some basic skill of seamanship, like how to determine wind direction, or basic sail and rope work, things that would make me more valuable and make the ship run in better fashion.

The Captain stood at the wheel, in a powerful stance, arms crossed, watching the horizon. His dark eyes always seemed fixed on that point where the skyline met the sea in the distance.

As the late afternoon sun set upon us, my duties were interrupted by a sudden call from the crow's nest, way up on the center mast, "Land ho!" And in an instant, the tempo on deck accelerated. There was a sudden level of excitement in the air....

--And an island was on the horizon.

We sailed past an old 'haunted' Spanish fort on the point, unmanned and dead and then into a lagoon, flanked by a township on the beach, and populated with three other frigates —each flying a variation of the 'black flag' or 'skull and bones' --and several smaller ships.

The anchor dropped into the water, water that was so clear that one could see the anchor hit the ocean floor below. I went to the railing for my first look at civilization in many weeks and saw many buildings and much activity. Part of the township had slid into the sea —and the buildings were damaged-- I was told this was from an earthquake that happened some years back. The damaged structures were now where a fish market stood. Some of the buildings, partially underwater, remained abandoned....

"Where are we? Havana?"

"No lad," Mister Harrow replied, "Port Royal."

"Port Royal" I repeated with a sense of wonder and my eyes became fixed on the beach ahead.

There were giant tents on the sand made of canvass sails. Docks, wharfs and beyond that, several buildings of wood, brick, and mortar. On the beach, a frigate was beached —on its side—with a massive hole in its hull, and it appeared to have been there for centuries, dead and decayed in the tropical air....

The men lined up with the pay master, Mister Lincoln --who worked with Mister Thorn and Mister Newcastle at his shoulder-- and they made their mark for their lot. Once collected, they made their way over the side, down the rope ladder and into the boats to be rowed ashore. The doctor supervised their departure "Enjoy yourselves lads, I'll be here to cure you of all your aliments when you come back aboard!" He chuckled.

I waited, unsure of what step to take. Was I welcome to go ashore? I felt like my friends were leaving but not sure if I was welcomed to leave with them. At that point, Mister Newcastle stopped me. "Mister Reed."

"Sir?"

"Let me see your hands." He commanded in a firm tone as he walked from the pay master to my position.

I did as commanded though insecurity made them tremble slightly. Unaware of what was to happen next, I watched him as he raised his fist and dropped some gold coins into my hands. I was, in fact, very surprised to receive them.

"Sir?"

"For your term of service," he said.

I was quite amazed. I knew I was to work my way to the next port but was unaware that I was to be paid as well.

"You've earned it lad." He continued, "All men get a share aboard The Venger."

I smiled to show both my surprise and gratitude.

"Now go, they have a place for you in the launch and a celebration is sure to start in town. Best of luck to you." There was a handshake and we parted.

"Come this way Teach!" Rajiv instructed.

'Teach' I thought must have been some sort of nickname for my role as a teacher. I made my way down the ropes to the boat where I was stabilized and helped aboard by Whitney, Mister Blair and the poet, Mister Clairmont. My actions betrayed my first thought which was to hide the fact that I had any coin at all however, a grin from Mister Cross, across from me, put this to rest…

"No need to be sheepish boy- no one will steal from you here," he said.

My next look must have betrayed my surprise because he leaned forward and continued with a deliberate and direct manner, "It is against the code for us to steal from one another. You have what I have, and our articles require us to allow you to keep it and spend it how you please."

I was relived but had to ask, "Out of curiosity, what happens to those who take liberties with the code?"

He looked at me as if to size me up again and with a smile, he dragged his finger across his throat as if to symbolize cutting it…

This I understood.

I splashed ashore in this new world and could smell the landscape around me, the cooking, the grog, the sweat of the people. I picked up a fist of sand and squeezed it through my fingers with a smile. This was land and I was on it again….

I helped heave the long boat out of the tide, then took survey of this fantastic place where civilization was in full heel. The town was very much alive with the smell of salt water, mixed rum –and cooking. Musicians on the corner, taverns a glow and balconies loaded with women of different colors all who appeared happy to see us arrive….

I must admit, I wasn't sure who to walk with into this unknown but felt the embrace and push of my shipmates in the direction of the King's Arms. This made me feel included and in I went with Mister Blair, Baako, Mister Blythe, Gordon, Mister Obal, Jagger, Irons, Locksley, Fury, Mister Miranda --who spoke several languages—Mister Nighthorse—a Huron native, Rabal ---the giant, Mister O'Shea, Lo-tan, in his bamboo hat that covered his eyes, Blackwood in his kilt and some of our Japanese comrades and we moved to make ourselves at home.

This building had windows but without glass, with palm trees growing around and up inside of its super structure to an interior second floor veranda. Young children pulled ropes that ran through the rafters and moved giant sheets of canvas like fans.

Another slap on my back forward and my attention was brought to the men around me and the company at hand. Another thought that again passed through my head was the fact that if I was back in England, most public houses would not allow natives or Africans or Asian warriors to enter –not that they could keep this group out-- but here, they practiced the 'social arts' right alongside us with no such animosity. In fact, it would be considered bad manners to leave anyone out. Bad, drunken behavior or mischief may get one blocked at the door but never your race or culture.

I made my way to the tavern bar where we were welcomed by the barkeeper. "Welcome lads, what will it be?"

It was to be rum all around….

"From The Venger I see--" he recognized the look of Jagger, Lo, Irons, Nighthorse and the ronin…

"Yes, that's right" I said with a touch of pride…

He nodded and asked, "And who might you be?"

"They call me Teach!'

"Teach?" was the response from the bar keep with a touch of bewilderment, "I thought you'd be taller!"

Curious statement I thought, then Irons put his hand on my shoulder, "Do not use your nickname here." He advised.

"Why not?"

"Because it happens to also be the name of another man who ventures into these waters, and we would want no mistake."

"Another man called Teach?" I was surprised. "Was there another teacher in the area? Maybe I could meet him? Exchange ideas? Talk of science?"

"His name is Teach. Edward Teach!" Irons picked up another mug, "They call him…BLACKBEARD!"

I was quick to spit out my rum in surprise, coughed, looked to the bar keeper, and immediately made correction. "My name is Reed!" I coughed out.

--Everyone in England knew of the killer Blackbeard.

The tavern keeper smiled. "Another rum then…Mister Reed?"

"Please…."

Rum appeared to be the beverage of choice and we were issued large servings of it. Pipe and tobacco was offered and because this was still somewhat new to me, it caused me to cough a lot, much to the amusement of my new friends. But I continued with the art and became more in tune with it.

Later, I began the process of discovery, I wandered out into the streets to survey the landscape. Plants crawled up the buildings, many lit lanterns hung from the trees to light the town and torches lit the doorways to taverns and brothels. Almost all the buildings were without windows or opened up to the night air. Some places were fashioned from shipwrecked parts with canvas sails used like tents. I even saw parchment, quills, and ink for sale which –as a teacher-- struck my fancy but I was unaware how long I could make my wages last so with regret, I passed on the purchase.

There were musicians on the corner of almost every street, playing wonderful melodies --this was a place of merriment.

There was boar –and beef-- on the spit for coin or trade, primed under the stars. Many of the ale houses and grog shops had bar tops and barrels right in the sand and these men from The Venger were welcomed everywhere…

Daws, Blythe, Hayte, Mister Nighthorse and Rajiv took to a new tavern with some of the ronin. Saxon, Mister Cage, Wilder –with his pet monkey on his shoulder-- Lau, Dakar, Kannon, Obal, some of the Aztecs and Duncan-Howe went to another. Howe with a woman under each arm. The Moors came ashore but did not partake in spirits --or tobacco-- their business was trading in the marketplace, oftentimes for literature.

Mister Strange was already asleep in the street –empty bottle in his fist.

I looked up as Prescott, Mister Ward, Blackwood, Watson –one of our officers-- and Mister Wicks found sanctuary on the balcony of a brothel that held down the corner of King Street. Mister Cage was already passed out with his body draped over the railing –like a casualty. I moved down the dark street opposite, lit only by a few lanterns and I looked around to suddenly find myself in a quiet part of town. No one was out on the streets here, only shadows.

A blacksmith's station was empty and there were only a few lights from any of the storefronts.

I entered the tavern across the street, walking under a sign marked 'The Pale Horsman' and made my way to the bar, it was a dark place, lit by candles and hardly populated though some of our officers Teague, Raeder and Wolfe were inside at a table in the corner, partially illuminated by a fire with an animal on the spit...

I nodded to them –out of respect-- as I entered, though I must confess those men struck a chord of fear in me. Teague especially, for there was a dark edge to his demeanor and if I was to describe his presence it would be like --Lucifer on Earth, subtle in manner but evil in intentions.

Raeder –pronounced 'Raid-er' was also ominous, with big shoulders and heavy hands like rocks and when his fists hit the table, the floorboards rumbled. He rarely seemed to blink; his eyes always fixed with almost no rapid movement. He was also a man of very few words.

I ordered a drink and was asked by the inn keeper if I wanted to eat. I passed on the offer for I already had roasted boar at the King's Arms, and I was also uncomfortable in this place so, I just took my drink in peace.

Of the officer's conversation in the corner, I could hear little --some ominous words like, 'Kill 'em', 'keel haul' and 'axe', 'chop', 'split', 'break' ...a conversation I did not have the stomach for.

Then, I turned and saw someone sitting in a lonely backroom corner of this place. A figure I could not quite make out. I don't know what possessed me but, I was curious and compelled to explore this so, I walked through a mix of shadows and candlelight and approached what was discovered to be a tarot card reader...

He looked like an Ottoman, the type that would have invaded Eastern Europe several centuries before. "Want to know your future?" he slowly asked though a thick accent.

I thought of the way my last few weeks had gone, 'Do...I...really...want...to...know...my future?' and confessed, "I'm not so sure."

He turned one card over. It was the image of a knife through a book. "You are and educated man. Dedicated to learning and ideas."

That much was true.

"But somewhat off course." He added.

--Curious.

He then slowly turned another card over. It was of a man and a woman. "Love is close by…."

Good. This was good. I liked this possibility….

He then turned the third card over, and it was the grim reaper. Eerie – somewhat frightening--and similar to the figurehead on The Venger. He paused and looked up at me as if genuinely startled. "Deeeeeeaaaaath." He hissed.

My blood ran cold, and I suddenly felt a sinister presence near me, and I quickly turned around to see Teague standing in the lantern light a few steps back. Teague suddenly pulled his pistol, slammed the hammer back and aimed it at the tarot card reader… "I don't like that card!" He said.

"No." The tarot card reader suddenly looked surprised and quickly changed his disposition from ominous to over-polite thanks to help from the gun. "My mistake, I meant to draw…this card." And a new card went down on the table. A card that pictured a gold crown, "Wealth?" The reader asked with an expression that appeared to ask if the card was acceptable….

"Much better." Teague put his weapon away and returned to his corner of the table….

There was a lesson in this, obvious to the reader I suppose that I, insecure in my standing and in a foreign place with little confidence was forced to ask the question of myself, would my insecurities help me fall victim to trouble and hardship? Possibly. Where Teague clearly believed he made his own future, and no pack of cards could –or would—dictate his fate.

He had firm belief in his abilities and the power of his application.

Later that night, I moved through the streets and under the trees, meeting up with Bishop, Flagg, Gray --who needed assistance from us to walk-- Irons, Towne, Java, and some other members of our crew as we roamed…

Some of the huts in this part of town were built under, on and even in giant trees, in their very branches --like tree houses made of ship decks. Lanterns and rope bridges marked the way to the top and there were people –sailors and women—in them drinking and celebrating. It was wondrous.

I continued forward, kept my balance, and crossed a bridge made of planks, roped across barrels that floated in a shallow waterway that led to the beach. There was an old smuggler's tunnel, and another system of huts and buildings on stilts by the lagoon. They were built like this, so the tide didn't overtake them during hurricane season. A lot of fishing was done here, and a small fish market was at work. Shark hung from the rafters to be carved. Octopus and shellfish in glass bowls, alive, if you wanted it. Fish and fish heads stacked up. Cooking was done by request and a stew made with all of it was what I tried. I could also purchase corn –which I had never actually seen before-- sugarcane and rabbit –alive or dead—also monkeys. Tobacco was very popular in all quarters and here the tobacco was favored with Jamaica rum…

It was not wise to go into all parts of town alone. Between taverns, I fell behind my friends and in the shadows of League Street a few moments later, a man emerged from the darkness and suddenly grabbed me by the neck --a knife blade was wheeled up to my face as I stumbled to react.

"Coin! Now!" He hissed in direct fashion, ready to stab me in the eye.

Looking at the point of the knife blade, frightened, I fumbled for my money as quick as I could but, as I offered it up, this man froze when he heard the words….

"Hold --let him go!"

My assailant turned to see Mister Irons and Mister Hatano –one of The Venger's rogue samurai-- standing just outside the shadows a few meters away….

"Why? What's he to you?"

Hatano locked eyes with this thief and slowly, very slowly crossed the street. Bishop was not too far off –in the shadows of the other side of the street --eyes fixed-- rubbing his index finger with his thumb as if ready in an instant to reach for his blade or gun. Flagg and Gray stood just beyond him, not far off –though Gray was drunk and useless.

"He's with us!" Irons reported.

"You? This man?" He said in a condescending tone "I find that hard to believe. Too much of a dandy this one."

"Enough talk from you!" Irons spoke through his teeth, "Now, you heard me –and I was clear. Let-him-go. Now!"

The man waited, then after a few moments that seemed to take an eternity, he did as instructed and released his grip on my tunic. I collected myself and got my nerves under control but as I started to walk away from this man, towards my friends, he raised his blade and moved to throw it into my back…

"Down!" Irons shouted and as I tumbled to the ground, there was a sudden, sharp, fast, yell as Hatano rifled something into the air that reflected in the moonlight —a hira-shuriken – and with a sudden sound, like a loud whistle, this blade cut through the air, zipped down the street and it struck my attacker square in the eye. His head shot back, and he stood for a moment before he fell backwards into some barrels --dead. Hatano then moved forward and reclaimed his weapon from the man's skull. He cleaned the blade on the dead man's shirt and stood up as if nothing unusual had happened.

Mister Irons stood there in a stance with his arms crossed through this entire encounter as if he had no doubt in its outcome. He looked to me, "That one will cost you Reed."

"Sir?"

"I believe you owe us a drink!" He smiled.

--And just then, Gray who had been drinking all night, fell face forward into the sand. Passed out cold.

Irons looked down at Gray and back up to me, "Well, those of us that can still stand of course."

"I-I believe I d-do." I was rattled, for I had never seen a man killed before much less in this stunning fashion but, if it was to cost a few drinks to keep my bodyguard around me, I was happy to oblige. However, before we could resume our tavern business, we had to make a stop by the undertaker. Here I had to offer up some of my pay to have my attacker buried. It was –of course- the right thing to do. I wanted to request that a coffin be made and that he be given a Christian burial but, my earnings only afforded a canvas bag and a pauper's grave --or mass grave. I had to be content with this.

--My hands continued to tremble for most of the night....

Later, we found Mister Blythe again, in the company of Mister Tabor, Mister Baltimore and Sam –two of the Huron Natives-- and some of the women from the town and it was agreed that we should enter into another tavern, The Witch's Den and here, men from other ships, such as The Warlock, The Revenge and The Marauder mixed with our own. Men from Ireland, The Azores, the South Pacific, North Africa even one who spoke with an accent from Italy. I was in the presence of men who were fortunate to be alive and their greetings reflected as much and here, I caught an interesting sight, a Spanish Captain –in the uniform of the Spanish navy— surrounded by some of his officers and Spanish Marines, sitting with our own Captain. I'm not sure why this caught my attention, perhaps because my homeland of England always seemed in a constant state of war with the Spanish yet here was a decorated commander drawing from a pipe and having a drink with our top officer...

I stopped Mister Blythe, "I thought this was a British port. Are the Spanish allowed here?"

"This port is British but for protection, the crown relies on privateers like us, which is why we are allowed here without malice." Blythe looked over, "And.... under the white flag, the Spanish are allowed ashore."

"Is that all it takes? A white flag?"

"No man is to be attacked under a flag of truce, if they come in peace, they may leave in peace." He smiled, "In most cases." And with that he continued to the bar where a drunk Captain Faulkner of the privateering vessel The Phantom was providing all the drinks...

Back at the Captain's table, the talk was about war and conflict but Captain Vasquez –and former Spanish privateer-- had a possible solution to all this --a commission from the Spanish Crown.

"I believe you should take the offer Essex." Vasquez stated in a relaxed tone as he ignited his tobacco, "You'll be given the rank of Captain in the Spanish Navy –maybe even made a Knight once you bring home a victory or two…you could…. buy a plantation and retire as a respectable gentleman in Havana or-Spanish Africa…"

"It is a solid offer I grant you and I'm honored to even be considered but…. fighting under the Spanish Flag, against England is one thing our crew will not vote for. Privateering yes, fighting under Spanish command –or anyone's-- is something quite different."

"I can assure you –as your friend—The Spanish government wants peace. Our temperament has changed, we've outlawed slavery, the crown has pardoned privateers who have acted against our interests--"

"You may have been pardoned for your past criminal actions Vasquez but then…you are from Segovia, and you will forgive me if I say that, since you are Spanish, your terms –and considerations—may be more favorable than mine."

Vasquez shrugged as if to almost concede the possibility….

"I commend your government on its condemnation of slavery, we both know the practice is in effect with the English and the Portuguese and that Spanish emissaries still participate in such an economy…."

"Making it law was but a first step," Vasquez exhaled…

"--And I admire you for it."

"--I hope that England and her colonies will follow suit."

"On that, we can agree." His eyes then seemed to lose focus if only for a moment and drift off into the distance, to a place in his past where slavery –and love-- may have played a part.

After a moment, Vasquez leaned forward "She did love you, you know." He said with sincerity as if able to read the man's thoughts. "Though," he continued, changing tone and pace as if to lighten the mood, "I cannot imagine why. But she was yours to be sure."

Essex looked to him, the candlelight flickering off his eyes. At first, he spoke not a word but, his eyes may have betrayed something as if they were seeking some sort of affirmation. "I often wonder if I deserved such affection."

"She owed you her freedom and she owed you for the life you gave her afterwards. If you were not deserving of it, then who?" He exhaled more smoke into the air, "Men like you and I, we have never played the part of hero of hearth and home well but, to have loved –if even for a short while— that is the real privilege. Is it not?"

Essex slowly nodded. "Your eloquence surprises even me."

Vasquez leaned back and pulled on his pipe. "Tis a skill I've mastered to be sure. How else would I maintain my reputation with the ladies?"

"Quite." Essex agreed with a smile. Then he grew serious, "Love may have no place in the world anymore. It's all war and commerce."

"You know Essex, your exploits are well known, you raid British ports and shipping as well--"

"I do." Essex was forced to admit, "But I do so under my own accord. Not under Spanish command." He added as he exhaled some smoke, "Joining the ranks of the Spanish Admiralty is something I fear, we cannot do."

Vasquez thought for a moment as if he wanted to press the argument but instead, he remained silent and stood up, "Very well…. you have my respect as well you know and …. I would hate to meet you in battle but, should it come to war between us, I will have no choice but to take action against you."

"Such is the way of things." Essex rose from his chair, "I hope fortune puts some distance between us."

Vasquez gave a slight smile and nodded in agreement….

"One last drink then…between friends?"

Vasquez smiled. "It would be an honor."

And at that, they both shook hands. A bar maid brought a round of mugs for Essex, Vasquez and all the officers. There was a toast 'to the future' and the mugs banged into each other and were emptied…

As Vasquez and his officers cleared, two more mugs were brought to the Captain who slid one down to the end of the table where Harrow, his second officer and steadfast confidant, gripped it.

Captain Essex was measured in all matters but particularly with acts of war where the crew, the ship and our futures were at stake. Using a candle, he drew upon his pipe in thought and exhaled the sweet stench of the tobacco and what followed was a long silence, uncomfortable for some but, not him for he gave his answers when ready, not when his audience wanted them. He finally put his thoughts into words, "It a shame really, I happen to like the Spanish, the women particularly." He looked to Harrow, "Go on, say it…"

"Far be it from me to disagree with you Captain."

"You think I should put his offer to a vote?"

"I believe you are correct in maintaining our independence from any imperial master…"

"But?"

Harrow exhaled, "It's war that concerns me…I don't like it."

"No," Essex looked out the tavern window, pushed the shutter wide so he could see his ship in the bay. "I never have either. Bad business."

It wasn't the violence of war that bothered them, it was the effect of war. It would bring thousands of troops into the region –from all crowns— to police the area. Commerce would give way to weapons and troop ships. Ports would become military bases and less vulnerable to raid. Bad business indeed….

The rim of my mug rattled against my teeth, nerves from my situation earlier out on the street. It was hard for me to get the rum down. There was no such problem with Hatano, Bishop or Irons, their evening progressed as if nothing had happened. I wondered if this was the road one travels in this business of privateering, to be so accustomed to violence to the point where it becomes something you don't even think about. Something that no longer bothers you, that you lose your humanity --and I was afraid that may –in fact—be the case here but, I tried to mask my concerns to maintain some sort of social standing and to keep what little reputation I had with these men, intact.

Back with my friends, gambling with dice and cards started up and became constant throughout the night for everyone except Johnny Kay. For some reason, Kay wasn't allowed in the gambling circles. He tried to get in on the game but was either pushed out or pulled out by the back of his collar. I thought this may have been because of his age. He was, maybe six, seven years younger than myself –around thirteen and because of this, our veterans seemed to keep him out of trouble –and gambling often leads to violence and that's why one of the unwritten rules of The 'Venger's code of conduct' was that our crew was not to gamble for money amongst ourselves.

Kay was someone I'd expect to see with schoolbooks back home, not weapons. I was somewhat concerned about how comfortable he was with 'the steel' but as a former 'runaway' from Albany I suppose he had to be skilled to survive.

Pharaoh was another member of the crew who was young. Schooled first as a powder monkey, then as a gunner –maybe the youngest gunner -- he was known to carry a jar of colorful marbles in his satchel –along with grenades and other needed items. Madds, Bolt, Bliss Monroe, Sterling, and the others seemed to make an effort to keep these two out of trouble when and where they could.

At this point, I could not assess the entire crew but of some key personnel I could offer this, Jack-Karr and Merciless seemed to have a dangerous edge and a wicked sense of humor. Daws seemed like a gentleman, Whitney seemed to almost have a strange sense of innocence around him and a logical comprehensive way in his manner. Rabal was clearly a killer and –as I have said—Teague I didn't like to be in the room with. Teague scared me.

More barrels of rum and wine were brought in as the tavern keeper was determined to keep this lot well supplied. I was surprised for a moment – in an evening of many surprises--- to hear Mister Nighthorse speak with

Bons and Mister Baltimore in their native language. It seemed like a simple, brief set of instructions but fascinating to hear, they then turned to some of French sailors and spoke to them in French to which they replied –in kind-- and they all laughed....

--Not so savage as one was led to believe, for that made three languages –so far—that I heard these 'natives' speak fluently.

Later, we played the card game 'Splinter', and I used my mathematics at cards, counting them to be precise, in subtle fashion to make some winnings for me and my comrades. This skill, I dare say, helped my popularity with my crew though it was not just skill alone, the drunken state of the opposition also worked in our favor. Coin –some stamped with Spanish markings and jewels traded hands and also paper. Letters of value and ownership. Mister Arson won a small fishing sloop, and he made exit for an inspection only to find the sloop under the tide thanks to a cannonball size hole in the hull....

"Blast! Of all the nerve!" Arson stood looking at the masts exposed over the tide,

"There's your prize Arson." Blythe smiled. "Not much of a future in the fish trade."

"Never trust a damn Capol." Arson said through his teeth, "They shame the art of gambling!"

Back at the tavern, the winning brought more rum...

"Nice work Reed." Jack-Karr said as he handed his winnings to the barmaid and a coin to myself as a thank you.

I smiled. "What would you have done if I got it wrong?" I asked.

"Probably cut your fingers off." He said in a direct tone.

I turned cold and tried to stutter some sort of response....

Then he smiled. "That was a joke."

I was relieved but still confused on where the real violence ended, and the comedy began.

The celebration continued and I found myself being marched upstairs to the second floor of this inn where the deck was populated by women, beautiful women of all types, colors, and languages, in dresses of different bright colors and material that shined in the lantern light. I managed to step through some fireflies and make it onto a balcony and into the company of the women there. I had been without a woman's company for many months and found my mind wandering. As the breeze blew through the island trees and onto our deck, I was able to appreciate the beauty that decorated this place. At home, at this time, my evenings would be marked with snow and cold but here, it is quite pleasant.

I turned and found myself in the presence of a beautiful woman with dark skin. She moved with a level of rhythm and directness that seemed to reflect confidence in her actions and when she got close, I realized that she had green eyes –with a tint of blue. I was momentarily taken aback by this. I admit, I was a man of little experience, especially with matters of the heart but, I had been schooled in the art of being a gentleman and found myself making a formal introduction to this woman which was, I gathered, unnecessary but she appeared amused and willing to play along as I introduced myself with a slight bow and she then replied in kind by lowering her chin in acknowledgement.

She introduced herself as Uralan.

"I am new to these parts, ma'am." And then it occurred to me how little I knew of my situation.

"That much I can tell," She replied with a smile and an accent I could not trace as she appeared to size me up.

"Is this island your home?"

"No. I come from a place called Barbados."

"And you live here?'

"I like it here." She looked down, over the balcony railing to my shipmates in the crowded street below. "You don't strike the fashion of a privateer."

I became conscious of my wardrobe and adjusted my tunic as if this would make me more acceptable. But I also realized that I had no weapons.

She appeared slightly confused, "How did you join the crew of The Venger?"

"By accident I suppose."

"You must be a brave man to sail with that ship."

"I'm not brave" I confessed, "Fortunate really, but…I would not consider myself to be a brave man. Fate brought me from England to an island populated by cannibals and…as it happens, these men arrived and saved me from what was sure to be a dinner." Then my mind came back around to her statement and in nervous fashion, I asked, "W-why must I be brave? Is-is the ship famous or –should I be scared or something?"

She smiled, "It's quite famous in these parts and far from quiet." She looked back out into the street below where Teague, Newcastle, Addo and some of the ronin were moving through, "It is said The Venger moves like a ghost, strikes fear in hearts of the Spanish commanders. That even the French and The Dutch in the South Pacific are afraid of her. The provincial governors have little choice but to be tolerant of its presence…." She turned to me, "Rumor has it, they just raided New Orleans."

"I found the men onboard to be quite tolerant really." I said, remembering my own ignorance when first aboard and how forgiving they were in ways….

"If you're not one of them, you should beware –they are savage."

This was an aspect of the ship's personality that I had not witnessed, other than the act of defense in the street and it made me think. She must have had some level of sympathy for me because she put her hand on my chin and raised my glance. "What is your business here?"

I stumbled for an honest answer, "Pleasure, I suppose." I was after all just happy to be alive. I am embarrassed to say, that I had seen very few people with dark skin. And in my recollections could not recall meeting one until I boarded The Venger. But here, I found myself in the most pleasant of circumstances with a woman I found to be quite beautiful. She said a few words in Spanish and a tray arrived with a bottle of rum and more tobacco. I put out some gold –waved off the tobacco for it had got the better of me earlier but I did take the rum and two mugs so we could have a drink in the night air and as I stepped closer to the balcony, I looked up at the stars. This was indeed a beautiful place….

I awoke the next morning in a damp heat. My friend was nowhere to be seen so I made my way to a balcony chair where I could sit and watch the activity of the streets below. Donkeys carried large amounts of bananas and coconuts and barrels of rum or molasses into town, coaches, and traffic moved below me. There was a mix of well-dressed proper pedestrians and then the very poor. On the corner was a man with a monkey on his shoulder I even caught sight of British soldiers talking with privateers in front of our tavern. How long had I been here? All night? All morning now.

I checked my pocket for what was now my life savings to find it still there –though a few coins short after last night. I was relieved it wasn't stolen and I doubt that would be equal case if I was back in London or Bristol under the same circumstances but here, my money was untouched, social debts not withstanding of course.

I had hoped that the remaining amount would be enough to purchase a trip to the Americas on the next ship and found myself down by the docks looking to book passage. This was not a proper place for maritime transit and there were no ships to set sail for the Carolinas or Boston. Instead, I was advised to take a ship to Hispaniola, Saint Margarite, or the coast of Spanish Florida where I could be dropped under the cover of darkness and then be allowed to make my way to a town –if I could survive the natives. From there I could find my way to the Americas. It was a costly enterprise. Too costly and credit was one thing that I didn't appear to have.

I had to earn some currency and I contemplated starting a school or offering some schooling to the island but there were few children, and my skills were not appreciated. My skills seemed inferior to other skills that seemed more important to the populace --such as carpentry, medical knowledge, or above all fighting skills. If you were a fighter, you could always find employment here.

Depressed, I explored more of the town from the customs house to the marketplace, a man was selling monkeys and tropical birds, birds that had personality they would repeat what was said to them. One could also purchase clothes, weapons, boots, almost anything --except slaves. The commodity, though quite popular in the colonies, was outlawed here. Captured slave ships even found a low price at the auction house for sailors disliked their histories, they were superstitious of them, and they did not like the way they were configured –with holding pins.   Often times, captured slave ships would be sunk in the bay as part of the underwater fixed defenses or taken a part for their wood paneling and metal. The cages were often re-fashioned to be brigs for the disorderly on ships or ashore. Sometimes, they were melted down into musket balls....

I did find my way through a cemetery –and tombstones covered in plants-- to a church, a church with Christian headstones. I was surprised that such a place existed here but felt obliged to go inside. The pews sat empty. The pulpit was bare. I took a seat realizing I had missed many Sunday school sessions and now, in the wake of my recent travels, could use some spirituality more than ever.

A sudden voice startled me, "Is everything all right my son?"

I turned to see a clergy man standing there, "Father?"

He gave me a nod and smiled. "I try to be a father to all things and a pleasant aid to all who seek some comfort."

I smiled....

"You are new to the island," He said in a matter-of-fact way, "It doesn't take much to recognize the traits."

I started to stand up, but he stopped me. "You are welcome here," he reassured me. "Sit and take peace."

"How do you come to bring religion to such a place as this?"

"Oh, I have been here many years, building hope and providing comfort when I could."

"Why? How?"

"I was an indentured servant in the Americas. My township was wiped out by the natives there." He paused and appeared reflective, "In America, the natives gain status amongst their own by--" He motioned his hand up to and against his forehead, "Cutting the scalp from their victims."

"I have heard of this during my time at university. They paint their faces."

"They do."

"Men on The Venger paint their faces. Many are from the wilds of the Americas. They're from a band called Ur-on! One is called a Seminole from Spanish Florida..."

I did not realize at the time that there was a H before the U, and it was actually written as Huron --but I hoped my shipmates would forgive my ignorance.

"Those men have taken a different path but, back in my township, the natives there were savage and un-wanting of any parley with those not of their kind," he paused, "I survived to make my way down a river to the coast. I bought passage home but fell victim to a press gang and was forced to spend several years in the service of his Majesty's Navy. One night, after a terrible firefight we were overrun by privateers, and I was given a choice.... enlist or be marooned.... The answer was obvious."

"You joined?"

"I did. I spent several years as a privateer aboard 'The Viking' until I decided to atone for my sins and... I looked up and built this place."

"It is an unusual setting for a church is it not?'

"Man needs God in all places. Most of all here, the visiting rate may be low at times but, I assure you, there are no atheists onboard a sinking ship."

I could not help but laugh at the truth of it.

"You are welcome to stay here as long as you want." He stood up "In fact, I may have another bible here if you'd like..."

"Please."

Moments later, he emerged from the church office with a bible, "Here, it was salvaged from the sea and it's missing some pages but....it should serve its purpose." He walked me out on to the front steps where he stood for a moment as if to appreciate his environment a new....

"This island could use a library."

He smiled, "An interesting enterprise my son, but only a few of the men here can read or care to read something other than naval charts or letters of marque."

At that, some Moors walked by. We watched them, in their black robes, black, tight head wraps that covered their head and faces except for their eyes, "We have men like that on our ship. They pray often."

He nodded, "As you no doubt know, they come from a desert country across the sea. Their religion has different requirements."

"Do you know about their practices?"

"I know very little but, all men who bow before God are worthy of peace and understanding. In some lands, there is separation of church and state, such as it is here in the Caribbean. The Spanish don't believe in it but here, man is content to allow another man his freedoms without trespass." He paused. "And we are all better for it. Now, I must report to the hospital where I volunteer, good day to you, my son. You are welcome here."

"Thank you."

Later, I continued to wander through the marketplace but had little to trade or barter. I walked through the tide and The Venger sat in the bay, accompanied by other ships. I remained there, at the water's edge until sunset. My mind drifted toward my new friend from Barbados. It was a relationship I could not foster back home but this was a new frontier and I had to admit, right –or wrong—I liked her company and I decided to make my way back into town....

I walked past the torches that lit the entrance to the Witch's Den and took a quiet seat on the wooden porch. I waited there until my friend came 'round to light the candles. "Ah, my schoolteacher!" she smiled....

"Yes-ah-yes." I stood to be polite.

"Back at the Witch's Den I see."

"Yes, I came to see you, actually." My sudden honesty surprised me. I wasn't usually so bold about my intentions...

She gave me a cunning smile, "And here I am."

"Yes, here you are."

And here I was, a world away from London society, a society that would tragically prohibit such a moment. "I hope you don't mind that I came back but, I wanted to-"

"Then this is where you should be." She made it so simple, and she waved to the bar maiden who brought a bottle of wine and glasses to the table.

I poured two glasses and thought I should say something or make some sort of clever toast but, the fact was, even though I was limited in experience, I was comfortable just to be in her company even if the right words didn't come to me. I was content to just sit in the candlelight and listen to anything she might say or even just listen to her breathing…

Many of the following days and nights blurred together.

After several days, I found myself without much in the way of money –my pay had dwindled--and in a foreign place, I began to calculate my position. If I remained on the island my money would run out soon, leading to a more than formidable hardship. But I was without the means to buy transit to the Americas. What should I do? I wandered the town depressed. I passed through the township shops, saw a tailor and a dressmaker –his wife—who was working up dresses of the most fantastic colors, deep red, emerald, dark blues and I thought of my friend from Barbados and how the red fabric would look against her skin and I started feeling in debt for her company, I re-checked my finances only to find that I would fall short of the asking price of such a dress. A slow solemn gloom grabbed hold of me. Is this what my life had become? A man in an island paradise with no employment and past merits that were all but useless. Was there nothing more to me?

I continued to walk the streets of the town, dejected when I saw some of The Venger crew outside the King's Arms tavern….

Mister Jagger had arrived with Mister Toombs who had been cut in the throat years back, robbing him of his ability to speak so he resorted to hand signals when communicating. There, I also found Mister Harrow. Mister Teague, Baako, Prescott, Standish, Whitney, Able, Tak, Jupiter, Wicks, Merciless, Fury and Mister De Leon all at the tavern entrance and as they prepared to depart, Mister Daws joined them, shirt in hand, from the brothel --and I saw Mister Rabal climb down the jungle ivy from the balcony above to join them....

I suddenly summoned some courage to speak. "Sirs....?"

They suddenly stopped their conversation, and they all turned towards me...

"Could-could you use another hand?"

"What are we now? Missionaries?"

I received a look one could only describe as bewilderment. Baako looked to Harrow "We do need skilled replacements."

"Yes," Jagger said, "But men who are good with the sword.... not schoolbooks."

I stepped forth. "I can learn."

"It's not the skill, boy," Mister Harrow explained, "It's the intent to use it!"

"We can teach you to fight but...will you.... when the time comes?" Mister Jagger asked. Arson remained quiet at his shoulder but, his expression seemed to agree.

-It was more than a fair question.

"No" Wicks barked out his vote, "The men need someone they can depend on in combat. Not him at our backs!"

My response rang of desperation, "I may find my intent with...proper instruction, sir?"

Harrow leveled his eyes and seemed to make an evaluation of what my soul might tell him. He knew I followed every command when working on board to the best of my ability. "Mister Daws?"

Daws gave way to silence for a moment then said, "The vote is yours Mister Harrow!"

Harrow's eyes darted to Able, Rabal and the others as if to read their thoughts, then he cut through the silence, "Very well, Mister Reed.... you may sign the articles and join the crew!"

"Thank you, sir." I started towards the shoreline.

"Mister Daws...." Harrow said as he watched me march off, "Make sure this man doesn't get himself killed."

V

UNDER THE BLACK FLAG

Mister Claixto and Java gave me a hand up on deck as I –and other elements of the crew-- reported back aboard. I found Mister Lincoln at his station on the quarterdeck and thus asked to sign 'the articles to live by' or --the code. He opened a large book and told me to make my mark. He seemed puzzled by my delay and asked, "What are you doing Mister Reed?"

I looked up, "Why…I'm reading it."

"You can read?" He seemed surprised.

"Yes, I was, I mean --I am-- a teacher."

Mister Lincoln gave a slight approving smile and said: "Very well, you may sign the articles when you are ready Mister Reed."

Looking at the code, most of it centered on the administration of the ship and offenses most of which were punishable by death or marooning.

I.

All men are equal in standing despite culture and language and shall obey civil command.

II.

Every man to be called fairly in turn, to an equal share of prizes –and money--earned. Stealing from the crew or general treasury is punishable by death.

III.

Weapons, always fit for service.

IV.

No crimes against women or children are to be tolerated. Violation of this act is punishable by death.

V.

Religion, if in want, is to be respected.

VI.

No stealing of ship's supplies or wares. The punishment for this act is marooning.

VII.

To desert the ship or station in battle, is punished by death.

VIII.

No striking one another on board. Every man's quarrel to be ended on shore, at sword and pistol under equal terms and under the watch of the ship's second officer.

IX.

Wounded men to receive special compensation. If any man should lose a joint, or become a cripple in the act of service, he is to have eight hundred pounds, out of the public stock, and for lesser hurts, proportionately.

X.

The Captain's authority and conduct and that of all officers onboard may be challenged at any time, by anyone, with a vote.

XI.

All men are to do their part to be fit and ready for combat.

XII.

Every man has a vote in affairs of the moment and has equal title to the fresh provisions, unless a scarcity makes it necessary to vote a retrenchment.

I looked at the list of signatures, most were marks or some sort of an 'X' all of them had a blood thumb print next to them. I looked up to Mister Lincoln and he instructed me to raise my right hand and put my left hand on a skull to be sworn in. Whose skull it once was I would find out later (although the rumor was that it was Lucifer's skull.) I did as commanded and followed his words with my own. "I swear to uphold the laws of The Venger and the commands of its Captain under fire, in the face of death, into war and through hell if necessary."

I signed my name.

He, then picked up what looked like a samurai dagger which I thought was a bookmark for the signatures and articles and exposed two inches of blade which reflected the sun…

I looked at him unaware of what to do.

"Your thumb print," he said.

I tried to hide my wince as I dragged my thumb along the blade edge and gashed myself. Then I pressed it into the book next to my signature….

"Well done."

I was now an official privateer and strange enough, I was not gripped by some dark, sinister feeling like part of my soul had died or had been sold off to Satan and I was not struck by lightning. In fact, I was more apprehensive than anything else and I was eager to prove myself.

"Welcome to the crew." Mister Lincoln said, "Report to Mister Styles for weapons."

"Thank you."

I moved below deck and reported to Mister Styles and Mister Standish —our armorers.

"Sirs, I was ordered to report to you for weapons."

Muskets were held in an on-deck armory, rigged to keep water out and only to be opened when the order for combat action came about but, here, with these gentlemen I could get pistols and my blades. Standish opened up a giant locker with hundreds of swords –of every type—from every part of the world, European, Chinese, samurai swords, even foils, many of them captured…

"Which one lad?"

I pointed to a large sword of German make and Mister Standish pulled it from the rack and turned to me but when he handed it off, it almost brought me to my keens with its weight.

"No?" Standish said and he took the sword back and racked it. He then pulled a cutlass. "Here," he handed it to me, "Spanish steel…great for killing!" He smiled. "You'll like it."

This blade seemed to fit. I pulled it from its sheath, stamped on the base of the blade was a Spanish inscription that read 'Feel no guilt.' I smiled and put my baldric and blade over my shoulder. I was also told to select a knife, and I pointed to a large blade that was almost shaped like a boomerang. "How about that one?"

Standish smiled. "Do you know what that is?"

I shook my head no.

"That," he said with a sense of pride "Is a Kukri blade." He picked it up and handed it to me.

It was true what they say, weapons seem to call to a man and this blade fitted me ---even though I had never seen anything like it. It was from Asia Minor and was as long as my forearm with a slight bend and an angle to it.

"Don't kill yourself with that." Standish smiled.

Styles handed me two pistols and ten rounds. "Do you know how to make shot?"

"For the pistol? No."

"Mister Reeves and our metal workers will teach you. I need to make some every few days."

I nodded and picked up my guns.

"And don't shoot yourself." Standish said "Or --any of us!"

"I'll try not to."

I passed Duncan-Howe on the way to the deck, he saw the Kukri blade and coughed up some tobacco smoke. "What the hell, are you gonna be hunting elephants so something?" he asked.

"No sir." I replied.

"Well keep that damn thing away from me until you've learned how to use it. You'll cut someone's bloody hand off."

I cleared the armory and then reported to Mister Newcastle at the wheel. "Looking to build a reputation as a privateer Mister Reed?" he asked exhaling tobacco smoke that seemed to smell like a touch of vanilla.

"I am sir, looking to work my way to the Americas."

"Very well, that work starts now. We need a man aloft if you please."

"Yes sir." I looked up to the crow's nest, using my hand to block out the sun. Now was not the time to confess to my problem with heights so I grit my teeth and started to climb the rigging as the rest of our men piled onboard. I climbed and climbed slowly with a tight, nervous grip, keeping my focus forward and up but, not down, if I could avoid it. I finally made it to my post where a cool tropical breeze brought the temperature down. Once I had hold, I could make a survey and from my view, the island –and the town-- seemed very small and so did the deck and everyone on it, below...

-Like ants!

Mister Hallock climbed up to my post to take the starboard watch and he, as the veteran between us, instructed me to take the port side --so I did.

The crew took to their stations, we raised anchor, the sails were opened, and I could feel the ship begin to move and we left the island in our wake....

I kept my eyes fixed on the horizon; it was the only way to make it through my watch. My knuckles became white and fixed –for my life-- to the railing.

Mister Hallock saw this and grinned. "Here," he grabbed some rope from panels at our feet, rope to be used if the rigging at our post failed and he fashioned a harness around my waist and tied it to the pennant mast behind me. "There…now, you can let go and should you fall, you can climb back in!"

This measure did make me feel more secure but, I was hopeful none of my shipmates would spot this as it was something of an embarrassment.

That night, several hours later, Mister Sunderland and Mister Miranda –a defector from the Portuguese navy-- climbed to my station and took over. "Don't forget to untie yourself!" Sunderland joked seeing my leash…

I did –rather ashamed-- and I was allowed to make a cautious descent.

My watch was at an end but not my day for Mister Jagger and Mister Teague decided combat training was something I was need of. Mister Jagger was a man to be feared, the rumor was that he was once thrown into a wooden coffin and buried alive by the Spanish after the battle of Vera Cruz. He dug himself up somehow and sought revenge on those who antagonized him, earning a new reputation --that of a ghost! A reputation he used to his advantage as he carried out a series of night attacks against the local population and patrols until he could leave Vera Cruz and make his way back to the Caribbean.

Jagger was good with a cutlass and gave me moves to commit to memory, thus fencing was the first of the combat arts forced upon me. Fighting and balance, strike and defend and for a time, most of my spare hours were spent in practice of this. When my duties where compete each day, I would also receive education in the making and packing of grenades followed by basic engineering tactics and pistols….

I also learned the value of my knife and I was made to always have it on my person. If the ship were to take water or, I was to be thrown overboard or tangled in the rigging, a knife could save my life if I needed to cut myself free or, cut the rigging free from the ship if it posed a danger. The condition of all the weapons was also of prime importance. Blades sharp and always ready for action. Muskets clean and powder dry and physical strength was prized. Killing was almost an art form with these men.

This training, I felt made me serviceable but, I was not allowed the chance to apply it. When we crossed paths with small merchantmen or sloops, the raiding parties were chosen by command or vote --and paid to match the risk --and I was not to be elected because my shipmates preferred to make war with more seasoned men. This, I could understand, and I must admit, I was unsure of myself when it came to taking someone's life. Could I take it? Would I? But I learned enough skill to have confidence in defense of the ship, should we be attacked and with this, I had hope that I could earn the fare to the Americas or survive the seas until we made port there --even if I was to be voted out of the action.

The Japanese onboard continued to practice with their blades each and every day and they continued my training. 'One never makes the horizon, it was always out of reach' they would say, in terms of swordsmanship, this meant, that you will never complete your training, you will continue to learn and will always continue to work towards improving. Their swords were of a different blade --metal, folded over many, many times from foundries in Asia. I was told by Hatano that he and his Japanese friends preferred this type because it helped in the art of making a clean cut when taking a man's head off --and the different blades seemed to have a sort of attachment to their users.

--Hatano had saved my life in town when he threw a blade down the block that pierced my attacker in the eye but, he never seemed to acknowledge it in any way. The other Japanese crewmen went by the names of Kai, Kato, Sakai, Akai-Dan, Tak, Takeda, Ono and Sanjuro-Tan who had a straight scar down from the left side of his forehead to his chin. The wound robbed him of sight in one eye --which had turned a faded gray-- but he was never deterred during combat training or combat. These men were onboard for profit and adventure, a self-serving change of pace after a lifetime of servitude to a shogun lord back in The Japans. There was more, much more to be earned on the high seas....

I was told of the samurai in my school days. Told about how they planned to meet an invasion of Genghis Khan, centuries before on the shores of Honshu, but these men went by a different name. They were called ronin and I was told that this meant without a master or lord, a 'privateer' of sorts. Many worked local conflicts as mercenaries. These men, with us here, left Japan because they were wanted by local authorities on charges that were not quite clear. Sometimes just being on the losing side could make one a criminal. Many of their number committed suicide back home at the end of their war out of shame…

My understanding was that Hatano and another man with us, from a Japanese Island off the north coast, named Mako Abe were, at first, not fully accepted by the ronin onboard because they were not a samurai. They were from a secret society of sorts, a clan of assassins –or—shinobi, in the north of Japan. A clan called the 'Black Scorpion Clan', covert agents, that dressed in all black and were paid to kill. They killed politicians, tax collectors, feudal lords –anyone who needed killing for anyone who was willing to pay and being paid to kill was considered dishonorable to the ronin and worst still, some of these samurai had fought different assassin organizations in the past so there was –for a time—a natural animosity to overcome but now onboard this ship, everyone was paid to kill so ill feelings soon faded away as the combined effort to earn a profit set in.

Mako was known as the Devil of Iga. He had burned a Lord's castle to the ground and was burned badly in the battle that took place in the flames. One could see the damage to his shoulders, neck, chest, and right arm when he removed his armor. Though he was still serviceable in a fight, he was quite scarred. The quiet word was that he had killed over a hundred men.

Mako almost never spoke, and I was afraid to make conversation with him but if I could read his facial features, I could surmise that he was quite dedicated, somewhat fearless, and apparently in tune with pain, meaning, it didn't really seem to bother him. Sometimes after evening meal, I would watch him insert a series of Chinese needles –dozens of them-- into his burn scars. This was a healing technique of sorts.

The Japanese trained with different weapons, one even used a spear and they also at times, used a secondary blade, much like the first but shorter for close quarter combat and sometimes they would throw and attack with what they called a hira-shuriken –the weapon Hatano used on the street when they saved my life. Mister Baako and the Africans called the hira-shuriken 'throwing stars' because of how they looked when launched in an attack –like stars.

Editor's note: Here the papers shift away from Donovan Reed's combat narrative to the Combat Action Reports on The Venger (Rumored to be collected from conversations with Mister Thorn, The Venger's navigator.)

FOUR YEARS EARLIER

THE COAST OF JAPAN....

Thousands of flaming arrows hit the castle. There was a sudden explosion --Mako was blown through the tower wall, kicking, and screaming --clothes on fire-- as he plunged several stories below and smashed through the ice, into the water...

Fire rained down around him as he punched to the surface. There were bodies adrift all around him, frozen and loaded with arrows. He pushed through them, confiscated a sword, and climbed out of the water as arrows –on fire-- zipped by like rockets. The castle behind him began to collapse as the flames cannibalized the support structure –samurai, and a few geishas, stumbled out of the building –their robes on fire –they died before they could reach the main gate.

By now, everything was a blaze. The snow on the ground was more, dark red with blood and ash than white. Bodies speared. Burning battle flags in the wind, everywhere was death.

Samurai horseman suddenly arrived, riding through the battle ground in hard-charging fashion. "Kill the assassins!" A captain ordered a squadron of cavalry to ride towards Mako and a few surviving ninjas and engaged. Spears cut through them and pierced some of them to the ground where they remained pinned. Those who were not killed, were boxed in and some of the ninjas tried to commit suicide to avoid capture. Those who failed –along with any other survivors-- were lined up and forced to their knees to be beheaded by samurai executioners…

Samurai warriors then splashed into the water and pulled some wounded ninjas to the sand for death and punishment. Mako was quickly brought to his knees to have his head removed with the others but just then, the samurai were counter ambushed! The samurai captain turned to see a sword blade swing at him at eye level taking off the top of his head—he stood there, from the jaw down, until his body finally collapsed backwards.

--More ninjas ran out of the snow-covered wilderness and engaged! Guns and archery brought the samurai riders down. One samurai captain stood, loaded, and pierced with dozens of arrows and bleeding to death but still took a battle stance, ready to fight in last stand fashion. As he rallied the wounded samurai around him to hold out, the black clad ninjas of the 'Scorpion Clan' rushed him. The metal blades took his body apart, piece by piece but now…The Scorpion Clan was out in the open. The one thing that had made it dangerous –and always protected it- was fighting in controlled situations using concealment, surprise, and ambush tactics as an advantage. Here, because they could not keep their vengeance in check, they emerged from the wilderness, closed on a platoon of samurai soldiers, and now found themselves surrounded by a battalion of armor-clad regulars who were waiting. From a league out, these samurai closed a combat square around them and moved in, tighter and tighter until the assassins were fighting almost back-to-back.

After hours of desperate fighting, on a frontier of chaos where arrows, blades and bullets cut everyone down, a wounded Mako, with a sword stuck in him crawled through his burning surroundings and plunged into channel waterway. He was close to death. He moved through the dead, lifeless bodies floating on the surface and managed to pull himself aboard a small fishing junk where he collapsed. The crew jumped over the side in fear for their lives as the junk drifted through the fog, out to sea and the next day, it banged up against the side of The Venger.

In the days to come, The Venger lit up the coast of Japan as it worked its way south. In the township Otaru, there was terror…

The bombardment continued and explosions raked the streets and buildings --people emerged from the smoke and climbed out of their hiding places to flee in a panic. A woman, carrying a baby, stumbled to make her escape, and passed by a samurai blade as it was rinsed in water —cleaned for killing. The Samurai General who handled it, looked at her, unconcerned, for her or her safety. She was after all a member of the peasant class, and he just watched as she and other civilians ran away through the fire and explosions to save themselves.…

Another samurai warrior then galloped through the flames, into the combat area. He quickly dismounted and took a knee to present a letter to this General. It was a letter from the reigning Samurai Lord…

誉
で
死

'Die With Honor.'

The warrior looked up and let the parchment leave his hands to blow away in the wind –like so many lives. Years of civil war, then battling ninja assassins and now this! It was a good day to die. The samurai survivors of his clan assembled around him with their armor and weapons. He shouted short, simple commands and they responded in unison with a yell and then a quick bow and they began to run towards the bombardment on the beach. The cannon fire continued to rip through buildings –and men—and by now, the entire town was on fire! The smoke blocked out the sun and the world seemed to turn gray…

On the beach, the samurai lined up in battle formations, ready for action and all set to die in their place as their code of conduct required. They made last minute armor adjustments and weapon checks as smoke rolled over their combat banners –and the battle flags on their backs.

On the horizon was the ominous shadow of 'the phantom' they had come to fear --The Venger—as it emerged from the smoke for a split second, just long enough for the Samurai General to see the skull and crossbones --and then, like a ghost, it disappeared in the smoke again and was gone.

This warlord wasn't even sure if what he saw was real until the ship suddenly emerged again from the smoke and smashed through some Japanese trading junks that were set ablaze in the bay –one junk sank in the tide as the crew jumped to abandon its decks…

--Death was here!

Suddenly, there was another flash from the guns as cannon rounds slammed into the beach, zipped overhead, and blew apart what was left of the trading posts, dock, and township buildings. Some of the samurai officers were blown off their horses –or vanished, blown apart, as cannon rounds cut through them on their way to explode in town…

Covered by cannon fire, fully-armed conquerors rowed forward, from the ship towards the beach as cannon balls zipped just overhead and screamed through the air to smash a target and explode. These killers pressed forward, through the smoke rowing closer and closer to the beach with rhythm and a wicked, collective cadence that sounded sinister in purpose…

The Samurai General shouted the command to brace for the attack as the privateers stormed through the tide, ashore and opened up with gunfire and grenades --some of the samurai charged forward to fight as lead rounds smashed through their ranks, cutting through armor, and cutting them down as several bodies dropped in the sand, dead!

The General ordered his legion into a defensive picket line with their guns but just as they formed up, Mister Arson fired a pistol round from the tide and the musket ball smashed though this General's helmet and hammered into his skull. Blood started running down, over his eye and when he dropped from his horse and hit the ground, his eyes had turned to a faded gray.

Samurai marksmen fired back, killing a few raiders in the tide but without concern for those who fell, the rest of these conquerors stormed the beach. They moved to close the distance, firing pistols from each hand, throwing grenades that streaked smoke through the air, and pulling their sabers.

Teague, used the teeth of his blunderbuss to cut down, kill and wound eight samurai in one blast.

Now --it was war!

The samurai and pirate ranks slammed together and merged into chaos. Tackling! Cutting! Explosions! There were sparks as cutlass blades banged into katanas…

Nighthorse ducked as a samurai blade swung above him, and he came back around with a down-swing of his tomahawk as the other Hurons clashed, banged, and cut into the samurai soldiers.

Jaffar moved under a spear and swung with his giant, curved blade almost cutting a samurai warrior in half, and he turned to slice-up two others, just as a grenade went off! The explosion blew Jaffar and the samurai off the ground and spit shrapnel into their bodies.

Addo and Jagger opened up with pistols as some samurai warriors tried to close in on them. They turned to blades with Addo gripping on samurai by the neck ultimately pulling his voice box out with his fist!   Some of the samurai around him were killed by throwing stars as The Venger's own ronin warriors stormed forward passing Addo just as he dropped his gasping victim to the beach.

"These bastards employ traitors!" A Samurai Captain shouted in his native language, shocked to see a battalion of former samurai charge through the smoke and storm forward, shoulder to shoulder with pirates. One even planted a massive black flag into the sand, its skull and crossbones blowing in the wind for all to see, as if to indicate that this beach --was now theirs.

The privateers then stormed into what was left of the town and moved on the Imperial castle…

A wounded samurai captain was dragged forward and dropped at Essex's boots. He was then brought to his feet, coughing up blood but when he spotted Takeda and some of The Venger's ronin soldiers he tried to lung at them to kill them but was restrained by Rabal and Wolfe.

"Your reign is over!" Essex said, "We're going to liberate your prison block." Essex continued as Takeda translated. "We're going to liberate your enemies, members of the oppressed peasant class and allow some of them to join our ranks, like this man…" He pointed to Mako "Who you left in the tide to die."

The samurai captain spit up some blood and said a few angry words.

Takeda translated. "This man is not samurai. He is a gangster killer." Takeda's eyes darted up to Essex. "Ninja."

"Well, whatever he is, he's one of us now." Essex was completely dismissive of this Samurai's prejudice and continued to make his point, "We are going to raid your warehouses, anyone who resists will be killed. Understand?"

The samurai remained silent but inside he wished to die.

Essex leaned forward, "Understand?"

Rabal bashed this warrior in the back of the head to make sure he heard the captain.

He mumbled a few words in Japanese. Takeda translated, "He understands."

"Good." The Captain and some of his officers began to get about their business when this samurai captain uttered a few words to Takeda. He asked Takeda to preserve his honor and behead him rather than allow him to remain a prisoner.

Takeda responded saying, "I will kill you when we leave –or when it suits me."

The privateers and their ronin allies stormed the palace –some crossed the courtyard to raid the other buildings. Essex, Newcastle, and the war captain Teague entered the palace gates. What was left of the palace guard was killed as they tried to fight their way out. The privateers liberated the sake stores, the warehouses were plundered for sacks of rice, plum wine, and dried seaweed of all things....

Jagger put his foot on the body of the dead man but, he could not pull his cutlass out of the ribs of the samurai he killed. Exhausted, he finally released his grip. "Damn. I like this sword."

"Leave it." Dax-Varrow said.

Jagger said a depressed goodbye to his favorite cutlass, moved into the castle armory as Merciless and the others stormed in, and took a fresh set of samurai blades off the weapons rack, something new and unused, from a foundry buried in the mountains up north. Wiley and Fury took new breast plates, helmets, and some other armor elements...

The armory was cleaned out and all the weapons seized along with armor and the barrels of gunpowder.

The palace superstructure was now on fire as they moved through the rooms and down a dark corridor. There, they found men imprisoned. Some in cells, some attached to different torture devices.

Essex looked at these survivors.

"Political prisoners." Takeda offered up, "Samurai of rival clans, samurai without masters, mercenaries, revolutionaries, some thieves.... awaiting execution."

Essex stepped to the wooden bars of the cage door and made direct and precise eye contact with the men imprisoned. He appeared to read the thoughts of some of these prisoners. "Release them!" He suddenly commanded.

The cell door was opened but as Essex started to move out, one of the samurai prisoners called out to him. Essex stopped and turned around. This man appeared to have some sort of military rank and after a moment·he spoke again. Essex looked to Takeda for translation. "He requests permission to settle a debt." Takeda said, "The Lord who occupies this castle subdued this man's wife and made her his own, He requests the honor of killing him." Takeda continued as the man spoke, "He says, in return, he and his men will offer no resistance as long as we do not cross the border into their fiefdom."

"His fiefdom?"

"He says his fiefdom is no more. His lord is dead but the land that was once his fiefdom is home to many peasants. He requests we do not raid there."

Teague who took orders from no one, save the Captain, put his hand on a pistol in his sash and –without removing it-- pulled the hammer back. The samurai saw this but raised his eyes back to Essex as if unconcerned and looked to the Captain for his answer. In truth, it made no difference to Essex who killed who in this fight so, it was an easy request to grant. "Fine. Allow this man the right to take the head of his enemy, then let us get about our business here."

The Lord sat in his massive throne room and waited for death. He knew this was the end.

The privateers and their newly liberated prisoner allies stormed the hallway outside where the last of the palace guards waited to make their final stand. Swords –and spears-- trembling in their hands. The action was quick --they were all quickly killed –save those that killed themselves and the throne room doors were forced open. Essex and this war party moved inside, leaving only the Lord and his two concubines to cower before him. He looked down on him as he sat motionless, waiting, and aware of his fate --ready to be beheaded. Essex then stepped back and out of the way as Jagger threw one of his captured samurai blades to this liberated prisoner. He caught it, pulled it out of its sheath, moved forward, muttered a few words in Japanese and then, swung it down with all the force he could muster.

--The lord's head then rolled along the hard wood floor.

This samurai prisoner then stepped to Essex, making the men around him somewhat nervous as they reached for their weapons but, he raised the blade with both hands and presented it back to the Captain as if to say thank you and gave a quick bow. Essex put his hand on the blade and lowered it as if to say, 'keep it' He then looked to the others, "Let's move."

They marched from the burning castle as it started to collapse behind them. Everything was being moved to the ship, sake –some of the barrels had already been punched open by the ronin-- wine, rice, gold bars stamped with the markings of The Shogun, weapons, everything and as the combat teams were moving back to load the ship the samurai officer who wanted to protect his fiefdom, called out to get the Captain's attention once more....

--Essex, Teague, and Takeda turned. Behind this man, some of the prisoners took to the countryside to flee but this samurai captain stood with eleven others at his back. He grumbled a few choice words in Japanese and then he and his men bowed, holding their position with eyes to the ground...

Essex looked to Takeda for an explanation. "This man says his name is Sanjuro-Jo." Takeda said, "He says, these samurai have lost their lands and have no loyalty to The Shogun." Takeda looked them over once more, "Some of his clan have been forced to become bandits and highwaymen."

"And?"

"They wish to repay their debt for the freedom you have given them and, they respectfully ask permission to join the crew." They would rather raid and fight on the high seas then rob their countrymen to survive.

Essex looked them over as they held their respective posture. He could see many had the same markings on their robes which signified a combined history or battle order...

"Ki Montoku clan." Takeda said.

"Ask them to assist us in loading the provisions then see Mister Lincoln to make the cut." He said referring to the cut and thumb print one made when they signed the articles.

"Yes Captain." Takeda turned to the ronin and shouted his instructions in Japanese, and they moved out to obey.

Back on board The Venger, Jaffar was a having cup of tea as the metal shrapnel was removed from his shoulder by Jopo. The other wounded were being looked after as the sake barrels were lowered in nets to the lower decks –the ronin seemed to celebrate this. Captured weapons were turned over to Standish to be inventoried. Sacks of rice and barrels of water were loaded onboard, and the galley stoves were already working....

"Where to sir?" Harrow asked from the steering.

"South –and let's be quick about it."

(Editor's note: Back to Reed's Combat Narrative)

THE VENGER. FOUR YEARS LATER....

I looked at hundreds of smoking needles piercing the burns –and slash marks—that rolled down the left side of Mako's body. It was the body of a killer that had been overtaxed by war. The ronin gathered around him with a cask of sake. Some removed their red and black armor, weapons, and tunics to reveal decorative tattoos of dragons, tigers, or koi fish –complex artistic messaging that meant something special in their ranks.

"They've fought everyone from the Chinese to East Indian Regulars to Polynesian cannibals." Wolfe said as he passed some tobacco over to the ronin and collected some sake in return. He kicked up the mug, took a sip and then passed it to me for a try. "Damn ferocious!" and he moved to the top deck.

What was this I was drinking? It tasted like something I could light on fire, and I tried to smile as the samurai watched me drink it as to not offend any of them...

"Watch out for this group Reed," Duncan-Howe said –long stem pipe in his teeth-- as he walked past with a few of the Hurons. "They'll kill ya' with that damn sake poison! Whiskey, from the Highlands, now that's my drink."

The ronin smiled and seemed to wave him off....

"Starboard watch aloft!" Arson shouted as he moved through the decks. "That's you Reed!" He turned to the others, "You too, Wolfe."

"Aye" He finished the sake and pitched the mug to Hobby in the galley. "Let's kill something today!"

"Cyril, Hallock, Hawkquez –on your feet. Dax-Varrow, move!" Arson ordered, "Where's Bolt?"

Cyril finished his drink and pointed towards the bow…

"Get him in place!"

"Yes, Mister Arson." Cyril returned as he stood up and grabbed his weapons.

"Are we gonna kill somethin' today or not?" Wolfe asked again.

"If the fates allow!" Arson continued, "Now move to your post, off you go!"

I worked the decks and continued to observe the rituals and habits of the men onboard. Here, as reported, a world at sea had different rules –and understandings—than that of society. For example, the Moor privateers – from North Africa, Istanbul, and Arabia—they wore robes, tight head wraps that also covered the face and they carried long curved swords with massive blades, but they preferred European boots to traditional sandals. They were allowed prayer time even in the event of war. Often under cannon fire they would take to the rug and prey to their God, which they explained was the same as my God, only, the practice of respect and worship was different. As a result, they were excellent fighters because they had settled all their godly business, and their souls were at peace and prepared to die. They also believed that their fate was written and there was nothing they could do to change it and because of this, they all seemed very calm even in the face of cannon and combat.

The ronin onboard prayed at a small wooden shrine mounted below deck between the cannon and their hammocks and only for a brief second and usually ending with a single, loud clap of the hands. They also maintained a vigilant practice of cleanliness with a wash with hot sea water –since fresh water was rationed-- from a giant kettle every night and every practice of theirs was worked to perfection.

Hair was sometimes cut short by the blade or tied back, out of the way of a man's vision. The fashion of wigs –powdered and popular with the upper classes back home--- was, shall we say, not practiced here. These men made no attempt to alter their appearance. They were real, battle scars and all.

Our Native American crewmen prayed for different things at different times, sometimes a prayer for the wind when the sea was without and sometimes for rain, sometimes for guidance in battle, sometimes for the health of others. Their weapons were also unique. Many had taken to the musket but also preferred the work of an axe called a tomahawk –and knife-- rather than a cutlass. Only Baltimore used a sword when working with his tomahawk. My impression was that when Bons or Nighthorse looked at a man, they already had decided where to slam the blade of the tomahawk --into his head, shoulder, or neck-- whether the situation called for violence or not and as a result, I was nervous around them.

The American natives wore European tunics, white, dark blue, red etc., with the sleeves rolled up to just below the elbow but they maintained their native look with their bracelets, tattoos and what they wore around their necks – decorative leather chokers and, of course some of them tied their long black hair back or cut it into what we, on deck called a mohawk and some allowed their hair to just grow long as a matter of fashion I suppose. Most of them spoke English and French – and some even spoke Dutch and they always seemed to add hand signals to their conversation.

There were quite a few heathen atheists with us who had no God but, between our decks the Christians were the largest group onboard and, as I have reported, the man of the cloth was William Rush. He would hold Sunday services for those who wanted to attend. Often the ship's work during such services was handled by our Asian, Native or Moor brothers. In turn, we did our share when it was their time to worship. And this was always done without question. It was expected.

Cowardice and lack of duty seemed to be the only cause for penalty here. Religion --or lack thereof-- was the business of each man on board.

And combat --sometimes for days at a time—was the responsibility of all of us and that made religious practices –and differences-- of small concern.

A good part of the crew was made up of former slaves. The slave trade was not restricted to Africans but also white criminals, many chained for lack of tax money or debt or sometimes trumped-up treason charges when political enemies wanted to remove each other. Many offered a certain set of skills rare in the islands like medical skills, accounting skills or teaching and language skills….

We had Africans onboard from the West Coast of Africa, the South of Africa and Africans that called themselves Masai and Zulu. All had exceptional fighting skills. Not always was this the case with the former white slaves, they were political prisoners and debtors, for the most part. They knew the manners of court and maybe dueling but hand-to-hand fighting was something many had to learn. They were sometimes put to work in other areas, Mister Lincoln was a prime example of this. He was once in debtor's prison, his family taken from him and put into a poor house, when the church refused to harbor them. Disease killed them during the first winter and he –Mister Lincoln-- was shipped off to work in the sugar cane fields of The Bahamas. Two years and several trips to the whipping post later, he was liberated when The Venger raided the island, took all the stores, freed the slaves, and burned the plantations to the ground. Prior to all that, he worked in an accounting house for a Misters Marley and Fezziwig and thus, he had skills The Venger could use….so he began to earn his keep.

On board, carpenters like Mister Crowe were also prized. He had the nickname 'Coffin' because he had been an undertaker in South Carolina. Repairs could often be made at sea –even mast replacement—and there were carpenters and metal workers –like Mister Reeves--on board along with other skilled tradesmen who were vital to the ship's survival and performance. And Crowe did in fact, make coffins from time to time when required.

Carpenters and medical personnel were not used to board during an attack. They were, by trade, too valuable to lose. They, the carpenters, received equal shares plus a bonus for their kits –and often they would have to assist the medical men with the wounded. As a man of education, I was glad to see our doctors had advanced past the practice of using leeches to bleed a patient and the use of strange powders. While garrisoned in Colonial South America, the natives there showed Johannis how to make new ointments and cures. Many made from leaves and tree bark. He was allowed a personal expedition anytime we raided off the South American coast to meet, trade and even speak with different native tribes about cures. For this he was reviled by society. In Europe, no one would hear of this. The idea that modern European medicine could learn from some heathens in the jungle was at best laughable. But our doctor persisted in experimentation, including a smoke, cultivated in the jungle and not unlike tobacco 'cept that it was more of a pain killer when inhaled.

He and the cook even shared a small garden off the port bow for herbs and vegetables.

One evening, I dropped below deck at the bow, where the officer's quarters were located. The doors were open. and I, curious, could see inside these narrow rooms. There were two bunks built into the side of the ship. One room –Teague and Jaffar's, had a table that sat under a lantern, on it was a chess set with a game in play along with some papers, pistols and books on engineering and mathematics. Opposite were racks of weapons, --originally built by the Royal Navy when this ship was theirs so officers could have quick reach of their weapons to put down any unrest below deck.

The other officers had similar cabins, two war chiefs per room, some further towards the front of the ship, some towards the stern or back. Arson and Rajiv, the gunner, Nighthorse, and Jupiter.

Sanjuro had no chair in his quarters, only a small mat on the floor where he sat next to two half barrels of his homemade sake. Sanjuro also had a game in his quarters that looked like a form of Japanese backgammon -- and he would play this with Duncan-Howe at his pipe until late in the evening…

Harrow and Newcastle as first and second officer had their own quarters with slightly more space. What kind of man was Harrow? Or Newcastle for that matter? One could tell by their personal belongings of hobby and as for Harrow, I surprised to see had paints and canvass by his window. Newcastle had several books written in French and Latin and something written on tactics and protocols of Marcus Aurelius …

These were the books, traits, and arts of men I would expect to see around Oxford, not the killers of the high seas but one thing was made clear and somewhat to my surprise, that these men were not average men in any way…

I was at the evening meal with Wicks, Irons, Addo, Bons, Dax-Varro and Standish –who was thought of as worldly because he had once been in a six-story building –that wasn't a dungeon or prison tower-- and a few others. Across from me was Mister Sampson-Rift, who wore a large scarf across his face –like a bandit-- where his nose and jawbone use to be, since that part of his face was removed by a musket ball in a firefight off of Cuba. His meals had to be churned to mush for only the teeth on the top of his mouth were intact and he could not chew or smoke for that matter but, he seemed polite enough, as far as my interpretation of his hand signals could determine ---since he could not speak.

At dinner, I scribed on my parchment the day's events much like a journal. I'm not sure what compelled me to make notes but something in the back of my mind told me it would be wise to remember details of this rather unique situation.

Wicks saw me writing and asked, "Are you a poet like this one?" He motioned to Clairmont.

"I'm afraid not," I smiled, "I don't have the talent."

"Then what is that?"

"It's a record of the day."

He looked at it with curiosity and I realized he could not read. Wicks had a wife on an island off Hispaniola, a woman from the West Coast of Africa and he had several children and a small cottage there. There was no real means to make a living 'cept privateering so here he was, with us. He would see them once or twice a year, depending on our voyage and target but, no more than that.

"Would you like me to show you what this means?" I said pointing at the letters.

He remained silent.

"Because if I do," I continued, "You can send letters of your thoughts from different outposts to your wife at home and have a conversation with her even though you may be far away...."

He gave a subtle smile and nodded yes. And with this I started an informal school of sorts below deck at mealtime for those interested. I focused on letters and writing at first, then science. These men had no knowledge of the basics but a grand knowledge of the world, topography, locations, maps, numbers, and charts and of course –weapons. They had command of different languages, local customs, and weather prediction. I did not dare enter into the education on our political system or religion for that would be an intrusion on a man's personal life and may cause offense. Likewise, politics was found to be something of a boring sideshow to these men. The very idea that a man could place himself on a golden throne and pass commands to those he regarded as beneath him was, by its very nature, cause of spark and anger here. A silly business! With these men, respect in the art of war or maritime practices was what was respected most. As I had learned, the man on your gun deck that would give aid to your cause in survival had more rank in a man's life than any king or governor.

At this time, my main specialty continued to be manual labor –cleaning deck guns, moving powder kegs--with combat training between shifts and meals and I was taught in all the combat arts when time allowed and ten days into our voyage, I was ordered below deck to witness gunnery practice with the 'Gun Tigers' or The Bengals. This was an art form. The gunners – who had good skills with mathematics and calculation--would load and wait for the command as the Master Gunner timed his 'firing order' with the roll of our ship and the roll of his target allowing for maximum effect. The trick was the speed in reloading –a round fired every ninety seconds--

and the type of shot that was to be sent into the enemy ship. Shot could punch holes and explode or cut the mast, rigging, and steering if that was the objective.

Mister Locke waved me forward to help his gun crew. This was in practice with the effort that all men aboard be taught to be their best in all areas if the need to replace someone was to arise. Gerard gave me my position and told me what to do upon his signal. Mister Rajiv gave the order to fire and out came the thunder as the blasts erupted. The cannons rolled back, Java looked to me, with his hands out and I heaved him the cannon ball for the next shot and down the barrel it went as Mister Gerard slammed it into place with the plunger. Then, she was made to fire and pulled back into place by the breechings or ropes Time and speed was what was most important, get the gun loaded fast so all three decks could unload on our target again and again in quick order....

Rajiv walked the deck bellowing commands and quoting the time in between bombardments. He then dropped down to deck two to supervise their work, then deck three before making the climb back to our deck and continuing. Load and fire! Load and fire! Again, and again.

I watched Java, Wilder –with his screaming pet monkey named Gunpowder on his shoulder—Saxon and the others, work and I tried to commit to memory their actions. The gunners were strong, stacked with muscles from rolling cannon into place and their forearms carried --the mark, burns up the forearms from hot iron, guns, and fuses...

--Many had become hard of hearing due to constant blasts.

We trained to the point of exhaustion, loading and firing. I almost collapsed because the heat was stifling --and fatigue. My face must have expressed puzzlement in the continued work and Mister Gerard smiled and said, "We train so the art of killing can be done, without thinking. Only reflex. You will get it soon enough."

Mister Locke gave me a hand up and he ordered me back to the guns...

I was also taught how to use the on-deck mortars and deck guns by Irons, Ward and Mister Bishop. Irons was a former cavalry officer with the Dutch military. He was –many years ago-- captured by the Prussians and pressed into their military, then he bought passage to the new world where he was recruited to take charge of a militia unit in Virginia. It was not the life he wanted so he ended up here where his skills would be appreciated, and he was free to continue to search for his meaning....

He would call Mister Ward to throw a 'target' off the port side rail then give me instruction on the deck swivel gun in how to aim, fire and hit it. Sometimes working until late into the sunset...

Mister Bishop supervised this, and he chuckled when I missed.

Irons threw out another target, which was a piece of wood, "Now," he pointed at the floating marker, "That's the enemy working into position to kill you! He's trying to fire at you. It's you or them and whoever hits his target first will survive the day."

I fired again and I did finally hit the target. Irons smiled and Bishop nodded his approval. Just when I thought practice was over, he said, "Keep at it." And we did until it was almost dark.

"Nice work Jans!' Irons said impressed with Bishop's gunnery –and teaching skills.

"Jans?" --What? Who was that?

"Yes" Bishop grinned, "Jans. It's my name."

"Then why do they call you Bishop?"

"Because I used to be a bishop!" He smiled as he worked with the deck gun.

"Gave up on God, did you?"

"No.... I didn't give up on God." He reloaded the deck gun and swung it back into firing position. "I gave up on man!"

That night, as the ronin drank sake of their own making on the deck, I took coffee under the stars –exhausted. After gunnery practice, I was still working to get my hearing back, I saw Pharaoh smiling, as he listened to some rather quiet music from Rajal and his sitar and Whitney working his violin, with child-like innocence. I also heard Duncan-Howe complaining about how he had to smoke dried seaweed once on a voyage when his tobacco ran out which put him in a foul mood for months. The Hurons and

Master Lau were nearby talking among themselves, and I watched Mako hand them a jug of sake as he passed by on his way to the helm.

I looked to the steering and watched the Captain work his charts under the light of a lantern, Newcastle and Thorn, the navigator, were with him and O'Shea had the wheel. Mister O'Shea was a man who fought against the British his whole life from bases in Ireland. He once even took over a coastal light house and removed the signal torch to get British ships to run aground on the rocks. He would raid them, turning salvaged weapons over to his Irish comrades while selling the cargo back to British merchants at a reduced rate…

Of the Captain, I knew little but, his presence was that of a man with firm confidence in his abilities. He had a directness in manner and tone with a touch of darkness to his character. I never spoke with him up to this point, I only saw him.

I was beginning to understand the command structure here, some of it, a carry-over from the officers that defected from the Royal Navy. Although our Captain put himself up for a vote every twelve months for the men to re-elect or replace him, it was a mere formality because he had earned too much respect to ever be put down.

Harrow was second in command and Newcastle –who wore his sword on his back when we were at peace --but not in action-- was the de facto third officer…

There was a unique command structure on The Venger beyond that, a sort of informal Warrant Officer type rank –or 'war captains' something I heard was on no other ship. These men served as a sort of non-commissioned officer -a sergeant type, if you will, to use the army equivalent —and they were elected or re-elected every twelve months and could also be put up for a vote of no confidence or replacement at any time –although this was also unlikely, for the men who had this rank were of a special quality and they included the German from the Baltic coast –Mister Reader –who struck me as more of a classic Viking type born in a different era. He was direct and dangerous and always seemed ready to strike. Mister Teague, Mister Jaffar, Sanjuro, Nighthorse, Duncan-Howe –our 'philosopher' of sorts-- Jupiter, Lo, Calixto –the former police constable from Lisbon, Watson –who had a hook where his left hand once was— Wolfe, Arson, Rajiv and Lynch were the other ranking officers of this cast. I feared to be in the presence of these men –with the exception of Lynch who was refined-- for they were of a very direct nature and didn't abide a man that could not hold his own so to speak! As such, they made it their business to build me up and teach me all I could learn about how to be an efficient, respect-worthy crewman here.

Mazatal, the Aztec, also had rank but he almost never spoke outside of the group of other Aztec warriors called 'Jaguars', except to convey specific orders. He did always seem to have a curious and inquisitive look to him, and he would answer if spoken to but, other than that, he was quiet and volunteered little conversation. Of the Aztecs, I learned that many had fought the Spanish missionaries who –with the help of soldiers-- tried to convert the tribe by force to Catholicism. Such were the policies in New Spain. The world was to be made Catholic. They, the Aztecs, more than any other cultural group onboard, seemed to run things in a democratic fashion. All the Aztecs had to agree on something before they would take action. Unless it came down from the Captain then it was 'a go' without debate. But if it was another issue and they did not all agree, they would not move. Unlike the Moors or Hurons who would issue orders to their battle groups and got immediate obedience. The Moors in particular, seemed to obey without question. They were killing machines for lack of a better term….

Rajiv –the joyous-- was the master gunner in command of all the deck guns with Mister Locke as his second in command. Mister Towne, Mister Tao –from Shanghai, Java, Saxon, Mister Tane –from the islands of the South Pacific-- and Mister Wilder always with his pet monkey on his shoulder, were the sub-lieutenants….

All the men on The Venger seemed to practice honesty but Nighthorse –more than most—could not shield his words, both good or bad, he spoke his mind and in the most minimal terms, never using any words that may be unnecessary. Baltimore on the other hand was somewhat more, friendly.

Another native went by the name Bons Iroquois. Or Bons. This I was told was not his actual name but the name of his tribe back home in Albany. For some reason, it became his moniker, and he did not seem to mind. Bons had a stern –almost mean-- way about him though, he could be helpful to me at times and would show me some combat tricks involving a tomahawk.

The other natives seemed to take English names like Sam who had an almost child-like way about him. He was a fighter but also, in a strange sense, seemed innocent. He was also young –nineteen, like me. There was also Mister Lamatan, George Big Sky, Jacques 'The Bear Killer' and one other whose name I would not come to know for he never spoke it or did his comrades ever call it –the crew referred to him as Mister Silence!

At night Mister Baltimore --and sometimes, the others-- seemed to practice a ritual with smoke, open hands to the sky and a native song. They would pass a long pipe around and they were not to be disturbed. The other men working around them, would give them space for this practice which only took but a few minutes. I was surprised by both the practice and the fact that they were allowed to practice without malice. This would not be the case in Europe or –I would guess—in the Americas where prejudice ran high. For our custom was obvious, break a man of such habits and make him more like ourselves.

-But not here.

It was better to respect a man's practices, then disrespect them and cause animosity in our operation, or worse—in combat. They were allowed their peace, as were the others onboard. The Christians had their time on Sunday mornings, the Moors like Mister Amir, Jeddah, Barak, Jaffar and the others a few moments five times a day. And again, of the Moors I knew little, they seemed serious, deadly and without humor. They too were fierce and had a traditional hatred for the Spanish that went back to the days of Christopher Columbus. The specifics of this I did not know nor was I ever comfortable in asking. These men were well respected as were all on board for I came to learn that only the best --the survivors of many conflicts— were here, on this ship, alive today.

As with all systems of society and government, there were also forms of punishment –most of which was reserved for captives. The plank was one. It was designed to scare a victim into telling the privateers what they wanted to know and once one did, they were usually permitted to walk back aboard the ship. However, at times, this crew would blindfold a man, tie his hands, and force him off the end of the plank so the rest of the awaiting prisoners could watch in horror and thus be made to speak more freely. If the intension was to be 'more cruel' one could be fastened with a prison ball and chain and then just kicked over the side so a man could sink into the ocean depths…

Sometimes, our victims would make things difficult after the surrender –which was a violation of trust. Once a surrender was accepted, any action after that was a violation of the terms and met with death. A death of our choosing. And the choice was usually of a nature that was quite severe as an example to anyone who may be harboring a similar thought of troublemaking. The 'prison ball' was a popular solution in this case. I pictured victims hitting the ocean floor, where the weight of the lead ball would keep them in place as they panicked and tried to reach the surface only to slow down and eventually die in the ocean depths…and remain there for all time.

More wicked still was the art of keelhauling. I use the term 'art' loosely. This was a practice as yet unknown to me, but I heard Watson describe it, where a prisoner would be tied by the wrists and ankles to a system of pulleys then dragged under the boat from the port to starboard side. His flesh would be ripped to the bone by barnacles --like razorblades--as he was dragged across the hull. Once was enough for both victim and witnesses alike but there were particular cases where a man would be sent around again and again until there was very little left of him.

--A harsh practice to be sure and I was unaware at the time that these tactics and the brutal practice of war was coming my way, on an apocalyptic scale.

VI

LET GOD BE YOUR AGENT

At dawn one morning, I climbed on the top deck into a still environment. The men on deck, Addo, the ronin, Jagger all of them were standing still, looking into the horizon off the port side bow…

I armed myself and stepped to Blythe "What is it?"

He hissed me silent and pointed up to the Captain on the raised quarter deck –looking through his spyglass near the wheel. I then turned towards the bow and focused my attention on a small object –a dot- - on the horizon that I could barely see –a ship!

I looked back to the Captain. He continued to survey the ship ahead and through his glass could see the giant flag blowing in the wind off her stern. "She's Dutch" he said, "Warship, roughly forty guns."

--FORTY GUNS!

Unknown to me, Harrow and our crew could calculate the number in their ranks based on estimated number of cannons.

I waited at my position, wondering if this day would be –thee day-- that would bring me my first action. And if I was ready for it?

Essex suddenly slammed his spyglass closed and said in a low tone, "Mister Harrow…."

"Sir?"

The Captain paused, then gave the order through his teeth, "Run 'em down!"

"Aye sir." Harrow turned with a wicked grin, "Action stations" and the men jumped...

A touch of fear set in against my bones. Every port back in England – and the Americans-- warned of privateers and the risk of sea travel. The government didn't like wide publications of plundering, but insurance companies did, for it aided in their justification to raise rates on shipping companies. Now I was about to be part of their problem...

Harrow belted out commands which were repeated though all the decks. Preparations for the attack commenced and the tempo shifted as men prepared their stations for war. I tried to mask my anxiety and work through it. The men around me showed no such fear but instead seemed to have a toughness or confidence or even a fun-loving eagerness --as they prepped their weapons and guns-- for what was ahead.

Mister Thorn kicked open a deck box loaded with captured flags from almost every nation and pulled out and unrolled a Dutch flag. He threw it to Mister Irons who hoisted it into the wind to disguise our identity...

As for myself, I tried to hide the fact that my hands were trembling, and I suddenly began to question my enlistment. "I'm a teacher" I quietly repeated to myself. "What the hell am I doing here?" It was a question I only seemed to ask myself now, now that the combat situation ahead of us was real --I may have made a very bad mistake signing up, without the full realization of what I was stepping into because here it was, now in front of me --hell on the horizon!

Bishop suddenly grabbed me and spun me around. In a firm and almost somewhat civil tone, he said. "Get a hold of yourself!' I looked at him. He knew my situation and he looked at me with a steel gaze in his eyes. "Do your job and we-will-win-this.
Understand?"

I gave a nervous nod in agreement.

"Good. Now move."

I jumped below deck –still scared—but the level of confidence of the men around me, in a strange way, seemed to make this situation a little more positive...

In the shadows below deck, Towne, Java, Wilder and the gun crews made ready. I watched as Mister Barak and the Moors ran their giant curved blades on the spinning sharpening stone. The curved blade was a mystery to me --although I had seen it-- I had no experience with its practice. Once the blade was ready for action, Barak would slice his forearm –which was heavily scarred—for this was his ritual, his sword could not go back into its sheath until it had drawn blood so even when sharpened –if there is no one around to kill—he cut his arm before loading it back into his sheath…

Another Moor –Mister Amir—looked up from the crank. "Give me your blade," he ordered, and I pulled my cutlass and turned it over to him. He checked the edge for cutting power and then ran it over the sharpening stone to increase its sharpness and 'killing strength'. Then he handed it back to me with a nod "Good luck today and let God be your agent."

I took my saber with a nod of gratitude and moved past the sick bay as the medical men prepared their operating space. Tables were cleared and covered in blood-stained canvas in preparation for the wounded. Their tools at the ready. Mister Crowe and carpenters joined them with their building kits and prepared to offer assistance. Sand was poured on the floor to help with traction against any blood that might be spilled…

As I stumbled forward to my section. Blythe passed me a crate of grenades that I was to heave to the deck so I moved back through the chaos –grenades in hand—through the movement of men pulling cannons into position, other men grabbing their weapons, to the deck hatch where I could pass this box of killers to Mister Baltimore and he and our Native contingent started to cut the fuses….

We repeated this action loading crate after crate of killing devices to the top deck, then, when ordered, we climbed up top as the deck guns were loaded with reserve shot hauled into position….

My nerves started to get the better of me and I continued to look to the horizon at our target. It was getting closer and closer. We maintained our attack principals --a practice I was to learn for the first time here-- which was to stay on the edge of the horizon, friendly pennant on the foremast, in this case, a Dutch flag, captured from an earlier action, then, once dark, open sail, gain speed and close with a vengeance!

Once we were under the cover of night sky, we picked up two, maybe three knots. No lanterns, fires or pipes allowed on deck –we moved in total darkness. I worked my way forward to the bow and watched as the ship in the distance slowly came closer....

From what I could tell, our target seemed unaware of our presence. For she did not change course or speed and there was no sign –or sound-- of panic or movement, the sound of which would have traveled across the waters to where I stood. I looked to Teague who slowly ran his thumb down the blade of his saber to test the sharpness and just then, the Captain gave command, "Run up the colors and prepare to engage."

The skull and cross bones was raised into the wind…

"Prepare to engage!" Harrow moved through the deck repeating the command in a low voice…

Mister Nighthorse and the Hurons applied their war paint. The Japanese adjusted their armor. Sakai fastened his helmet called a Kabuto and with it came a fierce face mask, the look of which was horrifying. Like a monster. The other ronin poured their ration of water on their blades and prepared for some killing.

Men checked their weapons which were always at the ready, some men packed three or four pistols in their belts. Other men, like Jagger had two, double-barreled pistols --one for each hand. Addo and the Zulu finished painting their faces like skulls then primed their weapons and took to their stations….

A fatal flaw lit like a fuse in my mind. Was I capable of the job before me? Could I do this? We were about to find out….

We continued to close the distance; the lights of the target ship were now very close…

"Roll out the port side battery…. quietly!" The Captain ordered. In almost total silence, hand signals were used to signal the commands, open the gun doors, and pull the ropes –or breechings—to put the guns into firing position. Rajiv gauged the target based on the position and distance of the ship's deck lamps and signaled Locke and Saxon to put the cannon rounds through the hull where the ship's crew would be sleeping, making an effort to keep all the shot above the water line so she would stay afloat when we boarded.

When we were within a league, Mister Harrow looked back to the Captain and got the nod, in calm fashion as he said one word. "Weapons!"

Tiger raised his large scarf to cover his mouth and nose. Mister Cage, Wicks, Baltimore, Ward, Irons, and a few others opened up the on-deck armory and the muskets were issued, two or three to a man. (Weapons were always issued at the last moment to prevent a misfire giving us away.)

Mister Bons, one of the Native Americans handed me my gun – ready to fire-- and pressed his index finger against his lips to say 'quiet' –a reminder that even at this distance, voices can travel across the water and alert our target....

Using signals, Prescott told me where to take position, next to him, in the third wave of the boarding party "Daws ordered me to keep you alive!" he said in a quiet, low tone.

I looked at him –his presence did make me feel better, until he added...

"It must be some kind of punishment or something." He pulled the hammer back on his weapon, "I don't remember doing anything wrong but here I am, stuck with you."

"Keeping me alive is a punishment?"

He shrugged, "There's better things I could be doin'!"

Arson repeated the command to get the combat teams on their mark even pushing Dax-Varro forward. The first wave –at the railing—was made up of some of our toughest and my eyes rolled over them --Teague, Baako, Hatano, Jagger, Lo-Tan, Toombs, Blythe, Cheval, Miranda, Bons, Nighthorse, Mister Barak, Rabal, Raeder, Lau, Manu, Lynch, Jaffar and the Moors, Newcastle, Cross, Sanjuro, Mazatal, the Aztecs, Kane, Jack-Karr, Addo, Wolfe, Merciless, Fury, Duncan-Howe, Sakai, Tak, Ward, Jata and a some others....

Then the second wave, with Blair, Gordon, Obal, Calixto, Hallock, Sterling, Dutch, Bishop, Blackwood, Takeda, Hazzard, Wicks, Abel, Watson, Kipling, O'Shea, Sampson-Rift covered with his scarf, Akai-Dan, Daws, Sancere and thirty others.... then me –in the third wave-- where I stood next to Mister Prescott who warned me to 'stay close...'
Now we were only a few thousand meters out from our target....

With us, in the third wave was Mister Rush, Clairmont, Amir, Standish, Sunderland, Tabor, Archer, Thorn, Sam, De Leon, Mister Foxx, Calderone, Whitney, Stamp, Cyril, Hayte and Therrinfall –the executioner--with some twenty or so more in our ranks....

Weapons were primed. My hands were damp, I gripped and re-gripped my musket and slowly pulled the hammer back with a click. I looked from man to man, all appeared determined, as if ready to charge through a brick wall.

Teague, Addo and Jagger armed themselves with what was known as 'a blunderbuss' a weapon which fired a load of several dozen musket balls at once. It was used to clear whole sections of ships of living people.

I looked to Dakar –a man the size of a small house-- holding a giant iron grappling hook in his massive hands. He looked back at me and suddenly smiled as if this was about to be fun. I tried to smile back but the tremble in my lower lip made it difficult....

The crates of grenades were passed forward. Mister Bishop aimed the deck swivel cannon. The Captain's eyes remained fixed on our target. The Venger was now within striking distance, only a few hundred meters out...

The silence was –in a strange way—deafening. My heartbeat seemed very loud to me and as we continued to close in, it was the only thing I seemed to hear...

The lanterns on the deck of our target were very close now. I could see silhouettes of people moving by their rail...

Now, it was about an hour before dawn and an early morning mist rolled over the black tide. The ship that had seen a friendly pennant on the horizon the day before had no idea what was about to come out of the darkness and slam deck to deck with it...

Our gunnery teams waited for the order to fire. I mumbled a short prayer for God to get me through this alive and the men around me were ready to jump...

Then, slowly, the giant grim reaper at the head of our ship emerged from the darkness, cut through the mist and --BOOOOOOOM! The sky suddenly lit up!

I went deaf for a moment as the cannons opened fire, rolling our target with a series of blasts and explosions that took their hull, deck, and rail apart. There was a second and third cannon strike as decks two and three opened up.

-Night became day.

With a high-pitched hum, my hearing then came back. I could hear screaming –as some of their crew were blown overboard. One shot smashed through the lower deck and exploded inside their ship, blowing a hole through the top deck as it collapsed the mast and a wave of splinters cut through the Dutch sailors...

Decks one, two and three continued to fire, punching holes into the side of this ship as our cannons rolled back with the recoil. More shots punched through and exploded between their decks taking the ship apart...

Another blast sent shot through their other mast –snapping it—and shots ripped through their sails, the rigging, and the steering, cutting the deck and wheel apart. We fired another round and loaded for a third before the frigate started firing back. A section of their mast came crashing down on our decks with the sails on fire. We held our positions and some of our men hit the fire with buckets of water –and sand--turning it to smoke.

Rajiv shouted commands and we fired again, a new round of blasts overturned cannons and killed several of their gunners –some blown apart—as the side of their ship caught fire. Another exchange and the Dutch warship fired back as two of the men standing close to me were killed by a chunk of our railing as it was turned into splinters by the explosion. Their blood splashed us...

Again, I was scared. Mister Newcastle moved through our lines offering encouragement –he put his hand on my shoulder, "Steady! Keep your wits about you."

Our cannon continued to fire, reload, and fire again.

Essex was calm under fire. "Hold firing, prepare to board."

Harrow repeated the order and roared the commands across the top deck, "Hold firing. Make ready to board!"

We were now only meters apart and up came our muskets and we fired a massive volley that cut into them and tore through their ranks. The first wave handed their empty muskets back, and fresh, loaded ones were handed forward for another volley, then pistols, dropping the enemy on their decks and into the water below…

We lit the fuses on several grenades and tossed them onboard to explode. Some exploded in the air and spit metal splinters and fragments down on the Dutch crew –one exploded and lit several Dutch sailors on fire after it blew apart. We used the blasts to cover us as we threw heavy grappling hooks across to take 'claw' on the ship's railing and rigging and we took hold of the ropes and heaved, in teams to pull our two ships close enough to slam together. Then, all at once, out came sabers, more pistols, and tomahawks and like a tidal wave, we stormed through the smoke and hit their decks making the jump over their railing and crashing into their ranks. I could hear metal clash and rip through flesh.

Some of our crew swung from ropes in our rigging above and across the water to their theirs. Others were blasted and fell into the sea below…

The first wave --made of our most feared fighters-- pushed the enemy back and our second wave pushed aboard. Axes dropped into shoulders and skulls. Close quarter fighting was the roughest, blades, axes, teeth tore into anything close.

As reported, I was in the third wave ---my skills not yet up to par—but I was expected to do my best and just as we climbed aboard Prescott had a few final words of warning, "If you die Reed… I'll kill ya' to death!"

I did not realize at the time that a Dutch sniper took aim and had me as a target. He pulled the trigger just as Mister Silence slammed his hand down in between the hammer and the pan preventing his gun from firing and saving my life! Silence then used his tomahawk in his other hand to swing down and dispatch this man by splitting his skull and killing him instantly. Then, with little or no regard, he continued to fight....

The ronin seemed like masters of close quarter combat, using their samurai swords –or sometimes two at once-- to slash their way through the deck, removing arms, legs –at the knee-- or even heads as they pressed forward. Sometimes, throwing metal blades –throwing stars—into the heads and chest of the enemy before closing in....

Lo cleared whole sections with his metal three section staff, a swing to the left and two, three or four enemy combatants were slammed into the mast, rail, into other sailors or...overboard.

I climbed aboard in a state of somewhat bewilderment and my actions were not my own for some force compelled me to hit my knees and help the first wounded man I saw, Mister Blair --he was part of our crew-- and had gash across his chest from a Dutch saber. I ripped his shirt into a bandage and put pressure on the wound, looking up to see men fighting and dying all around me and here I was, compelled to help a man. "Hold this" I said as I put his hands on the bandage and moved him a few meters out of the way –bodies hitting the deck all around us—then, I decided to press forward. As I left him, the body of an enemy sailor fell on him and, he ignored his wounds and tried to kill this man with his bare hands.

Two men closed in to kill me when Watson smashed into them. He fired a pistol round into one and swung his hook down to pierce the throat of the second man at the shoulder. The hole he ripped pumped a stream of blood into the air in what seemed to be the rhythm of the wounded man's heartbeat as he fell to the planks. His blood and other pools of blood on the deck made men slip and slide into each other while fighting. --The footing became difficult.

I pressed forward, musket rounds hitting the area all around me. A body was thrown into me, I turned as the man was killed by Mister Baako who picked up another man and just threw him overboard. Strength was prized in combat and when Mister Baako threw a punch, you could hear the bones in a man's face and skull snap and break. He slammed his elbow into a man's teeth as he tried to come up from behind, then Baako turned and pushed all the other attackers back...

Another man was killed, and another fell against me, screaming for help as we collapsed to the deck. He was finished by Mister Newcastle whose blade came down like guillotine, he then quickly turned and slashed at the Dutch sailors behind him...

--It was confused chaos.

I continued forward, crawling, then I got back to my feet. Mister Lau and Mister Nighthorse were fighting back-to-back, the clang of their weapons creating sparks in the collisions with other weapons. Lau swinging his butterfly blades –or— short swords in two different directions cutting and slashing, one victim walking away with one of the blades stuck in his ribs.

An enemy officer was crawling across the deck, his head bashed in and bleeding. "No, you don't!" He was picked up by Mister Rabal and Mister Miranda and thrown over the side. Another man was speared against a mast with a cutlass by Mister Cage.

Suddenly I was forced up against the ship's railing, a saber blade thrust came in and cut me across the shoulder and chest then pierced my shirt pinning me to the rail. My attacker could not remove his blade from the wood railing, and he reached for a hammer from his belt to crush my skull but just as he tried to swing it down on me, he was shot in the back and dropped. Mister Prescott stood there, smoking pistol in hand. He lowered his gun, gave me a disapproving nod, and disappeared back into the fight. I freed myself and got to my feet as a tide of our men pushed forward and we started down the decks below...

The next deck was filled with smoke. There was screaming. Here Mister Obal and our Moors were pushing forward. I watched Jaffar slash his way through the deck, hacking and cutting with bodies dropping to the floor, collapsing forward, and falling over cannon...

Some of the dead men on this deck were still on fire from our cannon bombardment earlier, their clothes and skin burning. I looked up as dark red blood was dripping through the planks from the deck above. I was suddenly tackled, a Dutch sailor pinned me to a cannon and gripped my neck, cutting off my air. Just as I started to lose consciousness, I heard a heavy 'whoooooooomp' as a tomahawk swung just over my head and smashed into the eyes and nose of my attacker! His blood went everywhere, and I was blinded by it for a moment. Jacques The Bear Killer pulled his tomahawk out of this man's head as his body fell to the planks and he held out his hand to help me up. Without ceremony, and before I could say thank you, I was back on my feet, and I was pushed right back into the fight…

We pressed forward and forward still, clearing this deck, killing everyone until, suddenly, hands went up and the last few survivors begged for surrender….

I heard shouts from above deck screaming "Quarter!" Followed by Mister Harrow's voice echoing through the ship "They've surrendered!" The combat –and the screaming-- seemed to slow down and eventually die out…

On my deck, once their weapons hit the floor and hands were raised, immediately upon the surrender, Jaffar turned and checked the men he attacked to see if any were still alive. I thought he was going to finish them off, but he found one and put his hand on his wound to stop the bleeding. Once the fighting had stopped, his work changed from killing to saving….

"Get their physicians!" Barak requested and Hatano and Mister Foxx moved to find their doctors and pull them down below to start their work. Both medical crews, theirs, and ours, would be very busy over the next few hours.

I watched Jaffar, in complete surprise at his actions. Barak and Blythe pulled a wounded enemy combatant to his feet and started to haul him to the infirmary, and I still stood, stunned with amazement. Jaffar cleaned his blade and slid it back into its sheath. He looked directly at me and must have seen my confusion. "What is it?" he asked in a very scratchy, deep voice and accent.

"I-I'm just surprised by your compassion."

He paused, then said, "If anyone saves a life, it shall be as though he had saved the lives of all mankind." He then started to move out of the hold...

I was astonished since I had heard Mister Jaffar speak not a word aboard ship, "Mister Jaffar, I had no idea you were a man of such profound statements and compassion."

"I did not create those words," he confessed, "They come from the Quran."

Mister Miranda, Newcastle, Tiger, Mister Obal and a wounded and bloody Mister Calixto started marching the unarmed prisoners past us and as Obal walked past, he said in his thick African accent, "Mister Jaffar, you are bleeding," Jaffar realized he had been gashed in cheek and forehead under his head wrap. He felt the blood with his hand, looked at me and smiled –slightly—then he regained his composure and followed the prisoners as they marched out.

"Why is he smiling?" I asked.

"Wounded men get more money" Obal said, and he put his weapon away, back in the sheath on his back and walked past me. At that point I realized that the blade of my saber was clean –for I had not killed anyone-- so I quickly put it away as to not draw any negative attention.

On deck, prisoners were disarmed, lined up and sized up. I made it up to the top deck where I found Mister Barak and Jeddah with Mister Jaffar a few meters in front of us. "Do you know what your Mister Jaffar said to me below?"

Mister Barak looked at me. "I-do-not."

I motioned it to him, "He said, 'If anyone saves a life, it shall be as though he had saved the lives of all mankind' --It's from your Quran, isn't that remarkable?"

Mister Barak smiled and some of the other moors laughed, "The Quran also says any man who kills...kills all of mankind!"

Mister Jaffar suddenly turned to us and said, "I did not claim to be a perfect Muslim!"

Jeddah let out a deep laugh and then went back to his work.

"Fair enough Mister Jaffar," Baako said as he walked by, "It's just fortunate for us, that you're a near perfect privateer!" The crew around us also laughed and we went back to our business....

"On that, we can agree...." Jaffar affirmed with a nod, "Minus the word.... near."

The Captain was having a meeting at the helm, "What's the count?"

"Sixty-one" Harrow replied.

Mister Lincoln took note. His platoon was still making inventory of the cargo, but sixty-one souls were added to his books on this date.

"Sixty-one," repeated the Captain. "Mister Rajiv, how many replacements do you need?"

"Our gunnery section is down sixteen men Captain but, we may get six back from injury."

"Right, Mister Therrinfall, ask for volunteers, prepare letters for those who are conscripted into service and put the rest in the hold until we make Saint Kristos. We'll turn them loose there." The letters the Captain spoke of was a letter to each man pressed into service saying he was drafted, against his will to join us –for the time being-- and therefor, should not be punished if captured or brought before a court. I had never heard of such a letter but was surprised when I was told that they were actually quite effective and respected by courts on all sides of a conflict.

As to the prisoners themselves, I was more surprised by that decision. "Turn them loose?" I said.

"Once they surrender and we accept, we're obligated not to kill them." Mister Newcastle said, "And, it serves us much better to be forgiving towards our enemies for if they ever serve on a ship, we strike again, they won't be so eager to fight to the death."

Had nothing I had been told about these men back in England been true? Pardons! Forgiving your enemies! Quotes from the Quran!

--What was all this?

The sun was now up....

The Dutch warship was burning in the early morning fog and our men, were quickly moving through her decks and into the cargo hold to raid for anything of value. Sugar, whale oil, barrels of molasses, rum, wine, gun powder, weapons, fresh water, food, bales of cotton, wheat and coconuts, bananas, mangos, tools –everything and as the process of off-loading the cargo –including prisoners—continued to The Venger, the Captain of the captured ship named Passchendaele, made his presence known on the top deck and asked for words with our Captain. The request was granted, and he was allowed to approach. He removed his hat and gave a short bow. "Sir, Captain Passchendaele at your service."

"My compliments on the defense of your ship Captain Passchendaele." Essex said, looking around at the blanket of smoke now covering a good part of the ocean, "And we appreciate your timely surrender."

"Sir, if I may, the cargo is yours but, I must beg for your protection of our passengers."

"Passengers?"

At that point, a regal group of four women, one man and a young boy who were hiding somewhere below, was brought to the top deck, and at their front was a man in proper European dress –and wig— who was blithering as it were and who identified himself as the Duke of Rodham.

"These passengers, sir." Passchendaele motioned.

Our Captain watched as this man –Rodham--caught sight of our Moors and without reservation, made his feelings known. "My God, there are heathens aboard. Filthy heathens! This is unforgivable. I will not have these ladies in the presence of these dirty animals!"

Jaffar's knuckles cracked as he gripped the handle of his curved sword and he looked to our Captain for permission to strike but our Captain looked back with a sort of unspoken code for 'hold your position.'

Bewildered, the Duke of Rodham made a survey of the deck where his dismay became even more evident at the sight of Baltimore and Obal. "Savages! Slaves? You have slaves aboard?"

"There are no slaves here Mister Rodham only free men" The Captain barked, "But, I promise you, they can be quite dangerous."

"It's Duke of Rodham, not Mister, I will not have you---"

"Rodham?" Harrow sized him up and suddenly placed him, "Rodham, the slave trader of The Carolinas?"

"The very one and I am a founding member of The Royal African Company and as such--"

"Mister Rodham here threw shackled slaves, women and children, overboard from the merchant ship Saturn last winter." Harrow reported just loud enough for the Captain and those close to him to hear...

The Captain had a look of wicked intentions in his eye, "Is that a fact Mister Rodham?" he slowly asked.

Jack-Karr scratched his cheek and chin, listening, then dropped his hands to the guns in his sash ready to draw them. Tiger checked the sharpness of his saber with his thumb.

"I don't answer to you! And it's Duke of Rodham you insolent bas-"

"There are no royal titles aboard our ship." The Captain said through his teeth, "Here, you are Mister Rodham, and you can consider yourself fortunate that you still have your head!"

"My head!!! Why you -- I will not forgive you for this. When the Royal African Company gets word of this raid, they'll grant me the pleasure of seeing you marched to the gallows for this act, you and your men will be tortured then join the countless other pirates we've hanged--"

At the mention of the word pirate there was a grumble of disapproval in our ranks...

"We are not pirates Mister Rod--" Harrow was stopped as this tirade continued.

"--You are correct, the term is too good for you and your kind." He then began to address the crowd, "Listen to me –all of you—I will not rest until you are clapped in irons for this offense. Every one of you here will swing from the yard arm in a body cage and then we will be rid of you...."

Captain Passchendaele looked down, slightly embarrassed. It wasn't just the actions and behavior of this man; it was his history as a known slave trader.

"A slow death is what you all deserve" Rodham continued, "And I shall be there to toast the executioner by God!" He motioned to the more worldly of our crew, "And I'll have these heathens in irons."

"Will you now….?" The Captain smiled "A body cage?" He paused for a moment, then stepped down from the quarter deck, "Let's have that drink now then, shall we?" He motioned to Mister Thorn who pitched the Captain a bottle….

"I'll not drink with you, you swine! Not now! Not ever! Your executioner maybe but, never you and your kind! The very fact, that you have these demonic heathens and slaves in the presence of ladies is maddening, do you hear me, maddening…."

"Mister Rodham, that won't be any concern of yours. I have no intention of making you sail on this ship, in the presence of these men for one moment longer…."

Rodham suddenly became quiet as if he felt a dark turn in the conversation and suddenly, he appeared nervous, "My-my title protects me from harm, and I am---"

"Enough!" Essex put his hand up as if to command a halt. "If sharing the deck with these men is so unbearable, then we shall liberate you from this burden…" He slowed his words down, "Please allow me to introduce you to a friend of mine --the plank!"

Rodham heaved and reacted with panic as Mister Rabal and Baako grabbed him and pulled him forward. The ladies in his party started screaming and out came the plank, rolled out over the side, and placed into position over the water several stories below…

"Mister Jaffar," The Captain continued "Would you do the honors."

Mister Jaffar gave a nod, stepped forward and grabbed Rodham from Baako and Rabal, by the tunic and despite the crying and begging from the women around him, he forced Rodham up on the plank. When he tried to step down, he was met with the point of a blade forcing him to remain in place.

"Per—perhaps I-I might be persuaded to show some leniency in this case…."

"Perhaps…if we were interested in that sort of thing." The Captain replied as he gave a quick signal, "But we're not!"

Our crew began to cheer as he was pushed further out on the plank and then slowly edged out by the blades around him, "Perhaps we can come to some sort of agreement, a reduction of sentence perhaps, clemency for your acts---" Each one of his steps seemed unsure of its place as he moved out over the water. "I beg you!" He looked down several decks to the ocean…

"We are not interested in your pardon Mister Rodham, nor your clemency, we are above such things here as we are above your elitist values and your laws." The Captain raised his bottle as if to toast Rodham…

"Certainly, you-you don't mean to put a gentleman to death like this…." The ladies in his company were horrified at this –and panicked- - but the decision was made…

Captain Passchendaele stepped forward, "Captain, I beg you, please do not do this."

"I'm sorry I cannot honor your request Captain, I cannot –and will not—leave a man alive who threatens my life or the lives of my crew! Forgive me Passchendaele but this man dies!" He then directed his attention to the deck, "Mister Arson, finish him if you please!"

"You won't be in the water long Mister Rodham," Arson assured him as he stepped forward "The sharks will make sure of that!" He used his blade to push this man further out as the plank began to bend under his weight…

Some hospital buckets, loaded with amputated limbs and blood were kicked off the deck to chum the waters beneath the plank turning the blue tide to red as an invitation to the sharks.

"Captain, I beg you…" Passchendaele pleaded. "Please."

"Be silent!"

I was horrified.

Mister Lo put his hand up, and across the Dutch Captain to keep him silent, distant and in his place.

Rodham's feet shuffled further out with Arson's blade drawing some blood. "Please sir."

"We can consider your life payment for the ones you built your fortune on. Small compensation for them, I know but, very entertaining for us."

Rodham stood there and for a moment, things seemed silent and still then, the cracking of the plank could be heard as it began to give way under Rodham's weight. His eyes betrayed a look of desperation and then the plank suddenly snapped, and he dropped into the tide.

One of the women screamed and lunged to the railing to see him hit the water. He popped to the surface grabbing at air and coughing up salt water, "Help me, please…" He begged reaching for some invisible lifeline…

"Mister Harrow, make sail and get us under way if you please…"

Harrow gave the orders, the men jumped to their stations and the ship began to pull away from the struggling Rodham –whose hand touched the hull of our ship as we rocked forward in the tide…

"Help him" the woman begged, "Please help him."

"He's beyond help." Newcastle said. "And take note ma'am, anyone who threatens us will meet with this end." And this woman was left at the railing, looking back at this man, grasping for life as we left him behind in our wake….

Mister Lincoln began the tally of the wounded and applied the appropriate accounting.

-Twenty-one dead!

-Forty-one wounded in the sick bay!

Severity of the wounds dictated the level of payment. Our doctors –and theirs—were busy. Our men aided their doctors in getting supplies such as water and saws and in the tearing up of cloth for bandages, whatever they may have needed to save the lives of our men first and then –soon after— their survivors.

Mister Crowe, our ship's carpenter was in the hospital, pressed into service with his tools. Other carpenters were already fashioning wooden legs for the wounded and the metal workers were making hooks to replace limbs and talons. Fingers could not be replaced.

I never made comfort with the sound of a saw when it cuts into flesh. The sound changes from flesh to bone but the screaming remains constant. I was told to hold down one of our men –Mister Sancere-- as Mister Johannis applied a tourniquet. Mister Prescott who had saved my life earlier in the day assisted me in keeping this man pinned. This was a hard moment for all of us but mostly for him and as the saw went to work, his body trembled violently, his screaming echoed off the rafters until he passed out from the pain. He would be paid for his leg and then dismissed from The Venger –if he didn't die of infection before the next port.

Other men around the sick bay, lost fingers, arms, or had holes made from blades and musket balls, there were also bad cuts, broken bones, and crushed skulls. It was a sad sight. Many men would survive the surgery only to die of infection days or weeks later. Crewmen re-shaped with hooks for hands would be compensated at the time of the wound but then be forced to work hard to prove they were still of value, in the hope that they would not be replaced by new recruits.

A lot of limbs, blood and bodies were washed over the side or tossed over in buckets. Then funerals were to take place. All men buried together and all men to attend. Men, sewn in sailcloth, were buried at sea under the watchful eye of their religious shepherd –if known. If his religious preference was not known, he was given a Christian burial and Mister Rush, or the opposing Minister would apply the service.

It was most respectful….

After a few holy words, Mister Rush closed his bible.

The Captain stood close by, "Well done Mister Rush." He said in a solemn tone…

"Thank you, sir." Rush returned his hat to his head and quietly left the deck.

The Captain stood at the helm for a few moments, alone with his thoughts before Mister Harrow approached with the thought of getting back on task. "Your orders Captain?"

Then came the command…. "North by west. Make for the Isle of Saint Noel to drop our passengers, then, The Dark Coast."

"Aye Captain," obeyed Mister Harrow, "The Dark Coast it is." Thorn was at the helm and the crew shifted their duties as The Venger sailed into the dark horizon...

Below deck, my hand was still trembling from the violence. I was horrified at the plank and what I had witnessed. I sat by the galley, looking into the distance with the sound of the plank snapping, over and over again, stuck in my skull...

Nighthorse, Addo, Merciless, Tiger, Irons and a few others came below deck, in good spirits and moved to the tables where I was sitting. Mister Hobby looked up from the galley stoves, curious...

"What's the matter with you?" Addo asked in his deep voice, bringing the laughter to a halt.

"I-I" I wanted to answer but something prevented me from putting my thoughts into words...

Irons splashed his mug into the rum bucket and sat down next to me. "It's the plank. I recon that's not in your schoolbooks back home, is it?"

"No, it's not." I admitted.

"The plank bothers you?" Archer asked as he slid a mug down to Addo and another mug across the table to me.

I held my tongue and remained silent.

Mako's eyes darted over to Nighthorse who used hand signals with the words, "It's done."

Merciless leaned forward towards me, "Understand, that man up there," he pointed to the top deck, "He would have killed you."

"Right! You, me, all of us, "Irons continued, "Privateering is a hanging offense and if your head is in a noose, no amount of begging will get you a pardon. The only solution is to kill a man like that now, rather than have him return to the world and employ all his resources to hunt us down."

This I understood. I just didn't like it.

"He was a slave trading bastard in any event!" Irons continued, "Dakar, show this man the scars on your back! Show him what the slave trade and the whipping post did to you."

Dakar just shook his head no, smiled and went back to his business on the other side of the deck….

"All from the likes of bastards like Rodham." Irons re-focused his attention on me, "The man threw slaves off The Saturn to drown! People! Families, women and children" Irons then tipped his mug, "He's made a fortune torturing people and now he's in hell --and the tables have turned!"

"Right," Wolfe walked past, "To hell with him."

"Look at it this way if you will…" Irons continued, "At least we didn't offend your schoolteacher sensibilities and throw the women overboard with him."

"Mister Reed," Tiger got my attention, "What do you call a hundred Lords at the bottom of the ocean?" I was without an answer, then he answered for me. "A good start!" He smiled.

All the men laughed. But me.

I was relieved we didn't throw the women overboard though I didn't doubt for a moment, that these men wouldn't do it if circumstances dictated, they should and I wanted to disguise my fear, that my acceptance here…may be fading.

Such as it was. I still had one foot back in the world. Civilization. I still questioned actions and balanced them with compassion. Not so with these men. This was –to them—justice and no one seemed to understand why this was even a discussion with me. When they put Rodham on the plank, everyone –save myself—knew why they were doing it. Their world was just made brighter by Rodham's death. One less enemy in the world for them to fight—

--And the notion of this took me to a dark place…

We now had the rest of Rodham's party to contend with. Mister Harrow gave up his rather small cabin so our passengers could have their privacy. He preferred to sleep in a rigged hammock on the top deck, in the night air in any event. There was no need for a guard, for our code of conduct protected them and prohibited the harassment of women passengers on any level. Their trunks and cargo boxes –the ones that could be saved--were brought aboard and put in place. We did not take from them.

By sunset, there was a knock on the door and Mister Archer extended an invitation to Lady Victoria Powell and her friends –the Lady DuVal and the Lady Winter-- to dine with Captain Essex, Mister Harrow and a few select members of the crew. It was a courtesy for I don't think the Captain was clamoring for their company but more for a moment to quell hostility.

--And why should the Captain care? It was my suspicion that he didn't care but, he lived by our code and 'Article IV' and thus these people were to remain unharmed, and I think that maybe, he wanted to change the impression of his men and ship enough to forestall any rabblerousing with the authorities these women might do when they got back on colonial property.

She fast refused as she did the next day and day after…

On the day after that, the Captain came to Harrow's door himself and knocked. The woman's voice behind the door answered, "Yes."

"It's the Captain."

There was a pause as if everyone inside looked at each other and wondered what to do or how to answer until Lady DuVal cracked the door open and revealed the left side of her face. "Yes Captain?"

"I've come direct to offer you ladies and the young lad dinner."

"I think not."

As she moved to close the door, the Captain slid his hand in the opening and even though she slammed it on his fingers his expression did not change. "Madam, I assure you, if you do not vacate this space even for a few hours, your party will be plagued with scurvy which could result in madness and death."

Her eyes widened with alarm though she tried to disguise it. "Very well then," she finally said, "For health reasons we will join you for dinner –for a short time."

He nodded as she slammed the door shut. The Captain straightened up, pulled his jacket close and started back to the top deck passing an eavesdropping Harrow along the way, "I hope you're happy."

"Scurvy-and-death…sir?" Harrow said with a questionable if not suspicious tone.

"It worked, didn't it?"

"Oh yes sir. It worked."

"Saves us from having to remove the cabin door and force them out."

"See you at dinner sir."

The invitation may have been reluctantly accepted and scurvy scare or not, confinement to Harrow's cabin was cramped at best and a little fresh air would be a welcome change even if the air was polluted by privateers.

Most nights, the Captain would have dinner with different members of the crew in his cabin, which enforced a feeling of camaraderie but, on this evening, he made an astute move and asked Mister Jaffar, Mister Nighthorse, Mister Jupiter, Mister Kon Boar –the Aztec— Mister Lo, Mister Lynch, Mister Sanjuro, Mister Harrow, Captain Passchendaele and myself as the school teacher to join the affair in a move I believe was meant to make these women familiar to these men of different cultures and –in a way—humanize them.

As it was a hot night, the captain ordered the table to be set on the top deck. Our party waited for the women to arrive and once they did, we made an effort to make formal introductions –Jaffar with a bow-- and then we waited until the ladies –and the young man—took their place at their seats.

It was silent at first, then Lady Winter made an effort at small talk as spirits were passed. She looked across the table to Mister Nighthorse "So, you are a Native of the Americas?" She asked with a sense of excitement, "Do…you…speak…English?" She said slowly and deliberately hoping he would understand.

"I do Miss." He replied with almost perfect pronunciation.

"And…they…. allow you to…. sit here at their table?"

"Allow?" He smiled at her quaint form of prejudice, "They do."

"It's as much Mister Nighthorse's table as it is ours, Madam." The Captain stated.

The uncomfortable silence continued until there was another feeble attempt to break it. The Lady Victoria, across from me asked, "So, Mister Reed, how long have you been a pirate?" She stopped herself with slight embarrassment but, the word had slipped.

"Mister Reed is a schoolteacher." The Captain corrected her.

"A schoolteacher? With these criminals?" Lady Powell said surprised.

"I assure Madam, I have these men to thank for my life." I confessed.

"These men here? They seemed more skilled in taking life then saving it."

I paused and searched for my answer, "At times yes but, I can promise you---"

"I don't wish to hear it." Lady Powell belted out, "I watched a man walk the plank a few days ago while others chummed the waters below. Lord Rodham may have been a crude man but, he deserved better than he got from you and your crew…."

"Did he?" The Captain asked, "He was a known slave trader who insulted this crew –my family-- and threatened to hang all of us. It seemed like good business to dispose of him and quickly as possible." And with that, the Captain raised a glass of wine and kicked it back.

"With his death, many African families were just spared a lifetime of torture in his slave economy…not to mention we secured our own safety." Harrow added.

She became silent.

"I ask you Lady Powell, if someone threatened your life, your family, what would you do?"

"I'm not a pirate."

"Neither are we."

"Your use of nouns bewilders me." She said with disdain in her speech, "You don't like the term pirate yet here we are, hostages in your company. Ship taken. Friends murdered…."

"If that man was your friend, you have my sympathy" Mister Harrow said, "And you are correct, your ship was taken --instead of burned or sunk with you onboard. You are here –your virtue intact—because of the way we conduct ourselves. I assure you, had another privateer in these waters taken your ship, you and your family would mostly likely be turned into slaves, shackled down, for the entertainment of the crew –then sold to the local brothel –or killed, the lot of ya! And it seems fitting to tell ya' that the

King's soldiers are no different in times of war but equal in their own barbarity towards captured parties."

"That is impossible to believe. The King's soldiers would never---"

"Ah but they would, and they have!" Harrow was very direct "It may not be in your local newspapers back home but, I've seen such barbarity with my own eyes."

There was another pause in the conversation. The Captain moved to get past this awkward moment. "You are my guests and as such no harm will come to you here." He assured them....

"As I said, I don't keep company with pirates." She used deliberate enunciation as if her intention was to offend.

"First...we're privateers. Second, yes you do. That man we sent over the side was a pirate, well-practiced in the art of destroying human lives. Most of the members of parliament are pirates.... they're not on the high seas but.... they steal.... They steal from the farmers, from families, from teachers and tradesmen, from honest people everywhere, to keep themselves in a life of luxury with a false title. They, Madam, are your real pirates...." He leaned back in his chair, "And, as of this voyage, there is one less in the world thanks to the plank!"

She sat fixed in anger and silence.

Our Captain stood up, "As Mister Harrow has said, if any other privateering crews in these waters were to stumble across your ship, your world would become a whore house. Your ladies in waiting would join you and the young lad, in your company, would be sold into slavery. That is the truth of the world you are now in. So, when you offer disdain, remember that it is I, Captain Essex, who will put you ashore unharmed and you may consider yourself lucky." He threw his napkin on his plate "Now, if you'll excuse me."

We took to our feet and excused ourselves as well and moved out across the deck. The Captain walked past Mister Newcastle, "That went well."

I hit the deck and found Jack-Karr and Kannon at the weapons station under the lantern light.

"Well Teach?"

"The Lady would like to put us all in a cage." I said.

"Too hell with that –and them!" Karr said.

As Karr spoke, I watched Rabal climb into a stationed long boat. "I-will-sleep-here-tonight." He said...

"What's the matter with him?" I asked.

Jack-Karr smiled, "You scared him. He doesn't like cages much."

BLACK THORN PRISON

CAPE PUNISHMENT AUS. HARD LABOR
PROVIENCE SIX

THREE YEARS BEFORE...

The fortress and its broken, worn-down battlements cut up into the moonlit sky like an old bear trap ready to slam shut on all who entered....

At the gate, the night shift was startled as something moved towards them from the darkness. The guards used torches to see and suddenly, wicked-looking plague doctors emerged from the shadows.

--There were six in all, two in the lead with four others carrying an ominous sign...a coffin.

"We need to remove a prisoner." The doctor out front handed over a letter of authorization....

"Dead?" The sergeant asked as he took the parchment.

"Not yet." The doctor waved the coffin forward. "The township has been sealed off. Your men should be confined to quarters."

The guard read the order, "There's no official seal on this." He looked again, "Nothing from his Lord Mayor, Constable Crabtree or his agent?"

"That's because agent died before the stamp." The doctor said.

Cautious and pensive, the sergeant looked at the letter again, "Let me call out the Captain---"

"--Word is the Captain is in the infirmary and if we don't remove this prisoner now, all of you—" He pointed, "Will get sick and be dead in fortnight."

The other plague doctor coughed and seemed to move close to almost cough directly on the sergeant though his mask.

"I can't just allow you to enter---"

"Sorry to say," The doctor replied, "---We're coming in any way!"

Inside his cell, Rabal looked up from his suspended cage box –a few feet off the floor—bleeding and with the sound of twisting steel, his cell door was pulled open. The doctors walked in from the dark hallway. Rabal saw the coffin, looked back to these evil looking doctors, and thought that this was to be his last few minutes on earth…

Then, in a split-second, they removed their masks --Jack-Karr, Kannon, Locksley, Bons, Kai and Merciless. They pulled pistols from their costumes and opened up the coffin to pull more guns….

"Jack!" Rabal smiled. "Good to see you."

"Save it. Let's get you outa here." He worked an 'impounded' set of keys into the lock, opened up the cage and Rabal climbed down.

"How'd ya find me?"

"There's a couple guards floating dead in the moat that could tell ya all about it." Kannon spit out.

"--The rest of the guards gave us some quick directions, then steered clear of us out of fear."

He pointed to the coffin, "Get in!"

Rabal hesitated, "You know I don't like small spaces."

"Now is a hell of a time to tell us" Kannon said, from the door, gun ready to blast anyone who might surprise them.

"Can't we just fight our way out instead?" Rabal asked.

"What? No. There's a battalion of prison guards—"

"Why didn't you just bring another doctor mask?"

"Are you questioning our plan?" Karr stopped ready to lose his temper.

"Six go in and seven come out—why the hell do think we didn't bring another damn outfit?" Kannon said, still watching the shadows of the hallway.

"Well," Rabal stammered, "Why doesn't Kannon get in?"

"Stow it! I'm not gettin' in that damn thing!"

"Why not?"

"Because I'm not the one who got captured—you did!"

"Rabal…we don't have time for this" Karr said, "Get in." He pointed to the wood box like it was an order.

With a touch of reluctance, Rabal climbed in the coffin and the lid rolled up over him as Merciless, Kai and Locksley started to hammer it into place and inside, with each blow of the hammer, more dust went flying into Rabal's face as he tried to keep calm.

They put their costumes back on. "Ready?" Karr asked.

Kannon nodded, then, the four others tried to heave the coffin but struggled with the weight and could hardly lift it. Rabal was a massive man.

"Good God! How much does this man weigh?" Locksley barked.

"Come on, come on," and with all the force they could muscle up, they lifted it up and slowly moved down the hallway.

As they moved towards the exit, a guard suddenly came around the corner with a lantern washing the tunnel a glow with orange and yellow light. "Ah, doctors" he said….

Startled, Locksley let go of the coffin and dropped it on its head.

There was a slight grunt from inside as Rabal hit against the bricks.

The guard's eyes darted to the coffin then back to Karr in the lead. With a touch of suspicion he asked, "Is…. everything all right here?"

"Yes, yes…fine."

Locksley and Bons moved to pick the coffin back up and heaved it up as Rabal let out another grunt--

"Is…there…someone alive in there?"

There was a moment of tension, Kai, slid his hand into his plague cloak and gripped his sword…

"Ah yes" Karr suddenly confessed, "But...He's not really well liked, and he'll be dead very soon."

"Very, VERY soon!" Kannon kicked the coffin out of frustration.

And then the guard suddenly changed his disposition, "Very well, better him than any of us hey?" As he hit Karr in the shoulder with a smile and dismissed himself....

They moved across the empty prison parade ground –the other night watchmen seemed to keep their distance –fearful of catching something-- and they were able to cross the bridge back to the gate without any further obstruction...

From there, they moved across the bridge, with four bodies—guards— floating in the shadows of the dark water, below...

As they entered the woods they dropped the coffin –exhausted--and Rabal let out another grunt. As they started to open it up, his fists came through it and shattered part of the lid in his urgency to get some air...

"Next time just bring another Doctor mask or... Kannon can get in the coffin."

"I told you, the man who gets captured doesn't get to make the plan!" Kannon barked.

Fury came out of the darkness with the horses. "What's all the racket here?"

Karr pointed to Rabal, "Ask him?"

"Rabal can't keep quiet."

"It wasn't a good plan."

"Really," Karr returned, "Well maybe next time you'd like to rescue yourself."

"Quiet, the lot of ya'" Fury hissed, "Now, mount up and let's move before the entire town comes after us."

They climbed on the horses Kannon and Rabal still pointing at each other with a touch of hostility as they rode off into the distance.

THE VENGER, THREE YEARS LATER...

"Here," Karr handed Rabal a mug as Rabal, clearly claustrophobic, made himself comfortable in the long boat with his weapons.

"Sleeping in the jolly boat again tonight Rabal?" Dos Santos smiled as be moved to his station.

"To-hell-with-all-of-you!"

The next morning as I moved to my post, I saw Mister Crowe, the carpenter, working on a new plank to replace the one that Rodham had snapped.

Over the next few days, Lady Powell was allowed to wander the top deck –with her parasol-- and given every courtesy though there was no real change in her attitude towards us.

Then came Sunday. I was about to take the climb to the crow's nest but was stopped by Mister Barak, one of the Moors as he put his hand up to hold me in position. "Today is your holy day," he said in his Senegalese accent.

I had forgotten what day it was.

"I will take your watch while you go to your church." Mister Barak said.

I nodded with gratitude and went to where Mister Rush was conducting services at the base of the quarterdeck. I felt that I may need some religion in the days ahead, so I went below and found the Bible I was given in the church at Port Royal, then climbed back above. I found a place to stand where I could hear the message of the scripture and caught sight of Lady Powell and her party also taking in the Lord's word. Mister Rush was poetic with the words but had a cough which was becoming more and more consistent. This Sunday, it seemed to also be causing him a little pain and I had my concerns for Mister Rush since he had been a real friend to me on this ship. After an amen that concluded the services, I approached him, "Mister Rush, sir?"

"Ah Mister Reed. Good to see you taking in the Lord's words this morning." He coughed again into his handkerchief.

"Thank you. I-ah-I was wondering....is there something I can do for you Mister Rush? You-you don't look well."

"All is as it should be --as the Lord wills it."

There was blood in his kerchief, and I sensed something very wrong with him. "Have...have you seen Doctor Johannis or Doctor Jopo?"

"I have. Rest assured young man, my path has been charted...and all will be well." He gave me a smile and a reassuring touch on the shoulder.

I took him at his word and after church services, I took my post.

At noon, I watched the Moors as they took prayer in a line and then bowed on their prayer rugs at the bow. It occurred to me that before my arrival on this ship, their practices were something I had never witnessed in person and for a moment I took heed of how far I had come from my humble beginnings in Bristol.

The next day we made sight of the Island of Saint Noel. A French base and trading post in the North Caribbean. The island was known to be pacified. Essex took a look at the beach through his spyglass and called up Captain Passchendaele and our guests....

"Good morning, Captain." He began as he pointed off the port side railing, "Saint Noel."

Passchendaele looked.

"We're going to put you, what's left of your crew and our guests ashore." He continued, "There's a French garrison there on the east end of the island. You'll be safe there until such time as some transport back across the Atlantic can be arranged." He then handed Passchendaele a loaded pistol and a few extra rounds. "Take this, in case the unexpected happens."

Passchendaele took the weapon and put out his hand. "I thank you Captain for your courtesy and I shall remember it."

"I should tell you, that some of your men have elected to stay on with us."

"I am aware, and may I say Captain, that they are fortunate to be in your care. I thank you again for your decency."

"Best of luck to you." They shook hands and the Captain ordered the long boats away.

As the women began the climb down to the boats, one looked up at me, "Thank you…for delivering us here safely." She said.

Although I was not the one who deserved credit, I gave a positive nod and helped lower her down. Lady Powell was defiant until the end. She climbed in the long boat with an act of angry defiance and Addo and the others began to row them ashore. Once there, he planted a white flag in the sand and launched a rocket into the sky to get the attention of the local garrison…

Once our shore party was back onboard, we secured the boats. Harrow stood on deck with the Captain awaiting orders. There was a feeling of two different worlds –together for a short time—then separated again, two worlds that would never understand each other but the Captain knew that whatever the opinion of these ladies may be, they were put ashore unharmed and that was the fact of it…

VII

ISLE OF THE DEAD

Days later, we arrived at our mysterious destination. A landscape eclipsed by fog. This was the Dark Coast. The Côte de La Mort –or-- The Coast of The Dead. This stretch of the Louisiana territories belonged to the French government but, that's not who protected it. This part of the coastline was protected by wicked superstition, the costal island of St. Jacques, in particular was known as L'île du Diable or…The Island of the Devil! This territory was protected by zombies and black magic. Fear kept most authorities away. Shore parties would scamper back to their ships with stories of painted zombies and voodoo sacrifices.

-Cannibal stories!

Silence was the order of the day when we arrived. I looked out across the water as the sun had started to set below the horizon and a strange fog continued to roll in. The deck became gripped by an eerie sort of quiet. Men stood motionless. Only the sound of the ship rolling in the tide could be heard as she shifted towards our objective.

At the bow, Mister Daws dropped a 'lead line' to check the depth of the waters. We were at "Twenty-one fathoms," he reported, and we dropped anchor….

The Captain gave his orders, his words were slow and deliberate, "Landing parties at the ready!"

Mister Harrow gave his instructions and pointed out the candidates for the landing party. Teague, Mister Jagger, Toombs, Lo, Gordon, Mister Irons, Mister Blythe, Cage, Mister Nighthorse, Lau, Takeda, Upatau, Mazatal and few of our Aztecs along with Baako, Obal, Tiger, Dutch, Sterling, Mister Baltimore, Watson, Rabal, Mister Lynch, Mister Therrinfall, Miranda, Standish, Bishop, Towne, Tabor, Sunderland, Bons, Wolfe, Raeder, Ward, and myself. We opened up the armory, pulled our guns, collected our weapons, and began to make our way down the rigging to the long boats…

Mister Nighthorse was at the front of my boat, and it was rumored that the American Natives had keen awareness when in it came to this part of the world...

This was a silent approach. We rowed –and rowed-- and moved through the fog and costal rocks where I was stunned to see skeletons, chained to giant wooden crosses, exposed waist deep in the tide, all that was left of victims of torture and drowning. It was a grim sight. This place was called the Dark Coast for a reason.

Through the mist, I began to see the shapes of dark figures, motionless ahead. Some of these figures stood in the water still, like statues –some motionless on the rocks. I continued to slowly row forward as the other men did, but my concerns –or fear—was perhaps more visible and obvious.

Other dark figures stood on the beach, like shadows in the fog, many in the tide, remained still as we slowly rowed past…

"Zom-bie" Baako said in a deep, foreboding voice as if he saw my fear and was content to add to it.

These dark shadows in the mist were men, of dark skin and covered in black paint on the shoulders and body but with white paint in the patterns of a skull and bones –much like Mister Baako and Addo wore in combat-- and now I came to know more about their history for this is where they came from!

'Was Addo some form of zombie?' He seemed alive enough.

Some of these men here had used white paint to draw bones on their arms and ribs, the mark of a skeleton…

We climbed from the boats and moved through the shallow water towards the black sands of the beach ahead. The sands of this place were littered with skulls and bones from enemy combatants.

At that point, Captain Essex stepped forward until he was face to face with a large dark figure on the beach.

My eyes searched the fog for these men, my fingers tightened around the handle of my cutlass, with hope that I would not have to rely on my emerging skills as a fighter to save myself –for I could make myself no promises if hell broke loose here.

Suddenly, Captain Essex and this foreboding character in front of him, grabbed each other by the forearm –a sort of handshake-- and smiled at each other with a greeting. I was equally surprised to see our Captain speak French to this character and –in French – was the reply. The Captain then offered our new friend some tobacco and drew his pipe and they continued their conversation with a little laughter.

Mister Harrow turned to Mister Daws, "Signal the ship, order Mister Newcastle to advance."

"Aye." Daws then took two torches, ignited them, and took position on the rocks in the tide and waved the torches in a fashion and pattern that sent a message back to the decks of the ship.

--Newcastle could see the signal, through the fog. He lowered his spyglass and turned to Mister Cheval "Lower away Mister Cheval, if you please…." and within a few moments other long boats arrived on the beach with some cargo –cotton, barrels of molasses and some silks.

I turned to survey my surroundings, of course, the stories of this place were circulated far and wide not by survivors but by the pirates and privateers –such as ourselves-- who found advantage in such stories. This coastal stretch --the Côte de La Mort-- itself had some decorative help, large scarecrows with a wicked, foreboding look were erected in the tide and along the coastline.

A population of vultures was brought to the island to signal death to visitors –and the bones on the beach. Fear kept people away and these men here –these zombies, were called the 'ferrymen' --like on the river Styx—for reasons I was about to learn.

Moments later, the supplies were brought through the tide and moved up on the beach, we carried them through the trees, under the Spanish moss to a bayou waterway that led through the swamps. Here boats –like native canoes-- waited for our cargo and we loaded them up….

Within this perimeter, there was a series of channels and waterways that disappeared into the landscape from this lagoon and a makeshift port – much of which was built on stilts. From here, supplies and cargo could be unloaded and in turn, hauled north to New Orleans and eventually up the large waterway that worked its way up the frontier of the Americas to a French outpost called Saint Louis. This was very lucrative and sensible, allowing the locals to take our captured goods and travel through the wilds of America by river --not in conflict with regulators or the French authorities—so they could sell them back to various markets. This made for a smart partnership….

Mister Lincoln went over the books and the numbers as more supplies arrived from our ship and this practice of unloading from the sea and loading at this swamp landing, continued. Some of the 'zombies' made count and inventory of our wares and helped us in the moving of the barrels. I was curious but spoke not a word for I had learned much by keeping my mouth shut and my ears open and once the last of the crates and barrels were loaded, these boats moved off into the darkness.

The dialogue continued in French with our Captain and the 'zombies' with more laughter and the zombies then led us to a series of huts also built on stilts that stood above the swamp. Lit with lanterns and torches we made our way forward until ordered to halt. Here the 'zombies' pulled on a rope and pulley system that slowly raised from the green swamp a massive rope net loaded with iron boxes. It was then maneuvered and placed on the dock where we stood….

"Here it is lads." Harrow said, "Grab hold" It then became our task to retrieve these boxes, open them up for inspection and inventory the gold, silver, and profits inside, then march then back to the beach. We moved them into the tide and loaded them on our long boats. Our commerce here had ended, and it was time to head back to the ship...

"Reed," Harrow called out.

I stopped and turned, as the tide rolled over my boots.

He used his thumb to point over his shoulder, "North, through the swamp about three hundred leagues is New France. If you want, these men will take you next time they make the trip north."

I thought about it, three hundred leagues of swamp and wilderness and with no real working knowledge of French, plus, somewhat scary natives and indigenous killers just to make it to a French outpost to hopefully start my life and teaching career from there? "It's all right Mister Harrow...if it's all the same to you, I'd like to remain with the ship."

"Suit yourself." he said as he climbed aboard the jolly boat. "Never let it be said we didn't give a schoolteacher a chance to save his own life." – and the men around him laughed.

I paused for a moment, then returned to my work. Again, I had the task of rowing. At this time, however, Mister Nighthorse and his habits became clear to me, for he wore no war paint on this expedition. Something I had seen him seek to apply every time we ventured into combat. Now it became known, that if he didn't paint his face, we were on a mission of a more peaceful nature. If he did paint himself, then, that was to be my warning – and Lord help us!

The next day we were hit by a warm tropical rainstorm...

After my watch, I dropped below deck as water splashed below, worked my way past the ronin at a table repairing their armor, turned to the far end of the deck to see the Moors –in prayer-- and moved past Mister Saxon's gun section, consisting of Thorpe, Flynn, Mister Temple, Pharaoh –the young man with a jar of marbles--and several others.

Many of these men here –the gunners-- were from various navies, including the Dutch, Spanish, Chinese, French, English, and other various countries, where circumstance --and quite often vicious treatment-- lead them to a change of employers.

The gun captain, Saxon --in the quarter deck division-- had survived the Spanish Armada both in battle and as a prisoner where he was shackled to a bench below deck and made to row when the wind had lost favor. There, after being imprisoned for several years-- he learned to hate drums. Drums kept the timing in such a place, drums kept the pace. Drums woke him up and made him work. Drums he hated. Drums he would always hate. He was, of course, rescued when his ship was sunk during the battle of Hook's Point. Many men died below decks as the water level rose to overtake them. He –however—forced his way to freedom…this is where he lost his foot. "Better a foot, than your life lad" was his sentence. Then his eyes seemed to drift to some far-off place in his memory. "The screaming a man makes while under water is something I can never –never forget. That always comes back to visit me in my sleep." He crossed his heart in the manner a catholic does, then pressed back to his duties.

I continued forward on my own, working my way aft, past the deck's powder magazine and deck armory and eventually to the galley. There Mister Hobby was baking bread and simmering a stew. Wicks arrived at the galley's seaside window and loaded in nets of fish caught by our underwater traps, "With the compliments of Mister Styles!"

"My thanks to Mister Styles." Hobby shouted as the chopping and preparation of such fish became the task. Everything, fish heads, guts, it all went into the stew. I pressed on, past the galley chicken coup where I found Mister Wolfe and Karr as they passed me….

"Reed...Mister Harrow is requestin' your presence on deck!"

I gave nod and made my way up the bow forward steps, above. I passed the Aztecs and approached Mister Harrow from the back as he watched the horizon ahead. "Mister Harrow, sir."

He turned and gave me a long look and then cut into me with the words, "What's this I hear about a school?"

I became nervous and stumbled for the right words to craft my response. "Sir –I-I sir…I thought it best to put my skills to work in an effort to help expand the intelligence of the men."

He looked me up and down as if to size me up, a practice he continued to make upon every meeting as if to measure my intent and value to the ship. "A school?"

"Yes-yes sir." Here I expected –and feared—punishment, my only hope was that it be swift.

Again, he was delayed in his response, which only increased my sense of dread. "Only at the evening meal, do not let it interfere with your duties."

I was surprised. "Thank-thank you sir!"

"And Mister Reed....an emphasis on mathematics and calculation, if you please."

"Yes sir. Of course, sir!" I was dismissed but with a new purpose for I was now allowed to apply my livelihood without clandestine measures.

I continued most nights at evening meal to apply my lessons and I am pleased to report that what started as a small crowd of students grew larger and larger with each evening. Since the world is not only mathematics, I applied what I knew of science and history which forced me to correct many a story and superstition these men had governed their lives by, such as Blythe's belief in mermaids or the legend that dragons had once existed.

The next evening, there was lightning on the horizon. On deck was another day of combat training. Fencing, then knife fighting. I hit the deck, blood coming from my mouth, my skull felt like it was split.

"On your feet. We go again!"

I climbed off the planks as Jagger closed in.

I hit the deck several more times, taking punches or being thrown to the boards and I continued to get to my feet and take this beating. If I was going to do anything at all, I was going to earn the crew's respect through effort. I may not have been a refined killer but, they could not break me or get me to quit. That was one thing I could control. It was also my theory that if I was going to be plagued by a conscious and in turn, hoping to inspire a conscious or a little understanding and kindness in the crew here, then I better have respectable fighting skills.

"Again." Jagger called out.

I wiped the blood from my mouth and looked across the deck to see more of the crew gather around, then I saw Newcastle step next to Hayte at the wheel, arms crossed, with some interest in what was happening.

Jagger closed in again but this time, I was gripped with a new level of determination and when we clashed, I held my ground. We fenced across the deck --this was my strongest showing, and I worked the steel with speed. The samurai slowed down at their work, Tak lowered a box on deck and stood there, hands on his hips watching, waiting to see if any of their lessons had taken hold…

Killing Bear and Merciless moved into the circle to see how long I could last –and then, with a move –a semi-circle defensive swing-- Jagger's cutlass was pried from his hand and shot into the mast nearby, piercing the wood right next to where Jack-Karr stood. Karr paused, coffee mug on its way to his mouth and he looked at us…

--I held my breath afraid he might charge at me for almost killing him.

Instead, he just said, "Leave it to Jagger to invent a new way of disarming himself." And the men all around us laughed. Even Jagger gave a slight smile as if impressed with my progress.

The practice continued and from there, Daws and Arson moved over to the small top deck galley to hold up by a lantern at the window. Toombs was not too far off. Rorry slid some rum cake forward and dropped bucket of coffee on the window countertop as Arson dropped his mug into it.

"We sail west."

"We do." Daws replied, "The Captain has an imperial target in mind." He said in a low tone.

"Under which flag?"

Daws focused on him, "Spanish. The target may be New Spain itself."

Arson looked to Kon Boar and the other Aztecs in a huddle around a small deck fire. "Our rebels will be happy."

Daws smiled before taking another sip from his mug, "As we all know, they may not love gold but, they love their cause --and the fight."

"As we all do."

"The Captain tells me, the Spanish are preparing for another war, they're out gunned and can't provide security for all their outposts. They want to conscript some privateers --and that the admiralty offered up a letter of marque."

Arson scoffed, "He was right to refuse. I don't mind killin' but I'm not killin' on their orders." He stopped himself, and turned from the flickering lantern light, "You don't think it's because he may be considering an alliance with the English?"

"Better not be the case," Daws looked back to Nighthorse and the some of the other natives on deck. "The Hurons will break us on the wheel." He smiled and at the moment, Jagger threw me face forward into the galley where they were standing.

I sat at the table for an evening meal –beaten and sore. With Mister Baltimore, Mister Wicks, Prescott, Toombs, Standish, Takeda, Dutch and Mister Lo –Tiger and Mister Foxx were working with weapons near-by.

Mister Lo-Tan, it became known to me, had been with crew for several years. His sailing junk –or ship-- ran aground during a local war in Southeast Asia. He made it ashore to fight in a nine-day battle which obliterated both sides. He was wounded, rescued, and brought back to life by Buddhist monks, and he would recover and work in their temple as a mason to earn his meals. Sometime later, the temple was sacked by the French, and he escaped into the countryside. He then made his way to a port in Indochina and signed up for something new, first on a frigate called 'The Tempest' that brought him to European ports where he had to learn to navigate the ways of the 'white man's prejudice' finding shelter in townships and small settlements run by Chinese people --like little Chinese towns. There he found life limited and went back to sea. The Tempest was sunk in the West Indies, he was adrift and eventually picked up by The Venger.

The different Chinese sailors onboard seemed to fancy customized weapons and blades. Lau –a former Monk-- for example liked these 'butterfly' blades that were short in length but wide and dangerous and he fought with two at a time. I summoned the courage to ask Mister Lo about his weapon. It was, he explained, based on a wax wood staff owned by a monk he once knew. The staff was broken in a fight with bandits on a high road, then for some reason repaired with rope. This –though odd—pushed this staff into a new evolution and it became the basis for the weapon –now in three parts—that he used today.

"But this is made of metal." I noted.

Mister Lo smiled. "Metal is better." He said, "Metal is better for breaking the bones of our enemies."

CHRISTMAS EVE

I climbed the deck, coffee mug in hand and stood next to Duncan-Howe, Java and Tane, the tattooed islander with Mister Wilder not too far off.

That night on deck, Lau and some of our Japanese compatriots were playing a game by the light of the deck fire. To me it looked like backgammon –a game I played with my fellow teachers over Christmas but, this was different –they moved pieces with sticks and called the game GO...

I passed to the rail. It was a warm night and the ocean seemed very calm. "It's your holiday today." Jeddah said from behind me, and I turned from the rail. "Your profit, the one from an-Nāṣira."

"Nazareth." I said using the Hebrew word.

Then he changed to a lighter tone. "I have been to Nazareth." He said with a touch of pride.

"You have?"

"I have. It is a small place. There is a school there were Jesus learned his letters." He paused, "The Romans burned it."

"Why would Jesus need to learn letters?" Jack-Karr said as he stopped chewing on his bacon to think. He looked at us, "Wouldn't he know his letters already?"

"What are you asking, Jack?" Jagger passed some mugs loaded with wine around to all of us.

"Why would God send his son on a mission, without teaching him how to read? Doesn't seem adequate."

"No?"

"Well not for the job he had to do!"

"Well, since you put it that way—"

"I mean, you send your son to save mankind but, he doesn't know the alphabet?" The more Jack talked the more he seemed to puzzle himself.

"Maybe it was so he could learn to be more like the people he was saving." I offered.

"Why don't you just teach him the damn alphabet, so he's prepared?" Flynn was now thinking along the same lines....

"And weapons." Jack-Karr added. "Teach him some weapons. That way he could give those Roman bastards a hard time of it –and not be crucified so easy. Kill some of those bastards in the process! Make a name for yourself."

"Make a name for yourself? Like 'Jesus the Killer'?" I asked.

"--He did make a name for himself." Rush said sparked with frustration. "The Lord Christ! And he wasn't supposed to give them a hard time. He was supposed to sacrifice himself!" He was now working a slight element of temper into the conversation....

"What? Like just give up? For people like us? So, we behave? Nay, makes no sense. Teach him weapons."

"What? Jesus The Avenger? Can't have that in our Bible!" Rush blurted out.

"Why not?" Jagger said passing a wine bottle around. "God helps those who help themselves, Father."

"By breaking commandments and killin'?" Rush shouted.

"Well Moses wrote those commands –and without authorization I'd wager. He most likely just made them up to keep his people in line." Jagger said.

"Needed to do something after wanderin' in the desert for four decades!" Karr continued.

"Do any of you heathens pay any attention to what I preach on Sunday? Any of you?"

"---Can't he resurrect himself in any event?" I asked as if I didn't hear the question about Sunday school. "So, if you kill him, he can come back to life."

"Aye and keep fighting!" Jack-Karr added, holding tight to the notion that fighting was better.

"That would be a very good skill!" Jeddah added. "Resurrection. You cannot kill him."

"But he can kill all of you!" Karr said as if he stumbled on to something.

Rush was now more than visibly frustrated. "He was meant to sacrifice himself, so we'd appreciate—"

"Nay, better to kill all those Roman bastards than sacrifice oneself."

"I agree."

"Yeah, me as well. Better to kill than be killed!"

"Merry Christmas gentlemen" Harrow said in passing, working his way down the deck, bottle in hand.

"Merry Christmas Mister Harrow"

There was a moment of silence as the argument seemed to settle then I heard some words from the shadows to my left. It was Cheval, the metal plate in his head reflected the moonlight. "I spent Christmas with my mother before I was orphaned" he said in a sort of quiet tone.

I was stunned. I had never heard him speak.

He then looked at me, as if to make sure someone was present to record this memory of his. "My mother was kind to me. And good!" He then looked away. "I should like to do something kind before my time in this life is up."

I smiled. "Your moment to make a difference is coming Mister Cheval. That I'd wager."

He looked at me with a faded, slight smile as if he hoped I was right. And thus, was my first Christmas aboard The Venger. Little did I know at the time, that we'd have a proper Christmas celebration by sacking Panama.

At dawn the next morning, I would take another beating. It was important to have skills in hand-to-hand combat and after my first engagement, I knew I needed more experience with this if I was to survive the days ahead. Different men would teach me different attacking and defensive skills each day. Mister Lo specialized in the art of what was called Kung Fu, an ancient art from India but adapted by the Chinese which consisted of striking from an uncomfortable stance with my toes pointed inwards. It was fast paced and involved kicking which I was in no shape to attempt. The ronin practiced the art of bending limbs in ways unnatural -- and tumbling. They called their skills Aikido and Judo. This always started with a bow before the lesson could begin and there was a hierarchy of sorts. They would throw me to the deck several times in demonstration of a move and then I would be allowed to try to move on them. But I was always thrown to the planks first in the practice of every new move. It was a series of painful lessons, and my teachers were unforgiving.

Mister Rajiv practiced something called Gatka –another killing art from India. Others had their own styles and habits, and combat practice was allowed and even encouraged. Sometimes friendly gambling –for shift duty-- even centered around it.

Mister Nighthorse also had a few combat tricks, but he preferred to fight with a knife and his tomahawk together at the same time. Never a sword. And he scalped his victims keeping the locks as a sign of conquest. He had fifty-one scalps at last count.

I found that combat practice and work on the ship was making me stronger though it was a slow process but, through much pain and discomfort I was becoming a new man. At home I would need assistance to move every little thing, here I was building real strength. The strength to haul things of a weight that I'd never imagine. My hands had become tough and work became very fulfilling in a strange way.

I collapsed on deck that evening, not too far from Mister Lynch, drawing in his book and looked out at the sunset as Mister Rush handed out mugs of wine to myself and those around me. The wind was blowing through my hair, and I looked out over the ocean and wondered what our heading was. It seemed to be west which I tried to confirm by position of the setting sun…

Destinations and targets were not always disclosed to the crew and our officers or 'war captains' went about their work without so much as a hint of our mission. If I asked Rush or Newcastle where we might be headed, Newcastle would respond, "Where the action is." or "Where the money is." As if that answered my question --and Rush would just answer by asking me if I was going to attend church the following Sunday,

Others would tell me just to get back to work or, "You'll know when you need to know" or "You'll know when we tell ya' and not before."

But judging by the sun we were definitely moving west and west meant New Spain and the Spanish Empire. I looked up; Rush was coughing over the side. His coughing seemed to be getting more and more frequent. He regained his composure and turned from the rail…

I took to my feet. "I can take over your duties in the galley Mister Rush if you need a moment."

He waved me off. "No need lad. I can manage." He tried to get his breathing under control and looked out across the water. "I do love the sea." He said as if he found a new –sudden—appreciation in it…

I gave a nod to agree and held a smile that was mixed with both worry for his health and happiness that he had something to appreciate….

Mister Newcastle made his way down the deck, past Mister Reader and Duncan-Howe to our position. "Mister Rush, Mister Harrow would like a word before we make sight of the coast if you please…"

"Right." Rush replied and he collected himself and started towards the quarter deck….

"Mister Newcastle?"

Newcastle stopped and looked down at me. "Yes?"

"What coast will we be in sight of…if you don't mind?"

"Panama." He said as he surprised me with a real answer. "Get some rest…. for it will be far from quiet."

Rush made his way to the helm to find Mister Harrow going over his maps under the lantern light with Mister Thorn, Sunderland and Therrinfall. Mister Flagg –the former mercenary—was at the wheel…

"Mister Harrow. You wish to see me sir?"

Harrow turned from the map, "How are you, Thomas?" He looked at him when he asked the question as if to betray some real interest in the answer.

"Fine sir."

Harrow turned to Thorn and Sunderland. "Give us a moment, if you would lads."

Thorn nodded and they cleared the deck as Harrow motioned for Rush to come forward. When he made it to the map table, Harrow picked up a jug and poured the contents into two mugs. He put one in the hand of Mister Rush…

"We have a bit of bad business ahead of us. Heavy fighting."

"I've heard rumor."

Harrow searched for the right words and then tried to lay them out, "The Captain and I think we may need some additional help in the infirmary once the action starts. We wondered if…you would mind lending a hand to Johannis and Jopo…."

"And…. not help with the fighting sir?"

Harrow made a frown and nodded no.

"Wh-what about Mister Crowe and the carpenters?"

"They'll be there to be sure."

"Then, may I ask…are you sure you'll be needing me in the infirmary…during the fighting? I'd like to do my part with the rest of the lads sir."

"I know and you will –in the hospital."

Rush seemed to search for the words that reflected what was on his mind. "Beggin' your pardon sir. Does this have anything to do with my condition?"

Harrow had known Rush too long to be dishonest with him and after a moment to think of every possible answer –honest and other—he finally told him the truth. "It does Thomas."

Rush tried to stand tall and upright as if he had just survived a physical blow to his structure and his face remained fixed as if he tried to overcome the hurt emotions that this line of honesty brought with it....

"The Captain and I think we owe it to you to keep you out of harm's way until---"

"Sir...with respect, is this an order?"

"Well," Harrow shrugged, "No but--"

"Then you can go to hell sir –respectfully."

Harrow's eyes went wide with a touch of surprise....

"I love this ship and the men aboard sir, you most of all and I'll be damned if my condition or –your sympathy—can keep me from doing my part to help them through whatever action may await us and God willing, I may die with a sword in my hand."

Harrow listened until Rush was finished.

"No sir, not me!" He then tried to realign his temper. "Ah- Is there anything else?"

Harrow shook his head, in a state somewhat like shock "No."

"Very well. Thank you for your time and consideration sir." And Rush dismissed himself.

Harrow smiled and went back to his maps in the candlelight, "God loves a rebel." He said under his breath....

VIII

THE STEEL MACHINE WILL EAT YOU

We were planning to have the coastline of Panama in sight in the next day or two and there was going to be a fight with the Spanish. The Spanish were excellent fighters on land –maybe the best-- so it was going to be hard work to say the least.

The crew was beginning to make their preparations. Weapons were checked, blades sharpened...

I worked with Mister Thorpe, Merciless and Dax-Varro –a man who had robbed a bank in Gibraltar—and we packed grenades and cut fuses and loaded them in satchels...

Below deck, that night, I watched as Mazatal, Upatau and his Aztec friends made darts and dipped them in a poison of their own making. He saw my eyes on his blowgun and picked it up and offered it to me for a closer look. This pipe of sorts was his weapon of preference –after the musket. A simple device from his homeland.

"You made this?"

"Yes. I make," he said.

Kon Boar took it from me and pretended to demonstrate how it was to be used in combat for me to see. I nodded. "Interesting." I looked at his darts and watched him dip them in a black liquid. "And what's that?" I motioned to it, "That you dip them in?"

He said a word in this native language followed by the word.... "Death."

"Death?"

"Death for our enemies." He said in his 'small' voice, "Death for Spanish."

The man next to him mumbled a few words. I was curious what he was saying....

"We use to fight the Spanish when they burn our homes. Spanish make us Cath-o-lic. Take away our women. Make us build their forts. They hurt us with ---"He needed his friend to translate. He looked for the words to describe what he was saying, and he had his companion show me his back. It was covered in scars and lash marks from a whip.

"The Spanish did that!"

"Yes. Spanish did."

When the King of Spain looked at his map of the world, he saw great sections that were under his flag but, at what cost? Was this happening everywhere? In New Spain, Spanish Florida, on the Southern American continent? And were the English, French, or Dutch much better? The answer to these men here, on this ship was NO!

I turned as Therrinfall suddenly shot up in his hammock. Sweat covered his face and he let out a panicked hiss. Therrinfall would suddenly wake up in the dead of night, clothes and hammock soaked. This was the price the man had to pay every night for his years of working as a hangman for the king –and the hundreds of people he killed now owned him. There was no mercy when he closed his eyes at night. The sound of the rope snapping straight, the echo of all those necks breaking from his noose, it made for a haunting line of work and...a haunted existence.

I had some compassion for Therrinfall but there wasn't anything I could do for the man. Some men called him 'The Executioner' as a sort of nickname but I was always afraid to call him that for fear of how he might react –and—because it seemed disrespectful.

I stepped up on the top deck waiting for the bell that would send me aloft. I looked and saw Therrinfall in the shadows by himself...

"How is it with you Reed?" Whitney asked as he roped down to the deck.

"Fine." I said, "The Aztecs are below making poison."

"For themselves or our enemies." He smiled.

"For themselves?"

"The Aztecs won't be taken alive if they can help it. Neither will the Hurons."

"Brave then."

"Brave yes but, that's only part of it." He turned to me, "Natives can't survive in a cell. If you lock them up…they die." He saw that I was confused by this but left it at that as he dropped below deck, passing Jack-Karr as he made up through the hatch.

"Have at it, Whit," Karr said as he took to his feet. He surveyed the deck, looked at the ronin melting down metal and making throwing stars by a deck fire, then to me. He then said something in the samurai language and Kai stood up and waved me over.

"Go." Karr said with a smile as he motioned with his head towards the rogue samurai, "Time for your next combat lesson."

I stepped to the ronin working above the sparks and saw the different blades being cultivated. Three-sided blades, four and five-sided blades. Round blades, even a square blade with the corners dipped in red paint. Kai shouted something down the deck and the on-shift crew seemed to clear out and step towards the starboard side. He then held up his index finger as if to get me to focus and raised a three-sided throwing star and in the flash of an instant, threw it, over-hand down the deck where it smashed into a fire bucket that was hanging from the main mast.

He then handed a blade to me and said something in Japanese.

It wasn't example enough for me to follow but, I was prepared to try so I gripped the throwing star but as I pulled my arm back to throw, the blade slipped from my grasp –backwards—and hammered into the rail at the quarter deck.

-The samurai laughed at my expense. Kai said something in his native language which I guessed was a joke at my expense –since there was more laughter, this time by both Jack Karr and Kannon and then Takeda stood up and stepped out of the shadows.

NO QUARTER! KILL ALL MASTERS!

Takeda who spoke perfect English said, "Hold it blade down, between your thumb and first finger." He said, "Put your other arm across your body." He got in a stance and demonstrated where to put my left arm, just below chest level. "Step forward to put force into the throw, when your right arm hits the left, release the blade." He gripped my wrist that was holding the star, "The blade will strike what your hand is pointing at."

I did as instructed, slowly at first to follow Takeda's checklist in my mind and the star did travel in the right direction –better than backwards— though it bounced off a lantern. Two more throws and the blade struck the fire bucket hanging at head-level from the main mast! My eyes went wide, proud of myself. There was some vague cheering from the samurai as if this was a victory and I turned around with a smile to accept the mild congratulations, then I got back to work on it.

Karr watched, arms crossed as I got more comfortable with the handling and throwing of these blades. I even advanced past the need to hold my left hand in front of me as a marker and started to point with it more like a veteran would. I actually got very comfortable with all this.

There was also a horizontal throw but stepping into a vertical throw gave the blade much more power when closing in on a target so –one thing at a time.

Later, that night, the windows in the Captain's quarters were opened up into the night air. The Captain slid the candle on his desk to the edge of a map. Harrow, Newcastle, and our warrant officers looked it over for evaluation. The unfinished –but still armed—fort that protected the harbor of Panama, the beach, docks, church, and the courthouse, all just off the water. But before any of this could be targeted, one defensive obstacle had to be addressed, any ship entering Panama had to pass by a small fort –or look-out post-- on the Reyna Coast that, if engaged, would use signal flares and cannon to alert the township of any impending danger. This post would have to eliminated before any attack on Panama proper could begin. Judging by the size of the look-out garrison, the ramparts could not house more than a platoon of Spanish regulars, maybe twelve to twenty men.

-That was if these captured maps, dated nine months before, were accurate.

The officers started to exchange killing ideas and as they did, the Captain focused on an old Spanish mission a league to the north of this outpost working different attack strategies in his mind. "We could disguise a raiding party as Spanish monks or…we could just let the Aztecs go in and kill everybody. Yeeeesssss, option two seems right."

The outpost stood on the water, Spanish and regional flags flying, above the mist, even at night. The stone works were lit by torch, with a sentry in the small tower built above the gate and with two guards and a sergeant out front to kept watch….

There was a sudden slight hiss as a sentry slapped his hand on his neck. Perplexed, he stumbled and then suddenly dropped dead. The two other sentries turned as Mazatal, and the Aztecs emerged from the jungle and used blow guns to kill them. Darts zipped through the air, a dart to the front of the throat and to the cheek, hitting the guard in the tower and his body draped over the spiked ramparts…

Mazatal gave a quick two-motion hand signal directing Kon Boar, Upatau and the Jaguars to move forward, quietly open the gate and advance inside to kill any others that may be around….

Acalan took the two torches by the gate and moved them in a pattern to signal The Venger.

'Guards killed. Coast clear.'

Daws signaled back from our decks, and we sailed past the outpost towards Panama.

The Aztecs made it back into their long boat up the beach, where Arson and Bishop waited for them in the tide. They piled in and rowed back to us, and we picked them up and heaved the jolly boat back to its rig without reducing speed.

I helped Mazatal and the others up the rigging to the deck as we picked up speed towards Panama and with the town lights in the distance, I stood at the rail in the wind, riding a privateering ship toward its target at full speed and I must admit –shame be damned--it was a feeling of pure adrenaline and excitement....

Captain Essex, Harrow, Teague, Wolfe, Raeder and Jaffar were at the bow. Essex used his spyglass to make a survey of the township. He looked to the un-finished fort –still equipped with twelve long range guns, then the town proper just off the water with lights burning and--   "My God--" Essex suddenly slammed his spyglass closed, "The harbor is empty!"

Harrow re-checked the same scene with his glass and then lowered it with a smile, "Fortune smiles on us sir."

"Indeed, it does. Get the raiding parties over the side. Stand by with the cannon."

"Right sir." Harrow shouted, "Raiding parties ashore!"

The commands were repeated below –and then through-- the decks. In rapid order, our war captains marshalled us over the side to make the climb down, to board the long boards and then, as teams, we started rowing towards our targets....

"Order Rajiv to run out the starboard guns, prepare to target the fort."

Below deck, Rajiv looked up as Therrinfall stuck his head into the hatch above, "Rajiv," he shouted, "Run out the starboard guns prepare to level the fort!!!"

"Aye" Rajiv shouted back, in his deep, grumbling voice and he started moving down the deck as his men jumped into action....

The gun doors opened up and the guns rolled out...

The Captain waited –as the ship continued to move forward-- until the range was right on the fortress walls. "Almost there,"

He waited...

And waited...

Suddenly a red flare shot up from the fortress –a warning flare that lit up the sky. We had been spotted!

"FIRE!" Essex shouted and the cannons opened up. Blasts and explosions hit the water, the beach, and the fort...

We watched from the longboats as flashes lit up our surroundings like lightning.

The Captain suddenly issued additional orders to adjust the firing and the cannons opened back up again. They fired and rolled back as Saxon, Wilder, Mister Temple, and the other crews rushed to reload and roll them back out....

As the cannons continued blasting the coast and punishing the fort wall, we rowed our raiding parties towards the beach. We could hear cannon balls as they zipped through the air just over our heads and hammered their targets, lighting up the night sky with explosions and fire....

A hole was suddenly blown into the fortress wall just as we made our beach landing, and we stormed forward. Jagger and Toombs, climbed over the giant, smoking bricks that had tumbled out onto the sand from our artillery work and threw grenades though the hole that had been ripped into the stone by our cannon --then Teague and the ronin stormed inside using the grenade blasts for cover...

There was an exchange of musket fire as the Spanish marines filed out of the barracks and walled up for a fight. Two of our crew were killed as we unloaded our weapons –musket rounds slamming into our targets, breaking bones, and punching holes—as some Spanish marines tumbled into the dust.

Teague moved forward, emptied both pistols and pulled two more from his sash and fired --killing four Spaniards as they ran towards us. The rest of us opened up our guns. The ronin ran past Teague towards the enemy screaming like devils....

Both sides reached for their blades, and we charged each other. Men were cut, stabbed, and bashed in a typhoon of metal and dust. A sword hit Takeda in the helmet with a claaaaaaaaannng and he countered by swinging his sword from the left shoulder to the right, slicing the man's hands off at the elbows!

Baltimore –armed with a knife and axe—made two quick striking moves, then brought his axe in on a Spaniard's knee dropping him to the parade ground floor then he gripped him by the hair, pulled his knife and made a sawing motion to take his scalp....

Ward fought his way forward with Manu, Sterling and O'Shea and threw a grenade into the officer's quarters --the explosion blew a hole in the roof and lit the building on fire....

A platoon of soldiers tried to remove two women from the fort in a mad dash --under fire-- to a carriage. Soldiers died to their left and right but, they did manage to get the women aboard and get underway even as one of the wagon drivers was shot in the back and rolled off the coach into the dirt. Some of our crew made chase but could not catch the carriage before it passed under the tunnel exit, then across the bridge, over a lagoon, into the unknown. I found myself relieved to see them make their escape, for I could not vouch for the conduct of my ship mates in such a combative environment.

DOWN THE BEACH...

The Venger fired on the town as she moved into the port --the bombardment along the coast was also designed to drive the populace to flee into the countryside for both their safety –and to prevent the civilians from obstructing us in attack. Blasts hit the buildings along the water, driving the defenders back and covering Newcastle and our raiding party as they rowed ashore and stormed up the beach into the township. Grey and Thorpe were killed upon landing and Kane was wounded. Irons, Merciless, Cage, Lo-Tan and the Moors unloaded from the boats, moved up the beach and brought havoc --with the blade and gun-- down upon the Spanish regulars as they tried to defend the cantina on the beach. Many of the Spanish were trying to find their units –drunk and dazed—and were cut down.

Jack-Karr sparked a grenade and used the blast for cover as it took apart the deck of the cantina. He motioned for Obal, Towne, Bons, Hallock,

Jeddah and a few others to follow him up through the smoke and they closed on the enemy for some close quarter killing.

--The sound a blade makes when it cuts is disturbing and when it strikes bone –or a skull-- it makes a sound no one forgets.

Our crew pressed into the town at full speed, running to engage targets as they emerged, sometimes giving them a slash, and cutting them down before they even cleared a doorway…

Mister Lau was moving –and cutting—with his two butterfly swords and he rifled one right into the back of a retreating Spanish Marine.

An explosion sent Spanish soldiers tumbling into the street on fire. Takeda slapped out some flames that were burning his sleeve and then went back to killing. Jata, Sanjuro and Calderone were all moving in between buildings. Jupiter had slammed his shoulder into the gallows, pressed forward and collapsed the structure using brute force.

Raeder cut though the Spanish but lost his sword when he could not pull it out of the body of a dead marine. He was tackled and had to fight with his hands to choke and kill his attacker --then he took his victim's sword away from him to press his fight forward into the street….

There were dead bodies all over the town square. Wolfe was drowning a man in a fountain that centered the plaza. He held him under the water until his body stopped moving, bullets hitting the stone statues and masonry all around him…

The fighting had, by now, spread throughout the entire township and some of the countryside…

From the fort to the prison block, to the town square there was action. In the plaza, the Spanish infantry formed a defensive picket line and fired into our ranks. Two of our Moors were killed, and Mister Cross took a musket ball square in the head –and another two in the chest and hit the ground dead --as he did, I grabbed his musket from him and checked it for a round-- I then looked down on him, he was gone, and I was compelled to close his eyes before I returned to the fighting…

The center of the plaza was no man's land. Some of our wounded were trying to crawl to safety. The Spanish regulars across the plaza fired another volley at us and –with sharp whistle—it cut up the terrain around me with lead. The Spanish held one side of the plaza and we held the other in what became a more classic type or... European type of fighting exchange.

But just as the Spanish became comfortable in a fighting style they knew, our native contingent –Mister Silence, Bons, Sam, the other Hurons, and Aztec Jaguars-- had got 'round and attacked this picket line --from the shadows, behind them and dropped in on them from the low, tavern roof tops above them, using pistols, tomahawks and swords to cut them down and wipe them out....

We pressed forward, killing what was left of this regiment and then we moved past the prison block, the prisoners looking through the bars on the windows to see explosions light up the town. The prison guards were cut down. Mister Flynn, Standish and others stormed the block house and began to open it up...

On our move up the main highway along the water's edge....
Mister Sunderland, Fury, Bishop, and our men fought as infantry and pressed the fight into a graveyard, using tombstones for cover in an attempt to press the Spanish back and ultimately force them towards a church to be cornered. The exchange of musket fire and grenades became intense, and the advance was reduced to a meter or two at a time –an explosion here, gun fire there. Whitney even tripped into an open grave on his advance. The Spanish marines were forced back --some carrying wounded and some crawling with blades and musket rounds in them-- and they moved to fort up in the church, bolting the doors and using the windows to fire from while our men used the graveyard for protection....

Having cleared the plaza, we arrived at the church to see our men holding and firing from the graveyard and the Spanish holding the church a few meters away. Mister Stylen crawled through the tombstones, up against the walls of the church and shoved a bomb through the window. There was an explosion, then smoke, He was tossed another grenade by

Therrinfall —fuse already lit—and in through the window it went - BOOOOM!

This time Spanish marines were partially ejected –some through the stain glass windows some through the front doors to tumble into the street –dead, uniforms smoldering. The holy building itself had caught fire.

Some of our men were killed in the graveyard –bodies draped over the headstones and on the ground-- but the others pressed forward and stormed the church. The flames, which started to bring down the rafters would not hinder us in our killing. Our men killed whoever was left and started to search and sack the building –as a Christian, this was a difficult task and I entered in an attempt to possibly moderate this but, once inside, I saw Jagger, Irons and Teague break down the door to the church confessional where a priest and some of the town's women were cowering inside. One of the women let out a frightened gasp, "PIRATES!"

The Priest, moved in front of them, arms out to protect them, white with fear but he tried to remain calm –and with a sudden look at our appearance and weapons he said, "No madam, these men are not just pirates, they're something much more sinister…" and with a touch of dread in his voice he hissed "Protestants!"

--And the women screamed in horror.

ON THE ROAD TO THE GOVERNOR'S MANSION…

Mister Blythe fashioned a bandage for a gash on his head now bleeding into his eyes and down his cheek. All around him was pure havoc, gunfire, and explosions! Men storming the sugarcane fields, ronin fighting with samurai blades in both hands! Tomahawks separating men at the shoulder and scalps being collected by the platoon.

Mister Lynch and his men crossed the highway and fought their way into the jungle as the Spanish took cover in the tree line. When the muskets were emptied, blades clashed with sparks, swinging into men –and trees— in sheer chaos. Lynch called for Mister Mazatal and asked him to use one of his Aztecs to send word to the Captain for reinforcements. He was about to push the Spanish through this part of the jungle and cross a plantation to the Governor's Mansion. Mazatal nodded, tapped Mister Kon Boar, and spoke in his native tongue –Nahuatl-- and gave instructions for Boar to be the messenger....

Under fire, Kan Boar began to run from the fighting on the edge of the jungle, across the fighting on the High Road where wagons were attacked --and defended—with a carriage on fire and men fighting all around. Kon Boar then moved over bodies and ran through the fighting there –dodging blades and gun fire-- to the far side of the road. He then moved across the great stone bridge –where Flagg, Miranda, Toombs, and others were fighting – The bridge was still contested by the Spanish infantry and here the fighting was intense! Kon ducked as Calixto's bolas shot over his head and wrapped around the neck of a Spanish marine killing him. Musket fire and blades claimed many victims which littered the bridge. Some bodies fell over the side and into the lagoon below, floating face down in the water --one with a cutlass stuck in his back –the bodies and wounds turned the water red.

Kon Boar made it across this bridge, under fire, then used his running speed to take him into town, where fighting continued in all quarters. He moved through the smoke, past a burning stockade with bodies impaled on the ramparts.... past the graveyard where some fighting continued –bodies draped over some headstones and littering the cobblestones-- through the plaza with its burning buildings and dead marines –and bodies floating in the fountain-- to the beach where dead bodies covered the sand....

He moved past a tent --a medical infirmary had been set up by Johannis and some Spanish doctors to work on the wounded –and there were hundreds of wounded from both sides piled up outside the tent and on the surrounding beach waiting for service. Some groaning, close to death, some just wounded, waiting in silence....

Kon Boar moved to another field tent, lit by lantern light where the Captain had set up his temporary headquarters. "Cap-it-tain" he spoke in what I would call his 'small' voice and a mix of English and his native language from New Spain…

Essex looked up, "Mister Kon?"

"Mister Lynch is driving his men to-toward the Governor's house. He re-qq-uests many men to fight through the sugar cane field."

"He does, does he?" Essex looked down at his map of town "Mister Towne, Mister Rabal, take what men you have, report to Mister Newcastle, muster a combined force and move to this point" He put his index finger on the map, "Cut through this terrain here," he tapped the map "Force the Spanish off balance here and press them. Then assist Mister Lynch and sack the Governor's mansion."

Towne grabbed his cutlass from the table "Aye sir."

At that moment, as Towne made his exit, a Spanish General and some of his officers approached under the white flag. Mister Standish –bleeding from his temple-- got the Captain's attention, "Sir, Spanish officers approaching...looks like a possible parley." Our Captain turned from the map and stepped forward. Here, as he often did, he would reflect on his years of military service under the British crown.

The Spaniard removed his hat, bowed, and introduced himself, "General Anza, at your service sir."

"General," our Captain bowed in return, "Captain Essex of The Venger. My compliments on your gallant defense of your township."

Anza did not seem to agree with the assessment but remained silent.

"You have done all that is necessary to satisfy the honor of your King. If your men lay down their arms, I give you my word, none of the people here will be harmed."

General Anza peered at our Captain as if to size him up and his intuition told him that Essex could be trusted to maintain order. "And my men?"

"Your men will be paroled. After our business here is concluded, the town and harbor will be returned to you upon our departure."

"I trust we can expect honorable treatment?"

"You have my word on it."

They shook hands and Anza turned to a Captain close to him and in Spanish issued orders to begin the surrender. His officers then matched up with our men, Harrow, Duncan-Howe, Wiley and, under a white flag they split up and moved to different parts of the township to report a cease fire and gradually, the fighting began to die down....

ON THE FAR SIDE OF TOWN...

Our men fought through the sugar cane plantation that caught fire during the fighting and lit up the far side of Panama. Spanish regulars retreated from the plantation –some with their uniforms on fire-- to the Governor's Mansion. The Governor had fled at the start of the battle leaving his servants to deal with the 'pirate' threat. The servants would offer no resistance and would therefore be left alive when his house was sacked. Some were even directed to flee by Mister Lynch. "You are paroled!" He shouted, "Take what you can carry and get to the mountains."

Spanish officers would arrive shortly after with the report of surrender and the surviving regulars –some burned in the sugarcane fire—threw down their arms, reluctantly --and in anger-- to quit the fight. The sight of their Governor's property being stormed was a tough image to take and one corporal threw his sword down and spit in disgust. Hallock took this as an insult, raised his cutlass and moved toward this soldier but Addo grabbed him and stopped him from killing this man.

Later, down at the beach, the survivors checked in to be disarmed. Weapons –swords and muskets—stacked up into a big, tremendous pile. The Spanish had fought bravely, as they always had but, our surprise and lack of 'gentleman's ethics' in battle gave us the edge and an advantage we pressed home.

The prisoners were to be respected and paroled –as promised-- once we departed. In the meantime, we looked after their wounded, their surgeons working in unison with our own, with help from Mister Crowe, our carpenters, and some local men of the clergy –Jesuits—who fetched water and helped apply bandages.

The town was now to be sacked proper. The store houses were opened up and we used wagons and carriages –many with battle damage--- to move the cargo to the docks. We took all the livestock and boar we could pin in the hold. We slaughtered many and started to salt it away, then we put more on the spit for a celebration about to start that would take days....

Everything in the customs house was impounded. Storehouses were raided. The treasury doors –though bolted-- were smashed open with a battering ram. A lonely clerk backed up in fear as we entered, torches and all, the flames reflected off his spectacles as he trembled --and we demanded the keys to the barred banking section. We took them from his shaking hands and opened the cage door to our prize. I stood amazed at the boxes upon boxes of money, some of it paper, some of it gold, some of it Spanish currency, some doubloons, and stacks of gold bricks.

"Sweet Jehovah!" Jack-Karr blurted out at the sight of this. He, Irons, Bons, Archer, Barak, Kato and the ronin began to load it up –even though they still had blood on their hands.

Outside, the sky was a light from the fires of burning buildings. Pillaging had started, papers and furniture being thrown out the windows and over balconies. Items of value were stacked up in the street to be inventoried and shipped off for division.

It was Mister Bishop along with Toombs, Hatano and Mister Rabal who stormed a warehouse to find it loaded with several hundred barrels of rum. "God help us!" was all Bishop could muster...

Jata moved through the township, cutting the dead open, from chin to gut, he would slash all the dead he could find wide open. I was horrified by this but –I was to learn—this was from his Zulu heritage. He believed he had to cut the body open so the spirit could flow to the heavens. It was a last act of salvation for his enemies. The Jesuits protested this behavior, one even throwing himself over a dead body to protect it. He hissed out the word 'heathen' at Jata and Wolfe –already drunk-- pulled his sword and lunged forward. "Do you want to lose your head over a dead man?" he barked. This move ended the protest and the Jesuit moved clear. Wolfe put his sword back in its sheath and moved forward along the water's edge past Daws, Prescott and myself.

"Threaten a Jesuit, Wolfe?" Daws said, "That just earned yourself a safe passage straight to hell!"

"My passage to hell was booked long ago Daws…though I thank you for your concern!"

For myself, I was surprised that he left the Jesuit alive….

What happened next was a carnival of sorts….

Our captive government officials were shackled and lined up inside the court building and Mister Sunderland –complete with a captured magistrate's wig-- began to preside over mock trials. Into the box went the first official, "You are being accused, of serving the king, collecting taxes and making life difficult for the common man…. how do ya plea?"

"This is preposterous," the shamed official pleaded in broken English as if his protest could regain order in the court…

"Guilty! That is all!" shouted Sunderland.

"Unhand me you brute…" the defendant shouted as Blythe and Hallock dragged him from the box to some unknown punishment…

Next in the docks, another gentleman of note, "You…" Sunderland began, "have been found practicing the king's policies and inflicting people with taxes…. how do ya plea?" A moment later, "GUILTY! Take him away!"

Next….

"You are accused of following the king and all the king's corrupt policies like a mindless drone. The sentence is death."

"What? Now just a moment---" and Miranda and Kipling pulled this defendant out of the dock.

Next….

The next man into the docks was trembling…

"Name?"

"Sir Juan Vasquez of Porto Bello!"

"On behalf of the citizens of Porto Bello that you have oppressed with your royal behavior, I sentence you to years of rehabilitation and torture....and then death...... followed by more torture!" The crowd roared. Mister Sunderland called for more rum and a maiden approached and poured from a cask that flooded the desk with the coconut-based drink to which he said to her, "You'll be punished for supply wastage later Madam, shackles and all..."

Duncan-Howe sat in the jury box, pipe in hand and laughed....

Terrified prisoners of all nobility and rank were brought up, one by one, to be embarrassed, harassed and sentenced. Sunderland even insisted that they address him as 'His Lordship.' How bizarre the title suddenly sounded to me. Had the title of 'Lordship' always been ridiculous and was I just now made to realize it under these circumstances? Lordship? Highness? Sire? Your Royal Highness? All now seemed like a comedy of oppression on the common man. Who were these men who made us call them so? And what made them worthy of making men like us bow down?

The hearings continued, the sentences were equal to what we as privateers or, to use their term, 'pirates' may expect and the drunk mob made up of our crew would laugh as these men were, one by one, dragged to the cells. Some were marched to a nearby tobacco wheel to toil under the crack of a commandeered whip....

Sir Juan Vasquez was sliced open with the whip before he was even shackled to the wheel, "But I haven't done anything!" He pleaded in pain...

"Aye," Stylen shouted as he pulled the whip back for another crack. "It's what we call preventive punishment! You get the whip now in case ya might be thinkin' of doin' something wrong!"

At this point, our Captain entered the courthouse with Mister Harrow and the room began to quiet down. "Mister Sunderland." he roared...

"Sir," he said, sorry and aware that he was being called out.

"Stop this farce immediately."

"Yes sir." Sunderland stood and removed his wig.

"I promised the Spanish safe conduct and we will not shame them!" He looked over the room to make sure his words landed with an impact and once they did, he quickly remembered that these men had fought and won a tremendous –and daring—victory here and he changed his tone, "Now, you men have earned a celebration but…instead of marching these men to the cells, march them instead to their bank vaults and homes."

"You'll not get one gold talon from me. I'll not bow down in fear to any of you," a shackled official said from the box.

"Then I shall offer you no quarter sir. You and your friends will be put to death. And this trial, such as it is, will continue…."

The man looked at our Captain, well aware that his tone conveyed a seriousness to it, and he reluctantly nodded a yes. "I apologize."

"Mister Sunderland, I request you make effective use of your time…. for Mister Bishop has liberated a rum warehouse on the edge of town and he is going to need assistance liberating its six hundred odd barrels!"

And with that, cheers and excitement took hold and the men stormed across town. Our mob raced outside --past a library where Clairmont and Mister Lynch had taken position on the steps with several hundred books and where Lynch was free to illustrate this scene in his book-- down to the warehouse….

The next evening, some of our men, put the cannon in the fort back into a defensive position. Guns that were blown over by artillery fire we put upright and Rajiv and some of his Bengals kept watch for the arrival of any unwanted visitors….

As this happened, the Aztecs loaded up a train of captured donkeys with weapons --muskets, powder, and swords. Their payment for the actions we had survived. Harrow was speaking to Mazatal and made it clear we would not be in Panama long –Essex preferred to make a quick departure after a battle. Therefore, the men from the Aztec platoon, who would venture into the countryside –to a point where the old Incan pyramids stood-- to deliver these weapons, would have to move fast. Mazatal understood, Newcastle waved them off and they moved out immediately….

"When do you expect them back?" I asked.

"In a few days' time. A Jaguar can cover ten leagues or more a day."

On the beach, the Captain began his administration from his large open tent on the sand. Under the lantern light, he, Mister Harrow, and Mister Lincoln had set about the business of appropriation when Mister Addo brought General Anza in before the Captain.

"You sent for me?" Anza asked.

"I did" The Captain motioned to a table loaded with food and wine. "Something to eat?"

"No, thank you."

The Captain then motioned him to sit, which he did. The Captain lit his long stem pipe and with a nod, a large canvas sack was dropped on the table between the two men. It was heavy and made the sound of coins.

"What's this?"

"The battle is over General. That is your share of the peace."

Anza looked at it and although temptation clearly had a hold of him, he said, "I cannot. Forgive me, I know the stories of Cartagena and other places where a level of collaboration was rewarded but I cannot accept this. I will return to Spain and face my judgement before the crown but.... I do thank you for the courtesy."

"Is that your final thought on the matter?"

"It is."

"Very well." Both men stood and the Captain held out his hand, "You have both my respect and my sympathies for what may await you back home."

"Thank you" Anza gave a curt bow and left the tent.

"Mister Newcastle."

"Sir."

"Fetch me the leaders of the Jesuit order."

"Yes sir."

Moments later Father Vaccaro was brought before the Captain by Newcastle and a squad of Moors. "Ah Father, how do you do?" without waiting for a response, he said, "This money is yours so long as you apply it to civil aid."

The Jesuit looked at the bag, his eyes widened, and he looked to the Captain in disbelief.

"We will leave a quarter of provisions in the storehouses which should last you six to eight months. By then, this base will be reconstituted by your government, I'm sure…"

"And then you'll be back?"

"One never knows, but if we should make it back here, I expect you to remember, that you received fair treatment from us –and-- should you show disdain for our good will, I assure you, you will never receive such courtesy again."

The Jesuit understood the message, slowly nodded, and summoned the courage to speak, "I-I may have other requirements…if you don't mind."

The Captain looked at him, with a touch of exhaustion in his eyes, "Requirements?" But he was willing to at least hear this man out, "Such as?"

"There are several women and children on the island, I would have your word, that they are not to be harmed."

"Very well…unless their occupation warrants it." Essex said, referring to 'women for hire.'

"--And…I would like some assistance from your doctors to help any of them who may be hurt."

"You shall have it."

The Captain tried to go back to reading his maps and papers but still, the Jesuit remained. Without looking up, Essex asked "What…is…it?"

"Your-your men b-burned our church."

The Captain looked up. "It caught fire in the battle and now it is gone."

At this, the Captain leaned back into his chair and looked at this man in thought –or exhaustion. There was a long silence before he called out "Mister Newcastle?"

"Yes Captain."

"Order the carpenter, Mister Crowe, ashore –if he isn't here already, along with a few extra hands. It seems we have a church to rebuild."

"Aye Captain" Mister Newcastle smiled and went to fetch the carpenter....

At dawn the next morning, the carpenter, carpenter's mate and several others had brought additional tools ashore, and the work began on rebuilding the church. Many of us started chopping down trees in the jungle, using horses to drag them back to town where we worked to turn them into planks. I, despite piercing head pains from the celebration the night before, was eager to help, for this work helped uplift my soul and helped me put things right.

Mister Crowe directed us in this project and once it became known what our mission here was, the town's people –those with a little courage-- almost seemed interested in our progress. I would swing a hammer and see some of the children watching me work from behind trees. When I would look up, they would hide like it was a game.

The town's masons were put to work making new bricks and salvaging old ones that could be used again and with the help of some Spanish marines and Jesuits, we built new frames and raised them into position. The women of the town would bring buckets of water and walk through our construction teams making sure we all had enough to drink. Even the Moors –great carpenters and engineers that they were – served a rare moment for me to witness, that of kindness between the Catholics and the Moors when the Moors got involved with the work.

--This kind of collaboration was not a common thing!

By the fourth day, the frames were in place and the Jesuits even assisted Mister Hobby and the cabin boy Rorry with mid-day meal and we would take to the tables and nearby steps, together to eat. I sat across from Amir and Barak and listened to them discuss how the construction should proceed, and I was some-what stunned to see two Muslims talking about how to build the best possible church...

The next day, we put the paneling in and then began the brick-and-mortar work. I was surprised to see Mister Rush so efficient with bricks. He told me he was a mason at one time who had built a school in Boston and thus had some practice...

That evening, the work continued under the light of torches. We took a respite –the same way we would if we were on the ship—and Raeder, Sterling, Dutch, Baako, Obal, Bons, Cage, Archer and their teams took over the work. On my way to the cantina, I walked past a corner of town where what was left of the book shop stood. The door was ajar and inside, Mister Lynch was drawing by candlelight at a shop desk. I knocked on the open door....

Lynch looked up, pipe in his teeth, "Mister Reed?" He smiled, "Workday is complete I see."

"Yes."

"Means it is my turn to get to the church to make sure the work carries on." He reached for his coat and weapons.

"What are you drawing Mister Lynch?"

"Have a look." He turned his book towards me. There were colorful images of the men of the Dark Coast --the zombies. There was a picture of Panama on fire. Then drawings without color yet. The church –burning and the new church, under construction.

"These are wonderful."

"Maybe you can have a count of them to go with your writings."

I looked up. "I would like that, Mister Lynch. Thank you."

He smiled. "You'll find parchment over there. Take what you need." And then he stepped out and started towards the construction site. I moved to pack up several hundred sheets of parchment, some ink, quills and then I noticed a book on Roman engineering. Inside was the design and construction of roads and the coliseum. It was impressive and I packed it up. On my exit, I left some coins on the merchant table and scribed a note. 'For parchment and book.' –in case the owner of this shop was ever to return for I had not become comfortable with just taking things.

I did find a table in the cantina –surprised to see Spanish soldiers and marines drinking with people like Wolfe, Jack-Karr, Fury and Mister Foxx like we were all on the same side. How the politics had changed over a week. I smiled at this and set up under a palm tree and went back to my writing...

At dawn the next day, we salvaged the church bell from the ashes, our metal workers cleaned and polished it up, such as they could and we used pulleys, a team of horses and men from our crew as well as some Spanish marines to heave it into the new bell tower. Once there, we finally managed to work it into place and then we allowed the leader of the Jesuit order to ring it for the first time. Once the bell echoed across the township, I retired, shirt in hand to my palm tree on the beach as much of our crew took refuge in the shade or the rafters of the cantina's outdoor plaza. Prescott, Towne, Temple, Flynn, Java, and the others looked up at the bell tower as the bell was struck again. We were quite proud of ourselves. We had done something good and in addition to this, I now, with this raid, had the money to get to a safe port and book passage to the Americas.

The construction work here in Panama delayed our departure for some time –a time much longer than made us comfortable. The Spanish navy would be back –on patrol—any day. Our scouts even ambushed and killed the members of a gold caravan sent down from a mine in San Cristobal who were unaware that Panama was in our hands. Nighthorse left the bodies on the Juventus Road, brought their weapons and armored carriages into town, and put the gold onboard The Venger, which by now had been over stocked with provisions. One would walk deck two or deck three and see rope nets loaded with supplies liberated –as Jack-Karr put it—from the Spanish township.

"When do we leave?" I asked walking through the galley.

"With the morning tide, I suppose." Tane responded over his coffee.

Then came the announcement "The Aztecs are back!" I climbed on the top deck as the Jaguars rowed across the port waters to be greeted with a cheer. They made it to the climbing nets and with a hand from Jeddah and Merritt, passed the top rail back aboard.

"Pleasant journey Mister Mazatal?" Harrow asked.

"Yes."

"Your friends received our donation?" Harrow asked, referring to the weapons.

Mazatal smiled.

"Then I trust, they are in good health."

"Yes." His smile became even more pronounced.

Then, with a return smile, "You may return to your station."

At dawn the next day, when the work was all but finished, there was a warning flare from the outpost on the coast. Mister Raeder's men had been on watch there and now, something was amiss....

Suddenly, Mister Standish came riding into town on a commandeered horse at a full gallop. "Captain! Captain Essex!" He rode across the plaza, past the fountain down to the beach command tent.

The Captain woke up in his chair where he had fallen asleep the night before and stepped out of the tent on to the sand, "What is it?"

"Sir, Spanish warship and two escorts coming in from the north-west. They're flying the banner of Captain Vasquez!"

"When do we expect them?"

"Six. Maybe eight hours."

"Very well, Mister Newcastle, signal Mister Daws aboard ship with the following instructions...."

--From the decks of The Venger, Mister Daws read the flag signals from the beach though his spyglass. "Mister Tabor.... raise the Spanish colors. Prepare the ship for engagement."

--And up went the Spanish flag....

Our men were ordered to disengage from the town and report back aboard the ship, immediately. Men packed up, kissed their 'hired' women friends goodbye and moved out. Essex rolled up his maps and collected the papers he wanted to take with him –just about everything else, including massive amounts of captured supplies had already been loaded onboard. As the Captain made his way out onto the beach, Father Vaccaro stepped out to meet him at the tide. "Captain...."

Essex stopped and with a mix of grace and speed he said, "Ah Father, sorry to leave you, ahead of schedule but, I'm sure you and the Spanish marines could finish the painting of your new church on your own."

"Yes, we should be able to manage it...Captain I--" He suddenly looked like he was searching for the right words to reflect his thoughts instead, he just put out his hand and cut through his confusion, "I wanted to thank you. I cannot condone your actions but, I will pray for you and your crew...."

He shook the man's hand, "And I thank you for it." He walked into the tide and climbed onboard the long boat.

"And when I say pray, I mean for you to find enlightenment and freedom from your wicked ways."

"Well then, God must work fast for I already have it."

Vaccaro smiled. "Go with God Captain."

Essex nodded from the bow as we began to row across the water and back to the ship.

IX

THE ROAD TO REDEMPTION IS PAVED... WITH TOMBSTONES!

We took to the sea with all possible speed leaving the Panama Coast behind us.

Below deck, I made a visit to Hobby's coffee bucket and found my place at a galley table and under the lantern light, I opened my book on Roman engineering, that I took from the small corner book shop. I looked closely at the drawings of the aqueduct of Segovia when I felt a sudden presence over me. I turned to see one of the Moors was looking over my shoulder....

--Jeddah. They called him Jeddah because that was where he was from. Much of the crew used the names of places or nick names for names. Like Tiger had the name 'Tiger' because he was rescued from a 'tiger prison cage' in a swamp in Indochina when he was young and Dakar, the former slave –who spoke French as a first language—was from the African base with the same name --Dakar.

Jeddah's eyes went from the text to mine with a look of curiosity mixed with intent. I edged the book out across the table with my fingertips so he could get a better look. "It's a book on Roman architecture."

"I can read English." He said in a firm tone and what may have been mixed with a touch of pride.

"Here," I raised the book from the table, "Take a look."

He looked at me again with a very slight smile and picked up the book. He looked through a few pages then slammed it closed and tucked it under his arm. He then pulled his red scarf –called a keffiyeh—from his neck. I looked at it and he gave me a reassuring nod as if to say, 'go on take it' and I did.

I did not intend to trade the book away, but I was not prepared to confess a mistake in communication, especially since the Moors were tough and intimidated me. So, I did what made sense to me at the time and I put the scarf around my neck. Some other members of the crew wore big scarves like this – even those that were not Moors. Some even wore keffiyehs when not wearing a shirt on deck. I confess that this gift, simple as it was, made me feel like a real member of the crew and when I stepped on deck at dawn the next morning, I had a new sense of pride in my attire. I saw Jaffar, Barak and a few of the Moors in a circle on deck and when I stepped into the wind, Jaffar turned, pointed at his scarf, and gave a nod as if to say he approved of my fashion sense. I felt somewhat accepted.

"Aloft Mister Reed if you please…." Harrow shouted, "Your penchant for the latest fashions doesn't entitle you to be late to your station."

"Aye sir." And I gripped the ropes to make the climb.

The first Spanish frigate was blown apart before it could get close. Essex then suddenly ordered us hard to port --Thorn cranked the wheel, and all hands went to work to cut a sharp turn in the water so all three-gun decks could line up on the other two ships.

"Send word to Rajiv…." Essex lowered his spyglass, "Hit that ship below the water line and sink it." He shouted.

The Spanish ship was hit hard and disabled…

In return, Mister Saxon's gun was hit and exploded killing the gun crew! Wilder was wounded –his pet monkey ran down the deck as the cannons recoiled. The discipline for the gun crews was exceptional. They stood in place, firing as the decks around them turned to splinters. Smoke blinded them and grapeshot and metal, cut many of them in half but they held, yelling commands to stay in the fight even as the enemy gun line came closer and closer, until we were exchanging cannon shots from just a few meters away.

Hammers snapped down and muskets erupted. I watched as Jagger would fire a musket, hand it back to be reloaded as a new one was handed forward and he unloaded it on a target, then I looked up to see a trail of smoke –a grenade—as it was tossed across to the enemy deck and exploded. Then another two dozen smoke trails as our crew threw grenades --with a vengeance—en masse. There were explosions all across the deck –and in the sky—blowing Spanish Marines and sailors off their ship. Metal fragments ripped through the others…

Mister Harrow took his instructions and relayed them to the crew. "Prepare for close quarter combat! Prepare to board!"

Then, the unusual happened. Two of the ronin started banging on the large Taiko drum they had brought on deck. Alistair began blaring his bagpipes, right in the middle of the fighting. This may have been done for morale --for I had heard about Scottish regiments going into battle with bagpipes blazing but to see it, on a ship, in the middle of this holocaust was truly bizarre…

Wolfe, Addo, Irons and the crew used grappling hooks to take hold of the enemy vessel. Even hooking a man, pinning him to the railing as we prepared to cross and board. The enemy crew used axe and cutlass in an attempt to cut their ship free but, it was of no use, we had this giant on its knees and now it was time to take the head….

"Now!" Raeder shouted, blade in hand, "Kill 'em all!" and our men roared as he led the first wave across…

We braved another volley of musket fire, pressed the attack, and tried to board their ship just as they tried to board ours, many of us collided with each other, some of us were killed instantly, some of us fell into the ocean below dead --or still fighting in the water.

Daws and Alistair Blackwood took a blast. Alistair was killed instantly --and so was his music. Daws rolled back, his jacket and clothes on fire, this man wasn't even aware of this, and he continued to fight, even with a burning jacket. One of our Chinese comrades hit him with water from a bucket, the flame turned to smoke as the fighting in that quarter continued....

Mister Teague threw an enemy combatant overboard only to watch him get lynched in the damaged rigging below. More grenades were thrown and, in some places, caught and thrown back to explode. Then, their deck caught fire, some men tried to put it out, while others just fought on or tumbled right through the flames. Some men --clothes on fire-- fell into the sea....

The ronin would slice off a limb at the forearm or swing down, across the knee, separating it from a man, leaving him to collapse on deck. The Hurons used their tomahawks...

I had my shirt pulled at the shoulder as a marine grabbed me from behind, his cutlass was on the down swing but mere moments before it could take my life, a native tomahawk smashed him in the face, punching his cheek and skull bones inward with a crunch. It rained some blood down on me but, I was relieved to have my life for a little longer....

Brute strength –as always-- played an effective part in the fighting as Cheval would slam a man's head into the rail before throwing sailors and marines overboard or pushing whole squads into the ocean below. He even raised one marine above his head and dropped him headfirst on the deck killing him....

The Africans, fearless, moved through the smoke with a vengeance. Addo slammed a grappling hook into a man's shoulder, then took the man's sword to engage more marines. Lau kicked a man down the stairs below deck. He stepped back as Therrinfall, and Barak threw two lit grenades down below after him. There was a double explosion, and they used the smoke for cover as they jumped through the hatch and descended below by jumping the ladder moving the fight into the close, compact spaces of the second deck.

The Moors' use of their curved swords and cutting power where the blade could be swung with the precision of a butcher was terrifying, removing slabs off the enemy in quick time. Barak's blade was covered in blood as he swung it at the head of a marine who ducked just as he planted his curved sword into the mast behind him. He then left his sword planted in the wood and used his hands to kill this man.

Suddenly the other Spanish warship –The Hércules --pulled along-side our starboard rail and their marines came over our side.   We were now trapped between two ships!!!

Jack-Karr triggered his blunderbuss in an explosion of lead cutting down a platoon of boarders as he and his squad rallied to defend the starboard side of the ship. Lo-Tan fired two pistols, pulled his three-section-staff, and gave it a wide swing knocking back six of the boarders. Wolfe, Tabor, Baltimore, Dutch, Foxx, Cage, and a few others shifted to that side of the ship and tried to hold off the wave of Spanish sailors as they collapsed all around them.

From the steering, Newcastle fired a deck gun loaded with nails and killed another six marines in the blast --but dozens of others swarmed the quarter deck. Some were gunned down, throwing stars cut into several others as Kato and Sakai stormed into their lines cutting and slashing in every direction....

Below, our gun crews jumped to the starboard guns and started firing --a few meters above their gun positions, more Spaniards were moving across to our decks using grappling hooks and ropes to swing across and storm us....

A grenade went off right next to me, the blast picked me up and slammed me back on deck and I was robbed of my hearing. The entire violent battle went silent. I tried to pull myself back together and started to hear voices that –at first-- seemed distant then slowly grew louder. I then moved to get to my feet when a marine closed in on me and I looked up to hear a –whooooomp-whooomp-whooooomp- and his head suddenly snapped back as Calixto's bolas killed him. Calixto then slashed another man down the back and then picked me up by the back of the shirt and helped me back to my feet...

--He then collected his bolas and swung them like a pair of iron hammers, one in each hand –smashing a skull to the right, breaking a shoulder to the left until he could throw them again.

There was another explosion and burning sails collapsed around Essex as he slashed a man against the steering. He then stopped amid the chaos of battle and looked at his decks as they were stormed on both sides in overwhelming numbers. "We're losing her!"

Below deck, on the León Del Mar, the fighting was hand-to-hand. Teague –aware that The Venger was trapped, and the Spanish were storming our decks-- made a command decision. He turned to Raeder, "Get our men off this ship –NOW!"

"What?"

"Back to The Venger, fast--"

"But-"

"-Do as I command-now!"

Raeder didn't like it but moved quickly to issue the command, "Everybody off!" He worked his way back through the chaos. "Now! Move! Back to the ship!"

Teague then turned to Jaffar. "Blow the powder magazine! We have to get this ship off of us now!" Jaffar nodded, pushed his way past the cannon and cut his way past few remaining Spanish survivors, stepping over –and on-- the Spanish wounded to the hatch and stairway that led down to the powder magazine. He turned – Sanjuro cut an extended fuse and tossed Jaffar a grenade. Jaffar then lit the bomb "Allah be merciful!" --And he dropped it down the hatch….

They moved –fast—back towards the top deck, helping some of the wounded forward and pushing them towards the exits as they moved.   At the hatch, Cheval who appeared to be the last man out, suddenly turned away from the ladder and moved back several cannon positions to pick up Sakai who was buried under several dead Spanish gunners.   He was dazed –his samurai helmet was cracked, and he was bleeding from his head. Cheval started dragging him back to the hatch when Prescott suddenly appeared in the hatch exit above and reached down from the top deck to help them up. "Here! Over here!" He shouted with his hand out. "Cheval come on…. hurry!"

--The fuse was burning away below deck in the powder storage....

On deck, our combat squads were running to clear the ship. "Move! Move! Move" Raeder shouted as most of our crew was moving off the León, jumping the rail or using ropes to swing back to join the fight on The Venger....

--The fuse below continued to burn....

Topside --despite the desperate timing, Teague couldn't resist slamming a wounded Spanish sailor in the crown of the skull –or gashing another with his cutlass as he w-a-l-k-e-d back to The Venger and roped back aboard. He dropped to our deck and looked to Raeder who was covered in blood, "All accounted for?"

They both looked back at The Leon as the men around them began to take cover from the upcoming blast....

But we weren't all accounted for, Prescott stretched out his arm as far as he could, "CHEVAL HURRY!!! THE SHIP IS GONNA BLOW!!!" Again, he extended his hand all-the-way-out "COME ON!!!!"

Cheval made it to the ladder, Sakai reached up and gripped Prescott's hand. Prescott smiled "Got ya!"

--AND BOOOOOOOOOOOOOOOOOOOOOMMMMM!

--THE LEÓN EXPLODED!!!

The entire quarter deck of the ship was blown apart –a fire ball sending thousands of wooden fragments across our decks –killing several of us-- and out over the ocean. Our ship shifted under the waves created by the blast and several of us lost our footing and fell to the planks...

Wood splinters ripped through Stamp, killing him. Bishop and Kato were wounded but Kato's samurai armor protected him from most of it. Chunks struck Hallock, Mazatal, Flynn, Cage and Mister Silence who began pulling them out of his body—and several others...

There was a secondary explosion, then a third! And what was left of the ship's skeleton was quickly pulled below the tide and as it sank below the waves, it made a sound like a dying monster….

Teague had a chunk of smoldering wood, the size of a knife stuck in his back shoulder. His clothes were on fire as he looked over the railing to the ocean below –and just then, Jaffar, Barak and a few survivors swam to the surface. Sparks, ash and burning wood raining down on them as they swam over to our hull and started to climb up the rigging….

Despite this catastrophic blast, other marines from the Hércules –on the port side-- continued to storm down on us.

I swung my cutlass down, only to miss my target and have it lodged into the wood rail. Panicked, I tried to dislodge the blade but, I had to duck to avoid a swing at my head. My attacker then grabbed the rail, reset, and prepared to thrust his blade into my ribs but Jack-Karr swung an axe down on his hand --breaking it and chopping part of it off-- and forcing him to drop his blade and clutch what was left of his other hand in agony. Karr then swung the axe up and struck this man in the chin. I went back to quickly trying to remove my cutlass and even used my foot to help dislodge it but, it was no use. I was then suddenly grabbed from behind and my head slammed against the railing. There was a flash-of-stars, and my vision became a blur. Before my head could be slammed a second time, Mister Kato swung his sword –just above my head—cutting my hair-- and striking my attacker in the neck, removing his head! Kato then had his attention drawn to another marine and attacked…

I was suddenly tackled against the railing, and, without my sword, I struggled to reach for my knife when suddenly Obal grabbed both myself and my attacker and slammed us together before focusing on him with a grip around his throat that turned into a snap. I dropped to the deck in an effort to figure out where I was –everything seemed to slow down—I saw Mister Nighthorse remove a scalp and I realized that blood was pouring from my own head and temple. My head had been gashed open when slammed into the rail and I tried to keep from blacking out. I could see our ship was a blaze. We were losing this fight.

Obal then picked me up and pulled me to my feet. "Get in the flight!" We were both suddenly tackled, and I tumbled down the steps below deck and landed on my back where the wind left my body! I tried to move before someone killed me and I slowly, in intense pain rolled to my stomach. Here I could see the port side cannon was still firing. Our crews trying to blow holes in the enemy ship only a few meters away. I struggled to get my breath back and tried to get to my feet with severe pain in my head and ribs --blood pouring from my mouth-- but I collapsed. I tried to crawl, but everything hurt –burning fragments and parts of the ship were coming down around me in what seemed like slow-motion.   Suddenly I was picked up by Java and Tane –two of our gunners-- who dragged me down the deck to sick bay where I was dropped on the floor. I turned –vision blurred—to see them run back to their cannon to keep firing and fighting….

In the sick bay there were wounded all around. Some men were getting limbs removed with the saw. There was screaming. There was constant screaming in this part of the ship.

Hearing all the combat clearly on the top deck, I tried again to make it to my feet and did but could not keep my focus. Not far from my position, the cannons were still firing, an exchange of fire at point blank range. Smoke made breathing difficult as I stumbled for the exit, but a cannon ball slammed into our side and smashed though the deck --the explosion lifted me into the air and slammed me against a cannon, the blast plastering the right side of my body with splinters. I fell to the planks.

I was dying and this battle was lost.

I was surprised to wake up several days later in the sick bay –alive! I had to blink, then feel my limbs and chest to detect a heartbeat –and—there it was. I was still here on God's Earth. I smiled and let out and exhale of relief. The damp tropical setting kept me in a sweat as my eyes tried to focus. The ship was still here. The men around me…still here. Slowly, I collected my senses and remembered I had been wounded. I looked --the splinters that had covered half of my body were removed and I had an extensive amount of bandages covering me. I tried to sit up. It was Doctor

Jopo who looked in on me and made me rest easy. "Slowly Reed. How do you feel?"

"I-I feel a lot of pain in my ribs and arm."

"That is to be expected" he said through his thick accent. "Some of your ribs are broken. Breathing will be difficult for a while."

I looked around at my surroundings, De Leon, Manu, Cage, Kannon Saint James, Dutch, Wilder –and his pet monkey, Gunpowder— were all in the sick bay along with a few others –Tiger was still unconscious –bandage around his head. Teague who had been wounded, was checking himself out of the infirmary. Then, my heart sank as I turned and watched Mister Addo and Mister Jagger pack up the dead body of Mister Prescott –what was left of his body had been blown from The Leon onto our top deck-- and as I watched them pack his body away, I was gripped by a serious depression for Prescott was my friend. He tried to protect me and like so many others, he had saved my life.

His footlocker –as was the custom-- was brought to the doctor to be opened up. In it was some coin and something that surprised us all --a letter! Doctor Johannis examined it, and his expression went from his 'working man stoic' to sad, "It's to his mother," he said, "Back in Wales."

There was a moment of reserved silence then Mister Teague –still wounded and in pain-- reached out, "Give it here," he said…

Kannon and Dutch followed the letter as it made it into the custody of Mister Teague.

Teague looked the letter over. He was silent for a long moment, then suddenly said, "I'll see that it gets there…."

Doctor Johannis nodded, for Mister Teague was a man of his word. He took the letter, threw on his overcoat and –still wounded-- dismissed himself from the infirmary.

I was impressed by this simple gesture –maybe because it was some kindness from Teague that I didn't expect. Whatever it was, I was moved by it…

I then watched them, stitch up Prescott in the canvass bag, the last stitch through the nose to make sure he was in fact dead and then he was to be heaved to the deck for burial at sea….

"I failed." I said watching this as my emotions almost got the better of me.

Mister Jopo looked at me, "Failed?"

"I got wounded and had to be saved again and again. I failed the crew." A tear began to roll down my cheek at the thought of all these men wounded and gone.

"Being wounded does not make you a failure." Jopo said though his thick accent, "You did what you could for our comrades, some live and some die but fate is not always in our hands –you can only control your effort in these matters, the rest….is up to God."

Wise words but they did not help me. For the first time in many years, I was compelled by my emotions to cry. 'Could I --if I-- had done, just a little more would some of these men be alive?' In a split-second my tears became uncontrollable due to the sense of loss and failure. Mister Jopo allowed me the courtesy to cry in peace, leaving me alone in a corner of the infirmary….

Later, I was allowed to collect my emotions and decided, against medical advice, to grab my weapons and visit the top deck. The sun was shining and blinded me for a moment, but the fresh ocean air did make me feel better and gave me some balance. I pressed forward, and in the distance, I saw the wreck of the first Spanish ship we engaged, sunk in about forty fathoms of water for its masts were still visible above the tide. What was left of the second galleon was a smoldering wooden skeleton that the tide had lodged on a sand bar….

I turned to the sound of hammering and repair work and, to my surprise, the battle which I had thought was lost was actually won! The other ship – The Hércules-- had survived a blaze and was now under repair from our men and some Spanish survivors/prisoners.

At the bow and –laughing—was Captain Vasquez and Essex. Sharing a bottle and some tobacco between them. The battle was over and, I suppose, the Spanish honor preserved and satisfied. His wounds had been treated -- Vasquez had a bandage around his head, a blood-stained tunic, and the cutlass before him, on a rum box which, I assumed was his, had been snapped in the fighting a few nights before.

I was quite surprised by this. "Vasquez?" I spit out at a near whisper.

"Yeah." Bishop confirmed, moving crates nearby.

"What's he doing here? I mean…I know they are friends but--"

"—The fights over son!" Bishop said in a definitive tone. "Once the fight's over. It's over. They did their best to kill us now, it's time to move on." He paused, leaned against a crate and looked at me, "And you? You seemed to have made it through all right. Where have you been?"

"In the infirmary." I said in a low tone marked by embarrassment.

"Ah. Well, you're out now, time to redeem yourself."

There may have been no malice in it but that statement…added to my shame. The very thought that I lay below deck in a cause I thought lost, only to find that my friends had taken victory from the jaws of defeat, took my thoughts to a dark place. Again, I had let them down and they won without me, and it was at this very moment that I made a decision, a promise to myself, that I would never again –EVER--let my shipmates down in combat. I would do whatever had to be done to be part of the solution and become the man they needed me to be.

Over the next week, both ships, the Spanish galleon and our own, were made serviceable with work 'round the clock. While I was in recovery, we had rescued several Spanish sailors and marines from the water and paroled them for repair work, on their word that they would not raise arms against us again and, in exchange, they would be allowed to live. Hard as it may be to believe, this protocol was obeyed, the Spanish didn't violate it.

Repairs on the Spanish prize continued --canvas stitched, and a new mast heaved into place—so she could be made seaworthy. The captured ship was renamed The Phoenix.

"What happens to this ship now?" I asked…

"She's to be auctioned off back in Port Royal…" Mister Harrow reported. "The earnings will go into a general fund, and you will get your share plus, a stipend for being wounded."

I didn't want it. I didn't feel like I earned it and I remained silent until the peace was interrupted by Mister Rush who closed in on us and got the attention of our second officer, "Mister Harrow sir, a word if you please."

"What can I do for you Rush?" Harrow noticed that Mister Rush stood in the foreground and had some of The Venger's Spanish crewmen along with Vasquez and some of our paroled Spanish Marines, at his back. "What's all this then, a Parliament meeting?"

"Given our venture and success here, I'd like to make a request of you and the Captain." He paused, "In private if you please…."

Harrow exhaled as if he didn't have the time but, was willing to make an exception, "Very well."

There was a knock on the Captain's door and after they received a 'yes', they were allowed to enter.

"Sir," Mister Harrow began, "Mister Rush and some of the crew beg an audience."

The Captain looked up from his charts and waved them forward as if ready to listen, "What can I do for you Thomas?"

"Sir," Mister Rush began, "You know my religious convictions and my medical condition if you will…."

"I do." He replied, "And… you have my sympathies."

"I appreciate that sir but given my current state, I'd like to make a request if I may."

"Of course," The Captain stood up straight, "How can I be of service?"

"As you know, the Isle of New Haven or what was part of the Spanish Triangle has been surrendered to the English crown."

"Yes, I know."

"Our paroled Spanish Marines and your friend Captain Vasquez have made a report—"

"—a report?"

"Yes. They tell me that the new administration there has arrested or evicted the local Spanish populace which has had undue atrocities committed against it. Some of a very cruel and unusual nature."

The Captain eased back in his chair as if he didn't like what he was hearing, "Your new Spanish friends told you this?" He asked, referring to our captured crews.

"Yes, but I dare say that Vasquez is your friend too, Captain."

Essex raised his glance as if he didn't like the direction this conversation was going and that his civility with Vasquez was about to come at some consequence.

Rush skipped over the particulars, "Captain, I beg for special permission to make venture there –in peace keeping fashion—and deliver supplies to the population, to prevent starvation of the families –and children— there."

The Captain surveyed the words he had heard in silence, then asked, "How would you purpose to do it?"

"I would like to forfeit my shares in exchange for temporary use of our captured ship and supplies."

Rush motioned to the men behind him a mix of Spanish prisoners and our own crew of Spanish descent. "Many of these men have families and relatives there and I believe, it would go a long way towards our political ends with these men here who, we've asked to join us in attacks against their own -ahem, former countrymen –the Spanish-- and again, it would allow them the means to grant some salvation to the people there…." Rush sized the Captain up and added almost as an afterthought, "And they're willing to forfeit their shares as well in turn…."

The Captain looked at Mister Rush in silence. He knew he was in poor health and that he, quite possibly might not have much time left and that this…. may in fact be, a last request in a way.

"I-have-been with you for ten years Captain asking nothing for myself save what our articles allow."

Mister Harrow listened with a keen ear as if he actually liked the idea but wanted to defer to the Captain.

"Tis a tall request Mister Rush and not without some risk."

"I know it is sir. I know it is."

"New Haven is but four days on the chart sir." Harrow said. "Four days there, another four back...could put the population on our side, if we should ever need their help or a base of operations."

At this the Captain raised his chin. His strategy had always been to win the hearts and minds of the population when he could --unlike our contemporaries who used terror and Essex seemed to only use terror as a last resort. There was a long moment of silence and Mister Rush clearly expected the answer to be no.

The Captain suddenly stood in a frightening manner that made Mister Rush take a step back. "Very well" He said, "You have eight days Mister Rush." He looked back to his charts. "Check with Mister Newcastle and Mister Lincoln and see that they give you all you require -save the water supply."

"Yes sir. Thank you, sir" Rush was somewhat overcome by emotion. "I will sir."

Mister Harrow smiled, then continued about the business at hand.

Rush made an exit and said, "I shall give my shares to the crew as promised."

"No need for that Mister Rush." Essex said. "You may keep your shares."

Outside, Harrow and Rush walked from the quarter deck, "With all our wounded, I can only spare a skeleton crew, so you should avoid any unfriendly elements."

"Understood."

"We can't parole any of the Spanish survivors for this, because they may try to kill ya on the way but, take as many of our Spanish crewmen as you need, they know the island and the language."

"I will sir"

"I'm also going to give you Mister Blair to navigate and Mister Gage to run it."

"Thank you, sir."

"And take a few of the Moors with you. As you know, they are excellent sailors and if you run into trouble well, as always, they'll be of service to you in combat." Harrow suggested the Moors because there would be some reluctance from our British and Welsh comrades to attack British regulars. The Moors had no such loyalty and of the twenty-six we had onboard, five would be picked for this venture and Amir --also known as The Baron of Morocco-- would be in command of these combat elements.

On overhearing this conversation on the preparation, I asked Mister Harrow, "Sir...are we to side with the men we just fought –the Spanish over the English?"

"There are no nations for us anymore. The Venger is our nation, son. We side with who we must, to do what's right for ourselves.   Understand?" Harrow then left me to my duties and turned away from me to face Mister Lynch. "Christ Almighty!" He said under his breath, "And he claims to be a schoolteacher!"

We washed the blood off the decks of The Phoenix and spent the rest of the afternoon loading supplies onboard. Flour, sugar, salt pork, coconuts, whatever could be spared –save water since we needed it and New Haven was reported to have its own fresh water source. We also tried to make the guns serviceable and there was still a supply of shot onboard.

Essex watched the final preparations from the rail, Vasquez stood with him.

"You should allow me and my men to go along."

"And risk you taking your ship back." Essex said with a slight smile as he kept his eyes on the work before him.

"I will give you my word, as a gentleman to try no such violence."

Essex turned to face him and leaned into the rail. "And typically, that would be enough for me. But, even if I could trust you not to try to retake your ship, your presence –and that of your marines—might spark an unwanted conflict." He took a deep breath, "Our men will go. The odds are better for Mister Rush, if they go it alone and you will be paroled on Pitchtag-Lota."

"Well, at least you picked some place pleasant."

Essex smiled.

That afternoon, The Phoenix was free to set sail and with a wave from Mister Rush, she disappeared over the horizon.

I admit, as I watched them depart, I felt very good about this mission. I was surprised the crew didn't vote against it, being that the supplies could have been dropped on 'The Dark Coast' or The Carolinas where they would be sold to merchant men then resold to the public. But thanks to our raid on Panama, profits were good at this time and Mister Rush and his mission did deserve special consideration after all, he was our minister.

We dropped anchor at Cay De Lota, a trading post –and illegal market. We unloaded some of our captured cargo in this corner of paradise –for gold—hit the taverns on the beach and waited for Mister Rush...

I spent some of the days, under the palm trees, teaching school for Whitney, Pharaoh, Johnny Kay, Tabor and Ward so he could continue to write to his wife –his letters were now scribed in an honest way that was becoming more and more sincere.

--Ten days later, there was still no sign of Rush.
--Fifteen days later –still nothing.
--Something was wrong.

Once he was twenty-one days overdue, the Captain ordered us onboard and asked Thorn to plot a course for New Haven and as Mister Thorn, the navigator applied his talents, there was some tension through the decks about this. There were some who thought this humanitarian effort had taken just about enough time and effort and –although always willing to help a shipmate—they were somewhat frustrated by the whole affair. I was still eager to keep my opinions to myself but, I was quite fond of Mister Rush and the compatriots who sailed with him so, I was prepared to look past this and ready to offer any assistance...

Still, I must admit, there was a strange feeling around this mission....

I climbed on deck –at sunset--a few nights later, to hear Archer and some of the other crew making music next to Nighthorse and the Native Americans. The Hurons were passing a large pipe around. I was surprised when they offered it to me. Although I struggled with tobacco, I knew it rude to refused so I choked it down....

I knew little about Nighthorse other than the fact that he was a good fighter and that he preferred the French to the British. He and Baltimore had fought the British in the Americas and I believe he was still fighting them in a way. Baltimore said the British would pay for Huron scalps but, this led to every trapper, scout, and militia man to kill any native, man, woman, or child –anywhere--and scalp them for coin. The British authorities would not ask questions or verify details about the scalp. As a result, many native families were killed –en masse-- for profit. I was afraid to ask Nighthorse, Baltimore, Bons or any of them, if they were directly affected by this but, it was obvious that they had hatred for the British that was of a very dedicated nature....

"I wonder," I moved to ask, "If would not have been better for you if Columbus had not discovered the new world?" I looked to him, "Do you know history?"

"We know." He nodded as he exhaled smoke. "And it's your history – not ours."

Bons said a few words in French and looked to Nighthorse. Mister Silence smiled.

I realized that they were talking at my expense. "What did he say?" I asked.

"He says that yes, it would have been better if Columbus was met with arrows instead of curiosity and kindness..."

"It would have altered history. No one would have attempted the same voyage for decades if Columbus was killed –never to return to Europe."

Bons continued with a mix of his native tongue and hand signals....

"Well?"

"He also said that the great grandfathers of his people tell a story about Norsemen finding their way to the Americas many years before your Columbus."

"Norsemen?" Blythe blurted out as he walked by, "You mean Vikings? Daft nonsense."

Nighthorse changed his posture as if about to get confrontational.

"Tis true." Wolfe said looking into the deck fire, "I fought in Sweden against the Russians –they tell stories of such."

"You fought for the King of Sweden?" Flynn asked…

"No." He offered a rare smile, "I fought for gold but, the King of Sweden paid it."

"No disrespect to ya Nighthorse," Blythe offered "But I never heard about no Vikings running through America if so…we'd all be speaking Viking."

"He at least discovered the world to be round." Flynn offered.

"That was the Greeks" I corrected him, "Or maybe the Egyptians."

Blythe by now heard all he could stand, "You've all been hit in the head too many times! The talk has gone crazy here…"

"Crazier still…." Raeder looked up from his blade that he had been sharpening in the shadows. "--This mission."

I looked to my shipmates wondering who would get the courage to ask so it fell to me. "What-what do you mean?"

He waited to answer. "I mean, we let our God-fearin' vicar, take supplies we could have sold on a peace keeping mission to an island we should raid and now…everyone is sucked into it."

Blythe gathered some courage, "But, the Captain –he thought it was a good idea to let him go,"

"—to make peace." Raeder said, "Rush was broken. Rush needed to repair his soul for what we had done." He growled in a low tone. "Better still, is to have no soul to repair." He said this with an evil look in his eye.

I looked to the others all of which remained silent. I tried to read their feelings on this matter but could only sense my own --for myself, yes, my destination was delayed, and profits may be slightly less but, I was still all right with this at the time.

X

NO QUARTER

At dawn, we sighted the island of New Haven in the distance, and we closed in. I looked at this curious island from the bow as it got closer –but with a strange feeling of dread! Why had Mister Rush never returned from this place?

At sunset, under a red sky, we dropped anchor in a cove about a league away from where our target –the town of New Haven proper--was supposed to be, in accordance with some captured Spanish maps. I was picked to be part of the shore party, the logic behind this decision was that Mister Harrow now believed that combat and experience was the only thing that would help my skills advance –after having to be saved several times in our fight with The Hércules. So, I jumped at the order, collected my weapons, and helped lower the long boats away….

No 'war captain' was to command this expedition. Harrow, our second officer, was to be in charge, which told me something significant –or sinister--was about to happen. The rest of the party was Baako, Jupiter, Mister Nighthorse, Mister Teague, Toombs, Blythe, Watson, Obal, De Leon, Mister Bons, Mister Lo, Hatano, Kato, Takeda, Kannon, Jagger, Merciless, Kon Boar, Lau and his butterfly blades, Sunderland, Rabal, Newcastle, Whitney, Mister Baltimore, Mister Styles, Wolfe, Mister Lynch, Strange, Fury, Jaffar, Raeder, Jack-Karr, Foxx, Cage, Mister Barak, Jeddah and some of the Moors, all under the command of Harrow and we shoved off under the moonlight and began quietly rowing….

I noticed, Mister Nighthorse --and the other natives-- had war paint on their face, across the eyes, black like the devil mixed with a dark red.

Handprints on the shoulders –except Sky, who wore a handprint on his cheek. Make no mistake, this was regarded as a mission of war.

Not a word was spoken between the lot of us. Jaffar who always had the look of concentrated anger, was also in our boat, many of 'his' Moors went with Mister Rush to bring aid to this fateful place. I tried to guess his thoughts at this time --for myself, I was now mixed between curious and scared.

As we moved closer to the beach, silence remained the order and we climbed out of the boats, picked them up and hauled them into the surrounding jungle to hide them. We then moved forward through the trees until we came upon the road into town. We moved along-side this road using the shadows and the tree line for cover until our scout, Mazatal, spotted a small guard house up ahead.

We closed in, this guard house, was lit by torches and protected by British sentries in their red jackets. Kato put his hand on my shoulder to keep me in place. I was to stay still as Obal, and the Moors moved past me like thieves in the night....

Mister Teague gave a series of hand signals and the rest of our boarding party closed in on the guard house from all sides. The only sounds were that of the saber slicing across its target –and the tomahawk, as it stuck in a sentry's skull, through his hat. The men dropped to the ground. Some of our crew –Styles, Wicks-- took their red coats and hats and assumed to look the part as British regulars. This allowed them to control –and kill—anyone on this road to town as the rest of us moved forward towards our objective --the only township on the island.

It was Bons who saw it first, he turned from the edge of the jungle with the township not too far off. Harrow looked to Teague and gave a nod. We formed a skirmish line, like infantry, and slowly moved forward. Step by Step towards our target. The town itself was quiet, not a soul on the streets but there was something unusual up ahead in the town square, an unusual shape in the shadows –a bit of architecture not common in a town square like this. As we got closer, my eyes focused to see that it was --a cross– and nailed to it was Amir! Crucified!

--A sign around his neck read: 'Heathen!'

"What the—" I was in shock but managed to keep still.

This discovery escalated the temperament of our men with a level of outrage and vengeance I had not yet seen. Mister Jagger spit –in anger--as if the sight had given him a bad taste in his mouth. Now, we were like chained animals ready to kill.

Harrow gave an order through his teeth "Muster the town!"

We advanced quickly. Baako, Nighthorse, Obal, Kato and the Moors went towards the quartering station where the regulars were housed. The sentry, outside, asleep, looked up just in time to see these men, charge out of the darkness at him and he was killed by an Arabian saber across the gut --before he could react, most of his organs spilled out as his body hit the sand in two pieces. At the entrance, Obal turned as Barak threw him a lit grenade, Nighthorse came up and kicked the door open for him, and Obal rolled the grenade into the barracks –under the cots! He quickly turned to catch another grenade –and Nighthorse another-- rolling them all inside where they exploded under the beds of the sleeping, groggy soldiers, blowing many up against the ceiling or across the room. Then we charged in through the smoke, to dispatch any wounded who may have survived the blasts. Men smoldering, some with clothes on fire were quickly finished.

Blythe, Wolfe, Mister Bons and Hatano went towards the block house. Regulars stormed outside –alerted by the explosions—just in time to be killed by the blade and musket fire, their bodies tumbled down the steps or fell into the sand. Hatano then moved up the steps and kicked the door open, two clerks were slashed and murdered, one, before he could stand from his desk, a third tried to crawl away, with a knife in his back and a fourth was cut and wheeled back to cower in the corner of the office. Our men stormed inside the cell block… the cells were opened so Spanish prisoners –those still alive-- could be released but our men were not among any of them. Mister Wolfe pulled the wounded clerk to his feet as he heeled at the pain. "Where are the men from The Venger?" He asked through his teeth….

"Si-Sir?"

"The privateers who brought supplies to this island, with the man you crucified," He shouted, "Where-are-they?"

"Th-the b-block house be-below" he pointed down the end of the dark corridor where a heavy wood and iron door concealed a stairwell to the dungeon....

"Mister Bons... thank our friend here!" Wolfe said as he released his grip and down came the tomahawk with a CRUNCH between the neck and the shoulder, hitting him hard and dropping the sentry to the floor...

We moved down the hallway, slammed open the door using the other wounded clerk as a battering ram and made our way down below. There, we found some of our men, many fastened to different torture devices of strange and complex engineering. Many were bled to near death. We moved to release them and give them some aid and water. We started to carry them out –for many had been deprived of their strength and could not walk.

--Mister Rush was not among them.

We made it back to the parade ground, were a number of prisoners, including some British regulars, town officials and British 'persons of note' were lined up and made to wait on their knees near our crucified friend. I had a bad feeling about this. Mister Teague was holding court in a way, arms crossed but with a pistol in both hands. Here a trial –of a different sort—was about to take place...

A British sergeant was grabbed by his jacket, dragged through the dirt by Jupiter and Mister Rabal and thrown down at the boot of Mister Teague in front of the cross that held our comrade. Once there, he was brought back to his knees –Rabal and Jupiter held him in place and Jaffar pulled his curved saber and placed it at the front of this man's throat.

"I want to know who did this?" Teague asked.

Despite the lovely warm temperature on this particular evening, this man was shivering and found it hard to formulate an answer, "I-I don't kno--" Before he could finish, Teague gave a nod and Jaffar dragged his sword across his throat, cutting him open and dropping him to the ground. He gasped for air as the life left his body....

Mister Teague looked down at him and said, "Wrong answer!" He then looked to Rabal, "Next?"

Another non-commissioned officer was dragged from the ranks. Again, he was held into position and again, Jaffar --without a word-- took a stance with his sword.

"I'll ask you the same question, I asked your dead friend here."

This man looked down to see his Sergeant, blood, voice box and most of the inside of his throat on the sand. He refused to make eye contact with Mister Teague.

"Who did this?"

He remained silent. Teague gave a nod and Jaffar pulled his blade across his throat dropping his body as it tumbled over that of his Sergeant.

"Next!" And indeed, a next man was pulled from the ranks of the restless prisoners and made to look at the crucifixion. Teague didn't like the look of this man so without asking the question, he just gave Jaffar a nod and the Moor in a split-second removed the man's head….

Sounds of horror erupted from the prisoners. Mister Teague now turned and addressed the crowd, "You know why this man came here?" He motioned to our brother on the cross. "Did you know his purpose? T'waz to deliver medicine and food to the people of this island who your Governor has seen fit to eradicate –and-- by killing him, you condemned the population here to starvation and death." He looked our captives over, "That was until we arrived… to remove your tyranny." Mister Teague's very cold nature made him the perfect man for this job for his very voice struck fear into all who listened –even me.

"Mister Rabal, fetch me another…."

The bodies were now piling up and Mister Rabal and Jupiter pulled another regular to his feet and brought him forward. "You know the question. Now give me my answer."

"It-It was done on the Governor's orders."

"I asked who? …Exactly?"

"Privates Talbot and Lawrence were charged with carrying out the Governor's orders, sir."

"Thank you." Mister Teague pushed the man back into the hands of Jupiter and the other Moors for safe keeping and turned back to his audience, "Now, do we have a Private Talbot and a Private Lawrence in the audience here today?" They were quickly rooted out by other regulars. Loyalty dies –somewhat quickly—at times.

Hatano and Bons grabbed Talbot and dragged him forward. "Move!"

Mister Lo-Tan and Blythe brought Lawrence forward by force. "You're coming with us!"

Teague looked these men over with a certain darkness in his eyes "You did this?" He asked.

There was –at first—no answer and Teague stepped closer. "I believe I asked you a question…and…I believe you heard me."

"Please sir," Lawrence answered, teeth chattering, "This man was nothing more than a heathen-"

Teague looked at them both and slowly said "For that…you die!" He motioned to us and just said two words, "The cage!" And with that, they were taken away and dragged back through the jungle to the beach. There, Mister Sunderland used flags to signal The Venger…

-Onboard, Mister Daws read the flag signals from the beach, lowered his spyglass, and looked to the Captain. "Mister Teague is asking for the cage, sir."

The Captain remained silent for a moment; his eyes fixed on the beach. Then he finally said, "Then by all means, send it to him."

And Daws passed the order below, "Bring up the cage…."

"Aye…bring up the cage!" The order was repeated below deck, and moments later a rope net heaved an iron cage up to the top deck. It was moved over the side and lowered into a long boat and rowed ashore….

On the beach, Private Talbot began the routine of begging for his life. "Sir, as a good Christian, certainly, you can find it in your heart to see our reasoning. One less infidel in the world--"

Wolfe punched him in the back of the head, then grabbed the private by the scalp. "The infidel-is-you!"

Moments later, the iron cage came ashore. It was maybe two meters by one and a half meters and shaped like a large coffin. It was heavier than imagined for it took six of us to heave it out of the long boat and guided by Mister Archer, we placed it on the beach at a specific point in the tide. Then, both prisoners were forced forward. They tried to resist but it was of no use, they were punched, kicked, and forced into the cage, the cage was locked and there, they would wait –and wait-- for the tide to slowly rise and overtake them.

With this task finished, we then moved back towards the town where the remaining prisoners were still in the town square on their knees.

"It's done." Archer reported to Mister Teague.

"Report to Mister Harrow," Teague motioned towards the Governor's mansion, and we started in that direction.

"What about the-the rest of us?" Asked a nervous regular from his knees in the crowd.

Teague slowly turned "For the rest of you ---No Quarter!"

As we moved towards the Governor's mansion, behind us, there was screaming as our men surrounded and descended on these prisoners and hammered –and slashed--until there was nothing left of them....

We moved through the gate to the Governor's mansion to report to Mister Harrow. There, the household staff was set free and allowed to depart in the Governor's carriage with all the supplies, silverware, and valuables they could carry. Inside the mansion itself, the wife of the Governor was on her knees begging for mercy. The Governor himself stood there –without his wig-- shivering in silence, waiting for Mister Harrow to make his next move...

"We-we have money." The Governor stumbled with the sudden courage to speak. "That's what you want isn't it? Money? A ransom? I can make you all rich men."

"And where is this money?"

"I have but to write a letter to the King and you will be paid. Please..." he motioned to his writing desk with a trembling hand,   "Please, a letter and it's done."

"A letter?" Harrow slowly stepped forward.

"Yes!"

"And all is forgiven here?"

"Ye-yes!"

"An intriguing proposition –ransom-- one we would normally entertain."

"All I have to do is write a letter and you may even name the amount."

Mister Harrow gave a slow, deliberate nod. "I wonder…" his eyes started to drift off, "Would such a letter bring our friends back from the dead?" And with that, our men closed in on the Governor and issued our own death penalty --I looked away but, turned to see the shadows of these men in the candlelight –as their weapons descended on these people.

Outside, all government buildings were put to the torch. Blythe, De Leon, and Kato opened up the customs house and used sledgehammers, to break open the supply houses making their stores available to the population, minus the gunpowder, muskets, weapons, and other items that we needed for our own supply. And ransom –though profitable—was not needed for we broke into the banking building and liberated about a-hundred-thousand pounds and some silver.

We burned the prison and stockade to the ground. We burned the surrounding sugarcane plantation to the ground and liberated the slaves there --one from the whipping post.

Once the damage was done, we started moving our stores to the beach to be rowed back to the ship. The loading continued as the sun began to rise and once the last barrels of fresh water and gun powder shoved off, our rear guard prepared to leave the beach…

The tide was now on the rise and had almost covered the cage. Private Talbot had very little space left to breathe. "Mercy! For God sakes, mercy," he cried, coughing up sea water and gasping for what little air was left. "Please sir!"

Mister Harrow stopped and looked into the cage. "Did you give our men mercy when they asked for it?" There was no response, just the sea water washing over the cage and back, choking their words. "--Thought not." Harrow said as we continued about our business of leaving...

"Have a nice day, gents," Blythe shouted as the last of us climbed onboard the long boats...

As we shoved off, the tide washed over the cage again and covered it for a longer interval before it washed back, soon it would overtake them for good –they didn't have long to live now.

Back on The Venger, we suspected some of our men filled a mass grave somewhere on the island but those we could find –like Amir—we brought back aboard --wrapped in canvas-- for a burial at sea, for they would not be buried in such a sinister place as New Haven. We always made an effort to not leave our dead or wounded behind and this foray was no exception. Harrow took to the deck and stood next to the Captain. There were no words exchanged but the Captain knew the matter had been resolved. He turned to Mister Flagg, "Get us underway, let's put this place behind us."

As the anchor was raised, I helped to stow the supplies and as I loaded and housed our freight, I asked Mister Irons about the cage.   "What's the cage used for, exactly?"

"The cage?"

"Yeah, what was it built for? I thought crab fishing and such?"

"Crab fishing?" He laughed, "The cage was made for just that. The iron workers made it for the sole purpose of torturing our enemies." He paused in thought for a moment, "I guess they'd better get to work on making a new one."

"It was made just to torture people?" As if to confirm what I was just told a second time.

"Yes."

The next morning in New Haven, the sun rose, and, in the streets, it was quiet --except for a few wandering chickens. Slowly, the surviving townspeople who were brave enough to venture outside and cautiously explore the devastation, found their Governor tied to the giant wheel of the creek side mill where his dead body was made to turn --round and round--

dunking his head and shoulders below the creek water line with every rotation. A gruesome example of retribution. Nailed to his body was a sign, painted in blood that read:

'Death To All Masters.'

XI

MAY THE STEEL BE MY SALVATION

The next morning, we were making good time with the wind rolling over the tide at about six knots. I made it on deck, Arson had just made it down the rigging and slammed on deck from his night watch. "Weather looks fair." He moved over to the coffee bucket where Rabal handed him a mug. He kicked it back in one swallow, "I want to kill something by God! I'm bent today!" He threw the mug back to Rabal. "I'm still angry at these damn Brits."

"Ease up Lazarus." Duncan-Howe said, working the ropes not too far off, "There'll be killing enough for all soon to be sure."

Suddenly, we noticed the Aztecs were in a close circle, having an up-tempo discussion. They would point at the sun, then talk some more, then point at the sun again. It was an argument of some sort.

"What do you suppose all that noise is about?"

I looked up and held one hand over my left eye --an eclipse. It was slowly becoming a pretty mesmerizing sight.

Mazatal continued speaking in his native language, but he was loud. For the first time, I heard one of the Aztecs get loud.

"What's his problem?"

"Superstition!" Foxx said as he moved past me on deck.

"Superstition about what?"

Foxx just turned and pointed at the sky with a smile.

"What's all this then?" Raeder barked making his presence known.

The Aztecs got quiet, but Mazatal stepped forward. "Huitzilopochtli is angry." He said and again he pointed at the sky.

-- Huitzilopochtli was the Aztec Sun God.

"We need to make sacrifice." Mazatal said in his broken English.

"What?" Raeder was stunned.

"You still do that kind a thing?" Duncan-Howe asked.

"Yes, must make sacrifice to make Huitzilopochtli smile again." Again, he pointed to the eclipse above.

Raeder, Arson and Rabal looked up with a squint, into the sun and then it became clear what they were dealing with. They seemed to be trying to pinpoint a solution and there was some slight mumbling between them like "How do you purpose we handle this?" And "Who can we sacrifice?"

--I, of course, took a few steps back so, I did not get any extra attention and be 'volunteered.'

Duncan-Howe seemed to strike an idea. "Can we get you a politician to sacrifice? Would that do?"

"Do we have a politician?" Raeder asked.

"No but we can get one."

"Do we have time to kidnap a politician?" Arson asked with a shout down the deck towards our officers at the helm...

"Is a politician worth a sacrifice?" Howe asked, "It seems like a low-grade tribute."

"Why didn't this happen when we were at New Haven?" Raeder asked, "We could have sacrificed the whole damn island."

Essex walked towards us, and our ranks parted for him to join the conversation. Harrow wasn't too far behind. "What's happening here?"

"Mazatal needs to rip someone's heart out to function properly today." Howe said tapping his pipe.

Essex looked at him. "Again? Already?"

Mazatal nodded. Essex looked to Harrow exhausted, "Didn't we just do this?"

"It's been a few months since the equinox sir."

By now, a crowd started to surround us with interest in this conversation. Essex looked to our scout, "Can it wait a day or two, so we can grab someone suitable?"

"How soon?" Mazatal asked.

"Well," He looked to Harrow, "Where are we?"

"St. Luca."

"Can't grab anyone there –it's a leper colony."

"What about Saint Jax? Or Port Anne? Can we take a hostage there?"

"We can but, it'll take us four days to get there."

"That marks Thursday!" He looked to Mazatal, "How's Thursday? Would that suit you?"

Mazatal shook his head no. "Huitzilopochtli needs his sacrifice by mid-day tomorrow."

"Well, we don't want to disappoint Mister Huitzilopochtli now do we?" Harrow added with a touch of sarcasm.

"Let's steer into the shipping lanes." Essex told Harrow and he looked to Mazatal. "Give me until mid-day tomorrow to find a solution for you." Essex said with a touch of reluctance.

Mazatal nodded and the Aztecs dismissed themselves.

"A sacrifice?" I looked to Jack-Karr, "What are we going to do?"

"Isn't it obvious? We're going to sacrifice someone."

I cringed, and he smiled, "Better make sure it's not you!"

"Better stay awake in your bunk tonight lad." Duncan-Howe added as he triggered some light laughter.

In the early morning hours of the dawn, we pulled alongside a merchantman listed as the H.M.S. Future out of the African port of Tibor (pronounced Tie-bor) with our skull and crossbones flying. A banner of the R. A. C. blew in the wind from the quarterdeck which identified this ship as part of the Royal African Company –a company which specialized in the slave trade, sanctioned by the British Crown. We expected to find slaves. But what I saw that day, I will never forget.

The ship surrendered without a fight, and we marched across the gang plank –Lau first-- to board. I looked up as Blythe, O'Shea, Manu, and a few others swung across by ropes to take hold of the Future's rigging. It was oddly quiet, onboard. There was a strange stillness in the air. Their Captain and crew stood in one corner of the deck, nervous, void of arms and scared of our presence as we stomped aboard and closed in, war paint and all.

Some of their crew trembled. This was now a sight I could expect. Essex moved to the forefront and his commands were direct and lacked any civility he traditionally allotted to a surrendered Captain. "Men of the Royal African Company, if you resist you will be killed."

The logbook marked this ship from the Ivory Coast. Our men started working their way through the ship for anything of value. We found the doors –and all the hatches to the lower deck were locked with heavy padlocks and cage doors and not wanting to search for keys, we blew them open with explosives. The Captain made his way below deck and then we saw the contents.

"My God!"

We expected something, but I was still stunned by the manner in which these human beings were being shipped –as freight—stacked on their backs, some on top of each other and some clearly the victims of extreme punishment and abuse. This gave us serious pause. Many of these people appeared frightened and apprehensive. Some remained strong and defiant and some –regrettably—were dead due to the harsh conditions. Their bodies left to rot in this hold. I saw a young girl, maybe ten years of age, the body next to her –maybe her father, maybe a friend—had been dead for several weeks and had begun to decompose on her. She just remained – forced-- in place, shackled. She trembled at the sight of us. Not sure what to expect.

I slid in, close to her on one knee, "I'm going to get you out of here." I said unaware that she probably didn't even speak English. "Hold on."

The Captain kept his composure as he overlooked the hold from the stairs, "Mister Obal?"

"Yes Captain" He replied in his deep grumbling voice.

"Get our doctors down here…"

"Right away Captain."

"Get these people unchained immediately and get some water…and have Hobby fire-up the galley." He started back for the top deck and passed Mister Newcastle, "Find me someone who can speak for these people and get them out of this hold…."

Newcastle nodded.

Later, on deck, these 'passengers' were given food, bread, bacon and water by Mister Hobby and Rorry which was much needed for many of these people had not eaten in days and the rations they did receive were shameful. They sat in huddles or groups talking almost silently amongst themselves unsure of their safety. Doctor Johannis and Jopo worked their way through their ranks to check for health issues like fever as our metal workers continued to remove their shackles…

"No fever" Johannis reported "But, they require some care." Johannis pointed out that many were shipped on their backs and had remained in that position since they started across the Atlantic so, it was hard for some of them to even move and some of them had to be carried to the deck --human beings had to be carried because of the abuse they suffered.

Essex surveyed this group from the helm, where Harrow, Teague, Newcastle, and Mister Lincoln waited with him, "What is your plan, Captain?"

"How many are there?"

"Two hundred," Lincoln returned looking at the captured manifest.

"Two-hundred-human-beings" Essex said in disbelief, "In a cargo bay built for forty bunks."

"The question remains, what are we going to do? If we leave them here, cast them adrift, they will die or be over-taken by the next frigate to pass through these parts." Harrow acknowledged.

"Aye and forced back into slavery most likely." Newcastle added.

Essex looked again at the group below, "Some of them appear to be families," he seemed to study the faces of these human beings. Some, young children holding on to their parents in fear. "This is a damned hard business, isn't it?"

"The smart play is to leave them," Mister Harrow said bluntly, "However," He exhaled and spoke in a more sincere tone, "I doubt there's a man onboard who could live with himself if we did."

"Agreed."

"Well, I could." Raeder said. "If it's between them or us. I choose us. We're not saviors, are we?"

"That is not the only option here." Newcastle said.

"We could land them in Spanish Florida or Havana under a white flag." Teague suggested.

"They'd have to fend for themselves….and that could be dangerous going."

"Even if we did that, even though the Spanish are out of the slave business, they'll most likely round them up, sell them to the Portuguese and profit while keeping up appearances…."

"Well, we can't sail them back to the Ivory Coast" Teague said, "Unless you want to fight the French –or Portuguese Empire."

"I never thought the French would make you nervous Teague."

"They don't but, the only profit in a fight in that region would be more slaves and we're not in the revolution business…." He looked to the Captain, "Are we?" he said it a way that made the possibility of a revolution almost sound intriguing…

The Captain looked back at him as if to almost consider it…

"When I was a boy, my mother tied grains of rice into my sister's hair," Jupiter suddenly said as he looked at the crowd of liberated slaves on our deck as if they were his own family. His memories seemed to put him in a trance as he spoke. "So many young children in our village went missing, that it became wise to tie up rice or grain so if the children were captured by slavers, they would have some small amount of sustenance on any voyage or forced march to keep them alive." He suddenly turned slightly to face the other officers, "My first sister disappeared when she was eight. My second when she was six." His eyes shifted to the deck then back up to

Essex, "Only one of my sisters survived to be a woman. All the others were taken off to some unknown place." He paused, "My mother still sings the prayer of loss and pain as she cries herself to sleep every night."

In silence, everyone quickly processed their thoughts, it may had been something Jupiter said –or—the situation in general but the overall conversation seemed to change gears at that point as our officers seemed to offer up –or almost invent-- reasons to sail East.

"A lot of those slave ports have rich treasuries." Newcastle said. "Big commerce for those brave enough to take it."

"And Hurricane season is closing in on us." Harrow added.

"Everyone is looking for us here," Teague said, "We can sail East, hit the slave outposts up and down the African Coast… burn them to the ground, then make for the Cape and raid the Indian Ocean,"

"And then?" Essex asked curious of what Teague was thinking…

"Macau." Teague smiled.

The Captain gave a slight grin at the prospect but went back to his business as if to not betray the fact that he liked the idea, "Mister Lincoln, what do your inventories tell you?"

"Eight weeks, full-compliment, six with the new passengers… maybe seven with rationing."

"So, we'd have to get to business immediately upon arrival to survive."

"That is –after all—what we do best!"

The Captain called for Mister Addo and Jata.

"Captain?" Addo reported.

"Ask if any want to join us…and begin training them immediately."

"Aye Captain."

"Mister Newcastle, strip this hulk clean of anything we can use, then set it a light. Mister Thorn set a course due East."

"What about the crew sir?" Newcastle asked as he motioned to the slave ship.

"Kill them --and be quick about it, we have a schedule to keep." Essex then corrected himself, "Wait, give one to Mazatal for his sacrifice then kill the rest."

"Aye." Newcastle looked to Jack-Karr "Jack, Kane, Foxx, Rabal, grab your weapons and come with me please."

Mister Rabal pulled an axe from his belt. Lau pulled this twin butterfly blades and with Kane, Foxx, Obal, Baako, Bons, Barak, Toombs, Jagger, and Wolfe they crossed the deck, closed in on the crew as they put their hands up and…. massacred them!

Amid the screaming and the cries for 'mercy' from the crew as they were cut apart, the captain was pulled aside and thrown to the Aztecs! "Make it quick, will you!" Newcastle ordered "And do it here. I don't want his ghost walkin' The Venger."

Mazatal nodded and as the Aztecs closed in on this man, his cries became more and more urgent but, it was no use, he was held by the arms --in a crucifixion like position—to expose his heart and out came the knife.

We moved our passengers –and anything of value—to our ship. I searched the hold below, with Bons, Dax-Varro, Arson, Jack-Karr, and a few others. There wasn't much. The food was cut with sand or a powder of some sort to make it last longer for the slaves and the water was tainted. As I stepped over chains and shackles, I could smell the stench of human waste –the slaves were not allowed to go topside for ANY reason.

The ship itself was reconfigured in a way that made it useless in a real fight and it could only be 'prized out' in a slave port –and we weren't about to get close to an English port after the incident of New Haven, so we took the sail, rope and mast elements for potential, future repairs….

Suddenly, we heard screaming from the top deck--the sacrifice! I looked up as blood from the victim dripped through the deck panels below to us. Through the cracks in the deck floor, I could see his body violently shaking as his screams became choked with blood and a still beating heart was ripped from his chest and held in Mazatal's fist –my eyes went wide with terror!

"And there you have it" Arson said as he walked past me, in a tone that showed him to be unconcerned for this killing. "One less slaver to worry about."

"Come on, let's get the hell of this blasted ship." Karr ordered. "Kannon, move."

We swung over the water, back aboard and landed on the panels. "You won't make the new world any time soon Mister Reed." Duncan-Howe said as he exhaled some smoke. "The destination is Africa."

"Africa?" I was somewhat sad about this but, as I looked around the deck at the people we had liberated, I became aware that Africa may be something of a much-needed detour.

Just as we were about to set sail, Rajiv and a gun crew put a cannon round through the Future's hull, below the waterline and this villain slave ship, slowly began to twist into the depths….

I tried to focus on the situation at hand –not what I had seen-- but what was before me. This was hard at first, the image of the still beating heart and sacrifice forced its way back into my head, again and again but as I worked to train my thoughts on the situation and the people around us, I started to get more and more intent on the present. There was, after all, a humanitarian crisis around us.

I slowly walked through the ranks of our new guests who still appeared cautious, scared, and concerned. I looked at their faces, tried to read their histories and imagined the savage road that led them to this point. There was the look of apprehension on some of the younger people, the ten-year olds, the twelve-year-olds, in an unknown place –with an unknown future. Some had been ripped from families they feared they would never see again. What were their mothers back home thinking? –Feeling? I felt a sudden emotional connection with my own humanity that reminded me of who I really was --and a strange sense of pride in our officers for the decision they had made on this issue. It would be said that heading for Africa was what would be best in the interests of the ship and our crew after the New Haven incident –not the slaves. But I knew better. I knew that THEY DID factor into this decision. Sure, the prospects of raiding the African coast were intriguing but just as intriguing was the idea of putting something right with the world –however small for us –or however big it may be for the children on our decks now. Maybe, we were changing what we were about as men.

Baako and the other Africans used their dialect to give instructions and clarify our intentions and many of these people seemed relieved or even excited –one woman broke down in tears!

Doctor Johannis walked through the ranks addressing medical concerns. One young woman, not more than maybe twelve years of age had deep gashes on her back. Cut apart by the whip! What could a woman so young have done to get lashes like that? Some of the other women were abused –and used for entertainment by the crew we had just killed, and I regret to say –before God—that this made me feel better about killing them.

Without instruction, I reported to the galley for it was where I wanted to be. I had given almost no thought to the slave trade before now and having seen this horrid affair, first-hand, I felt compassion for what these people had been put through –the hatred –the agony inflicted on them, including the children. It was hard to bear, so I got the attention of Mister Hobby, "Could you use another hand sir?"

He turned from opening a large cask of broth and gave me a yes. I served meals and more meals with water. Standish suddenly emerged next to me and pulled down nets with bananas. Then, Therrinfall, Kannon and Sanjuro arrived and started opening up supplies –with Rorry directing them on what to pull together. Before long, Lo-Tan, Manu, Java, and many of the Moors were helping in this effort, preparing plates, and passing out food. With Addo, Calixto and Sterling moving through their ranks with water buckets.

I even saw Jaffar do a simple magic trick in front of one of the young children, where he made a coin disappear only to pull it from her ear and give it to her when she smiled.

--I smiled too.

I dare say, I saw another smile or two from our guests when I handed them a plate and when I cut the bread, I, at first, put the knife at the ration mark where we would cut for each crew member but as I saw the woman before me who appeared to have been without food for several days, I moved my knife to make a larger piece --I looked over my shoulder to Mister Hobby for approval and he gave a nod as if it was the right thing to do, before he continued in his work and I made a wider cut for all I could....

We would work until late in the evening --and we, the crew, would eat last. In these efforts, I felt the strange presence of Mister Rush –or perhaps something even more holy-- for this work did in fact 'restoreth my soul' and it was the path through New Haven that put us here.

At midnight, when I finally managed to make it back on deck, I found that many of the liberated slaves wanted to sleep on the planks in the open air. Maybe because they felt free there, in the wind and the elements seemed to breathe life back into them. A simple request after spending weeks stacked on top of each other. Some of the younger ones looked up and pointed at the moon almost as if they were surprised to see it again...

I looked around and saw Pharaoh playing with his jar of marbles with some of the children and I stepped to the quarter deck where Mister Foxx exhaled tobacco smoke and managed the helm with Thorn at the wheel. "Well Mister Reed. Done with your tavern duties?"

"For the night, yes."

"Then have some coffee" He motioned to the bucket with the long stem of his pipe.

I filled a mug and leaned against the rail still wrapped with a slight smile on my face. "It's a fine thing we did today." I said.

"It was. Sure, it could send us all to the gallows but—"

"That's of small consequence" Thorn interrupted "Since most of our actions bring a death sentence in any event."

"But this is The Royal African Company –it's different."

"How so? The gallows is the gallows!"

"I'm not speaking of the method of killing but the intentions behind it. The R.A.C is a highly motivated lot and that's what I have to say on the matter."

"Fair enough Foxx." Thorn said, trying to end the conversation as he refocused on his steering.

"Don't you agree Thorn?" He then looked to me, "Reed?"

"I believe we have to stand up to any force that wants to inflict a genocide on the rest of us. Whether it be the Royal African Company or the British government. Authority be damned!" I said –though I could hardly believe the words that came out of my mouth.

Both Mister Foxx and Thorn were stunned and looked at me in silence. Finally, Foxx managed to put a phrase or two together, "My God Reed! You may be a privateer after all." He smiled and they both laughed.

I tried to chuckle but my smile faded as I turned away so they could not see. I looked out on the ocean, I may have talked tough, and I meant what I said but I was fearful of who I was becoming.

XII

AFRICA

DAWN. DAYS LATER....

Once our guests started to recover and get some strength back. Twenty-six of them –known as Masai––joined our ranks. They appeared tough -- and a shade away from being physically fit––and after a day of basic deck work with the brush and bucket –where I started, Jagger, Bons, Addo and the ronin began to train them on the top deck in the use of different weapons. I would later find that they did not adopt the practice of painting a skull on their faces for war –instead, they applied a dark red paint over their eyes. This was their tradition, something they did when hunting back home.

--These men could practice with the weapons late into the evening, without getting tired. And they remained almost totally silent, very little talk.

The other liberated slaves helped where they could along the way and for the most part, kept to themselves the way any kidnapped survivor would. For my part, I kept to my work by day and made an effort –with the help of Juta and Dakar––to include these people in my small evening school but, there seemed little interest in western learning. Still, I was grateful for the opportunities I was afforded and did what I could to educate even if school with these people became dominated by the Moors stopping by to do magic tricks and making the children laugh.

Food was rationed at this time but every day or two, Mister Hobby would allow me a banana or a few coconuts from the galley –if I threw some coin into the ship's general treasury fund –controlled by Mister Lincoln-- and I would give this to some of the 'liberated' children up on deck. Mister Rabal caught me doing this and I was sure this would work against the 'hard' reputation I was trying to earn, but he followed suit and for a small amount of coin, he also bought coconuts, cracked them open and gave them to the kids. Eventually, Whitney and Abel became our accomplices, and this made the trip a little more pleasant.

One night, I caught Mister Lynch drawing some of them in his book under some lantern light. The faces he drew were of a near perfect resemblance. Lynch looked up, caught me watching and smiled. He had several pages of drawings dedicated to these people.

"You must get this published Mister Lynch…someday." I had discovered a printing press and publisher of naval charts in Port Royal, so I believed my suggestion to be sound but, Lynch seemed to have no real interest for his drawings other than drawing them for himself…

Mister Duncan-Howe made his way past me, offered me some of his tobacco --for it was my time in the look out-- and he too caught sight of the book and illustrations. Sucking on his pipe he said. "What's this then? An illustrated history of our adventures?"

"Aye, it is, in a way" Lynch replied.

"You're a true artist Mister Lynch both with the quill and with the gun. Proud to kill with ya! God bless ya'" And he moved down the deck into the darkness….

At sunset the next day, I started my deck watch at the helm under the command of Mister Newcastle with Jagger and Mister O'Shea. O'Shea was a man who fought against the British his whole life from bases in Ireland. He once even took over a coastal light house and removed the signal light to get British ships to run aground on the rocks. He would raid them, turning salvaged weapons over to his Irish comrades while selling the cargo back to British merchants at a reduced rate –an art we practiced now.

He stood at the wheel, with myself not too far off. Coffee from the galley made the night watch easier and as I drank it, I looked at the different flags we had racked at the helm. British, French, Spanish, Dutch –almost every national flag to disguise the ship one could imagine. We even seized the R.A.C. flag off the 'Future' so I asked, "Are we to be warring against the Royal African Company now?"

"We war against everyone lad. If a war against the African Company serves our purpose, you can wager we'll unleash it!" Jagger said.

"These men are not only British," O'Shea added "But, they profit on sale and exploitation of men and women, and this disturbs my soul and-" He leaned back to dip his mug in a bucket of coffee, "I'm also for anything that brings the damned Union Jack down!"

I passed the steering, took a seat at the rail, and looked up at the stars, listening to Mister Thorn and Newcastle talk at the map table. "Have you always been privateers, sir?" I asked.

Newcastle stopped his conversation and looked at me, "There's no sir here son. That's reserved for the Captain and the habit is a holdover from our days in the Royal Navy" He directed his work back to his maps, "And one is not always a privateer, one becomes a privateer out of necessity or when tyranny drives a man to it. No, I, I-" He suddenly stalled and appeared to remember his past, "I brought Christian charity to the heathens of La Rochelle by bombarding them into submission." He said with a smile, "You know, the Lord's work!"

I scowled in thought "La Ro-- You mean, the Catholics of France?"

"I do. As an Atheist, I can tell you in confidence, that once your King orders you to war on some nonsense religious grounds, it doesn't take long for one to –wise up—as they say."

"Well," O'Shea added "Longer for you, then the rest of us, Newcastle."

"See," He motioned to Mister O'Shea but spoke to me, "That's an Irishman for you –always fast and loose with the truth. We'll have none of that vocal treachery from you Mister Reed, you're not to share your countryman's disdain for the facts –understand?" He turned with his cup of coffee.

I smiled sensing the warm feeling behind the sarcasm and I had come to like Mister Newcastle. I suspected that he had quite a normal life before becoming a privateer. I pictured him as a local sheriff or land baron, a man who had real responsibilities who may have enlisted himself into royal service at a time of war and who had become disenchanted with the cause. I imagined some set of tragedies that forced him to leave service and never return home....

If I offered any hint of asking about his past he would always reply with the words, "I had a simple life." And leave it at that. This created only more mystery about him. I was told that his Christian name was Warrick, and that Newcastle was not his real name but where he was from in England. Hence the reason some of the crew, who knew him for years –like Mister Harrow—would call him 'Iron Hands' in casual passing but Newcastle was the name he used now...

Any romantic sense I had about Newcastle's past was put to rest when Kannon Saint James told me he had in fact been a contract killer....

AUTUMN

THE BANKS OF THE EASTERN HUDSON.

TWO YEARS EARLIER

The lantern over the signpost read...

THE TAVERN OF THE MIDNIGHT PHANTOM

A storm was rolling in. Lightning lit the way across the frontier...

A platoon on horseback moved in, the Huron native, Nighthorse emerged slowly out of the darkness, black and red war paint across the eyes. He was followed by other figures covered in long highway coats and scarves, then Newcastle, sword on his back.

They moved slowly, past a wicked looking scarecrow, towards the lonely tavern building as smoke piped into the sky from the chimney. They were met by a man at the edge of the road, a local contact named Brom. "He's inside," Brom reported, "with the local militia commander." He then raised a canvass bag of what appeared to be money.

Newcastle held up his hand to hold him in place. "After it's done."

Brom nodded and the platoon moved past him and continued towards the tavern. There were three men out front —a security detail— standing guard with the horses and carriage –and a tomahawk for each of them.

The barkeeper looked up as the tavern doors were thrown open and in walked what appeared to be shadows, dark figures flickering in the candlelight. They moved inside and spaced out, "We don't allow Indians, military scouts or otherwise." The tavernkeeper said.

Newcastle's eyes darted up to him as he and his 'highway men' made themselves comfortable up against the bar. The look was something that brought silence to the situation and the barkeeper did not press the issue of his prejudice. "I suppose, just this once." He said as he put a jug down.

There was a conversation near the fireplace between the magistrate and the local militia commander.

"I am aware, but I need better enforcement from you and your men. I plan to continue the tax until all the farms along the Carfax Road are in forfeit—"

"Then yours through a rigged auction?"

"Rigged or not, the property will be mine –every farm. Now your men must use force and evict every family---"

"--Excuse me." The dark image of Newcastle was suddenly revealed in the candlelight as he stood nearby.

The two men took pause, somewhat startled by his presence, then almost swayed to anger by his intrusion.

"Are you Magistrate McConnell?"

"What is the meaning of this interruption?" The militia lord asked.

"Yes, yes, I'm McConnell—"

"Then we have business—"

"See me at my office –and during office hours when I return to work in three weeks' time."

"I'm afraid, that my business won't wait for your recess."

McConnell's temperament seemed to change, "As a member of the civil administration, I decide when I am available to the people and when I am not and right now sir, I am unavailable. Now, be off before I have my men remove you."

"Your men outside are dead!" Newcastle moved his head and as he motioned in the direction of Nighthorse over at the bar, Nighthorse raised his fist into the candlelight to reveal three bloody scalps….

The militia commander seemed jarred, "Who are you? A land agent?"

"No, merely an agent from The Venger."

His eyes went wide –and he moved for his weapon just as there was a sudden flash and blast from Newcastle's gun. The blast blew the top of his skull off as his body collapsed back on his bench, next to the fire… dead.

A gun was suddenly pointed at the barkeeper to keep him in his place.

McConnell froze, hands up. He slowly put his words together, "Fire another shot and every person within the county will come running."

"Not tonight."

"So that's it then, you mean to assassinate me."

"Yes." Newcastle said in a direct manner as he pulled a second pistol and as he did, panic shook McConnell…

"Now, wait a moment---" He pleaded as the situation became both real and definitive.

BAMMM! The blast put a lead ball through his neck, shattering the picture behind him. He stood for a moment, trying to speak –but his voice box was now splattered all over the wall behind him—and then he fell forward to the floor.

Newcastle and his men cleared the tavern and as they did, Brom turned the money over. Newcastle then took a look around, the landscape was completely deserted, not a soul to be seen. "Looks like the rumors I asked you to spread, paid off." He smiled.

"Yes, with help from you man's action tonight" Brom replied, he turned and looked down the dark highway. "Here comes your man now."

And out of the shadows rode a frightening, ghost-like figure –a headless figure—in a burned and tarnished military uniform. This headless rider galloped out of the darkness, pulled the reigns, and brought the horse to heel just under the lantern light. Then, suddenly, the shoulders, cape and jacket were removed revealing Johnny Kay underneath. His small proportions matched with a wooden rig that fit on his shoulders so he could wear the overcoat in a way that made him look indeed --headless! Like a cannon ball had taken this rider's head clean off. "That's that, then!" Kay said, "Every farmer and shopkeeper for six leagues is hiding in the shadows of their own home, bolted behind their doors –scared to death the come outside" He smiled.

"Nice work."

"--And if I'm good enough to scare the countryside, then, I'm good enough to be used in a fight hey Newcastle?"

"Gun section."

"What?" He said in angry disappointment.

"You heard me, Kay."

"Damn officers!"

"Take it up with Harrow when we get back to the ship, I'm sure he'd love to hear all about it. Shore leave is just about over in any event." Newcastle then turned to Brom. "Here," he threw the costume to him, "Just in case you ever need to scare the local population with a headless ghost again." He smiled.

TWO YEARS LATER

BACK ON THE DECKS OF THE VENGER

There was lightning on the horizon. Merciless climbed down the rigging as the first rains hit the deck. I helped Archer, Manu, and a few others as we prepared the deck for the storm. We tied everything down and tied guidelines so one could hold onto something while working from bow to stern. I finished my coffee by the deck galley window and with a nod from Merciless, I took my shift and started my climb to the crow's nest.

Less than an hour later, Newcastle, the ship's 'storm rider' was at the helm with both hands on the wheel. The wind was already howling and so was he, as the ship gained speed and descended down a massive wave --he would hold tight to the wheel and scream like the Viking God of War...

The storm started to make things difficult to say the least. I had to ride the crow's nest as bigger --and bigger-- waves rolled underneath us. I would shift my position –and was even lifted off my feet as the ship slid down the face of a wave then, I'd hold on --for dear life-- as we rode up the face of another, water splashing our decks. I was then thrown forward, out of the crow's but caught by my harness which choked the air from my lungs. As the ship shifted, I was thrown to the left and then to the right before I could grab hold and try to climb back into my post. Whitney reached out for me as the storm suddenly lunged the ship –and us— forward. He extended his arm. "Come on Reed." He shouted as he reached out, "Grab hold!"

As I swung from the left and back to the right again, in my harness, I looked down at the men on the deck below -like ants moving around the lantern light- then I looked back up to Whitney, reached out as I swung past him and grabbed his hand. He heaved me up as we hit another wave that slammed me against the crow's nest and over its railing back inside with a slam to the floor. Coughing and in pain, I tried to roll off my back and I slowly got to my feet. "Good God!" I said, "Am I alive?"

Whitney smiled, "Yes" he nodded. "You're alive. For now."

At the end of my watch, I washed below deck with a lot of water. Here, under the lanterns some of our ship mates were playing music to lighten the mood and get us through the weather. Water was already dripping below from the deck above. I moved forward, Rajiv and his men had housed the cannons in place and gun doors were closed and sealed. The ship would creak as it would rise on a wave, shift, and drop down swiftly….

And the weather only got worse….

"I was once on a ship that capsized in a storm like this," I said.

Duncan-Howe froze, mid-action, stuffing tobacco in his pipe, alarmed.

"Damn Reed! What are you trying to do to us?" Irons said, mad that I mentioned such a thing under these conditions….

I was nervous about the conditions but, I'd look around the deck, as the ship rocked, and I'd see scenes of relative calm. The Moors were at prayer, Lynch was drawing, Jack-Karr was asleep in his bunk and some of the ronin were quietly playing the game GO under a lantern, and I saw Mako and Sanjuro invite young Pharaoh to sit and learn the game, acting as if there was no storm at all.

The night watch made up of Bons, Hayte, Lau, Locksley, Rabal and a few others, marched past me, and up the steps into the storm, unafraid as a bolt of lightning struck close by and lit the hatchway up…

"Monsters strike in a storm…" Dax-Varrow said, cautious as more water came through the deck panels from above. "The Kraken! The bottom of the ocean is a graveyard, littered with sunken ships and men, who march the reefs and dark ocean floor as ghosts, trapped under the waves of the sea!" He looked at me in the lantern light, "Bad luck to go down during a storm."

I made it over to the galley, late that evening for coffee, took a seat and started a dialogue with Mister Hobby when Mister Teague suddenly came below deck and appeared at the galley deck window. He dropped a mug into a bucket of coffee and drank. "Damn-it-to-hell Hobby!" he suddenly barked, "The coffee's gone cold!"

"Apologies Mister Teague, if you'll give me but a moment, I'll remedy the situation with a new bucket."

Teague gave a nod and held his post. Rain was blowing in through the window where he stood…

"It's the devil out there tonight Mister Teague" Rorry said referring to the storm as he unloaded bread from the stove. He cut a piece for Mister Teague, but Teague waved it off...

"The Devil and I have always been close." He said in a low voice with wicked confidence, "And if it's a storm to take my life –then it will have to be a storm much meaner than this."

Hobby smiled as did I and so did Teague, slightly, for it was his way to stamp fear out of us. All things to him were survivable. Once the new coffee bucket was placed before him, he filled his mug and took a sip. "Aye, good work Hobby. Good thing you have Rorry here to keep this galley running in proper form."

Rorry smiled and Teague went back out on deck...

Mister Hobby could see my mind wandering as he threw a plate of bacon in front of me. "What is it lad?" He handed me a mug of coffee...

"I-I was curious, I heard a story about him, Mister Teague and--"
Hobby made a frown and nodded no. Rorry appeared concerned and silent. "Best not to ask boy." Hobby said, "Here upon the Venger and man's past is his own affair, and we are not to judge him by it."

I gave a nod and agreed to this principle even if curiosity was my devil....

The next few days the ship pitched on the waves. Sea sickness forced some to run for the deck but for the most part, we made it through....

The waves slowed and the rain eventually stopped, the rolling slowed down and steadied. The skies cleared and that evening I went below deck and as I walked through the weapons sections, I saw Teague with some of his platoon, making lead rounds over a fire and sharpening his blades with sparks blasting in every direction. I'm not sure where my sudden courage came from –perhaps my easy conversation with Newcastle-- but out came my question without stammering or fear. "They say you took the head of a judge." I suddenly said to him.

Teague stopped sharpening his cutlass, remained still, and looked at me, the lantern light hiding most of his features in the shadows and his eyes appeared almost black. "And what do you say?" He asked in direct fashion...

Now came the fear for some reason and I stumbled to repeat the ship's principles, "I believe a man's past is his own and therefore we should leave him be with it...."

"A sound principle to be sure." He put his blade back against the block and continued his work as the sparks went flying.

"You must forgive me...as a schoolteacher, I am always curious." And with that Teague cracked a slight grin for it became evident that curiosity was the point --if people wondered about this man and the limits of his temper, then, that was a good thing in this business.

"A man arrives...five minutes before he arrives." Teague said. "Understand?"

I did in fact understand.

He then added a wicked touch of psychology, "Stay awake in the dark and wonder if I'm coming to kill you or not." Teague then turned his dark, black eyes towards his blade and continued to sharpen his cutlass, content to make one wonder if he would strike out of the shadows or let one pass...

I was grateful when Mister Arson moved through the deck, stopped the conversation, and put us on task, "To your stations, this is a warship, not a tea party."

I regripped my coffee mug and began to move on, "Thank you for the nightmares, Mister Teague."

At dawn, there was an early morning mist with moisture in the air. Therrinfall had been up all night again and looked tired....

I finished working in the galley serving breakfast and as I finished, I took a plate for myself and sat down next to Ward, Lau and Irons who was asleep –head on the table--after his night watch. Ward said Irons 'had the gift' as a former cavalry officer he could sleep anywhere, against anything.

From my table, as I started to eat I watched Calixto working with his bolas...

"That's a south American weapon." Ward said as if he detected my curiosity. "Calixto learned to use it when he was stationed there. But I've seen it in other places…." He said as he continued to eat…

"Where?"

"At the top of the Pacific, there's a land covered in ice. The natives there call themselves Inuit –tough bastards—they use that weapon as well. It's a mean piece of work."

"Inuit. I have read about them." I chewed…

"Yeah. They build houses out of bricks of ice and live in a place where it could be dark for most of the hours of the day or several weeks at a time. Tough people! Savage place!" He looked at me, "I'll never go back there…."

What Ward was doing at the top of the Pacific Ocean? I was told he was a missionary once upon a time and had traveled north through the Canadas, to the top of the Pacific seeking passage to the land of Czars. A place called Siberia but, in hearing him talk about it, I could not help but wonder why a man would desire to make that journey. Mattis said that Ward's ship became locked in the ice in a place called 'The Straight' and the crew turned cannibal after a time, and he escaped and ventured out on foot until he almost died. Fortunately, he was saved by some natives who used a sled powered by a team of dogs to drag him to safety then, gradually back to life….

Four weeks and two days in, the fog cleared, and we made sight of the continent…. From the top deck, I got my first glimpse of Africa in the distance --and it was magnificent. The heat was stifling but the air was different. Addo seemed quite happy to see this place again for he double-timed his work on deck, and he hummed a little louder….

I climbed down the ropes and hit the deck amid a crowd of liberated slaves at the rail and as I slowly moved through their ranks, I realized what we had done –I could feel what we had done--for there, they stood. staring at the coastline, some clutching their children close. Others just stared in reverence at a land –a home—they never thought they would see again.

A slight surge of emotion took hold of me as I moved down the deck, looking at the coastline with a half-smile. I got to the quarter deck and even though the target had been called out, I sill said: "Africa Captain!"

"Indeed, it is Mister Reed." Essex replied without looking up from his navigational tools at his map table....

"It's Africa." I said again...

"Do you realize we're in Africa yet Mister Reed?" Harrow asked from the wheel as Archer maintained command of our direction.

"I do sir." Just then Raeder passed me on his way from the quarter deck. "We made it." I smiled.

"Aye" He looked at the continent then back to me, "Maybe we're saviors after all."

In North Africa, I went ashore in an Arabian marketplace, intense heat, sweat and an architectural blend of European design mixed with the African frontier outlined the horizon. This was a wild and lively place. Elephants carried men and supplies on their backs. Camels were sold near the docks and festive, lively music from the region was on every street...

Blacksmiths were working with spark and steel on the corner. Blacksmiths didn't just work on horseshoes, they also worked on ship parts and weapons. Blades could get bent when they struck human bone, and a blacksmith could hammer it back into place with a little heat. Many of these smiths were former privateers now wounded and earning a living ashore --so they had their combat stories.

This place –Algeria-- was a colonial possession of the French and there was a presence of French soldiers in the street but, they wore a unique uniform different from the other French marines or soldiers I had encountered. This division of troops was called the 'Foreign Legion', and it was made up of all different nationalities ---many rumored to be criminals-- who sought a new life and identity or, French citizenship through service in this military unit. This base in North Africa was their headquarters, this was their territory.

I saw Mister Jaffar and Nighthorse –who both spoke French-- conversing with some of these unique soldiers. It was a conversation I could barely hear –and not understand-- but it looked like some sort of agreement had been struck for the conversation ended with a round of handshakes...

At the docks, I waited and there was a great deal of commerce –and dust-- in the streets. Mister Harrow emerged from the crowd and ordered Daws to pull his flags from the case on his back and use them to signal the ship to bring the harbor tax ashore and release the crew for shore leave....

--The Africans would not get freedom just yet. They would have to remain on board for the time being so they would not be captured and re-purposed in the marketplace.

After Newcastle supervised the off-loading of provisions, the long boats brought the cargo to our docks. Dax-Varro, Bons, Sanjuro, Rabal, Barak and some of the others heaved it onto the planks –several barrels of whale oil, sacks of sugar, and a small chest from our onboard treasury –our general fund-- from which all business of this sort was transacted, under the accounting and inventory of Mister Lincoln. This 'harbor tax' allotment was to be divided into two with a portion for the local French Governor and half to the local Muslim Cleric who –it was rumored—controlled a great part of the population....

We knotted and fashioned big nets out of rope and with some local help we heaved our tax load onto the backs of several elephants for they were the only beasts who could move cargo through the terrain outside the town, to the cleric....

That afternoon, Mister Jaffar, on orders from Mister Harrow, pressed some local guides into service and we –as armed escort-- moved our caravan off into the horizon. Mister Bishop was on the back of the lead elephant, Watson and I marched next to this beast, down through the sand and through a green waterway, knee deep...

The sweat was stinging my eyes, but I found this place –the topography— with the plants, trees, and the sounds amazing to comprehend. I stopped for a moment and looked around as giant birds scattered from a tree then and as I found myself being left behind, I stepped up my pace and caught up with Watson…

"I don't mean to offer offense but, why do we pay the harbor tax?" I suddenly asked as we waded through the water….

Watson marched, one hand on the handle of his sword, the other – former hand—now a hook by his side. He looked at me with his left eye—his right closed by the sun. "How do you mean?"

"I mean why do we pay the tax? Is it a law or something because, we're the only crew I've ever seen, do it?"

Suddenly Mister Harrow interrupted as he marched past us, "What's all this talk?"

"The Prime Minster here is seeking an education in the harbor tax Mister Harrow…." Watson said with a spit and a grin as he continued forward…

"What about the harbor tax?"

"I-I know what it is, and I believe I know why we pay it –but we're the only ones I've seen make offer of it?"

"It's a business practice we like to keep to ourselves…."

"But why?"

"Since it's our philosophy to make you the best shipmate we can, I'll educate you…. The harbor tax is payment –advanced payment—for freedom of the township, local protection and for any information that may pertain to our business…."

"Such as?"

"Such as, one: information on any potential target, such as treasure ships in the area or any treasure ship that may have recently departed along with information on their present course, crew and weaponry. The harbor masters give that information to the local authorities, the local authorities give it to us. The tax also pays for your protection Mister Reed—should you run afoul of the law while you are here. The tax is your fine and payment so our trained and valued crew mates can stay out of prison and avoid the hangman. And should any of the colonial authorities arrive here looking for us, the harbor tax impairs any memory of our visit, if you get my meaning. In simple terms, it's good business boy…"

"Does that answer your question, Minister Reed?" Watson smiled, with a piece of long grass in between his teeth.

I nodded yes but now was made to wonder if Prime Minister was the latest friendly insult or my new nick name.

We made it through the edge of a small village, across another wide – but shallow—water canal and down a sand bank where we were stopped by a sentry, in robes and on the back of a camel. He had a musket across one arm and raised his other hand to order us to halt. Once we stopped, he removed the wrap from his face and gave us a peaceful greeting "As-salāmu ʿalaykum" – which I came to learn meant 'Peace be upon you.' But it was also code for 'What is your business here?'

Mister Jaffar gave a response in kind, "waʿalaykumu s-salām."

From there, it was business. We had the tax and we, after a brief description of our intentions, were allowed to pass. We marched forward into a patch of tents under some palm trees, by an oasis. Here we cut the cargo down and delivered it. The hospitality of the Muslim community was of a very polite and serious nature. Upon arrival we removed our boots and entered a tent where we were considered guests –something taken quite seriously in Muslim society-- and with a clap of the cleric's hands, we were offered tea and food which was presented to us by the women of this community…

We were told it was rude not to accept, so we did and although it was exotic –lamb meat, rice with some sort of leaves-- I actually found it to be quite delicious.

We were also allowed to rest and remain for as long as we wanted and –as guests we could make any request although none of our number took any liberties. After a brief discussion and exchange of formalities, the Cleric presented us with some gifts and said, "To your Captain with my compliments and please, thank him for his kindness and generous contribution."

"I will sir and thank you." True to his character, Harrow rose to his feet and made our visit friendly but short. We had been given fresh water, food stuffs and some silks and blankets in return for our 'donation.' This was the first time to date that our tax garnished an immediate return, and we climbed the backs of the elephants for the march back to the township. I had never been on –or even seen—an elephant before this day. I knew about Hannibal and the Alps, and the power of these beasts made me quite aware that that campaign was not fiction –but fact—Hannibal had crossed the mountains on elephants to invade Rome.

Once back in town, we passed our gun crews as they worked their way through the streets. Tane –from the islands of the South Pacific—Rajiv, Locke, Kipling, Gerard who had purchased –or impounded—a hookah that he was smoking from as he carried it, Wilder with the monkey on his back and the others, taking in food and drink and partaking in some of the local 'entertainment.' We passed on their invitations to join them for the time being for we had to report back to the Captain.

Harrow and our party found Essex at a table under a large canvass tent in a tobacco shop close to the water's edge but as we approached there was a sudden commotion. We all turned as two Captains marched up to us, Armitage from Wales, and Rochambeau from Le Harve on the French channel coast for what appeared to be a duel…

"Ah, I was hoping I'd find you here Essex, I need a second." Armitage threw his hat like a disc across the sand and pulled his pistol to check it.

"Spare me Armitage, for I've only been in port a day and I have no need to witness this folly."

"Folly? This? This Frenchman has insulted our King."

Essex turned as Rochambeau stepped up, "Good afternoon, Essex."

"Rochambeau." He paused as he sized up his silhouette in front of the sun, "Good to see you."

"You as well."

"I thought you were in Havana."

"I was but, the Spanish authorities, you see…such an angry lot at times. I'm afraid, I wore out my welcome."

Essex smiled. "As we all do from time to time."

"Are you just going to sit there Essex? This man got in the way of my afternoon drinking and insulted our King."

Essex looked back at him, "He's not my King."

Armitage looked confused, "He's not your-- damn it man! You may have gone rogue but you're still an Englishman."

"He's not my King. I have no King." And he added under his breath, "Nor will I ever have again."

"Well, he's my King by God and this man insulted him so stand and witness as my second." And he rechecked his gun and took a few steps out onto the beach.

"All I said was that your King exploited the populace and plans to being genocide to his colonies." Rochambeau held his hands out as if to offer no offense.

"Sounds right enough." Essex agreed.

"Damn it all. Have you all gone mad?" Armitage continued to bark.

"Don't you gentleman have something better to do with your time." Essex asked.

"Not me. This is it."

Essex looked to Rochambeau, "You too?"

"My honor is now at stake." Rochambeau smiled and took to the sand. "Shall we say ten paces?"

"Agreed," Armitage replied.

"Very well" and Rochambeau raised a pistol and pulled the hammer back.

"Essex?"

Essex went back to what he was doing, uninterested.

"Perhaps you, Mister Harrow would be good enough to--"

"Captain Armitage, you are a man of some quality, but I can't abide dueling... least of all over an offense such as this."

"Have all of your men gone insane Essex?"

"Afraid so. You want to kill this man, that's your business --none of us will stand in for you."

Armitage then looked to Rochambeau with a look of slight embarrassment, "Perhaps we can rely on one's honor in this case, Captain Rochambeau?"

"Of course." and the two captains turned back-to-back and started to pace off...

One...

Two...

Three....

Once they reached ten paces out, they turned and fired but both missed! And at that, they both followed the 'old rules' and pulled their swords and moved in where they banged together and engaged.

--Harrow looked exhausted –and bored—watching it. Essex didn't look up from his reading.

Another clash, Armitage swung across as Rochambeau stepped back and then thrust his cutlass forward. Another 'clang' Rochambeau swung down as Armitage moved to his left to avoid damage and he let out a laugh as if proud of himself only to be caught suddenly in the arm as Rochambeau swung back.

"Damn." Armitage looked down as blood soaked his sleeve from the shoulder...

"That's it!" Essex stood up. "In accordance with the old rules, blood has been drawn. That's the end of it."

"So, it is." Armitage exhaled, he wiped the sweat from his brow and put out his hand for Captain Rochambeau. "Well done."

Rochambeau shook hands with this captain, and now with this work done he said, "Please accept my apologies."

"Indeed sir. A drink then?"

"Yes of course."

"A damn fool business." Essex grumbled as the two Captains moved off to a tavern on the beach.

Harrow closed in. "I didn't realize we still did duels."

"There's an idiot in every port Harrow. How was your visit with Ali?"

"Polite as usual. He sent back some gifts."

"Did he? Divide it among the crew who has gone above and beyond as a thank you for their service—and make sure to include Hobby so he knows his work is appreciated."

"I will." Harrow turned to the ship sitting off the beach. "What about our guests sir?"

Essex turned and looked back at the ship....

"We could bring them to the beach, protect them with a shore party."

"And invite a fight with any slavers here? Two-hundred slaves in the Algerian economy would welcome some cutthroat attention –and could start a war." He shook his head, "Best leave them aboard for now and keep their presence quiet."

Harrow nodded...

"Still...let's not stay here long."

That night, as the Captain was a half-bottle into his evening and losing a game of chess to Mister Jaffar, a North African rider rode out of the dust on the back of a camel and arrived at the Captain's command tent on the beach.

The rider was stopped by our sentries --Merciless and Kannon-- and identified himself as a messenger from Cleric Ali on the High Plain. Essex waved him forward and the rider dismounted and bowed. He used the customary greeting and Essex returned in kind and asked –in Arabic-- if the rider wanted anything to eat or drink. The rider declined –and just as Harrow arrived from a tavern at the edge of town sensing something amiss and coughing up rum, the messenger presented a scroll.

"What is it sir?"

The captain unrolled the scroll and began to read it, "Our good Cleric pays us in kind," he turned the scroll so Harrow could see it. "Word just reached him from a village to the south of the Wadi that a French trading convoy is on their way to Mozambique. Four days head start...."

"They most likely need to stop and resupply off the Ivory Coast we could catch them off San Pedro...."

"If we leave now."

"Aye, if we leave now."

"How long to resupply?"

"Four days, maybe five."

Essex nodded. "Give the order for a rapid departure...."

Harrow turned, "Mister Lincoln?" he yelled down the beach for our quartermaster who turned, mug in hand, from a circle of musicians around him. "Rapid evacuation if you please...."

And Lincoln scrambled....

The Captain then stood and looked to Mister Jaffar, "You're a lucky man, Mister Jaffar," he motioned to the chess board, "this business has just saved you from immediate defeat here—"

Jaffar just shook his head well aware that the Captain was about to lose but let it be.

"If any of your Moor brothers in this township wish to offer up their services, now would be the time, we could use the replacements."

Jaffar bowed and then dismissed himself to carry out his task. He would later make the beach with nine more volunteer replacements –all Moors – all armed with curved swords, guns and robed and marked with a particular silence that I had come to know as a sort of trademark for the Moors. One, named Shaddam was very large and 'head-length' above the rest of us. Another, named Mandagan the V –or Fifth-- carried not one but two curved swords. He had scars up both forearms, I came to learn, that he had a personal code, similar to Mister Barak, to not put his swords away until they drew blood so every time he would practice, he would cut his arm before he could put it in his sheath....

Others carried the names Volkan. Ozan, Laban and Khan El something or other –for now, just Khan. An intriguing lot.

Essex asked Newcastle, Daws and myself to add some hands to the resupply effort for we still had a lot of people on board to feed so we supervised, as long boat after long boat arrived with water, sugar, gun powder until deep into sunset. This work continued through the night and into dawn the next day and it would continue beyond that without a recess until we were reloaded and ready.

Four nights later, aboard The Venger, I watched Jaffar –and Barak-- talk to our Captain at the helm. Once the conversation had ended, Jaffar nodded and walked down the deck to my position, he ordered me, Jagger, Toombs, and Wicks into a launch, then looked across to Mister Lynch, sketching under the lantern light by the main mast—and asked him to join us as well. We climbed down the ropes and boarded the long boat and we rowed silently towards shore. What our mission was, I did not know but, I felt an improved sense of confidence because I was asked to take part –and by one with such respect as Mister Jaffar commanded—for this had me convinced that my standing with the crew was improving....

When we made the shoreline, we kept the boat in the tide, and we waited in silence. Moments later, a few figures emerged from the darkness, members of the Foreign Legion including the men Jaffar had spoken with when we first made port. They wished to defect from the legion and use The Venger as a way off the continent. There were six in all under the command of a corporal named Le Clerk --I would later come to know them as veterans of foreign wars from all over the French Empire, including Central Africa, The Canadas and Europe. Now, they would fight under a new flag --the skull and bones.

They climbed aboard and with their assistance we rowed back to the ship. We worked our way up the rigging to the top deck where Mister Arson met them and gave a statement on what was to be expected and under Mister Lincoln's supervision, one at a time, they each placed their hand on 'Lucifer's skull' and then signed the articles of conduct.

"Your old government no longer exists" Lincoln said, "This code and these men here --the crew of The Venger-- are now your king and country. Understand?"

Le Clerk and the others nodded.

"Now report to Mister Harrow for your duties."

We then made preparations to make sail. I found, in my subsequent conversations, that men found the French Foreign Legion a hard life –as if designed to get them killed. Many were criminals or prisoners of war and as such considered expendable by the Crown. I was also told that if they tried to desert on the continent, that they would be hunted for weeks or months and –if caught—would be dragged back to face a firing squad so, defection by sea gave these men the best chance to escape. They were qualified for war, unlike myself who was unknown to this art when I joined, these men had seen more than their share of combat so, they were assigned –based on a short conversation about their experience-- to different sections and divisions of the ship. Two –Lambert and Favreau-- to the gunnery section under the command of Mister Rajiv because they had fought in a French artillery battery. The other four –Roux, Laurent, Giroux, and German named Blix-- all former infantry men, were for the deck where we needed replacements and there, we would eventually find out what caliber these men actually were….

We set sail in darkness, and we sailed down the African coast making the best possible speed. I would have preferred more time in Algeria given the time invested in crossing the Atlantic but every move we made unfolded with more and more interest so I could offer no argument when we departed –not that I had any say in the matter.

XIII

BACK FROM THE DEAD

We ventured down the coast and on the sixth day, we spotted a ship in the distance under a British flag. It was obviously not part of the French convoy we were after but, we would seal this ship's doom none the less....

The tactics of The Venger were always the same, trail behind a target under a neutral flag at reduced speed until nightfall, then cut loose, gain a few knots, close in –run up the black flag-- and strike from the dark. This attack was to be no different. The Captain preferred to time his attack to just before dawn so the opposing ship's crew would not have all their wits about them...

We maintained an order for complete silence as we closed in and when we were less than a league away from our target, we could hear the crew – or passengers—on the ship's decks talking, singing, or carousing as we approached. For whatever reason, the Captain preferred not to use a broadside bombardment this time –though our 'gun tigers' were at their stations and ready.

Our target was unaware of us closing in, until we slammed alongside her and seemed to almost tip her over, throwing the crews from their hammocks and cots. Their watch, above in the crow's nest, must have been asleep for he tumbled out and fell into the ocean. Moments later, we were already on her deck. The first wave of our boarding party was quick to the quarter deck, when their officers emerged from their quarters still trying to get their uniforms on. There at the wheel, this Captain found himself surrounded by our cutlass blades and muskets. He was bewildered and shocked as Mister Harrow approached from the darkness, "Who's in command here?"

"I am sir, Captain Avery of Sussex. Master of The Ballantrae." He was nervous and somewhat in shock as he watched our men plunge below deck for a search....

"I congratulate you Captain," Harrow began, "On managing to keep your crew and passengers alive. You have a man overboard –your lookout—with your permission, we'll retrieve him."

He gave a nod and stood there, a dejected man. This officer had a look of shame on his face. How can he face his masters back in England, cargo and ship lost without even a fight?

Our men were already starting to move through the lower decks and hold. Captain Avery watched this and motioned to ask Harrow, "Sir, if you'd permit me. I will offer you our ship's manifest and cargo, but I request I be allowed to retain my ship for I am on a mission—"

"Retain your ship?"

"It's my first captaincy sir, to lose it to pirates— "

"DO NOT CALL US THAT!" Harrow barked.

Captain Avery seemed to reposition himself at attention out of fear. "I am sorry—I-I"

Harrow regained his temperament and continued, "Look lad, you saved the lives of all onboard. There's no shame in that but, there the victory ends!" He watched as our men emerged back on deck with some of the ship's inventory. The unloading had begun. "Go back to England" Harrow continued, "And regale your audience in the local pub with tales of heroism and survival at the hands of privateers! But your ship is ours." Harrow then turned to us, "Stand by to put his crew into the long boats."

At that, this Captain looked down to the panels with a touch of almost sadness. He now appeared to be a broken man and he started to make his way back to his cabin...

We set about our work. We pulled the lookout from the water, opened up the cargo bays and stormed the cabins for anything and everything of value. We used rope and pulleys and started to move the captured cargo to The Venger one load at a time when suddenly--

--THERE WAS AN EXPLOSION!

--Blowing out the glass of the quarter deck windows below. The captain had killed himself with a grenade! We looked over the aft rail as the smoke rose out over the ocean....

The report reached Mister Harrow. "Damn fool!"

"What's worse, the blast blew a hole below the water line...." Hallock stated from the entrance to the deck below....

"Can we pump her out?"

"Yes."

"Do it then....and get the first mate of this ship up here now" Harrow commanded.

Mister Rabal and Mister Lynch brought the first mate forward.

"Your name?"

"Briggs sir."

"Very well Mister Briggs, we're taking your ship. You and a skeleton crew will remain aboard and help us sail to the nearest port, in exchange you and your crew will receive a share of the profits from the auction block—and you will live. Now, we expect no mischief from you. Give us any trouble and we'll blow you and your ship to hell. Understand?"

"Yes sir." This man had grasped the threat as real.

"Do I need to make an example of my intentions?"

"No sir."

"Good, Mister Rabal here and small contingent will remain on board, their authority supersedes your own." He looked to Mister Rabal, "Rabal, pick your boarding party."

Rabal nodded and then nominated Blythe, Sterling, Takeda, Bons, Tak, Mister Hayte, Clairmont, Abel, De Leon, Standish, Addo, Jagger, Wicks, Therrinfall, Merciless, Bolt, Fury, Dax-Varro, Hallock and Sampson-Rift to retain their weapons and hold post onboard this craft....

"You stand here." Hayte directed a sailor to the wheel. "Move only in a direction I tell you. Do not try me for if you do, this will be the last post you ever serve."

Below decks, Baako, Gordon and Roux –the former French Legionnaire—pressed the crew into some repair work and we stopped the flooding below deck using canvas, blocks, and a hammer. Mister Sunderland ordered some hands to the pump, and we began to pump the water out of the hold. An hour later, Baako reported the ship as stable, and we prepared to make sail….

Two days later….

We arrived at the coastal town of Rio De Oro. Here, we did as promised, the ship was turned over to the Harbor Master who, in exchange for a share, took it off our hands for the next day's auction. We put to shore briefly for supplies and once loaded were allowed a night in town…

There was one more bit of business, the landing of our liberated slaves. We had twenty-six new volunteers from their ranks, but the rest had to be put ashore soon and this raised a debate, would they know how to traverse this continent back to their homes? Would they be safe there? Would slavers find them again? Or had we done enough, and should we now leave it to them to figure it out on their own?

"It doesn't matter what we do," Kannon said just as he tested a musket ball in his teeth. "Leave 'em here or drop them on the doorstep of their village –it's of little consequence. As long at the trade exists, they'll always be in danger."

Maybe it was their sense of excitement to be close to home, but they clearly preferred to take the risk and try to make their way back. Baako reported that some of the men in the group could lead these people back to their villages even though –by our own estimation—their villages may be three hundred leagues away or more…

Essex deferred to Mister Baako, Jupiter and Addo and he remained silent in this matter –Manu and Obal also had some say and all agreed that the liberated slaves stood the best chance to make their way from here --

the Port of Dakar-- for further south were the slave ports and the slave traders were very aggressive in moving though that part of the continent. But, if they moved east to Spanish Africa, where the trade was outlawed, then south to the frontier, they might just make it.

Manu requested his dismissal from our service in order to serve as a sort of guide or protector. Two other men from our crew –both Africans-- wanted to go too and also requested to be released. Essex agreed to let them go and he also agreed to arm the liberated slaves and equip them with food and water to help them with this venture and with that, we started to put them ashore just south of the township so they could start to cross the country towards home…

As we rowed through the waves and tide, I looked at the faces of our guests and it was true, an expression can tell you all you need to know. Many conveyed a look of apprehension. Some appeared to smile with excitement.

I took a long, captivated look at a young woman '–Would her mother still be there when she ran back to her home? Would the mother cry at the vision of her child running back into her arms having once feared the worst?'

–It was obvious that many never expected to see this country again and that a miracle had happened here –executed by the most unlikely of heroes. Men who few—if any—expected any shred of good or decency yet they defied logic in this regard.

Valor may rise from combat or valor may rise from circumstance, but one can never underestimate the human spirit. Any man may rise up and surprise you when a unique set of circumstances are on the line. The world may say one bad thing after another about the men of The Venger but here, I witnessed something special, something few could have achieved, something noble and something that above all …was life changing. The future of the people here, even generations from now, would be different, lives and destinies would be completely different. From the shackle to the open sky there was now a sense of promise....

We pulled the long boats ashore and helped them disembark. From the water, I watched them walk up the beach and start off into the rising sun, Manu turned to us and raised his hand in farewell, I found myself waving back though he and I spoke hardly a word on the ship but, I could not help but feel some happiness in this moment –and pride in what we had done, and this made me I smile…

--I smiled, hit by a thunderbolt of emotion –not just by this act of kindness but the knowledge and awareness this act triggered --a new almost religious sense of purpose, I was like someone back from the dead with a renewed sense of life. However dismissive the men of The Venger may be about this deed—I felt the impact and for the first time in my life I had a clear vision of the world around me. The laws that make us. The economy and society that shapes us –it was all wrong! The world I had been a part of was wrong –wicked and evil and built that way to exploit all of us. Strange how it never seemed to affect me before, how I never seemed aware of it until now--and it took this moment here, this visual, this first-hand experience to make a blind man see.

"Why are you smilin' Reed?" Arson barked from the rudder.

"Because I'm proud." I confessed unaware of who I may offend and unconcerned if I looked weak. "I'm proud of what we've done. Proud of myself, us --proud of even you Mister Arson."

Arson took a moment to size me up, "Well… for God sakes just don't smile, it will ruin our reputation for bein' frightening and scary."

I let out a laugh, shook my head and smiled with even more emotion, for I did not care. "No sir, you can't ruin our reputation with this. This is too good a moment and –if anything—this action here has made my reputation."

–The slave trade was a dirty business but, I was surrounded by the heroes who would help bring that system down.

The next day, at dawn –after a serious celebration in town the night before-- Mister Baltimore and Toombs found me under the palm trees where I had fallen asleep and I was ordered to report to the customs house where Mister Obal, Roux, Dakar, Nighthorse, Blythe, Tak and Irons formed a defensive ring around the building. I entered and walked into the inside loading dock to find, Mister Jagger, Teague, Jata, Standish, Hallock, Lynch, Sunderland, Calixto, Miranda, De Leon, Baako and a few others under the command of Mister Newcastle down by the water's edge and there we stood watch as the Harbor Master's men opened up the warehouse doors to reveal a hundred sacks of gold coins…

"Good God!" I found myself saying almost as a reflex for it was more money than I had ever seen in my life.

"Aye" Standish said from close by, "It does make one find religion, doesn't it?"

The Harbor Master and his men took their share then, we checked and loaded each sack into iron boxes which we locked, the keys were put in the custody of Mister Newcastle and we brought the boxes --all ten-- down to the boats at the inside dock and we began to row them out of the building –through the water way doors—outside the building, down the canal and towards the ocean and the ship….

Once we arrived, Sanjuro, Addo and some of our African partners pulled the ropes and heaved the boxes aboard. Mister Lincoln made the inventory and did the math in terms of division. As we all gathered around, he reported the 'share' amount to the Captain who made the announcement on the total profit, and this was met by excitement from all hands with fists in the air –this was a good day.

One, such as myself, had to think for a moment on the Buddhist concept of karma. That fate –and destiny—was the result of one's previous actions. To be plain, I had just had a hand in reuniting families on this continent and now I was –in a modest sense—a rich man.

Half of the money was to be cached to our treasury, the other half to be divided among the crew immediately and at that time, the former First Mate of The Ballantrae, Briggs, who we promoted to Captain --though Rabal was the real acting Captain—was given his share as promised –and a share for his crew who assisted in sailing the ship without conflict. It was more money than many of them made in a year….

Briggs appeared grateful although he had a slight look of bewilderment and he asked Mister Harrow, "Should I—should I return home? I-I mean with this" He raised his hands that held his gold.

"That decision is yours but, if you do go back, may I suggest a low profile upon your return."

"Is this ship --are you headed to England?"

Harrow turned, "I'll never see England again boy."

Mister Addo stopped Briggs, "We're preparing to set sail, are you going ashore?"

He seemed to have no answer. He looked over the rail to the town of Dakar. The city, this frontier, had many unknowns for this man and he looked to Mister Harrow, "May I remain aboard sir until you reach a more suitable destination?"

Harrow turned, it was true, this man had obeyed orders and delivered the prize –without resistance—to this port and since he did such, he deserved some consideration. Mister Harrow pointed to his money. "You either work your way –or pay your way. Understood?"

"Yes sir."

"See Mister Lincoln on the quarter deck…"

He gave a nod and was off….

Lincoln was going through his books when this man caught his attention…

"Sir, I was told to report to you."

Lincoln looked up….

"Briggs, sir…first mate of the Ballantrae. Your Mister Harrow said you were in need of replacements."

"Prior to our introduction, what was your experience Mister Briggs?"

"I- I was a Naval Academy graduate. I specialized in navigation."

Lincoln spun his registration book around –quill in between the pages, "Sign the articles and report to Mister Thorn at the helm, please…."

He did so as we made sail to continue our move down the coast…

XIV

VENGEANCE ON THE EDGE OF HELL

Six days later there was a war council at the helm, that included our Captain, Mister Harrow, of course, and our primary 'combat captains' and key personnel, including Newcastle, Mister Teague, Jupiter, Mister Jaffar, Mister Thorn, Rajiv, Lo-Tan, Nighthorse, Sanjuro-Tak, Mister Locke, the gunner's mate in battery two and Mister Lynch. We were about to round the coast of Porto Norvo, a slave trading –and shipping—outpost that was part of the Portuguese Empire and we were planning to burn it to the ground....

Porto Norvo was protected on the north side by a fort with massive guns and unlike Panama, this fort was complete and ready for action. There would also be ships at anchor and elements of the Portuguese Navy close by. The township itself was estimated to be about sixty percent military or 'slave administration'. Few, if any families would take residence in such a place and the ones that did must have had relations to the slave trade itself --and because of the slave economy it supported, Porto Norvo was also rumored to have stockpiles of gold.

I watched in the moon and lantern light as the conversation progressed from the deck, a few meters away –and—since there were no real secrets onboard the ship, the conversation was, in a sense, open to the public. At issue was the fort. A pounding match with fixed defenses and a garrison was not promising and any military ships in the harbor could work to dismantle us. Even the aggressive Mister Rajiv was concerned and his mathematics on range, distance, versus gun caliber and size was not inspiring any confidence....

We were fortunate that onboard The Venger, ambition was met with equal parts creative thinking. "Why face the fort at all?" Essex asked, "Why put ourselves in that position?"

Teague, Lo and Jaffar preferred to fight ashore —so did Jagger, Newcastle and Toombs --as was their skill set. So, a daring plan was put forth. Two leagues north of Porto Norvo we would land a shore party at dawn, under the cover of the early morning darkness. They would move through the jungle countryside to the fort and launch a surprise attack at nightfall. Once the fort was taken, The Venger would raise a Portuguese flag, move into the harbor and under the gunnery of Mister Rajiv —and Locke-- destroy any ships docked or at anchor there, then, we would storm ashore and sack the township….

Something was quite different about this war council meeting than the ones previous. The mood was different. There was real disdain for this place and there seemed to be an unforgiving attitude towards it. I got the impression that this mission would be absent from our previous rules and regulations of conduct. There was no forgiving element to be had in this – no charity to be had here.

Teague was to be given command of the shore party and, looking at him, I made the appreciation that he knew exactly how to go about it. He elected some of the more 'fierce' crew members among us, including Jupiter, Baako, Addo and a few of the liberated slaves we had been training since we left the Caribbean, Jaffar and a few of the Moors, Lo-Tan, Mako and two more of the ronin, Nighthorse, Bons, some of the Aztecs, Raeder, Ward, Calixto, who spoke Portuguese, Abel, De Leon, Merciless, Lau, Toombs, Fury, Jagger, Duncan-Howe, Mister Strange, Jack-Karr, Wicks, Irons, Sunderland, Dakar and some sixty others for the mission. I was surprised to find myself among their number for Teague had governed some of my combat training but never betrayed any real admiration for me and --in truth, as reported-- I was in fear of him. None the less, I planned to earn some respect ashore….

Nighthorse applied his war paint. Baako and Addo painted themselves in black body paint then added the white pattern of a skull to their face and bones down their arms and across their ribs. This always made them look vicious –and they had some of their new 'ex-slave conscripts' do the same. For them –our new conscripts—this mission was a reprisal. Addo made it clear to them what the mission was --that part of the very institution that had packed them into crates and brought them to the new world could now be destroyed.

Lo-Tan checked and packed his three-section staff on his back and grabbed his bamboo hat and guns. Calixto packed his bolas. Mako and the ronin put their armor on, tied on their bandanas or, in the case of Tak and Kato, a helmet –then they stopped by their wooden box to clap hands and prey.

Jack-Karr, Ward, Shaddam –the new Moor who was the size of a small house and myself packed grappling hooks and climbing claws. Most of us carried rope over our shoulders --and we all loaded up on pistols and handed out grenades, muskets, and ammunition.

"It's war time!" Karr said with a smile, and we moved out.

We rowed ashore, through an early morning fog and made the beach, with weapons, ropes, grappling hooks, water, grenades, and about two-thousand rounds between us. We immediately made for the tree line and moved into the surrounding jungle. Teague wasted no time, once every man was ashore, he sent out Mister Kon Boar –the Aztec—as a scout and we started our march south. I looked back, through the trees and saw The Venger –flying a Portuguese flag-- in the distance and as we walked farther and farther away from it, I had a thought that I might never see her again....

As we moved through the trees and though a shallow swamp, silence was the order of the day. I looked up to see the early morning sun blinding us through the treetops. Sweat --and moving through a wall of constant heat--had already drenched my tunic. An hour later, Teague suddenly put his fist in the air –the signal for our convoy to stop and immediately we all froze in our places...

Jupiter quietly moved up to him, "What is it?"

Teague pointed ahead several meters where our scout, Kon Boar was standing motionless. Sweat dripped down his face and covered his Jaguar tattoos, but he remained still, like a predator.

"He senses something." Teague said in a low tone. He then used a hand signal to order us to remain in place and he and Jupiter moved up to Kon's position. Kon Boar slowly led them forward through the trees, then pointed ahead to a coastal road maybe sixty meters away where a Portuguese military carriage and a squad of Portuguese troops –and cavalry escort-- were trying to repair a broken wagon wheel. A high-ranking Portuguese officer –fanning himself with a handkerchief—waited for the repair work to be completed and a soldier was holding a parasol over him to help with the mid-day heat…

"I count forty hands" Jupiter whispered as he tallied their ranks. "We can try to go around."

"We either kill them here or kill them in town." Teague replied keeping his voice low. "So, I say we do it now and be done with it."

Jupiter reaffirmed what we all already knew- "If they hear us, if shots are fired or…if anyone gets a way to warn the fort, then this party will be for nothing."

"Let's make sure we're thorough in our work then." Teague then used hand signals and we quietly moved forward to his position and fanned out into an attack line. I watched Mister Nighthorse pull his tomahawk and nod to Mako who pulled a pair of throwing stars. There was no discussion about what was to happen next, everyone knew these men had to be killed, there was no going around it….

Just as a Portuguese soldier stood up from his repair work to wipe the sweat from his brow, several throwing stars came whistling in, killing him, and wounding three others. Several others were killed with Aztec blow guns and a split second later we stormed out of the wilderness, closed in on them and brought down the blades. Nighthorse dropped his tomahawk into a man's skull but could not dislodge it so, he quickly pulled his knife and threw the blade into the back of a Portuguese soldier who was making a run for it.

--For the most part, it was over quick...Except, three soldiers quickly mounted up on horseback and took off to escape towards the township. One rode into Jaffar's curved sword as he stepped out in front of the horse to cut him down --the rider was thrown! The other riders made for the road, Toombs raised his gun, but Raeder slapped it down and pressed his index finger to his lips to signal quiet.

It was Bons and Sanjuro who jumped to mounts and rode off after them at a gallop....

Karr, Jagger and Mako walked over the ranks and speared any survivors with their swords. Nighthorse pressed his foot against his victim's skull in an effort to finally free his tomahawk. It made a crunching sound as he withdrew it. Then, he, Abel and Wicks checked the wagon for anything useful....

"Let's move." Teague ordered. "Fast."

I looked to the riders that took off towards town. 'Was the fort going to be warned of our presence? If so, would we attack in broad daylight, under fire?' We're we going to be killed on approach?' Whatever it was going to be we moved out quick to meet it.

On the road, the two remaining Portuguese riders moved at a full gallop to warn the fort, with Bons closing in on them. One rider veered off the road to take his chances in the countryside but, he rode into a low, heavy tree branch that hit him across the chest and he was thrown from his horse. He tried to crawl away, coughing up blood but he looked up as Bons's shadow rolled over him.   It was the last thing he saw....

The last remaining rider had Sanjuro at his heels. They splashed through a waterway slowing the chase down, allowing Sanjuro to catch up and when he was side-by-side, he used his samurai sword to take the rider's head off. Sanjuro dragged on the reigns to command his horse to splash out of the water and back towards the road –leaving the head and headless body of this Portuguese soldier to drift down the waterway. Then he dismounted, pulled the body from the water, and dropped it –and his head, under a tree, covering it with giant palm leaves to hide it.

At dusk, we passed under the last few trees and made sight of the fort. Torches lit the top wall a-glow, giving us an almost clear view of the number of sentries on duty –in the watchtowers and walking the ramparts. This also allowed us to calculate the best possible position for our grappling hooks, away from their stations so we could try to make the climb undetected….

I wished for a rest but was also gripped by a sense of excitement and the risk of being detected was far too great to wait around. Teague also seemed to smell blood in the water, that is to say, he wanted this fight now –not later.

Teague had fought in Gibraltar but, he wasn't in command there. His battalion tried to storm the fortress at Devil's Point. They tried to slip past the gate house watch command –it didn't work. The defenders mounted a picket defense, held the gates. Killed most of the attackers and the fort remained in enemy hands. Since that lesson, Teague learned, never have just one point of attack. Strike the gate --take the walls at several points, come down on the enemy from the ramparts above and descend like hell from all angles.

So here it was, 'war time' as Jack-Karr said pulling his weapons and gear…

"Have you taken a fort before?" I asked in a near whisper.

"I was with the 22nd when we stormed the fortress at Saint Augustine during the war." He said as he tied up his grappling hook.

"And what happened?"

"Well…most of us were killed!"

I swallowed and started to tremble a little bit.

We emerged from the palm trees, made ready with our grappling hooks, and moved to tackle the giant, eight-meter stone wall. Addo removed the rope from his back and tied a double half hitch knot. Jack-Karr, Mako, Toombs, Lau, Bons, Barak, Sunderland and a few others picked up the heavy hooks and quickly moved out of the trees into a low position by the base of the massive stone walls --covered by shadows. We followed and positioned ourselves along the west wall of the fort.

--So far, so good. None of the sentries on the top wall had seen us.

At this time, Jupiter, Jagger, Wicks, and De Leon advanced on the highway and waited in silence meters from the squad guarding the north gate.

Teague stepped out of the shadows with Acalan and Kon Boar and waited. His eyes scanned the top wall and when he saw the shadow of a sentry move under a torch, he pointed and Acalan raised his blow gun, rocked forward, and fired dart that cut through the darkness. The shadow moved, then quietly dropped out of sight. Teague then shifted his eyes to the southwest corner as another shadow emerged. He gave a nod to Kon Boar who moved along the shadows to the fortress wall, got into position, raised his blow gun, and fired a dart that seemed to strike this shadow in the chin –and he dropped.

Teague then gave us the signal and we jumped into action…

Our hooks were thrown over the fortress wall. The metal made a 'claaaang' against the stone, but we did not wait to see who heard it, once the grappling hooks took hold Barak, Addo, Jack-Karr and the others started to make the climb in fast order. Hand-over-hand, boots working the stone. On the far side of the wall, Bons, Toombs and Sunderland were working their way up. Once they climbed past the half-way mark, another six of us took to the ropes and started up. All the rigging and rope work on the decks of The Venger had conditioned me for this --physical work I would have thought impossible a year or two before. And as always in daring moments like this --for a split second-- my mind flashed back to my former days as an innocent schoolteacher –back to now-- a privateer, climbing a fortress wall.

--How does this happen?

I shook the question from my head and continued to press upwards on the ropes. Close to the top, Toombs put his blade in his teeth as he, Bons and the others silently made it over the wall and on to the ramparts. Barak and Addo moved out to sack watch tower number one on the southeast corner –Addo 'The Skull' appearing out of the darkness behind one sentry, breaking the man's neck as Barak used his curved sword to slice down and quickly split the other watchman from chin to belt.

Bons planted his tomahawk in the skull of the sentry inside watch tower two…

Sunderland removed his hand from the mouth of his victim and pulled his knife out of his lower back dropping him to the rampart floor. Watch tower three was clear.

Karr slammed another sentry's head against a cannon –twice for good measure.

As we cleared the ramparts above, down below, Jaffar, Shaddam and some of the Moors suddenly emerged from the tree line with Calixto and his men to kill the guards at the gate as quietly as possible and then storm the guard house to kill the platoon playing cards and sleeping inside.

Outside the guard house, Shaddam banged the heads of two soldiers together --splitting their skulls as Jaffar went to work, wielding his curved blade –as it reflected in the moonlight—left, right and down, quickly killing another three of the Portuguese regulars.

One soldier made a run for the fortress gate. Calixto turned, pulled his bolas and before the runner could scream there was that familiar 'sound' that got louder --the 'whooomp-whoomp-whoooomp' as the bolas cut through the air, wrapped around this man's neck, and snapped it before he could scream!

As this was happening below, we continued to move along the ramparts above, killing the sentries as silently as possible using knives, swords, and tomahawks. One soldier was thrown over the wall to the trees below and let out a short scream before his body hit the ground with a thud. His scream stopped some of the soldiers on the parade ground below who seemed to look around and ask each other if they 'heard something' then they went back to their duties as if there was nothing to worry about.

--Lazy security.

We helped Raeder, Ward, Dakar, O'Shea, and the others over the fortress wall and then moved down the ramps to the ground floor and split up. Addo and Baako moved to unbar the heavy fortress gates and allowed our men to enter from outside and help us silently storm the parade ground.

--Suddenly a shot rang out!

All our men froze!

Wicks had surprised and killed a sentry as he cleared the outhouse, and his gun went off and now, their men started to wake up and move in the barracks.

"Kill everyone, quick!" Teague quickly gave the signal and Sunderland, along with Toombs, Merciless, Standish and Sanjuro moved to spark the fuses of several grenades and roll them into the barracks where they exploded, blowing bodies out of their cots and into the rafters. Those who survived --some on fire-- stumbled out and were killed by our blades as they cleared the doors…

Sanjuro swung his blade across the stomach of a soldier who was stumbling to make his exit from the burning barracks –his uniform smoldering. The cut opened him up and most of his guts fell out as he fell into the dirt. He slowly crawled forward, across the parade ground in pain --leaving a trail of dark blood-- and he grabbed hold my boot. I looked down and he looked up just as his eyes went lifeless as he died there….

Across, on the other side of the parade ground, the officers' quarters were also blown up, with the blast blowing part of the roof off! There wasn't going to be any negotiations here so, Teague wasn't interested in leaving anyone alive but, the explosions were lighting up the fortress and the surrounding area --and the sound of the blasts was echoing across town.

In Porto Norvo proper, the blasts got everyone's attention in the streets of town. The troops quartered in the township stormed into the chaos of the town square, some still throwing on their uniforms, some stumbling out of whore houses and some tumbling out of cantinas. Captains tried to overcome the shock of a sudden attack, muster their men, and made an effort to quickly pull their troops together.

--They were alarmed but not really aware of what was happening around them…

Back inside the fortress, we killed any survivors who resisted and those crawling around wounded. Stab. Cut. Slash. Hammer. We raided the armory, discovered the fort's treasury and payroll office where we liberated the Portuguese of their finances and holdings of gold. Calixto cracked the whip on a team of horses and brought a captured wagon forward so we could load the gold and weapons onboard. We seized all the other military wagons and horses housed by the fortress livery and loaded everything up to move to the ship when the time came…

We also opened up the powder magazine. Teague stepped inside and took a visual inventory, sixty-some-odd barrels of powder maybe three thousand rounds of cannon shot, and a wall of muskets equipped with bayonets. We moved in and opened up another magazine cell block to make a discovery –barrels painted red and black!

Raeder read the warnings on them, "Good God!"

"What is it?" I asked unable to understand the Portuguese markings.

"That" Teague said, "Is Byzantine fire!" He looked to Raeder, "You know what to do!"

"I do."

"Then get started."

Raeder called a platoon together that included, Duncan-Howe, Blythe, Wicks, Baako, Jagger, Shaddam, Dakar, myself and a few others and we started rolling the barrels out….

Teague then called for Mister Addo, "Turn the fort batteries on the ships in the harbor and open them up…." Addo smiled and with a nod, was off to the ramparts where he re-shaped some of our shore party into gun crews and had them man the cannon…

Loaded and ready, Addo took sight of his targets in the harbor below and ran the mathematics in his head –allowing for what he believed the velocity of the wind to be, then he ordered some slight adjustments on the targeting. His attack plan was simple –use all twenty-four batteries on the Portuguese war ship at anchor. The four frigates at the docks were not in position to return fire on us at the fort and would have to sail out and reposition themselves in the bay to counterattack and by then, we --or The

Venger—will have blown them to hell. The other slave ships would be destroyed at our convenience throughout the night....

Teague made it up the ramparts just as Addo was ready. "Ready to fire Mister Teague!"

"No need for any ceremony here" Teague returned, "Blow them to hell!"

With a nod, Addo gave the command, "FIIIIIIIRRRRRRRE!!!!"

We lit the fuses and the fort guns erupted sending cannon balls through the siding of the warship and snapping the mast of a slave transport. Explosions ripped into her side, hit the water, and smashed the quarter deck. The alarm continued to ring out on their decks as our second volley came in, hitting the bow and --by wild luck—a round hit the powder magazine and suddenly blew one ship completely apart. The explosion lit up the harbor --and the entire coast—as wood and splinters rained down on the town forcing the population to take cover...

Addo's men moved from gun to gun with torches lighting fuse after fuse. Mister Addo wasted no time in loading for his next volley, issuing rapid commands for a sight adjustment to target the ships at the docks as their crews panicked to get under way. It was of little consequence for the cannon balls started to smash their way forward and shatter their decks – and the docks—lighting them up and turning them into splinters.

Teague surveyed the damage through a spyglass –he watched the sails on one ship catch fire as cannon blasts hit the water around another and shattered the deck of a third! Some of the sailors had been blown off the decks –clothes on fire-- and were swimming for the beach. "Keep the pressure on them!"

Meanwhile, we moved though the south gate, outside the fortress walls --under the cannon as they fired into the bay-- and into the field and hillside that separated the fort from the town below. There, Duncan-Howe ordered us to stop and Baako, Blythe, Nighthorse, Wicks, Jagger, Shaddam, O'Shea and myself started to bust open the barrels of Byzantine fire and we poured it out in thick lines across the field. Barrel after barrel was poured out –and more was rolled out from the fort. We continued to place it until a dim light painted the field with the coming dawn and at that time, Kon Boar, acting as our scout caught sight of Portuguese regulars and some militia elements assembling at the edge of town preparing to march up to our position and engage us....

Duncan-Howe saw this and smiled before he ordered us back within the walls of the fort. We closed the gates behind us –leaving some thirty odd barrels of gun powder at the door—as we climbed to the ramparts...

By now, the Portuguese battalion formed into a picket line under the early morning sun and started marching towards us. Officers on horseback, their Imperial flags, and banners in position behind them with drummers hammering a marching rhythm. Standard European thinking at the time would have one believe that the Portuguese officers were convinced that this situation favored them. There were no fort guns positioned to face the town to the south so their approach would go unopposed by artillery—and they undoubtedly thought they could make our skeleton crew surrender based on this display of force.

Each step they took towards us built more and more tension inside my skull. I had never faced a formed-up combat force this large but –outside of myself—no one in our ranks seemed apprehensive or nervous. They only appeared confident as these soldiers closed in.

–We waited!

They made it to a mark seven hundred meters out...
'Where was the Venger?'
At six hundred meters out, I nervously looked to the men on my left and my right but still sensed no fear with any of them.   "Damn it all!" Duncan-Howe suddenly blurted out, making me jump. I looked over "I'm out of tobacco!" He looked at me –angry, "Damn sorry way to fight a war! Now I'm really mad!"
At five hundred meters out, the infantry came to a halt and the drums suddenly stopped. A rider came forward at a gallop and pulled his reigns

just under our position on the wall. "Attention, inside the fort!" he shouted with a heavy Portuguese accent. "Who is in command here?"

"I am! Teague… of The Venger!"

The rider seemed to size Teague up quickly, then continued, "This fort is the property of the Portuguese Empire and by order of our King –and local Governor-- we order you to surrender it to us now, and your lives will be spared. If you fail to do this, then we will have no choice but to take this fort by force and execute all of you!"

Mister Teague appeared unmoved. He spit the taste of gun powder out of his mouth and gave his answer, "Now you listen to me. If you –and your battalions—lay down your weapons and surrender now, along with everyone in this town, I promise…I'll do what I can to save your lives."

The rider looked bewildered. "If we surrender?

"Yes! You! All of you –surrender now. If you don't, then I promise you, not one of your men will leave this field alive today!"

The rider still appeared confused, then upset, "How dare you talk to me in this manner— "

Teague's voice overtook his, "YOU HAVE MY ANSWER! IF ANYONE SURRENDERS HERE TODAY, BELIEVE ME --IT'S GOING TO BE YOU!"

The rider took off, in anger and rode back to report to his officers.

I was amazed at Teague's audacity to respond to this Portuguese officer's demands as he stood there with an army behind him --with a threat of his own. We watched the rider make it back to his battle lines at a gallop and ride up to his commanding officer and we needed no spyglass to gauge their reaction --anger met with exaggerated amazement.

The drummers started back up and the Portuguese troops continued their march forward in formation. They stopped at two hundred meters out, dropped into firing formation and launched a volley in our direction. We took cover –all except for Teague—as shot plastered our surroundings. The Portuguese formations then fell back into their ranks and continued to advance, marching to the drum…

We collected ourselves and got back into position and waited for orders only --there were no orders. Teague remained silent.

The Portuguese again took up their firing positions and opened up on us, rank by rank. A musket ball hit the bricks next to me. Again, they stepped back into formation and continued their march towards us. Teague checked them with his spyglass and took what seemed to be a prolonged survey of their position. "Mister Nighthorse?" Nighthorse looked back to Teague as he slammed his spyglass closed, "Burn them out!"

Nighthorse signaled Baako down by the south gate who, with the help of Roux, Raeder and Bons opened it up and then started rolling barrels of gun powder down the slope and into the field towards the troops. I watched as these barrels tumbled towards our attackers, and once the barrels rolled into the Portuguese ranks, Toombs, Jagger, Karr, and a few others took aim and opened up with their guns and the barrels suddenly exploded killing most of the frontline troops immediately. Some troops caught on fire or were blown into the air....

Nighthorse then lit a grenade and dropped it over the fortress wall where it exploded in a patch of this 'Byzantine' tar and in a split-second the entire field seemed to explode and was ablaze. We were almost blown back as a rolling wall of fire moved down the field --like an avalanche of flames and destruction-- and incinerated the surviving infantry. The screams were deafening!

Teague looked for a moment as the silhouettes of these soldiers twisted in the flames then he gave the order for us to open up with muskets –and end the agony. An act of mercy as the last of the survivors stumbled –or crawled-- back towards town, most of them burned or wounded with uniforms smoldering.

At this time, The Venger made its presence known and as it came around the point it raised the SOLID RED FLAG...

–NO QUARTER!

Essex from the top deck commanded Rajiv to run out the guns and fire! The cannon cut the surviving infantry to shreds –even blowing apart a casualty clearing station-- and once, their numbers were reduced, Teague ordered us on the field. We opened the gates back up, moved through the smoke and into the dying flames to cut the rest of the Portuguese survivors down and the advanced on the town....

The Venger's bombardment came from all three port side gun decks, the starboard decks fired on the surviving ships in the bay still at anchor then Essex turned our guns on the town! The attack was heavy, unforgiving –and excessive. It was as if Essex wanted the slave port flattened and all its inhabitants blown to hell! The beach front buildings were hit, the customs house, slave docks, a cannon ball even dropped through the roof on the local tavern and exploded inside....

Explosions hit the beach, as more rounds ripped through the town square and warehouses, even people who were running for their lives when they were hit and blown apart.

Once most of the town was on fire and the slave ships sinking in the bay, Essex and Mister Newcastle brought their war party ashore. With them came Rabal, Dutch, Mister Cage, Tiger, Le Clerk and 'the Legionnaires' Archer, Gordon, Merritt, Lynch, Kato, Akai-Dan, Daws, Kannon, Clairmont, Dax-Varro. Baltimore, Watson, the scary Sampson-Rift, Hallock –all the killers-- and three hundred more, leaving just our gun teams and support staff aboard the ship....

These men hit the beach with the intent of destroying E-V-E-R-Y-T-H-I-N-G and they moved up the sands under cover from our guns and into the streets –cannon blasts smashing into the buildings before them as the surviving civilians tried to flee into the smoke towards the outskirts of town and into the surrounding fields. Essex pulled his saber and once he did, he barked the order, "No quarter!"

"NO QUARTER!" Harrow repeated with a shout over the concussion of the bombardment....

"NO QUARTER!" Newcastle and the other 'war captains' screamed through their ranks as the weapons came out and –like dogs who just snapped the leash-- the killing began in town proper...

We moved through the flames and arrived on the north edge of the township. The visual image of us, men of different cultures --with a curvature for war, hell bent on savagery-- as we moved through the smoke and into the streets, against the populace, must have been terrifying and our anger seemed to get the better of us...

We cut our way through what was left of the Portuguese soldiers and militia --killing even the wounded as they tried to crawl away. Mister Nighthorse and Bons Iroquois were making quick work of some the Portuguese infantry with their tomahawks, and they were also talking scalps. They did not wait for men to die, a slash with the dagger, a swing of the tomahawk and a man would be crawling away in pain to save his life only to have Nighthorse walk up on him, grip his scalp and with one clean, slow gash, take his scalp off, allowing time to do the rest as the victim would slowly die.

"Tis a savage practice!" I winced upon witnessing this, a man crawling, skull exposed, dark blood running down his face --and shivering in place as death slowly seized him....

"Aye," replied Wicks, out of breath with some explosions behind him, "But then... so is all of it!"

We started moving through the township and no one was safe. Administrators, running to evacuate from their offices –papers in hand— were cut down or shot at close range by Jagger, Miranda and Obal as Standish threw a torch through the front doors to burn their office down...

Shaddam swung his curved blade up on a soldier and his blood splashed a 'crescent moon' on the brick wall next to him as he froze in place for a moment, then dropped to the ground dead...

Blades and axes took civilians and the panicked militia apart. The sun reflected off of Takeda's sword as he swept it from left to right, cutting his way forward through people in the street. One militia captain dropped to his knees with his hands up to surrender. Takeda saw the 'slave whip' on his waist and removed the man's hands with a rapid horizontal strike – cutting them clean off-- before he brought his sword down vertically into his head --the man's eyes turned grey, like the color of fog-- from the impact of the blade as he dropped.

Other administrators tried to hide only to be dragged out in the street and killed. Find them here, kill them there! Their papers –the sale receipts for thousands of Africans—left to blow through the streets in the wind…

At one point, a man walked out of a storefront with his hands up, "I'm just a humble solicitor. Please! I'm just a solicitor!" And Jack-Karr turned, pulled his gun, and put a musket ball right through his neck and the ball shattered the window behind him.

The solicitor stumbled for a few moments, clutching his throat as the blood pumped out before he dropped to his knees and eventually fell forward dead….

"I hate solicit-solicit—what-ever you are?" Karr spit.

"Solicitor!" Duncan-Howe said, with pistols in both hands. "It's a man who uses the law to take money, misery and most-often ruin you."

At that point, Jack-Karr raised his second gun and shot him again –a second round right through his dead his body. "Take that! You law-wielding bastard!" And then he got back to the business of killing, leaving Duncan-Howe to roll his eyes at the overkill.

We moved into the town square where the bodies of troublesome slaves had been lynched and remained as an example to others. I had not seen a man hanged before and it was a sight –so grim—that I knew, in an instant, that it would stick with me until my grave. Harrow did not have to order me or the men to cut them down for we moved to do it on our own accord. The lynched bodies dropped to the ground, and I found myself fixed on them, the sons, and daughters of families far away, once children with great hopes pinned on them for their futures --now dead, brutally lynched! What a wicked, nasty business this was and as I watched my ship mates take through the streets with violence, I understood their vengeance, for so many of them had been slaves in one way or another --this was their payback-- and…. I am not ashamed to say, that I wanted this vengeance for them. This so-called town, this port of commerce that destroyed so many lives --and families-- made my ethics give way to my anger and rage. My preference for non-violent solutions was lost in this moment for I too wanted these people to pay....

Essex himself was at the stockade by noon as we raided the slave compound. We moved through the brick-and-mortar tunnels and dungeons and opened up all the cells. Some of these people were held three hundred to a cell built for sixty. They were suspicious and frightened at first but soon came to realize that this was their chance at freedom....

We liberated some from the stocks and crude pits in the ground with fabricated cage like lids. Others were held in various hanging cages like animals, the variety of which were familiar only to those involved in the Spanish Inquisition. Many that we freed were children with no idea where their families were. Murdered? Shipped to the new world stacked in the hold of some transport or crucified for a slow death? Some of the children would run through the violence looking for their mothers, their fathers – anyone who would help them.

We fought our way back outside and then opened up food warehouses and the water stores for starvation had been a weapon in the act of suppressing these people and many had not had anything to eat for days....

Mister Daws pulled his flags from the case on his back to signal the ship in order to have Doctor Johannis and Doctor Jopo put ashore to begin to administer aid to these people. Once we moved these people to the clear, Essex ordered Mister Rabal and Shaddam to put the torch to the whipping posts, stocks, and what was left of the slave docks and the buildings. He wanted them completely burned out....

As this was happening, our men continued to move through the streets killing anyone and everyone. More buildings were put to the torch and in the chaos, some people ran through the streets, clothes on fire. Others were thrown through windows and off balconies. Those that begged for their life were not spared –they were killed on their knees –and in the most brutal fashion-- while crying for mercy.

The devastation to these people was complete...

Then a Portuguese general emerged from the smoke with his young valet – a former drummer boy-- behind him, holding up a white flag of surrender....

"Here Captain," Lau got Essex's attention and pointed to the officer as he moved forward...

I watched as Essex raised his stare to fix on this officer as he approached....

The General removed his hat and gave a curt bow. "I am here to ask for terms sir." He said in English but, through a heavy Portuguese accent...

"Terms?"

"Yes, your articles and code of conduct are well known, I have come to offer you our surrender and---"

Essex planted his cutlass in the sand and slowly walked towards this officer. Harrow and Newcastle watched closely as the situation developed. Essex came within a few meters of this man and slowly spoke through his clenched teeth, "You have to be a privateer for the articles to apply and-you're-not!" And with that he suddenly pulled his pistol and fired, putting a musket ball square into the general's forehead. His head snapped back as he dropped to the sand and twitched on the ground for the musket ball smashed into his skull but failed to make a clean strike against the brain -- a small amount of lead was still visible in the hole in this man's forehead, and it was going to take several minutes – or hours-- for him to finally die.

Other prisoners were put to the axe. Even the wounded and I was surprised to see Africans in their ranks.

"Slavers." Harrow remarked under his breath. Slavers --selling their own people into slavery for profit.

"Much like a politician, hey Harrow." Jagger said as he spit some gun tar from his teeth.

Harrow looked to his left, to the war captain Nighthorse and his gang of killers standing in the smoke nearby and with a nod, they closed in on them, axe blades came down on these slavers from all sides. Skulls, shoulders, necks –even a face plate-- split by force.

Now, to build our legend. Here, Captain Essex made a traditional move. Despite our red 'no quarter' flag on The Venger, he ordered the general's valet, a young boy not more than twelve, left alive –he always left one survivor when he could, to tell the tale of what they had witnessed and to help spread fear though the populace and, on this day, it was to be the valet. So, he gripped him by the collar and pulled him close. "Look around!" He instructed as the lad took a nervous, scared look. "Everything is gone! Destroyed! Your soldiers and administrators are dead. The people are dead. Your fort, town and stockade have been eradicated from the face of the earth! Tell anyone you find that Essex and his terror troops from The Venger did this and tell them we'll destroy every slave outpost on the African coast and kill everyone! Everyone will be put-to-death! The women! The children will all die.'" He released his grip, "Go now!"

Harrow marched through the street as burning ash rained down. He and his men worked through what was left of the customs house and the auction house where some financials were found, then they raided what was left of the treasury and banking offices and there, true to our suspicions –in the bank-- was a fortress supply of gold. A great deal of business had been done here in this port and now, the profits had been liberated.

"Congratulations lads" Harrow addressed us, "You're all rich! Now let's get these cache boxes out of here."

We went to work, two men per iron box removing them as quick as we could and running them down to the beach where they were loaded directly on the long boats. Once the two hundred or so boxes were removed, we then removed every possible item of use, supplies, canvass, tools, weapons, powder –even cocoa beans. Also, all the private household savings were raided --gold coins, plates, jewels, rings, even clothes.

Barak, Rabal, Nighthorse, Cage, Briggs, and Sampson-Rift forced open some warehouse doors to discover the rum and wine stores. "Ahhh!" Barak barked in disappointment as he slammed his curved sword back into his sheath. He turned and walked away into the smoke behind them....

"What's the matter with him?" Briggs asked.

"He doesn't drink. It's against his religion." Rabal stated.

"Well, more for us then."

Our men moved through the docks and climbed aboard what was left of the transports and sacked them for anything of value –rigging, canvas, iron, rope, candles, tools, whale oil –everything. Then they were set alight and were sunk in the bay where they would serve as a harbor obstruction for anyone who wanted this port's services in the future....

Hours later as we continued to load raided supplies, Kon Boar and our scouts reported a slave caravan approaching the edge of town --wagons dragging slaves behind them, roped by the neck. Despite the smoke billowing from this burnt-out city, they continued to approach under the crack of the whip. Essex asked Baako, Jata and Dakar to assemble a welcoming party to go out to meet them and extend a 'hello' from us and kill them all. They did so and brought Kan Boar, Rabal, Jack-Karr, Baltimore, Hayte, Kannon and a few others with them to wait in ambush on the 'Odalisque Township Road' and as the caravan approached, they jumped them from the wilderness and put the escort troops to the knife. The slaves were cut free, and the rope used to restrain them by the neck was repurposed when the slavers bodies were lynched in the trees on the side of the road as a warning to other caravans that may approach this port in the coming days or weeks...

The captives were freed and took to the countryside.

The Captain wanted to make a quick departure for this port was the site of large amounts of maritime traffic and he didn't want to risk another engagement with the military. Everything was loaded on board, even cattle, rowed to the ship in long boats, hoisted aboard in rope nets and lowered into the cargo hold next to the galley to be pinned together in our make-shift corral as it was being extended and built larger by our carpenters. Mister Hobby was already sharpening his cleavers....

Chickens –to be caged for eggs until it was time to make a meal out of them along with lamb and boar by the dozens, all confiscated and put aboard along with everything we could unload from the provisions warehouse like salted pork, flour, sugar, coconuts, bananas, limes, mangos and hundreds of baskets of bread, rum, plum brandy, and cheese. The tobacco stores were also confiscated. "I'll take that." Duncan insisted on moving the crates of tobacco himself, "This work requires the delicate hand of an expert."

All weapons, powder, whale oil, what was left of the Byzantine fire – even several hundred cannon balls were loaded in. I had never seen The Venger so packed with supplies, netted to the ceiling of every deck, into every hold and some supplies even strapped to the top deck.

Then, every township structure was put to the torch. We took a few liberated slaves who wanted to join our ranks, maybe sixteen, the rest were free to take to the countryside and try to make it back to their homes. We then raised anchor and set sail with the tide, leaving the burning town in our wake....

--It was total devastation!

That night in the galley, spirits were high. Food, rum, wine, and music flowed through the deck. Despite the violence of the day, we were merry. We believed –I believed—we had done right and had been rewarded for it in what we had seized. I also smiled at the thought that those in cages days before waiting to be packed on to ships for a painful voyage to America were now crossing the African frontier back home. Although the possibility of recapture would always exist, tonight --at least--they were free, and I had a small hand in this…

Even Teague, a man who always appeared with dark eyes –and a dark attitude-- had a smile on his face though he sat somewhat apart from us, on a captured, red, throne like chair by a deck fire but, his disposition seemed somewhat more pleasant than usual and with that, I ventured over to him, bottle, and mug in hand to say a few words of gratitude....

"Ah Mis—Mister Teague?"

He looked up at me from his chair. I raised the bottle and motioned it forward as if to ask if it was alright to refill his mug which he then raised. I then took this moment to speak, "I wanted to thank you Mister Teague for having confidence enough in my abilities to nominate me to your shore party for the fort!"

He gave a slow, single nod that one could interpret as a 'you're welcome.'

I smiled with a surge of confidence, "My skills and training must be starting to inspire some level of respect---"

"--Don't get ahead of yourself boy!" Teague cut me off, "You still can't fight worth a damn but, you're smart and sometimes….it pays more to have a smart man along, then just another fighter."

And, just like that, I made a recovery from my initial dejection and found a sense of pride in this honest –if somewhat backhanded— compliment. "Thank-thank you sir."

I left the bottle with Teague and returned to sit next to Whitney, Duncan-Howe, and Mandagan the V. All were telling stories of their side of the raid. Though Mandagan's English was very poor, he seemed to smile, laugh and understand what we were speaking about. This was a good day.

At that point, the Captain came down and as he appeared through the tobacco smoke, the deck became silent out of respect. He looked around at all of us and asked, "May I join you lads?"

"Please Captain," Addo stood up and motioned to a bench for our Captain to take a seat and as he moved to it, all the men on his path smiled, nodded, or removed their hats out of respect as he passed. Instead of taking Addo's place he motioned for Addo to stay in it with a hand on his shoulder and Essex stood tall.

"Here Captain," Daws handed him a mug.

"Thank you, Mister Daws and may I say, fine work from you today…."

"Thank you, sir."

The Captain then turned his glance around the deck, "Fine work from all of you…"

We smiled and said our 'thank yous' and then became silent again to allow the Captain the floor.

"It was a rare and special thing we did today. A thing, uncommon –yet-- righteous in its action. Whatever history may make of us, you can rest easy, knowing that your role today has put you on the right side of it." He paused for a moment, "Few men can claim to be the salvation of others but today.... you can!" He smiled with pride, then suddenly turned with a motion so fierce that Daws and the others took a cautionary step back as Essex then continued his speech, "It's to you men here who have my respect --and admiration—that I drink to tonight." He raised his mug, and we did the same in kind as he took a heavy drink from it unleashing cheers from us all....

I smiled, proud of where I stood and proud of what we had done....

The Captain reset his mug –after Hobby refilled it—and raised it again, "And to Mister Jaffar..."

Jaffar gave a bow and a rare, ever so slight, smile. "To Mister Harrow and Mister Newcastle, whose steadfast character has led this crew forward and Mister Teague... whose audacity was outmatched only by his bravery in his actions taking the fort..."

All the mugs went up, "To Mister Harrow! Newcastle! And Mister Teague!"

"No!" Teague roared and rose to his feet. There was a moment of silence. We were unaware of what was to happen next and got quiet as Teague stepped forward. He slowly began to speak again "Any man can take a fort with the likes of these men here at his back but, it is you Captain, who shaped this ship –and this crew. It was you who defied convention and devised articles to live by, better than any legal system under the crown and 'though I must confess that I offered resistance to your civility at first and was defiant--"

Essex smiled as if to remember earlier days with a defiant, rebellious Teague.

"I can say now," Teague continued, "Without any doubt, that I was wrong to do so, and it is YOU.... who has matched wits with the devil and won! And I am damn proud to know you!" He raised his mug, "My respect sir," He turned to our crowd, "To the Captain!"

And all our mugs went skyward, mine highest of all, for I belonged.

XV

THE ABADDON CIRCLE
AND THE ARCHANGEL OF THE ABYSS

Ten days later –with still no sight of the French treasure convoy-- we made for the Cape Colony, the temperature had been dropping gradually each day and although it was considered late in the year to round the Cape of Good Hope, we still made that our intention. We locked the ship down and crashed through the rough seas. The ship would pitch and roll –and at times feel like it was about to ride sideways on the rail but, we pressed on. We know the Portuguese Empire had by now, discovered the destruction of their slave port and their next move to be to search down the coast so, they would be, in effect, closing in behind us and making a late run around the cape was a good way to force them to remain in the Atlantic for another few months, rather than take the risk of coming after us late in the year.

Nature always put me on edge, the sheer force of it and the waves off of South Africa were a sinister reminder that nature was our god, and we were at her mercy. Men moved down the deck, using lifelines and worked despite waves crashing on our deck –as if the weather was just a minor inconvenience. For myself, I had been washed off a deck before, so I had no shame, I tied a lifetime around me on every combat shift –like a leash.

Things eventually slowed down, and we made it 'round intact...

The first marker beyond the cape –as the weather improved—was 'jawbone' an old shoreline battleground and cemetery that had cliff rocks that looked like the remains of skeleton's jaw.

Just beyond this landmark, we raided a small Italian trading vessel off the coast of Mozambique during a lightning storm. It was a dry environment, and the bolts lit up the sky. The Italian crew was allowed to live and keep their ship –for it was of poor design. The cargo was –of course—impounded.

Jata and I, along with Tak, Hallock and a few others were packing cotton along with sacks of captured spices and grain into the hold. Addo was humming some words in his native Zulu language when he passed us. There was no hostility between Jata and Addo but I could detect something, something less than friendly.

"Are you Zulu?" I suddenly asked Jata.

"No" Jata said, "I fought as a scout for the imperial forces against the Zulu." His English was good but, his accent was ever present. "I was translator as well."

"Yes," I said, "Your English is good."

He smiled.

"We're you paid well as a translator?"

"No. I was promised money but once the tribe we fought was destroyed, they thanked all of us by selling us into slavery. I was sent to the diamond mines in Lankan Prime. These men," he motioned to the men on our decks, "Saved me when they sacked it."

"Diamond mine? Now that's an excellent target."

"Many men died that day. Many soldiers and many privateers – hundreds! The fighting went into the mines," the look in his eyes suddenly seemed distant, "I saw an officer thrown into a mining car and kicked down the tracks. The privateers used grenades, and the mines collapsed into rocks. Many men were buried down there alive." He looked at me, "There was screaming-- I will never go into a tunnel again."

The Venger turned towards the sun and moved up the coast. We raided the East Coast of Africa and conscripted some Zulu revolutionaries on the run from the English –who started to teach me some Bantu—as we continued our journey past Madagascar.

We burned shipping in the Persian Sea, sacked a silk and spice trading outpost on the Arabian Coast and on the eighteenth of that month, we collided and fought with Moor Privateers from Arabia, working for the

French government. The killing lasted two days and the tide on the banks of the shoreline was red with blood...

As the fighting died down, I moved through the town.

In the burning wreckage of the port and fortress, the Moors took prayer, the smoke and burning embers rolled over them as they took to their mats and I watched, exhausted, black ash marking my face and hands and in this fatigued state, I turned to see the head of an enemy combatant roll across the wooden planks outside of the burning apothecary shop followed by Mister Teague. He paused for a moment, then slapped the fire out of his tunic sleeve, looked at me and then disappeared into the flames like the devil....

NORTH AFRICA

TWELVE YEARS EARLIER...

After the battle of El Alegra, there were only six survivors left of second platoon. There were, in fact, only thirty-nine men left out of the original six hundred in the 52nd Regiment. The fighting, all across North Africa left hundreds dead and had burned-out several fortresses, towns, and desert camps, turning that part of the continent into a barren land, littered with bodies, mass graves and a landscape...populated by ghosts.

Known as the Iron Soldiers, what was left of these men would be unceremoniously released from duty and Teague, though young, still held the rank of sergeant in what was now a 'dead' and unwanted military outfit when he, and what was left of his platoon sailed for Gibraltar...

--The dust from Cyrenaica, Sicily, and Malta, still mixed with the dried blood that had become the fabric of their uniforms and now, their lives....

--But something happened during the war and with the hardships that followed and the government's general disrespect of the veterans who kept their empire together in one colonial conflict after another fostered an element of anger and rebellion in the ranks and Teague—gifted as he was at killing--- went 'dark' in a way...

As the disrespect and injustice seemed to mount, this man –who had a short fuse to begin with-- decided to forge his own path—whatever the consequence may be, and when he saw crippled veterans begging in the street, spat on and kicked from one alley way to another, he made his move...and the next morning, the doors of The Grand Imperial Bank of Colonial England were kicked in....

Corporal Raeder moved left; Private Jack-Karr blocked the door as Private Rift –whose jawbone hadn't been blown off yet—along with the other survivors of 2nd platoon moved right to cover the room. Teague entered through the early morning fog and moved forward. "No one move!"

The clerks backed up, terrified with their hands raised --no one had the audacity to rob a King' s bank before and some of these men actually appeared to be former soldiers to the upper-class administration which, made the situation all-the-more, confusing...

"Now I want your cooperation," Teague shouted raising the scratch in his voice up an octave. "Give it and you'll all have a story to tell your grandchildren. Resist and –just so there's no mystery here-- I'll kill ya!"

"Wh-What do you want?" The administrator asked.

"My pension, for six years of war." Teague said as he pushed him back and moved behind the counter to the massive steel vault.

"Your pension?"

"Yes, damn it mine! And the pension of every other veteran you hold in your vault, Now open up!"

"I will not" said the defiant clerk, "I'm charged with administration by Lord Edward Thatcher, and I will not stoop to the will of a common criminal—"

--BAM! Teague shot him dead and through the smoke from his gun, looked over the rest of the room, "Anyone else want to object?"

--The sudden sound of gunfire sent the townspeople in the street, running for cover...

Teague turned to another clerk and raised his second pistol, "Is this where you want your life to end?"

"No-no sir." And he opened the vault.

The sacks of coins were removed but something else was discovered, a black iron box.

"Open it!"

The clerk pulled the key and opened the box up. It was loaded with what appeared to be sealed documents, parchment, and letters. Karr stepped to Teague's shoulder "What the hell is all that?"

"Mortgages, debtor records, loan receipts, pending foreclosures."

The clerk reported.

Teague started to help himself to a fist-full of documents when the clerk tried to stop him…

"Please don't" The clerk held his hand up, "Those are the only records we have of such business, without it, we will not be able to hold any of our debtors accountable!"

"Is that a fact?" Teague asked and he kept his eyes locked on the clerk as he sparked the fuse of a grenade, dropped it into the iron box and closed the vault door for it to explode, igniting all the paperwork.

The clerk tried to advance and put the fire out but was pulled back by Karr who gripped him by the back of his collar, "As you were!" He waited until all the documents had been burned and the room filled with smoke to release him.

Suddenly there was a shout from outside. "Hello inside the bank?"

Raeder looked out the window. "Local authority," He reported, "Militia, six men." He peered a little further to the left, to see two more men –civilians—in the alley close by, "Resurrection men!" He said in an even tone with a touch of curiosity.

--Resurrection men, men who collected dead bodies to sell, instead of just robbing graves.

"Resurrection men, for us?" Rift said, "A tad early don't ya think?"

Teague sashed his two pistols and went for the door—

"What the hell do ya think you're doin'?" Raeder asked from his position at the window.

"Having a conversation." Teague opened the door with so much force that the militia squad jumped back out of caution.

Teague emerged from the smoke that the grenade had stifled his surroundings with and stood there for a moment, waiting --waiting as if he actually wanted to hear what this militia commander had to say and maybe—fixing a little too much 'dangerous' attention on him.

The commander pulled together enough confidence to stutter out his question, "Sir…if I may ask, what-what are your in-intentions here?" He asked with a slight shiver.

Teague appeared to take a long, almost uncomfortable moment to size the man up then answered, "I'm robbin' your bank, in case you hadn't noticed."

This militia officer was stunned by the brute honesty but still tried to maintain some civility. "We, we can-can't have that sir."

"Can't we?"

"No sir, we cannot. However…" He looked at Teague's guns and his army jacket and recognized him as a man of some military skill and thus began to talk his way out of a confrontation, "If you and the men with you, lay down your arms. You have my word, that I will speak to the magistrate on your behalf and request a minimal sentence for your, misdeeds--"

Teague paused, then said, "I have a counter-offer for ya…if you and your men --along with this whole town-- lay down your arms and surrender to us here-and-now, then we'll allow you to live."

The militia captain was baffled, not sure if he heard Teague correctly…

"Talk it over amongst yourselves!" Teague suddenly stepped back and disappeared back into the smoke and slammed the door shut.

"What was all that?" Raeder asked, weapons ready at the window.

"A slight obstruction out front, we're going to have to kill those men so get ready!" He turned as Karr and the other members of the platoon loaded up their satchels with bags of gold coins. Teague pointed to the bank clerk, moping over the smoldering ash that was once his foreclosure documents and said, "Bring him here."

Karr grabbed him, "Come on," and he pushed him forward to Teague as he regripped his gun.

'Wait!" The clerk said in a near panic, "You promised not to kill me!"

"It actually wasn't a promise, it was just an idea and I've since thought better of it," Teague grabbed him by the back of the scalp and looked to Raeder, "Stand by to open the door."

--The platoon went for their weapons and braced for a charge.

"Hello outside…" Teague shouted.

"Yes?" Came a timid voice from the street…

"We're coming out to kill all of ya! Prepare yourselves!"

"WAAAAAAAIIIIIIIIT!!!!" The clerk shouted as he was forced forward and the bank clerk was thrown head-first through the doors as the street erupted in a blizzard of panicked gunfire, blasting the clerk, and killing him as his body tumbled down the front steps of the bank and into the street.

And just when they realized who it was, it was too late --they had all discharged their weapons and looked up as the 'iron soldiers' stormed outside, blasting. The militia members out front, took rounds to the head and chest. Once their guns expired, Teague stepped forward with a horizontal strike across the neck of a militia officer cutting him open--as his men switched to blades and brought their sabers down, inflicting all the damage they could --separating a shoulder at the collar bone, taking an arm off, or splitting a man's skull with a drop cut.

"Wait!" The officer in charged wheezed, wounded with a blood-covered hand up to draw a halt to this action, "Wait…stop! An assault on the king's soldiers is the same as an assault on the king himself."

Teague peered at him, "GOOD!" And he speared his saber in a downward thrust that went through the man's eye and out the back of his skull.

Jack-Karr sparked another grenade and tossed it to Teague who threw the bomb into the building to blow it apart and ignite it into flames.

The men hijacked some horses and rode out like bandits but, as they made their way out of town, a canvas bag marked with the emblem of the Grand Imperial Bank was dropped into the beggin' tin of a crippled veteran on the corner of Concord Street.

As the warrant posters went up on every signpost and tavern wall, the master of darkness practiced his vengeance in sinister and unconventional ways. Other banks and imperial institutions were robbed and violated. The rich, moving from one township to another, across the King's Highway, were robbed and the entire countryside was made to feel unsafe and dangerous.

--Strangely enough, it was the first time in recent memory that the veteran's hospital, the medical convent, and the local school were actually well funded though –no one can seem to remember exactly how.

One morning, as the sun rose over the horizon, a trigger point was reached, and the 'imperial rage' was in full effect. The County Judge – Hardwick-- who believed that his very self-esteem was threatened with such lawlessness, ordered a rough search of the township. Front doors were kicked in, families disturbed at dinner or while they slept –and-- unlawful arrests made, with the idea that the populace might be harboring these criminals, and some harsh interrogations and abuse might bring about the information required to put an end to it. This was followed by a violation of the countryside that lasted into the winter –that is, until the honorable Judge Hardwick who had authorized this campaign of imperial terror, was riding in his carriage down the Lexington Road and came face to face with a roadblock in the form of a tree that had collapsed across the dirt—with what looked like a large, burning scarecrow, three meters high, in front of it to light up the landscape…

As the carriage was brought to a halt, Rift jumped from the nearby trees onto the roof and with the help of Jack-Karr and Raeder --the coachmen were killed!

Before Hardwick could even look out his window to see what the obstruction was, his door was thrown open with so much force that it came off the hinges. Panicked, the judge slid back in his seat and held his breath.

Teague, then emerged from the shadows awash with the flickering light of the burning scarecrow and asked, "Judge Hardwick?"

"Ye-ye-yes!"

"I'm here to take your head!"

THE VENGER...

TWELVE YEARS LATER...

Eventually we sailed into the Indian Ocean. Our next stop was Madras in the Bay of Bengal. This was paradise. Mild weather, thick jungle threaded around the town buildings and shoreline temples and encased it with a tropical marine layer. In short, it was beautiful.

Many privateer settlements along the coast of India were run by liberal governors who –for a fee-- would allow anyone to dock. One such settlement was even constructing a fort, designed by a former military engineer, a Scotsman, with the British 71st who turned privateer. Here, they used elephants to haul the stones and captured cannon into place.

The Governor, Arjun, was a friend to privateers –if they had the proper tribute. So, upon landing, Mister Harrow instructed Mister Rabal, who knew the local language and custom better than most of us, along with Akai, Mister Wicks, Toombs, Mister Gordon, Obal and myself and a few of the Bengal gunners, under the watchful eye of Mister Lincoln to procure a wagon and supervise the delivery of the harbor tax to the governor's warehouse. Here the British regulars used an augmented force of local Indians called Sepoys. They wore British uniforms but with a head wrap much like our Mister Rajiv. A detachment –under a British officer—was to escort us and this officer, a lieutenant was found at a local tavern, called Lord Khan's Public House, where he was into his spirits and quite drunk by the time, we found him. He still managed to take charge of his platoon of twelve Sepoys, filed outside and keeping his balance, we started our march out of town towards the Governor's castle…

The road became dark as we moved out of town and into the jungle countryside. Part of the road was lit by torches every few meters, or old lanterns and the jungle trees appeared like giant claws in the shadows beyond and, as we moved, my imagination took hold –and I thought I saw something in the shadows move…

--I re-focused to take a sharp look when suddenly a giant rope net sprung up in front of our horses and spooked them to heel! I fell off the wagon as we started to take musket fire from the countryside all around us…

"Bandits!" The blasts started to light up the topography….

Some of the Sepoys were hit and killed. We moved to fight along-side them but, they tried to form a picket line –making themselves easy targets-- and took heavy causalities as they fired a volley off.

Toombs returned fire with several pistols as the bandits charged out of the jungle and fought with a determined ferocity. Akai swung with his samurai sword almost cutting an attacker in half. Mister Lincoln took cover, Mister Obal fired both his guns. When all the muskets were emptied, we switched to blades and engaged…

Rabal flipped a bandit over his back, speared his sword down into him, twisted it, then turned and took a swing at another one as he charged out of the darkness. Mister Gordon sparked the fuse to a grenade but was shot before he could throw it and he dropped it! It exploded, blowing the wagon over, killing Gordon in the blast and some of the Sepoys. They hit the ground with their uniforms smoldering from the explosion. Mister Rabal was wounded but continued to fight. With the explosion, the bandits began to retreat, maybe with the belief that our cargo had been destroyed in the blast –or-- that more grenades were coming. Rabal tried to chase a few down, he slashed one bandit in the back, swung at another then, ultimately walked back to our position…

We checked the wounded; Mister Gordon was lost –dead! As my hearing returned, I helped a Sepoy to his feet and with the help from

YOUR ROAD TO REDEMPTION IS PAVED WITH TOMBSTONES!

Toombs and Wicks, we pushed the wagon back over on its wheels and found it still serviceable. We loaded the wounded aboard –and the tax-- and moved back down the road towards town…

Back in town, we found the Captain on the balcony of The Bombay Tavern, jug on the table, pipe in hand and an attractive Indian woman not too far off. We arrived to make our report and he saw we were exhausted, dirty, and rattled, "What is it?"

"Sir…we were attacked on the Raja Road. Bandits! We made short work of some of them but lost part of the cargo in an explosion."

"Anyone hurt?"

"Mister Gordon, sir, killed….in action."

The Captain looked down at the news…

"I apologize sir." Mister Rabal said in his gruff voice, his large frame blocking out some of the lantern light and his tunic still smoldering from the blast. "I took my eye off the mark as it were sir…."

"The fault is my own. We know the countryside is owned by rogues. We should have assigned more men." There was a pause then he gave the following command, "Mister Rabal-"

"Sir?"

"Have Mister Teague report to me immediately."

"Yes. Sir."

Later…

Back at Lord Khan's Public House, the front door was suddenly kicked in getting the attention of all inside. Mister Teague slowly walked in -- Baako, The Dutchman, Mister Cage, Foxx, Mister Jaffar, Mister Lo, Tane –the tattooed islander--Jagger, Hatano, Sampson-Rift and Jack-Karr stood at his back, like a mob, just inside the door.

The kick gripped everyone with a sense of shock and Teague took a long look around the room before he began to speak. Finally, deliberately, his words formed up. "My name's Teague… of the warship Venger." The patrons seemed fixed on him, one man swallowed nervously, as the tension was thick in the air. "Tonight, some of our men were ambushed on The

Raja Road." Teague slowly started to pace the room, "Now.... anyone know anything about it?"

The room was still. Tension was high. I had seen this before in New Haven. Teague asked the question and if he didn't like your answer, he killed you --immediately.

Baako stood silently in the lantern light, his 'skull war paint' alone made the patrons shiver. Jack-Karr slowly moved out to his left, in a wide circle, with slow and direct steps that signaled a man looking for the specific point in which to draw and apply his weapons.

Teague slowly walked through the tables of seated patrons and looked directly down at some of the people who, clearly felt the shadow of evil roll over them. He then took a few more steps, "Now these bandits killed several sepoys and....one of our own...and one of the men killed was a British lieutenant who was in here –drunk--before he took to the highway...." Teague continued to move, slowly and he seemed to try to read the expressions of the men he was talking to as if something would give his target away. "Now, we have no fight with honest men...." He scratched, "But if one of you knows something about this wicked business, well...." He looked the room over and with his sinister tone he said, "Then I'd say it now!"

--He dropped his hands to the handle of his cutlass and one of his guns.

Suddenly a man flipped over his tavern table and lunged at Teague but was shot before he hardly left his chair. Jaffar –who anticipated this might happen-- lowered his smoking pistol. Teague stepped up and put his foot on the throat of his victim to get a good look at him and make sure he was dead, then he looked up at the rest of his present company. "Anyone else have anything to say?" The room was quiet, the tension could be split with a blade and Teague continued, "Well, there's only one way to be sure we got the right man here." And with that, Hatano, Foxx and the others pulled their weapons, stormed the room, and began to cut the tenants apart. Outside, the silhouette of the killings could be seen –through the Khan's giant front window-- against the brick wall of the alley outside....

At the same time, Mister Harrow along with Sunderland, Mister Watson, myself, and several others led a heavily armed group up the Raja Road. Anyone seen on the road was killed and this time, the tribute arrived. We rode through the gates of the Governor's palace, dismounted, and announced ourselves to the guards and were escorted forward through the front doors by a servant.

Inside, were several Indian women lying about. Their religion didn't seem to apply here. Neither did proper government politics. "It appears our Lord Governor may be occupied." Harrow observed.

Then the Governor appeared in the candlelight. He appeared 'used' by opium but managed to greet us. "Gentleman."

"Sir," his valet began, "Men of The Venger with the…. ah…. harbor tax, sir."

He seemed to stumble for his words but managed something of a sentence, "Ah yes, wel-welcome gentlemen."

"My Lord, I regret to tell you, some of your soldiers along with one of your lieutenants was killed in an earlier attempt to deliver this…tax."

"A pity." He became distracted by one of the women present, "Died doing his duty I suppose." He said in a nonchalant manner and then quickly put the thought from his mind and turned back to Mister Harrow. "I hope you will enjoy your time here as are our guests."

Harrow appeared to disapprove of the Lord Governor's response, --a consequence of the government system in place in these parts-- and his lack of civility –or care--towards his subjects, provided yet one more reason to live and work outside the law. But Harrow did manage a 'thank you' and bid him goodnight.

We left. As we rode back, we passed some children begging on the Raja Road. I looked at them and pitched them a few coins that I had in my pocket –for they looked hungry and must have had families some place-- and I thought of the immense wealth we left behind in a palace for a governor who had starving children, begging just outside his front gates. "Why don't we use our profits to help people?" I suddenly asked.

Harrow pulled his horse to a halt as if stunned. "What?"

"Why don't we use some of our profits to help people in places like this?"

"Are you a missionary now Reed?"

"Well, no, but I—"

"Stop with the kindness –you're starting to frighten me!"

"We've been helping people too much if you ask me." Sunderland barked. "Look what New Haven got us! An entire relief party killed by these imperial bastards –and very little profit to show for it."

"I just thought we should win the hearts and minds of the population instead of—"

"--Do you want to save the world Mister Reed?" Harrow asked.

I didn't answer.

"If you do, you're in the wrong line of work."

Sunderland and the others laughed at my expense but, I couldn't help but think of ways I might be able to do better for the populace. Maybe it was the ghost of Mister Rush. Maybe it was my own upbringing and the words of my mother back in Bristol. Whatever the trigger, I couldn't really let the thought go…

We made it back to port and found a tavern open to the night air right on the beach. Here much of the cooking was done on a big open fire with curry and it could take time to get accustomed to it but, being from Great Britain, I had my experience with Indian food and that night, with the crew, I would eat steaming bowls of it with lamb meat and vegetables. I sat with Whitney, Jack-Karr, Tiger and Rift –who smashed his food into mush and ate through a hole in his throat since his lower jaw and been blown off— and we celebrated being away from the rigging for a while.

There was music made by a sitar, sepoys, sailors, and women of a particular trade. Our men struck up friendships with these women quite quickly and sometimes with more than just one.

I admit that Jack-Karr, as dangerous as he was, was good company and I did tend to gravitate to this group, Whitney, Tiger, and the like when at port. These men, in a strange way, had a shade of good in them different from some of the other killers we had onboard –and Duncan-Howe and Lynch were also good to be around when we were lucky enough to get their company. So, I was content for the evening.

The next night, I had watch back on the ship with a skeleton crew of twenty-five men under the command of Mister Bishop. We made a deck fire, and I stood close to our warning flares to keep a weather eye out. Indian merchants rowed up and brought food and wine to our rail. They would cook right onboard their long boats and give you any request. Some of it we would trade for or buy. They offered us the company of women but, we had an article that forbit this kind of thing on our decks –on land, that was another matter—but not onboard and never on watch for if I was caught, I would undoubtedly be thrown overboard.

The next day, after a quiet night, I was allowed back on the beach after Hallock –his head pounding from the party the night before-- replaced me.

Not far from Madras proper was a killing ground. A fighting arena right out of the past like the gladiators of old. They called it The Abaddon Circle which was Hebrew for 'The Place of Destruction.' We entered through the gates of the first floor. It looked like an old theater in the 'round, there was balcony seating. gambling –and the crowd-- was in full roar. A fighting match was about to start so our crew pushed for position on a few benches.

"What's happening here tonight exactly?" I looked to Raeder who motioned me to be silent as a man took to the center of this sand-filled arena.

This man raised his arms in a motion to quiet the crowd. "Ladies and gentlemen --if we have such in our ranks-- for our next action tonight we have something you might all enjoy…." He raised his voice and motioned to a tunnel "From the prison colony on Tasmania comes one of the toughest criminals the new world has to offer. He's big, he's bold and he's an expert in dispensing pain, please salute the Cyclone of Terror, The Maelstrom of Madness --Ash De Vacca!"

--The crowd erupted as a man –or small giant emerged from the shadows with a skull tattooed to his face, massive shoulders and armed with a trident.

"And…out of the inferno of war on the high plains of Africa and Asia Minor comes the Messenger of Death, The Madman from Malta, The Master of Torture --Mister Tiberius Longshanks!"

There was another loud roar from our crew for it turned out, many in our ranks knew this man and had fought with him….

A set of heavy doors opened up and out walked the challenger -- Tiberius Longshanks. Tiberius was armed with a heavy ball –the size of a cannon round-- attached to a metal chain almost like the kind of ball and chain we would punish people with when we chained them up and kicked them overboard.

The fight started and the warriors closed in on each other and engaged. The trident worked as a blade on one end and an attack staff on the other making Tiberius dodge and move to reposition himself. Tiberius dropped back, weapon in hand and when he swung it, it suddenly took out a heavy wooden support beam dropping a section of the balcony above and all the spectators in it came crashing down to arena level. They panicked to get out of the way of the action, ran and dove into the crowds sitting ringside on the ground floor.

He threw the chain which wrapped around the handle of the trident and with a heavy pull, it was ripped from the challenger's hands, sailed across the arena, and slammed blade first into the woodwork next to where I was standing….

--My eyes went wide with this near-death experience!

Ash De Vacca, now unarmed, did a somersault over to the weapons rack and pulled a combat net and an axe before jumping back into the action…

The two worked in a circle pattern. Then Tiberius started to swing his weapon round and round over his head. It was so heavy and powerful that those of us in the benches up close could feel the wind coming off it. Suddenly his challenger moved to charge under it when he brought the ball down and struck the man's skull separating it from his body and sending it into the seats –where it landed in a woman's lap!

--She screamed!

But there was a roar from the crowd –except from myself, for I was still something of a human being and I was appalled by this –but our crew loved it.

That night in the tavern, our men, Teague, Raeder, Wolfe, and the others stormed inside in a celebratory mood. I sat next to a fire trying to forget what I had witnessed --and waited on wine and bowl of curry. Tonight, was yet, another stark reality of this new world and killing still made my fingers tremble. I was almost relieved that I still was not comfortable with death.

As I sat in place, I realized that I had now been ashore on almost every continent –and several islands and mostly in peace. Most townships were populated by those much like ourselves, privateers. Sometimes navy from different countries or marines and natives. Sometimes slavers or bureaucrats on their way to lay claim to some distant plantation or resource. Most passed with no offense. Every once in a while, one would turn up missing, with a little help from our crew. Sometimes he would be found later, floating face down in the harbor or bleeding to death in the street. But other than the rare incident, the work and release in town continued….

We mixed with other notorious crews. The men of The Revolution, The Eclipse, we met with men of The Black Witch out of Salem and their Captain, Rafer-Davies and even a woman who was a Captain named Anne. Everywhere, the rumblings were the same --war and a sense that our world was being run down and forced to become smaller and smaller….

"I fought the Spanish for ten years, one colonial war after another and in the end nothing changed." Merciless complained. "The rich got richer. They took over more islands, more commerce and what did we get?" He preached to the men of The Witch as he kicked the bottle up, "We got poverty and despair handed out by the government like a bad case of the plague. Now they won't stop until we're all dead." He looked to me, "If the crown had their way, I'd be a gardener back in Dover."

"And a right terrible one at that." Duncan added, "The only flowers we'd be good for are the ones we push up when we're dead!"

Davies, a man with a distinct scar weathered by the sun and dark hair and features exhaled his tobacco smoke from a hookah with some women not too far off. I tried to size him up, he had a slight, almost wicked grin and both he and his first officer, Balack -a man who had lost an eye to be replaced by a patch-- both seemed driven by something. Something unseen. Though they were present here and now at this celebration, I could sense something abstract about their manner, like they had pressing business.

Suddenly, there was cheering by the door of this tavern and a steel box was suddenly dropped on the table next to me and as I looked up, the shadow of Tiberius rolled over me as he took the seat across from me. He held out his hand across the table "Longshanks!" he smiled as people around still hit him on the back with congratulations for his victory earlier in the evening....

"I know" I took his hand "I saw you fight tonight!"

"What with this?" He opened the footlocker to reveal his cannon ball type weapon it still had some blood, skin and.... hair on it. "It's just for show."

"For show?" I was put off by his casual nature and the casual reflection on his killing.

"A circus instrument of sorts." He motioned to the weapon, "I rarely ever fight with something like that in the real world."

"I thought your arena was the real world."

"What? The arena? Na, that's just a way to kill prisoners for profit."

"How do you mean?"

"We're paid....to fight and exterminate prisoners. Rapists. Murderers. Sometimes pirates. People like that."

"Is that what all this is?"

"Once they've been sentenced. They get to choose between the guillotine or the arena. The gambling works up the economy and justice -- -however crude—is served."

"So, you do this killing?"

"A man has to make a living boy!" He must have read my reaction for he continued, "It's not God's work I know but, it does give me a purpose and pay the bills so to speak."

The bar maiden arrived with a bottle of wine, which he helped himself too –without the use of a mug. "Another!" He ordered, "And one for my friend here a Mister? Mister?"

"Reed."

"And one for Mister Reed." He tilted the bottle towards the ceiling then gasped for air. "So, Master Reed, how long have you been with The Venger?" Before I could answer, he continued, "No matter, any man in that's ship custody is bound by its articles and must be a good man. What were you before, in your previous life?"

"Previous life?" I almost thought he was asking about reincarnation; it had seemed so long since my days in the classroom and this actually made me reflect a bit....

"Were you a soldier, a prison guard or something?" He slammed his hand on the table, "I know, an executioner."

"Why would you think that?" I wondered.

"Well, The Venger is home to certain talents."

At that point, Duncan-Howe emerged from the crowd, drink in hand. "Ah Tiberius, I see you met our schoolteacher. Mister Reed."
Longshanks looked at me. "Schoolteacher?"

I was prepared to be insulted, for my craft was obviously not considered the bravest.

"A schoolteacher, well that's remarkable! Smart man that Essex to employ some professors onboard, teach the men a thing or two about the world."

"What?"

"Yes, makes them better men I say. Smarter. More intella—intella-"

"Intelligent?"

"That's it. Ya see, this man is already payin' dividends right at this very table."

"Tiberius use to be our quartermaster."

"Really? What happened? Why did you leave."

"I got captured in Istanbul."

'Captured? But I thought the Venger went back for its men?'

"--By a wife!" Tiberius finally roared as all the men burst out laughing.

"And how is the woman?" Duncan-Howe asked as he lit his pipe. "Still unlucky enough to call you, her husband?"

"Aye, unlucky indeed." His smile faded. "She was killed by the pox last winter."

Howe waved his match to extinguish it and he became equally reverent. "I apologize. Bad humor that." He put his hand on his shoulder. "You have my sympathy –and my respect."

"I know –beautiful woman --and it was good while it lasted, God be praised! But we're here now –in a new world--in a new place in time."

"Indeed." Howe exhaled. "Ah, Tiberius," he continued with a tone of curiosity, "At the risk of offending you twice in one evening, may I ask, what does your future hold?"

"More killing I expect."

"And this killing –ah—profitable, is it?"

"Not really. Not enough to build a future on. Day to day tavern livin' is about all it's good for."

"And this tavern living? Good, is it?"

"See for yourself Duncan." Tiberius held his arms out. "This is all it ever is."

"Then I may have something to offer you."

"Yes?"

"A chance to return home."

"Me?"

"Aye, you were always good with a map and a gun –and The Venger needs to restore its ranks with real fighting men." He threw a quick glance to me, "No offense Reed." He looked back to Tiberius "So, what ya say, shall I put in a good word with our deck officer?"

He thought about it for a moment, his eyes seemed to drift off to a distant place or memory, then turned to Duncan, "I'd be obliged."

"Good, you'll have your hand on Lucifer's skull in no time."

DAWN. THE VENGER...

"Name?" Mister Lincoln asked as he kept his face in his legers and picked up his blade to carve a thumb print.

"I think you know my name." Longshanks smiled as he raised his scarred thumb to scar it again.

Lincoln looked up from his books, "Tiberius. I heard you were killing convicts in Calcutta."

"You heard right."

Moments later in the Captain's cabin, Harrow was pacing, making his thoughts known. "We can't have a man on board who was paid to kill prisoners –and he's difficult to control."

"Therrinfall was paid to kill prisoners."

"That's different. Therrinfall was commanded by the King."

"And that makes it different?"

"Therrinfall was a different person then. Young. His eyes not yet open to the way of politicians and their wicked ways. Longshanks is more seasoned. He knows right from wrong."

"This doesn't have anything to do with that business in Alexandria, does it? That business at the Pyramids?"

For a split second, Harrow's mind flashed back to the north African desert when the men of The Venger formed a defensive battle square, and riders charged them –through a sandstorm-- from all four sides by the thousands. Then he snapped back to the present... "No!" Harrow suddenly stopped and looked to Essex. "Well, maybe," He confessed. "Possibly."

"That battle was several years ago Harrow and we're not sure it was him who was responsible--"

"Yes, yes, I know and although I cannot prove Tiberius to be responsible, those civilians did die a horrible death in his custody." He looked out the window to the sea and mumbled the words, "Children too."

The captain finally stood. "You command the deck Harrow; the decision will be yours –and I won't go against it. If you want to deny his enlistment, I'll support it."

"Well, that's a good way to shame me into saying yes." Harrow said under his breath.

Harrow stepped out on the quarter deck where Tiberius stood as if it was a showdown.

"Mister Harrow."

"Tiberius."

There was an uncomfortable silence. "I bear you no ill will Mister Harrow and you have my word, that if you permit me to join the crew, you'll get the best I've got."

Harrow took a deep breath with the sound of acceptance. "Of that I have no doubt." And with a touch of reluctance he said, "You may sign the articles, then report to Mister Rajiv for a gun section assignment."

"Guns? I'd prefer to raid."

"I said guns damn it!" Harrow barked. "And you'll raid upon authorization and under authorization only. Do you understand me Tiberius?

"Yes sir." He said with reluctance, "I understand."

"Good, now get below."

As it happened, The Witch was leaving port and passed close to our decks at that time, and she was under the black flag.

"Where too?" Harrow yelled.

"Back to Jamaica" Rafer shouted. "If there's gonna be a war, I want to fight in home waters and not die among the corsairs."

"Good luck to ya then and bring the hell!"

"I will. Travel safe Venger."

One afternoon, towards the end of our first week in port, we got caught up in a game with some of the local children on the beach. The game was one the ancient Greeks played –though the Chinese in our crew claimed their countrymen had invented it. It was played with two teams and a ball we made from leather. You could only use your feet --not your hands—hands were not allowed but, you could get help from members of your team in trying to kick this ball in between two posts to score a point. This required a lot of running because the targets to kick the ball through were a hundred meters apart but, it was fun. The ronin, Bons, the Aztecs, Dax and Whitney mixed up with a few of the local children, so we had equal teams with children on both --and they seemed to have just as much fun as the rest of us….

The days dragged on and our stay in Madras was coming to a close. Arson issued the orders for all of us to wrap up whatever business we still had in town and prepare to leave for the ship by sunset so we could sail with the evening tide…

That afternoon, I was in a tent-like tavern on the beach to pass my remaining time ashore. The sun was low in the sky as I ate meat speared on a wooden stake. Lamb. I also had tea for the first time in months and I don't know what it was, but it wasn't as good as the tea we had sacked off the Coast of Africa. I was concerned by this notion. 'Was that tea better because we had raided it? Because it was stolen? No. That wasn't possible. Or was it?'

After dinner, once the afternoon sun started to descend and I was several rums into my evening, I decided on one more round before I was to report to the ship when a group of aristocratic gentlemen walked in and took a table not too far off. Not unusual in these parts but not together common either. I could hear talk of the East India Company and of the Royal African Company. They had several bottles of wine between them and became vocalized about plans for business and commerce. They discussed shipping objectives, new plantations, warehouses, not just in Madras but Siam and Java…

I tried to make a mental note on all this when their fire-side talk turned to the dirty business of politics. Things like, 'Which Parliament official should be bribed for a vote or government contract? What was the value of a slave? How to price out a human being for the auction block.' Others talked about 'stealing territory from France –and starting a war to do it.

What would a declaration of war cost? What reasons for war could be created to sell it to the citizens back home?' and 'Not to worry because the poor and the ignorant would fight it.'

Another asked, 'How long do you think before we destroy the American savage? Would prisoners from New Spain or South America make quality slaves? Or should they just be killed in the art of territorial expansion? How can we control the newspapers back home --and in the colonies-- to suit our means and our own narrative?'

--This was a dark conversation that started to get under my skin.

The talk then turned to killing privateers –and how much they seemed to enjoy this. Offer them a letter of marque then revoke it when it suited them. "Kill 'em all I say" One offered, "No need for a trial, we know the outcome already." They continued to talk about the sound a man's neck makes when it's snapped. The screaming a man does after a few days locked in a body cage or hung by a yardarm for the birds to pick apart. They laughed at the idea of this....

I finally had enough. I couldn't stomach anymore, and I blurted out, "Cowards!"

They all looked at me. Some stunned, "Are you speaking to us sir?"

"I am!" I continued with a little assistance from the rum bottle by my side, "You talk and talk and talk of buying politicians and killing as if you enjoy it –have you ever killed a man yourself? Or do you just pay someone to do it for ya?"

--There was a fair amount of shock about this confrontation.

"It's easy for you, isn't it? Just buy a politician. Start a war. Control the populace – it's all good for you as long as you make money --and more money than a man can use no doubt!" I spit out some rum for I was now sick to my stomach. "What do any of you know?" I said as my frustration began to wear me out, "You just hide behind your pocketbooks with entitlement and watch the world decay into profits!"

One man smoked from a hookah as if board with my words.

"You make me ashamed to be English –but then I'm not English anymore, am I? I'm a man of The Venger. The Venger is my country now!"

One man peered at me, "The Venger?" he slowly asked.

Suddenly, I was fighting for my life. These men were beating me with fists, all six of them --and one with a cane. I made a fight of it, punching and kicking back but, they got the better of me and I collapsed. They started kicking me once I was down and I started to lose focus. Moments later, I was dragged outside where the beating continued. I threw what punches I could as I took a serious blow across the head from a walking stick that almost knocked me senseless. I struggled to remain conscious and realized that I was being dragged down the dirt street --bleeding from my mouth. I tried to focus so I could call for help, but I just couldn't put the words together. As I was pulled through the dust, I thought I saw Briggs in the shadows of an alley way, but I could not get a good look or manage to call out. Before I knew it, I was thrown in a prison cell. "You be hanged in a few hours!" Was all I heard my jailor say and I collapsed –out cold!

At the beach, our men were preparing to make their way back to The Venger to make sail and leave India. Mister Arson was standing in the tide, waving the last of the men aboard the long boats.

Suddenly Briggs came running up...

"They got 'em!" He said in a near panic. "Reed has been captured!"

"What?" Arson asked.

Duncan-Howe removed the pipe from his teeth, "By who?"

"R.A.C. Officers." Briggs said, "They beat him senseless and dragged him down the street to the Botswana Constable Block."

"R.A.C.!!!" Arson answered. The Royal African Company –slavers! "Pirate bastards!"

"Can't be! We paid the tax." Howe replied. "We're exempt from this kind of hostility."

"They overstep!"

"This must be about Porto Norvo!" Addo suggested.

"If it is, we're gonna have a war here!" Lynch added.

"The Portuguese must've issued death warrants on us!" Addo said, concerned.

"What?" Duncan remarked, "In addition to the warrants we've already got? One more damn government warrant isn't going to make a difference where our careers are concerned! Besides, R.A.C. officers don't have the guts to enforce a criminal warrant. This must be something else. Something personal."

"What do we do?" Briggs pressed.

Duncan-Howe turned to Teague, standing in the tide a few meters away, with some of his combat regulars, unaware of the conversation, "Teague!"

Teague walked through the water, followed by a few more of the crew, "What is it?"

"Reed's been imprisoned by R.A.C. officers" Howe explained.

"They're gonna hang him!"

Teague looked to Briggs.

"They were bragging about it as they dragged him down the street." Briggs explained.

"And yet you did nothing?"

Briggs tried to stutter out an answer, "There-there was too many of them, I couldn't---"

Teague shook his head, grit his teeth, and motioned as if he was ready to strike Briggs out of frustration. It wasn't because of any special affection for a schoolteacher, it was the idea of any man from The Venger being taken against his will --that angered him.

"You did the right thing Mister Briggs. Best to get help." Duncan-Howe mediated the situation and tried to bring a sense of calm to the conversation –but this didn't make Briggs feel any better. Duncan-Howe then looked to Teague, "You're the ranking officer Mister Teague –we paid the harbor tax, do we put this to the Governor?"

Teague thought for a split second...

"By the time we get word to the governor, Reed will be dead!" Arson said, clearly maneuvering for a more immediate and more aggressive solution. "Those R.A.C. bastards will have the satisfaction of killin' him – and braggin' about it all over town! We'll be mocked!"

"Aye" Merciless barked, "And I ain't in the business of being mocked."

Teague gave a slight look over his shoulder to Mako, Tak, Sanjuro, Takeda and Hatano who just stood there listening. Then he suddenly said: "Go get 'em!" and the samurai, without a word, moved out, weapons ready.

I sat in a prison cell, wounded and bleeding. My head hammered and thumping with my pulse like a rhythmic pain vibrating through my skull. The R.A.C aristocrats were having drinks with the officers of the law as they taunted me here and there with some wicked –pompous—laughs. They stuck around only to see me hang and the hangman was on his way....

"Pity it's just the one pirate. Maybe there's a way to drag this hanging out and make the experience last longer."

I looked up and was jarred as the front doors of the constable's office suddenly slammed open and in walked Mako and the others.

"Ah Orientals." The constable stood, as the others watched the ronin enter the room, "Don't see many of you in these parts. How can I be of service?"

--He had no idea the ronin and I knew each other, and I gave no hint. There were no words from these samurai, only an awkward silence. Tak looked around as if to size up the other officers in the room and then I watched as these killers seemed to slowly space out....

"Do you, speak the King's English?" The officer asked puzzled by the lack of response.

Mako smiled at this question –English and King in the same sentence. His eyes then seemed to size this naive man up as a target...

"Do...you...speak...English?" He said slowly with a touch of frustration.

"It's no use. Ignorant, Oriental, monkeys." Another R.A.C Officer said with obvious disdain as he leaned his chair back against the wall by a small fireplace.

Something suddenly started to feel very wrong to these gentlemen now. The silence stretched out into almost painful awkwardness and a strange sense of foreboding seemed to creep in....

The constable raised his hand to grab Mako and throw him out when --in the blink of an eye-- out came the steel and off came his hand with a sudden swing --zzzzzziiiiiiiiiiiiiiippppppppp! He screamed clutching the bloody stump of a wrist and as he collapsed to his knees the ronin jumped into action with a series of quick, rapid strikes and all the officers were cut apart and cut down. The moves were so quick, that I couldn't even see the swords in action, only the reflection of the blades –like lightning-- in the candlelight with the sound of 'the zip' through the air followed by the 'slllllliiiiittttttttttt' of the cutting and the 'thump' as severed arm or hand hit the floor. Even a jaw was cut off, separated by a blade through the 'jaw hinge' in the face as the blade cut through it --and dropped it to the floor.

After the bodies all hit the floor, I then heard a rolling sound move over the floor planks and as it got louder, I looked to see the Constable's head wobble over to the base of my cell door.

--I jumped back as my cage door was suddenly thrown open. Mako looked at me and smiled. "Teacher, time to go!"

I made quick about it.

We stepped outside into the street just as the hangman suddenly walked up for his appointment saying, "I think that's my prison---er--"

--He was cut down mid-sentence.

The samurai formed a protective square around me as we moved down the block, through the dust. The civilians moved out of our way and, in some cases ran back inside their shops, one that didn't was pushed out of the way by Takeda....

We marched out of town and onto the beach where the rest of my comrades waited. Arson looked at me as I walked into the tide, "You're late."

I smiled and climbed aboard the jolly boat with the ronin, beaten, in pain but far from dead.

The moon moved behind the clouds. One of the castle guards was asleep the other two were slowly moving aimlessly around their post when the throwing stars zipped in, killing all of them. Once they dropped, we stormed across the bridge and opened the perimeter doors…

--Like shadows, we moved towards the palace, killing any guards that stood between us and the front doors. One guard even took a throwing star in the turban –and with a crack, he stood upright, his turban wrap turned a dark red and blood started to drip down his temple. Sanjuro finally pushed him down to the bricks and pulled the throwing star from his head!

Moments later, our men rode into the courtyard on horseback, dismounted, picked up a guard and used his head as a battering ram to open up the palace doors! Some of our crew rode their horses directly inside the palace waiting room…

--A valet came running towards us "What's the meaning of this?"

Jack-Karr dismounted, closed the distance between him and the valet and then grabbed him by the neck. "Do you recognize us?" He asked as he squeezed.

The man stumbled for words….

"I won't ask again."

"Ma-men of The Venger."

"Right. Do you know why we're here?"

The doors to the main bed chamber were kicked open, Baako, Rabal, Jeddah, Toombs, and Cage stormed in. Toombs removed the expensive whore from the bed as she awoke with a panicked scream, and he tossed her out of the way as the others seized the Governor and carried him out of the room.

Moments later, he was brought to the barred holding room where his treasure was kept. The heavy lock was opened with the help of an axe and Rabal and Kannon heaved the two massive, carved, wooden doors ajar. Harrow stepped to the front of our ranks. He looked at the treasure and then to the Governor, "We paid the tax and one of our men was almost killed, lynched by pirates of the Royal African Company. Are you aware of this?"

The man gave a nervous swallow and shook his head no.

"Now you know. You can consider yourself lucky if you survive this night. In the meantime, we're taking a refund." He then turned to the men. "Take the tax and just our tax. Leave the rest, understand?"

Jack-Karr gave a nod and the platoon started to pull the iron chests out and loaded them up on some of the horses and wagon that were brought along.

As our men started to muster out, Harrow climbed up on his horse and pointed to the Governor, "If the likes of this was to ever happen again, we're gonna ride up here and kill ya! Understand?"

He man gave a petrified nod in agreement.

"No tariffs for The Venger ever again –or the master dies!" And with that, he turned his mount, and we galloped off....

Harrow climbed over the railing at dawn and almost seemed to storm aboard, still angry about the night's events. Essex stopped him, "What happened?"

"Agents of the R.A.C. imprisoned Reed and threatened to kill him."

"What? How?"

"They pressed ganged him from a tavern."

"He's a schoolteacher for God's sake!"

"He was a schoolteacher--" Harrow seemed to say this with a tone designed to remind the Captain of the ship's principals --that a man's past was his past and no longer applied once aboard. "--Now he's one of us. They recognized him as a privateer and seized him."

"How did they recognize him?"

"He identified himself as being from The Venger in a confrontation and they beat him senseless."

Essex seemed to reposition himself and straightened up with a deep exhale. "Was anyone else hurt?"

"Just Reed." Harrow said, "Teague sent the ronin to liberate him. They killed a few of these R.A.C. criminals."

Essex nodded as if to accept this. "Well, I can't get angry about that."

"And there's one other thing."

"What?"

"We rode to the Governor's palace and reclaimed our harbor tax."

"You what?" Now Essex was angry but, he tried to keep his voice down and not provide any entertainment to the deck.

"We stormed his household treasury and took what was ours in retaliation for the actions against Reed."

Frustration seemed to mount with the Captain, "How many?"

"How many what?"

"How many men did you kill? --Don't fool with me."

Harrow paused then finally gave his answer, "Eight sir."

"Damn it, Harrow! You killed eight men and raided the Governor's palace without my authorization."

"I did as I believed you would do Captain. Our man —such as he is-- was set for the gallows. The harbor tax is supposed to prevent this. When it didn't, our deal with the local Raja was void. I took the action that I though was required and.... I took the action that I thought the men would respect, sir."

"Are you the Captain here Harrow?"

There was a moment of silence between them.

Harrow finally spoke up, "Would you have done any different sir?"

"No" He finally confessed, "I would not." He exhaled with the words "Killing Governors is starting to become a habit here."

"Not a bad thing."

Harrow seemed to get some satisfaction in this. but Essex moved close. "We have to demonstrate a chain of command. With these men here, with their temperament, we have to show them that decisions —and actions-- are put together in proper fashion with proper intent." He looked at the deck, at his crew, at the men around him who climbed over the rail to board and take up their stations. Men like Rabal, Jagger, Teague and Mako. "If we, as officers start acting without authority, on impulse and out of anger, how long do you think it will be before men like Teague, Arson and Reader take the law into their own hands without command or justification and start doing what they damn well please?"

Harrow seemed to take sudden sense from this. He hadn't thought that far ahead. He only believed his actions were just and should be supported and indeed, they were but, when he heard the logic of the Captain, he knew he should have gone about it another way. "I apologize sir."

"I don't want your apology, George. I want a God damn second officer who understands the psychology of the men around us."

"And I do sir."

Essex seemed to reign in his temperament. He exhaled, "I know you do" He finally said, "You're a good man Harrow, even if this one got away from you--"

Harrow seemed to buck up with these words....

"Our job is not an easy one."

"No." Harrow's eyes darted back up to Essex. "It-is-not."

"If anyone asks, I gave the command to raid the palace. Don't let the men know that you took action on your own accord. Understand."

"I do sir."

"Otherwise, we'll have men killing anyone and everyone just for the hell of it." The Captain started walking towards the quarter deck then stopped and turned back, exhausted he said, "And Harrow, divide the harbor tax among the men."

"Yes sir."

Essex suddenly stopped as he caught sight of me by the quarter deck with all the signs of a rough day and the Captain straightened up, "Reed? How is it with you?"

I mustered a response, "I'm fine sir."

"Glad to hear it. Get below and let Johannis have a look at you."

I stumbled below deck, made my way past the galley and into to hospital.

Johannis turned as I entered, "Making friends again Reed?"

"Trying to Doctor." I said as I took a seat for him to check my skull and eyes. Kojo, the new orderly --whose shackles were broken on the deck of The Future --brought some tools forward to assist the doctor and as he did, one of the blue and yellow deck birds flew into the infirmary and landed near me. I looked at it and –strange as it may seem—I thought of its ability to fly anywhere it pleased while I sat there wounded. What clicked in my head as I saw this, was our code. The crew felt obligated to get me out of jail and things almost spun out of control from there with Harrow forming his own command to take to the Governor's palace and if things went south there, a war could have been sparked between us and the local authority – and only Harrow seemed concerned by this and only after the fact when he spoke to the Captain. The rest of the men seemed unconcerned about the prospects of a war. None of them even seemed to be bothered by this possibility.

XVI

LUCIFER'S HAMMER

OFF THE COAST OF SIAM….

Flares lit up the sky as we engaged the French treasure ship Bon Roi….

A long-distance exchange of cannon fire opened up, a bombardment and cannon exchange that would go on for two days before we could sail in to close the gap --and once we did, all hell broke loose. Therrinfall, Flynn, Irons, Clairmont, Archer and a few others climbed towards my position in the crow's nest as I dropped down and we met on the lookout platform just below my post. Therrinfall had a roll of guns and satchels of grenades. "As you were Reed." Therrinfall shouted, ordering me to keep in place.

"Shouldn't I get to a combat station on deck?"

"No." He passed out the guns. "We're going to start the fight from right here –sniper duty!" And he thew a gun up to me. I caught it but I wasn't a sniper --and I had almost no experience with a long rifle.

The cannon started slamming into our side –or bouncing off-- until one ball shot through an open gun door, zipped through the deck, and exploded killing the crew of battery number twenty-six. Rajiv had large splinters pierce him all up and down his right side.

He pulled some of the splinters out and left some of them in as he called for gunner replacements which came running…

Timbers was slowly crawling across the floor panels with splinters in his back the size of knives. The wounded were dragged out of the deck section as there was another explosion. "Damn tyrants!" Mister Tane shouted as Mister Hayte dropped a fresh cannon ball in the cannon for him to plunge into place. "We shall pay them back in kind!"

The master gunner waited to time the firing with the rolling tide for maximum effect. "On the up roll," He shouted, "FIRE!" And our guns again, erupted....

Blasts shattered along their hull, railing and top deck and forced sections of their mast to come crashing down –on top of us and our deck-- with part of the sail on fire. Dakar and Rabal began to chop it away and with the help of Jata and some extra hands pushed the flaming mass overboard to clear our decks.

There was another pounding exchange of cannons. Gun sections were blasted apart and turned to splinters. Wounded men crawling away, some torn open with chunks of wood and metal. Where the gun crews had causalities, other men climbed into their place and manned the weapons.

The French marines were firing at us from their ships rigging and crow's nest. We fired back, some of their men fell from the top of the mast, into the sea, dead –others were wounded—at the cost of some of our own. Mister Irons hit and dropped his target as Archer took a round in the shoulder, he fell from his post and got tangled in the rigging. Claremont started to climb down and pulled his knife to cut him free....

I fired and watched the ball from my musket splinter the railing of the 'look out' across the way, on the Bon Roi just as both our ships slammed side to side against each other, their 'look out' fell over the railing of his observation post to his death below. A moment after that, their main mast snapped under fire and all the men on it plunged to their deaths as it crashed across both our decks.

I looked down from my 'look out' position to see the combat and havoc below. Our crew was fully engaged. Mister Irons lit a grenade and tossed it down by their wheel where it exploded. Another was dropped on their quarter deck and blew two men overboard. He repeated the action. I picked one up, but he stopped me, "That's enough, anymore and we hit our own men when they board." I looked down as our men were now swarming their top deck.

Therrinfall raised his weapon, "Use the guns!"

Irons fired and hit a sailor, then reached back for another loaded gun. I fired and missed, hitting the woodwork by their wheelhouse. Irons kept hitting his targets that would fall and roll across the planks....

Then, there was another --sudden—explosion and our position shifted like the deck had moved. I grabbed hold of the railing around our lookout post and caught my breathe, "What the hell?" Our position suddenly shifted again and then I realized what was about to happen. "Oh no!" The mast we were on, had been snapped! We all quickly grabbed hold of something --anything-- as the mast slowly tilted backwards –with us at the top of it. I screamed for my life as we started gaining momentum until it fell back and slammed into the sea....

I plunged into the water, and everything went dark, silent, and faded away. The cannon blasts, the screaming, the gunfire –all drifted far away as the force of the mast plunged me deeper and deeper into the dark depths and the air had escaped my lungs. Finally, I pulled myself together, snapped out of it and started to swim back to the surface. Against the force of the current dragging me down. Above my position, in the dark, I looked up and saw the yellow flashes of fire and cannon and as I made my way back to the surface, it grew louder and louder until I splashed topside and was back in the action. There was fire and the world was exploding all around me....

Whole sections of mast and rigging were blown into the water with men attached. They'd scream until they hit the surface of the ocean and were dragged down. I swam over and grabbed hold of what was left of the mast and tried to catch my breath. I saw a hand reaching up in the tide and quickly moved towards it and grabbed hold of it. It was Clairmont, trapped under the water, tangled in the rope, and rigging. He was fighting to get some air. I dove under -the water was dark, except when an explosion lit up the sky and ocean near the surface, then I could see, and I pulled my khukuri knife and began to cut the rope as fast as I could. He was gasping, taking water into his lungs. I sawed through the rope and pulled him to the surface where he started coughing up water...

"Are you alright?" I shouted over the cannon fire.

He slowly nodded and struggled to speak, "Th-thanks lad!" He coughed, "I'm in your debt."

Therrinfall and Irons also splashed to the surface. "Damn bastards!" Therrinfall shouted. "They're going to try to drown us to death!"

"Where's Archer?" I shouted, realizing he hadn't come up from the water. Therrinfall and Irons both dove under the surface to find him, so did I. I swam along the submerged rigging and the sails looking for him -- nothing! I couldn't see much in the dark water but there was no trace of him.

"He's gone!" Therrinfall shouted as he splashed back to the surface. "Archer has gone to the locker!"

Suddenly there was a giant explosion on our deck –that lit up the sky— and got all out attention. "We need to get back on the ship!" Therrinfall shouted.

I looked at the mast, though it had snapped, it was still attached –barely- - to the base on our top deck. "We have to make our way back onboard." I looked to Clairmont, "Can you make it?" He was exhausted and out of breath but nodded yes. I climbed up onto the mast and pulled him up, then, with the others, we turned and started to climb the mast, out of the water, back towards The Venger's deck…

Some explosions hit near us as we got closer and closer to the deck and the action. I made my way over the rail and back on to The Venger's planks. I helped Clairmont off the mast and onto the deck, and with Therrinfall and Irons, we crossed it to where the action was. I found some of our men, Addo, Kato, Fury –bleeding from the temple, Standish, Lynch –who was bleeding from a knife wound— Roux, Miranda and a few others forming another battle line ready to cross onto the enemy ship…

"Where the hell have you been?" Standish asked as he caught sight of us.

"You'll never guess!" I pointed to the mast.

He looked at it. "Good God!" Then looked at me, the winded Clairmont, Irons and Therrinfall all drenched and exhausted. "Are you still up for a fight?"

I nodded yes and pulled my cutlass…

"Then let's go!" Standish shouted, "Into the breach lads!"

"Well, time to die historic!" Clairmont said with a touch of reluctance.

I summoned my courage, grit my teeth and we moved across our deck –through the hand-to-hand combat where heads were bashed, people were gashed, skulls cracked, and men pinned with grappling hooks-- and we made the jump across the water and into the chaos on the French frigate but just as we climbed to clear the rail --Standish took a sudden cutlass square to the head! The blade lodged in his skull and snapped at the handle so the French marine could not retrieve it and he was now without his weapon. I moved forward and looked up just as this man pulled a pistol, inches from my face and pulled the trigger but --it misfired with a spark! I moved my cutlass just as Kato emerged from the chaos and used his samurai sword to remove the man's head –the tip of his samurai blade cut my cheek as it swung clear though the victim's neck—and the head rolled in the air before tumbling on the deck like a cannon ball…

--His body remained standing for a few moments before it buckled and collapsed.

More marines stormed forward, I pushed Mister Barak out of the way as a sergeant slammed down his cutlass and snapped it on the rail –the sergeant was killed by a gun blast from Sampson-Rift, but Mister Barak was in shock, "Oh no!" He suddenly said, distressed.

"What?" I shouted, having just saved his life and wondering what the disappointment was.

"You saved my life."

"I know." I smiled proud of myself as bullets ripped up the area all around us.

"But now I owe you a life debt."

"What?" Bullets zipped by…

"Yes," he said, alarmed, "Now I have to save your life in kind."

"Oh, you don't have to---" I ducked as more gunfire and lead hit the jolly boat I was using for cover.

Jack-Karr, emptied his pistol and laughed, "Damn Moors."

Suddenly an explosion blew them both clear of the deck and into the ocean below –I was blown up against the mast and other French marines suddenly piled on me as I collapsed to the deck. I was taking punches from every direction --then a metal ball swung in with a loud 'whoooop' and slammed into them. Blood rained down on me and a French marine fell to the planks with a collapsed skull. I looked up to see Tiberius as he pulled his chained weapon back and continued to clear the deck with this tornado type machine.

A circus instrument my ---?!?

Baako pulled the marines off me, broke one's neck and threw two others over the rail into the ocean before he picked me up and pulled me to my feet....

Another grenade went off killing several more sailors nearby and filling this section with smoke.

I rolled to one knee and looked up, as Mister Lo-Tan used the staff weapon from his back and swung these rods with a vengeance and it craaaacccccked across four French marines knocking them back…breaking bones and clearing men like the blade of giant fan. This weapon, --the three-section staff-- in action is hard to describe, Lo used it to block swords or sometimes, he swung the top rod in one direction with his left hand, using the center section to block as he swung the third section in a completely different direction with his right hand. Almost like having fighting sticks in both hands with a middle section to block!

I froze, paralyzed for a moment....

Lynch reclaimed pistols off the deck and fired both of them, then he pulled a third pistol from his sash and fired it before drawing his cutlass to engage, the men around him. Mister Jata had an enemy combatant under each arm, and a saber through his stomach and I watched as he suddenly jumped the railing --with his victims-- to drown them in the ocean below....

Jeddah was fighting with a grappling hook stuck in his back, he slammed his knife through a man's hand pining it to the wood railing before Jagger stepped forward with a 'down-swing' from his cutlass and cut the man's arm off, leaving the hand --still moving-- pinned to the woodwork as his body fell to the planks...

Attackers and defenders slammed into each other, cutting, hammering, clawing --struggling to gain advantage. A man fell on me with a tomahawk stuck in his skull. Sam removed it and gave me a hand to my feet just as he was blasted by a musket ball and fell backwards –dead! I turned as the sniper who shot him was tackled and killed by a blow to the head from a cannon ball, the only thing Mister Daws could get his hands on to hit him with....

There were several explosions on deck where gun powder had been ignited, blowing men aloft and overboard, and sometimes into other combatants....

Hazzard and Fury threw another man over the rail.

Wicks was throwing grenades below deck causing explosion after explosion... The quarter deck was swallowed by flames as our Captain emerged –sword in hand—as he moved through the flames like the devil himself, killing everyone in his path...

Khan kicked one marine down below deck, and we stormed down after him, with Dakar, Kane, Bons, Cage, a wounded Volkan, Rabal and several others. Here we crossed blades and fought some of their gunners. The enemy gun crews tried to reposition their cannon to fire within the deck -- at us-- and kill everyone in the interior with 'grape shot.' We charged and closed the gap fast as a gun opened up and cut through our ranks –killing Laurent, Stylen, two others and wounding Cage....

"Move!" Rabal drove us forward towards the guns and before the rest of the cannon could be positioned to fire, all the enemy gun crews were cut down with exception of one which got their shot off...

We fought our way forward, past the ship's medical quarters –their doctor was not to be harmed, for he would be needed later.

Enemy officers below deck tried to barricade themselves in various cabins for protection but our gun fire made them pay as we shot through the doors. Those who did not collapse to the floor –killed by splinters and musket fire-- had to listen to the sound of the axe and tomahawk cutting their way towards them. Surrender entered the mind of every man cornered. Some of the enemy crew climbed through windows to make their escape and take their chances on the ocean surface. Many dropped their weapons and raised their hands in the air.

At one end of the deck, the Moors fought their way through to the rum stores and after a momentary survey, sheathed their swords, turned, and left the stores to their Christian counterparts who were all too happy to sample the wares and begin to load 'em up –even as the fighting continued all around them.

At the aft end of the deck, Lo used the chain in between his sectioned staff to choke and man and drop him to the floor. Then he unleashed it in a wild swing that bashed it across another four French marines knocking them back! Lo-Tan may have been a monk –but he was a particularly vicious one when angry...

Most of the French crew had retreated to a fabricated section of the hold where heavy wooden cargo doors could be closed behind them --like a shield-- to protect the section. Addo and the others ran up against them, but the doors would not budge. Seconds later, one of their officers opened an eye slit and nervously looked out this shutter just as Toombs slammed his saber blade into it, killing him as his blade smashed into his eye and through his skull...

Hatano, Baako and Blythe started taking the door apart with axes. Once they had punched a hole in it, Hallock, Sanjuro and Wicks moved up with grenades.

"Here, give it here" Newcastle turned as Sanjuro lit the fuse and pitched it to him. The first grenade was shoved through the hole to explode. We lit and pushed additional grenades into this section. Blast after blast erupted inside –and we heard the screams of the men in between explosions....

"Open it up!" Newcastle shouted....

We went back to work on the doors with our axes. We had to work fast for the deck was now on fire and one spark could ignite the powder magazine. We cut a hole big enough to storm inside this compartment and we charged through the smoke. Baako first –with his axe-- followed by Blythe and the ronin, then I moved up and went through the hole. Inside this compartment, I saw the bleeding, dying combatants in pain. Wounded French marines crawling across this deck --and blast work everywhere. The damage was complete....

As we searched, we also found an iron trunk fashioned with a special three-key lock. Newcastle immediately recognized this box as something of importance because of the configuration and he ordered it and other trunks removed to The Venger. He then ordered us to clear out fast, taking anything of value on the way....

The fire had weakened the deck and caused it to suddenly give way. Several of us –while fighting—suddenly fell through the floor and plunged to the deck below. I landed on a cannon and tumbled over in pain. Abel dropped through this section to the next deck below, Lynch landed on an enemy combatant and Calixto had hold of the planks above where we fell and managed to heave himself back up to the deck we were on. I collected myself, found my sword but saw that O'Shea had fallen through the deck and been speared on a large piece of jagged timber which was still on fire even after it had impaled him. He was bleeding from the mouth but still alive. Lynch killed the combatant he dropped on, then kicked and snapped the timber that had speared O'Shea and helped him to his feet. O'Shea could not stand without aid. Lynch looked to me, "Pull-it-out!" He motioned to this timber spear still stuck in O'Shea, "Pull it out Reed. Now!"

I summoned my courage, gripped the blood covered stake, and pulled it through O'Shea's body. The blood was dark which told me that a vital organ had been pierced but I took him from Lynch and tried to move him to safety. "You'll be all right!" I screamed as I tried to move him away from the fighting....

He coughed up some blood, "Don't lie to me boy. I-I've lived on borrowed time for years and now the devil's come to collect!" He smiled as more blood shot from his mouth, "It comes for all of us.... does...it... not?" And with that, his eyes went lifeless....

"No! No! Come on" I shook his body, "Don't die on me!" but it was no use. He was gone.

Lynch helped Abel up from the deck below. He slapped the fire out on his tunic and helped him to his feet. We picked up O'Shea's body and we moved towards the top deck when Raeder came through the hold with some of his men. "Move through the deck" He ordered, "Get anything of value –we're losing the ship--so move, fast!"

Lynch looked at me and we put O'Shea down. We started moving though the different holds as smoke started to cloud the decks and stifle our breathing ---then, we uncovered something quite new to me, boxes with Asian markings. My shipmates called it The Devil's Claw --I knew it as opium! We impounded it. The market price was quite high for something like this –some of it would be turned over to Johannis for the wounded— the rest would be sold off and I would be warned not to use it by Lynch...

---The price for such property was low in Asian ports where it was quite common but, it fetched a high price in the Caribbean and in the Americas where it was harder to come by. This was also the job of Mister Lincoln, not just the inventory and accounting of impounded goods but also market evaluation. If profit on an item could be doubled in another part of the world, then it would be stored until we reached that market versus a fast offload.

On the top deck, nets and pulleys pulled loads of captured supplies off and over the water to our ship. As was always the practice, everything was taken, guns, food, barrels of fresh water, apples, mangos, packed spirits, cotton, candles, medical supplies, and medical men, were brought aboard to cooperate in patching up the wounded. As I have reported, this earned the doctor his life until we reached the next suitable port for his release –

and—in the meantime he was given a letter from the Captain, stating that he had been pressed into service against his will, in case he ever went before a magistrate.

Other items hauled on board were animals, chickens, goats and even a steer which would be our evening meal. Rope, tools, rigging, canvas all taken. There was almost nothing left but a wooden skeleton that was slowly sinking. It was the end of this ship's life. Its resting place was now the dark depths of the ocean and there it would remain until the end of time.

As the French survivors started off to the next port in what was left of their long boats, Crowe and our carpenters were already working to refit our damaged mast and using pulleys and leverage to hoist it out of the water while other carpenters removed the damaged base and prepared to reset this massive obstacle....

Our wounded were carried below deck for treatment, the doctor cutting and sawing through the wounded as fast as possible. He would pull giant splinters out of our crew and use the metal claws to remove musket balls and shrapnel while shouting instructions to his aids and pushing for the most out of his staff.

Johnny Kay and Bolt were removing buckets of severed limbs and blood to be thrown overboard.

During all this, Newcastle ordered Fury and myself to bring the iron case into the Captain's quarters and we placed it on his desk. He looked at it and focused on the lock. He too recognized it as something important....

A three key lock meant, of course, three keys, one for the ship's Captain, one for the Governor of the courier's destination and one for the King's representative back home. Essex sent word for the iron workers who arrived with tools and began to cut the box open and once it was opened up, Essex rose to his feet as we all peered forward....

It was loaded with what looked like French letters of marque and other royal documents –some of them coded and marked for different ambassadors across their empire...

Essex, who knew both French and Spanish, started going through the documents, and then he suddenly stopped, like he froze for a moment. He suddenly shifted through all of the other documents and then stopped again. "Master Newcastle, get Mister Harrow immediately."

Moments later, Harrow came through the door, "Sir."

Essex turned over a document, "Take a look at this."

Harrow began to read it, mumbling every other word or two in French to himself, before he stopped and looked back to the Captain. "Is this?"

"It is." He exhaled, "Another war on the horizon –and keeping the peace is going to be even more difficult—"

"--And violent."

Essex continued, "As part of the condition to maintain peace, every privateer or former privateer who served in the colonial theater is to be turned over to the King of England for execution."

"What?" Newcastle asked with a sudden touch of shock.

Essex held up another document, "And here are the death warrants to prove it. Captains like Revere, Sloan-Stannis, Van Guardian, Faulkner and the Mediterranean rebel Dorian Vai –all of them, raiding all over the world have been sentenced to death."

--The death warrant wasn't unusual, acts of piracy carried a death sentence but privateers --many who served as independent commanders for one government or another in a time of war--were usually allowed to fade away or disappear. Here was a unilateral order for all of them to be arrested as a condition to keep the peace.

"The killing has probably already started." Harrow said going through the paperwork, "And here…" he held up another letter, "The French crown has offered to comply and assist in these matters."

"What do you mean?"

"Right here," He pointed, "In exchange for sugar concessions and part of the tobacco trade out of Jamestown, the French have agreed to arrest and turn over any of the captains they catch or employ, in any French port, for execution."

"They'll target the trade routes and The Caribbean."

"Do you think the Spanish will allow that?"

"The Spanish will lie in wait, like old enemies often do. They'll play nice and strike when the time is right."

"Even still, after Panama, we can expect no grace from them." Harrow concluded. "They're more likely to turn us over to the damn British –and take our ship-- then help privateers like us."

"Then, what do we do?" Newcastle asked, referring to the other privateers, "We can't leave them to their fate."

"Some of them, most of them perhaps have already been arrested and killed by imperial authorities."

"Well, the date on this execution order is less than two months old." Harrow looked to the Captain, "It's a new authorization."

"Captain, what do we do?"

Essex looked back to Newcastle, "The only thing we can do…warn everyone we can."

Below deck, our wounded men continued to be worked on. The sound of sawing was constant, and the sound changed from flesh to bone as it always did.

--The screaming echoed through the decks.

I was patched up, my two wounds being minor but something of a badge of honor. To be wounded in combat was, at times, credit at the tavern –and included a cash bonus but it didn't matter too much at this time due to the pain I was in. I was a long way from my schoolbooks now and I made myself busy by joining the infirmary crew, swabbing up the blood – and sand, used for traction. Cauterizing wounds, holding men down for amputations. We worked until late into the night under lanterns and candles…

I was sad to see Stylen and Jata pass on to the next world –and Standish, with a saber blade in his skull, was still remarkably holding on though, fading through his final moments. I held his hand. His sight had been robbed of him during the battle –his eyes had turned a faded grey-- so, I gave him my name and my hand and gave reassurance that he would not die alone. Strangely, my mind wondered to other combat predicaments like, 'what happened to the men who jumped overboard? Did we save them all or, are they still afloat out there on the sea somewhere with nothing to grab hold of nothing but a prayer until they go under? And the other wounded combatants, on the sinking ship --maybe crawling below deck as water rushed in –trapped--as the she went down. This grim end was what awaited most of us and now, all of this flashed before me....

--After having a saber blade stuck in his skull for almost two hours, Standish had finally died.

Once Standish slowly released his grip, I stood up and turned away to take a moment to myself for I liked Standish, he had humor and wisdom for a young privateer, and I would miss him. My only choice now was to try to force this moment from my head with some distraction and get back to work helping those that I could here in the sick bay and maybe come to grips with this loss later but, I had hardly turned around before his body was gone. Strange!?! Why would someone remove Standish so quickly with all the other work here to be done? Maybe they needed the table space for more amputations. Still, it was curious to throw a causality over the side so quickly.

Some more wounded were rushed in, including Barak and Jack-Karr who were carried into the hospital having been pulled from the water. Barak was hurt badly and unconscious, Karr was angry about his injury – bleeding from his head-- and was almost fighting Kato and Sampson-Rift for bringing him to the hospital to be stitched up. In fact, Johannis had to calm him down.

The hours passed. The work continued through the night. More stitching done under the glow of lanterns. Mattis was hurt –bad! Deck splinters from an explosion had plastered his face –and eye sockets-- robbing him of his sight and there would be no saving it. He had his head bandaged and lay in the infirmary in depressed silence. We were all concerned but I, for one, could not find the right words to comfort him so I just read from my bible.

When Johannis walked through the section, blood on his hands up to his elbows, I asked if I should stop reading and return to the work but,

Johannis shook his head no. "Continue with what you're doing lad for it helps more than you know."

I gave him a nod and continued....

Others among us had battle damage, Kipling with his missing hand which, with help from our metal workers would be fashioned into a hook –and this injury would transfer him out of the gun decks to a different division since all gunners required two hands. Others now had various eye patches or limbs removed. When and where we could, we'd keep these men in our service and re-assign their duties but blindness –like Mattis-- was a difficult one and only the best could overcome it. It was heartbreaking to me because Mattis was considered reliable and in an instant, he was robbed of the trade. He could still contribute to society of course but in terms of our business he was out.

He had my sympathy –although he did not want it and would not hear it.

Once the work had slowed down, the Captain made his way through the wounded to make his survey. He asked his men if there was anything they needed, waving other men forward with grog to ease the pain of some nearby patients. He stopped to converse with our surgeon Johannis where he received a full report on the dead and wounded. A report he did not take lightly. Essex then turned to the captured French surgeon and gave a slight bow upon making his introduction, followed by his thanks for the valiant effort put forth to save his men despite their national differences. This was followed by the presentation of a letter --thee letter—which, as reported, explained that the doctor had been pressed into service against his will and should he be brought to trial for piracy –if such events were to unfold—he could present this letter to the authorities and expect an honorable acquittal. Again, I was reminded this was commonplace when artisans were conscripted.   And quite often IT DID allow for an acquittal.

The captain then asked if the doctors needed anything and then bid them goodnight as Rorry and a few volunteers ran down some food and buckets of coffee to the sickbay.

The next morning....

I moved through the lower decks where the carpenters were hammering repairs that prevented the deck from being flooded. The pumps were in action.

I made it to the top deck. In the armory, the men were loading in the new weapons and sharpening blades. Roux and Le Clerk were taking apart muskets, cleaning them, and refashioning them with new parts where required. I walked past Hallock, then Watson and Bishop as they loaded in a new swivel cannon --captured from the enemy ship-- and I found Mister Harrow…

"Report to Mister Crowe if you please, Mister Reed."

"Yes sir."

I found Crowe –our ship's carpenter—at the prow. "Mister Crowe sir?"

"Reed. We're short-handed." Crowe shouted, dividing his attention between me and whatever he was looking at over the side.

"How can I help?"

I was given a tool belt and lowered over the side of the ship by a rope harness where Irons, Jeddah, Tiberius, and other men were working to repair all the battle damage to our side just above the surface of the ocean. I noticed an unexploded cannon ball stuck in our hull and I used my tools to dig it out of the wood and drop it into the tide. What made a man-of-war so dangerous was the thickness in its sides matched with the number of guns giving it its punching power.

Heavy panels were lowered over the side to replace some of the damaged siding and once in place we lowered some paint over the side to bring up the ship's appearance…

Tiberius and I worked on the paint in the Siam sun, and I happened to look up to the rail to see Harrow looking back at us. It was as if he didn't trust Mister Crowe to supervise us -as if he needed to see us do the work with his own eyes.

"That's unusual."

Tiberius looked up, then went back to work, "He doesn't quite trust me."

I continued to paint, "Care to elaborate?"

"Since you asked, I'll tell ya. --we fought the war lords of Egypt a few years back. Killing at the Pyramids. During the fighting, I was sent on a mission, to safeguard some children and move them away from the theater of war. Well," he breathed, heavy "I hated to leave with a serious fight to be had so, I got them to a safe place –or at least I thought it was safe-- and I ran back to the action."

"Doesn't sound so bad."

"Well, I was wrong ya' see. I got back to the fight quick enough –did my part but those children," he stopped painting for a moment, "They were killed." He spit, "Bastard war lords don't discriminate!"

I looked back up but, Harrow --was gone.

We continued to refit off the coast of Siam and worked around the clock. Men would labor for twelve hours then take to the shore, rest, and investigate the Coast of Siam for the other twelve. The people of Siam were friendly, and we traded with monks from a local Buddhist temple. In the evenings we would share meals with these monks –and some of the locals-- on the beach. They made rice with pineapple and nuts also, fish that was loaded with local spices but, one would gain a taste for it after a few days of refit and hard labor….

One night, after I was coming back aboard The Venger after dinner with the monks ashore, I climbed the ladder to find Therrinfall at the rail, staring off into the dark horizon. He was alone and this wasn't his watch. He was having bad dreams again, so I stepped to him and because I didn't feel it was right to check up on him, I instead offered him some of the stew I brought from the local temple. It was an act of simple charity, nothing more. He looked at it for a moment, then with a mild nod, took it and kicked a sip back.

There was then a moment of –somewhat—uncomfortable silence and I was suffering so I choked up a few words. "Maybe you should go ashore for a few hours."

He just shook his head no.

My next sentence, in retrospect, seemed naive. "I...I don't have a past like yours—"

"No...you don't!" He said as if already fatigued with my presence.

But my next batch of words was already out, "But...I too, have a hard time getting bad thoughts out of my head."

He peered at me, the way a sniper would look over the site of his gun. "And what would a schoolteacher know about it?"

"Not much I suppose." I looked out, over the rail and out to the sea. "I saw my grandfather die, in a hospital bed from infection...not the same I know but...still hard to take."

After a long pause, he suddenly said, "What I would not give to have that as my only experience with death."

I nodded, without words.

"Ya know why they hang people Reed?" He suddenly said.

I shook my head no and he turned to me. "Because we use to kill 'em with an axe and take the head off." He said, "One day the county clerk decided to make a study, science he said it was –so he brought a young man to the chopping block, not more than nineteen maybe. He was to be killed for treason with the French but, the rumor was that he was, actually romantically involved with a lady of the court --a woman who was the property of Lord Drax-- and this was just a way to get rid of him. So, they trumped up some charges, beat a confession out of him and I got the job to bring the axe down—"

"You...don't have to tell this story."

"You should know what keeps a man up at night. So, listen...and learn. This boy, who probably believed in love at one point, was loaded onto the block, so I took position and prepared myself. Ya see Reed, when you're the executioner, you don't get to close your eyes like the audience does, you might miss the neckline and put the blade into the skull or the back. So, I didn't get to escape anything ya see. I lived through every-moment-of-it."

This conversation made me tense but, I couldn't disengage and leave him alone to deal with this.

"I took my position, and thought, I'll make this merciful and quick so, I slammed the axe down and when his head rolled across the planks, this bastard, clerk called out this boy's name and...." Therrinfall looked at me, to make sure he had my attention, "--His eyes moved! When his name was called, his eyes seemed to focus. There was recognition in what he heard –after-- his head was removed! Regardless of the so-called experiment the clerk wanted to conduct, he knew --they all knew—what had happened to them after their head was taken off." He scoffed with some disdain for his past actions, "And here I thought I was being merciful this whole time and making for a quick out for the criminal --I wasn't! It was never that. Soon after...they switched to ropes because, they thought that would be 'a kind and gentle' way to execute everyone moving forward. So, ya see, killing people now when associated with a corrupt government or company....is easy. Forgetting my past is hard."

With that, I pulled the rum bottle out of Blythe's hand, interrupting his conversation at a nearby deck fire and I tipped it skyward. –causing Addo and the ronin to laugh at me.

The next morning, as I worked on The Venger's hull, I watched the Captain climb down to a long boat and with Lynch, Lincoln, Java and Tane, row to the beach. There was no security or shore party, just a few men and once ashore, he met with some of the monks. A day later, I found out what this mission was about. Some of our wounded –that were either too damaged to be of further service or dying of infection-- were going to be put to the beach as Lincoln cashed them out for their wounds –as was our code-- and our Captain matched the funds and even went one step further, he rewarded the monks from the local temple to look after them.

One man who would stay was Mattis --now blind by splinters with his eyes wrapped in a bandage, he was offered a post in the galley. Hobby had to show him where everything was, pots, pans, wood for the stoves and placed his hands on the items so he could get a sense of it all. The training continued day in and day out...

Newcastle saw this training in action one evening and watched for a few moments and he wasn't sure if this situation was going to work. "Gentlemen...getting along all right?" he asked.

"Yes sir," Hobby smiled as he moved Mattis' hands like a puppet from stove to pantry.

"Mattis?" Newcastle asked, concerned.

Mattis turned in the direction of his voice and tried to be positive. "Learning. Sir."

Newcastle looked to Hobby.

"Happy to have the help sir." He said as if to reinforce the decision to keep Mattis around. "He'll be a fine cook and a valuable hand in this here galley."

Newcastle kept his eyes fixed, then gave a reluctant nod and left the deck...

XVII

DEAD MEN TELL NO TALES?

On the evening of the 22nd, we shoved off towards the Pacific Ocean, leaving Siam behind us. As we sailed away, there was lightning in the distance. The ship was quiet. The decks had a strange –almost eerie— silence about them. I thought it was because of a specific reverence for the brothers we lost --the causality rate had been high. So many of us had been killed or wounded and although we were able to recruit some French marines to our ranks the feeling on the ship was one of remorse. I made a note of this on my parchment, then closed my book and loaded it into my footlocker. As I moved to the top deck, I realized that the galley –and the gun sections—were almost deserted. Just a flicker of lantern light and a few men here and there but nothing like the usual commotion or joviality.

I climbed on deck, and it was quiet there too --except for the sound of the wind which carried with it a haunting howl of a sound. Clairmont was scribing some poetry under a lantern. Sterling was replacing the strings on his cello and Duncan-Howe was packing tobacco and talking with Nighthorse and Bons about the Americas –more specifically, they were arguing about a pub in home of the witch trials –Salem, New England

Merritt was with us but, he kept to himself conversation-wise as was his usual way. Mazatal and some of the Aztecs were in a huddle around a fire down deck a-ways. Mako, Calixto and some of the others were also taking in the night air…

There was the occasional flash of lightning in the distance to keep us company…

I stood at the rigging looking at the stars when Blythe slowly emerged on deck. He had the look of a man in troubled thought –perhaps confused-- as if his mind was working to figure something out. He finally spoke and his words were the first to break the silence around us. "I didn't realize that Standish had survived that cutlass to the head," he said.

Duncan-Howe removed the pipe from his lips, "He didn't," he said with an exhale of smoke.

Blythe looked even more confused…

"Doctor Johannis tried to remove the blade from his skull, and he died in the sick bay."

There was yet another moment of silence, "But, I just saw him down in the quarter deck division." Blythe stated.

Baltimore stood next to this conversation in silence but seemed to be perplexed by Blythe's statement. Indeed, I turned from the rail, and we all started to listen….

"Na," Duncan-Howe exhaled more smoke. "He's dead! We lost him. Damn shame too, he was a good man with both gun and blade--"

"--And the ladies!" Clairmont looked up from his writing.

"Aye, that too." Duncan-Howe agreed. "I fine compatriot he was."

"But…I just saw him by the guns." Blythe continued.

"Not Standish. Therrinfall maybe or… Locke but Standish has passed. This I can attest to."

Calixto nodded, "Right, Miranda and Tak dragged him to the infirmary. He died a moment or two later…."

"I was there when it happened." I said softly as Duncan-Howe quickly removed his hat and placed it against his heart and looked quickly to the sky in a show of reverence. Just as quickly his hat went back on his head. "A noble shipmate you are son!"

Blythe shook his head. "But I could swear— "

"Did you break open some of the opium boxes?" Howe asked.

"Stay off the grog Blythe for it makes you see things" Clairmont said, a statement which triggered laughter from all of us –because it was what many of us were drinking at the time.

Blythe himself smiled but it was the kind of smile that still reflected some confusion and puzzlement.

"Rest easy Blythe, it must have been something else you saw lad... for I was in the sick bay when he passed and I can assure you, no sorcery could keep that man alive after a wound like that, poor bastard."

"Split skull, bad business that." Sterling said as he tuned his cello.

"Let us remember him in good times lads for there were many...."

I looked at Blythe as the conversation drifted into the distance and I wondered about the man's mental state for I saw Standish die. Blythe appeared able but his look was something different –as if his mind was in a different place.

We traveled the jungle waterways of The Orient. We traded with natives – and tried to avoid headhunters. Sometimes we'd be attacked by colonial troops and their native allies with flares and rockets...and we'd send some artillery back and cut down a few trees...

We avoided the coastal villages but raided the colonial outposts and ports, sometimes the ship would collide and run over junks when on the attack. The main prize in these parts was the devil's claw –or opium – Which we would uncover in massive amounts...

OFF THE COAST OF JAKARTA

We opened up on the Dutch fort. Smoke and gunpowder rising off the still ocean surface. A Chinese junk was burning in the harbor. Its crew jumped into the tide –clothes on fire. Survivors tried to swim for the beach...

Below deck, our guns fired and rolled back –and fired again. Rajiv making adjustments as required to keep the pressure on...

The fortress watchtower was hit and exploded. Holes had been blasted in the walls and some of the garrison buildings were on fire. Newcastle's shore party was already on the beach, storming the nearby village. Most of the population had fled into the jungle with their children.

As we rowed towards the beach with Mister Jaffar, explosions lit up the village ahead of us, Mister Barak, just back from his injuries leaned forward to me with a look of wicked intent and said, "I pray someone tries to kill you tonight, Reed."

I was somewhat alarmed by this....

"I pray they try to kill you very hard."

"What?"

"That way," He continued, "I can kill them and settle our debt. So please, do something dangerous, very dangerous if you would not mind."

I swallowed some nerves, "I'll try."

"Good." Barak said. "Please try very hard."

Jaffar and the Moors protected the Buddhist temple outside of town with a defensive square –from new crewmen who may not be up to speed on our code of conduct when it came to a pacifist element –such as these monks. And since the Moors did not take part in any celebration it made this task easy. They preferred to meet the monks actually, exchange texts and literature and information or even have a philosophical conversation over tea on the temple steps –and these conversations or tea parties would begin –and continue—during the sacking of the town all around them as if oblivious to it –even with fires and explosions nearby....

The monks would also join forces to help the local populace after the action was over...

--Raeder ordered his combat party to halt at a jungle tree line -allowing some people to escape in the wilderness. We never gave chase into a foreign jungle unless we had to. The local contingent knew the terrain and that marked us at a serious disadvantage for possible ambush so, we held at the jungle's edge and then we were ordered back into the colonial part of the town for a sacking....

I walked down the street as a burning rikshaw rolled past me. The sugar mill and opium den were on fire but still being raided for goods despite the flames. I was not surprised to see buildings burning but, the red candle district –and whore houses were untouched. I'm sure this district figured into our immediate plans after the battle was over....

The sounds of warfare could still be heard in the distance as I walked through the smoke and stepped over body after body, -I saw the Buddhists among our crew –from Siam and China praying. Two worlds, death, and religion –together in the same aftermath. Fury, Hazzard, Jagger, Kannon, and the others sat on the temple steps, dirty and exhausted from the fighting –weapons still visible. Sterling with a bandage wrapped around his head covering his left eye. Duncan-Howe sat in a smoking rickshaw. There was blood on their hands and clothes and their faces were covered in burnt ash.

I collapsed next to my crew. Without a word, Merciless handed me a near empty bottle of rum to aid in my recovery and not too far off, the ronin, having pillaged the marketplace, built a small fire and were having tea of all things and a quiet conversation.

The politicians we found alive we anchored with a rope around the neck from man to man and we used them, like cattle to move the plunder to the docks and the beach. There Mister Lincoln made his inventory. "That's twelve thousand sacks of rice, sixty-two hundred sacks of tea leaves. Nine hundred cases of wine, six hundred crates of pineapple," --And there were crates of plums, monkeys, pigs, birds and as I kept moving, I saw coffee, silks –some wrapped around our crew-- gold plates stamped with the writings of the Orient on them and weapons –of course--all captured.

My combat group was ordered back to the ship to stand watch. As we walked into the tide –the beach was still lit up by the occasional explosion—and we climbed into the long boats and started to row back to the ship.

Suddenly, Barak appeared from the smoke and yelled from the beach. "You did not try hard enough to get yourself killed, Mister Reed." Again, he pointed to me in angry fashion as I pulled on the oars "No one tried to kill you and that makes me very, very, angry! YOU make me very, angry Mister Reed." Then he looked up to the sky in frustration, "Allah forgive me."

I apologized with a wave to him…

"What the hell is all that?" Kane asked from the oars behind me.

"He's upset that my life wasn't in enough danger tonight."

He laughed loud as we rowed towards the ship, and we left the noise of battle behind us.…

As we got to The Venger, the wind came up. I climbed the rigging to our deck along with Whitney, our officer Daws and nine others to replace Bishop and his team who would go ashore in our place while we watched the deck…

This was a lonely watch. The ship was quiet. The ocean was quiet. I took my post in the crow's nest where I could see the countryside a blaze but no sign of any other ships, imperial or otherwise on the horizon. At midnight, my shift ended, and I descended the rigging from the crow's nest and turned my duties over to Hayte who made the climb up in my place. I surveyed the deck; Lynch was in command at the helm with Thorn and Daws at the steering –we were at anchor so there was nothing more than a quiet conversation between them at their station.

At the rail gun by the bow, Duncan-Howe slowly paced the deck, smoking tobacco and keeping his eye on the horizon for any sudden arrivals.

I descended into the darkness below deck. It was dark and quiet in this section at this time –most of the gun crews were ashore—there was a little lantern light but before I could move towards it, I was startled by the sudden squawk from one of our tropical birds as it suddenly fluttered up in front of me. I clutched my heart, collected myself and I worked my way through the shadows, past the cannon and hanging supplies to the warm glow of the galley…

Mister Hobby suddenly shot up and looked at me from his hot stove – he seemed startled to see me but then breathed easy. "Oh! Mister Reed. It's you."

"Evening Mister Hobby."

He swallowed, as if still trying to get his mental balance after I surprised him ---and his eyes seemed to bolt to the left or right as if looking for something but, I was the only one on deck here. He then told me to keep an eye out while he ran a bucket of coffee to the men at the helm above. I agreed to do so, since Mattis was absent, and Rorry was now asleep in his hammock for the night –and so he left me alone.

The night breeze came through the shutters as I drank my coffee, cut into some rum cake, and sat there, observing the sights and sounds as the ship rolled in the tide. I was tired and exhausted. The lantern light created haunting shadows and shapes on the walls as the ship rolled and I could feel tremendous fatigue setting in –and-- as I started to drift off, I heard footsteps slowly coming towards me. I was too tired to look at my shipmate who took the place on the bench next to me. I didn't acknowledge him but, I did slide the cake to my right for him to take a piece, only--.

--A moment later, the plate slid back to me. Untouched.

"No rum cake then," I turned and looked up but there was no one there! Only shadows. No one on the bench next to me and no one in the deck section. It was completely vacant --empty! I picked up the lantern and turned to look down the deck towards the darkness and suddenly lit up what appeared to be Mister Standish, just as he –and his gray eyes-- turned away to disappear into the shadows....

Instantly, I shot to my feet --jarred! "Stan- Standish?" I swallowed some nerves and slowly moved down the deck, lantern rattling in my hand, past the guns, through the darkness and finally to the steps that led to the top deck –the only way Standish could have gone-- and made my way up top outside but there was nothing there –just an empty deck...

I looked around and saw De Leon and Lynch –with a pipe—at the railing. They looked towards me as if they expected me to say something, but I couldn't frame up any words. Lynch cut through the silence. "What is it Mister Reed?"

"I-I...I thought— "

"Yes?"

"You look like you've seen a ghost." They both laughed.

I realized that the words that I wanted to say may affect my standing on this ship, that fatigue may have played a part in what my eyes had seen --

and that perhaps it was best to keep what I witnessed to myself until I could make sense of it. "Nothing" I finally said, "I'm…. sorry, I thought I saw something" And I went back down below….

--Once I dropped below, a hand slapped over my mouth as I turned and suddenly bumped into Mister Silence. He put his index finger to his lips as if to order me not to speak –or even make a sound, then he sparked a fuse and started burning some sort of plant below deck, directing the smoke to cover certain areas along with the cannon, the supplies, the hammocks….

--This was curious.

I watched as Baltimore emerged from the shadows next to me. He said something in French and then told me, this was a way to 'cleanse' the deck of evil spirits. The natives from North America had their superstitions and used plants and wildlife to combat wicked elements….

When Mister Silence was finished, he stood straight up and said a few words in his native language. This was the first time I heard his voice since I joined The Venger, Baltimore replied, turned, gave me a nod and then the two left the deck as if their work was now done.

I, on the other hand, grabbed a lantern and positioned myself against the port side wall where I knew nothing could sneak up behind me and there I would wait, keeping an eye out until I passed out from fatigue at dawn…

I woke up in the damp tropical air later the next morning with crewmen working around me. "Aye, there he is." Dutch and Cage gave me a hand to my feet. "Enjoy your evening?"

"Huh?"

"Better get some food" Cage pushed me towards the galley, and I started wondering how long I had slept? What time was it? And what had I actually experienced the night before?

"Back to your duties, all of you." Harrow barked as he moved through the deck. "Aloft now. The Venger doesn't sail itself!" As the men scrambled to take their stations, I looked at the galley, still empty as it was the night before, but I was perplexed. What happened there?

We spent the next few weeks raiding shipping and damaging the opium trade off the coast of Indochina. Not every craft was blasted, one evening, we pulled along-side of a Chinese junk and –in a peaceful manner—we traded supplies for spice, silks, and other things. I looked up at their flag that blew in the wind. A skull but with two spears where the bones should be and Mandarin markings –markings that protected them from our cannon.

These Chinese privateers liked Spanish tobacco from Cuba, sugar, and salted pork. Here Mister Lo-Tan and Lau seemed at ease in conversation and talked –and laughed—with some of these sailors in Mandarin. It turned out this 'battle junk' had been raiding prison convoys out of the East Indies and had just made it through a six-hour fight with the Spanish and was now on its way to the Xi Jiang River, close to our destination of Macau so – because of their banner and markings—we offered this boat a chance to sail alongside us, up the coast for the next two days and so…it was!

XVIII

MACAU

We passed some ships, wrecked on the reef from decades before...

There were red and green fireworks in the sky as we dropped anchor -- guests of our Chinese and Indochine compatriots. The port itself, lit up the coastline for several leagues in every direction. Every port we visited had its own culture, its own look, its own blend of the native and the traveler and every place created its own sense of excitement and Macau was no exception.

We made preparations to go ashore. Here –as always-- we planned to share in the local food and custom but the moment we made port, upon arriving at the docks, the Port Authority arrived in a rickshaw with some Chinese soldiers behind him and stopped us in our place. This agent had a parchment with him so, the Captain called for Mister Lo to translate. Lo read the document and looked to Essex. "It seems The Venger was seen by a look out and our Captain is expected –with his harbor tax—to meet the Marshall at the local fortress known as Sin-Hawk Castle." Lo then passed the document to the Captain for it was stamped with a special seal, a fist with two Chinese swords behind it in red wax –the mark of Bo Chen!

"Very well' Essex said taking the parchment back, "Bo Chen will not be disappointed –Mister Lo, form a special detachment if you please." As Lo started to move, Essex continued, "Make sure the shore party includes our officers and --our schoolteacher."

Lo understood and gave a nod. Orders went out to commandeer a wagon, a team of horses and some additional steeds and Mister Lau picked up his dual blades and took charge. Once the wagon arrived, it was loaded with a metal chest that included a modest amount of gold, jewels, and coin –most of it raided from the Portuguese slave outpost, some from the French. We also loaded up tobacco, whale oil and a few casks of wine....

I got the detail, along with Mister Harrow, Mister Newcastle, Mister Lynch, Jaffar, Mister Baltimore, Hatano, Jupiter, Mister Rabal, Lau, Mister Barak –who still seemed angry with me-- and Mister Lo and we were to be escorted by the local Macau militia who used Asian lanterns to light the way...

The Captain prepared to deliver the harbor tax personally, not to the local governor but to a local fortress and headquarters of a Cantonese privateer –and legend-- Bo Chen.

On the way, I came to learn that this woman Bo Chen –known as The Empress-- had direct command of a local fleet with over four hundred junks and almost forty thousand sailors but, she was in charge of a much larger Asian confederacy across the Pacific with about fifteen-hundred ships and upwards of a hundred-and-eighty-thousand 'privateers' and she had united them with a code, much like our own --or-- maybe even the basis of our own.

Article three of this code was that her commanders would be beheaded for stealing from villages and villagers who harbored and supplied her privateers. Other articles detailed orders that profiteering between the fleet's seized goods, would be balanced out between all ships, including those who were unsuccessful in their raiding. Also, there were strict guidelines against taking women captives and rape, both punishable by death.

She had fought every empire, The British, French even the Qing Dynasty –and won! She had forced the Portuguese out of Macau and fashioned it into a privateering capitol. She was –quite clearly-- the most successful privateer in history...

Our Captain preferred to ride a horse and our shore party mounted up, leaving Mister Rabal and myself to man the wagon. "Hold on!' Rabal said as he cracked the reins, and we rumbled off.

The road took us through the streets of Macau…

This appeared to be an interesting place. The town was aglow by Chinese lanterns and rickshaws were moving in every direction and it smelled of spices –almost in a sweet way. We passed through a town square with a massive Buddha head, several stories tall in the corner, then over a bridge and in the water below, there were hundreds of floating lamps...

The road took us out of town and into the jungle, then up along a cliff towards a giant ancient fortress that marked the horizon in the distance. This castle overlooked the harbor and as we got close, highway guards stopped us by crossing lit torches in front of us. They wore Cantonese armor and battle dress, had long hair tied together in a single braid down their backs and –like our own men—battle scars of all sorts. Another sentry came forward and in his local language he asked us our business. Mister Lo responded and the Captain handed him the letter we had received at the docks. After the sentry read it, the path was cleared and we were allowed to proceed, past a tower as we rolled across a draw bridge through the fortress gate. Here we were stopped by more guards who ordered us to check our weapons. We looked to the Captain and he gave us a nod to obey this command and so we did. All our weapons were turned over to the guards --pistols, sabers, the three-section staff, more guns, grenades, even knives-- and loaded onto a dragon looking table. We also removed our hats.

From here, we were marched through two giant wooden doors -- decorated and carved with dragons and falcons --doors that took several guards to push open and from there, we stepped into a large throne room lit by hundreds of candles. There was a square mat in the middle of this giant room and two massive Japanese wrestlers –covered in tattoos-- called 'sumo' were engaged. Beyond this, up a few steps was a giant red throne and there, sat the Empress in a red dress, tight to her form with long black hair, tied back tight with a large gold needle pierced through it. I marked her age about fifty and though her stature seemed small, her presence seemed very, very, big.

We all bowed –our Chinese compatriots bowed but also placed their right fist against an open left hand and she gave us a slight nod back.

She looked up from her hookah, and slowly exhaled smoke into a ring and motioned for our Captain to approach. As he moved forward, so did I but, I was quickly stopped in my place by Mister Lo, who put his hand in front of me --for the Captain was to approach alone.

This woman looked at him with a cunning smile and held out her hand. I watched the Captain take this woman by the hand, bow, and kiss it, at which point, the greeting seemed to become more familiar with a smile and a laugh between them --though I could not hear what was said.

Eventually we were all invited forward, and we advanced with the tax and placed it at the steps of her throne, but this queen seemed uninterested in it, as if it was just a formality. She had seen many treasures in her time to be sure...

One by one we were introduced –as if we stood in a regal court-- when I approached, I heard Mister Lo tell Bo Chen my name and...something else. She responded in an inquisitive way, and she seemed to have a sudden shine in her eyes when she looked at me. "Your Mister Lo tells me you are a school teacher." She said broken but understandable English.

Lau and the others smiled...

"I am, that is- I was."

"Not many schoolteachers survive as a privateer."

"I assure you Madam," Mister Harrow said as politely as possible, "Mister Donovan is proving to be a very able privateer."

I suppose she was right in general but, here I was standing in a fortress in Macau.

We were ordered to take our place at the large table a few steps below her throne. The table was low to the floor, and we sat on giant, colorful pillows as servants brought out food on very large plates –some of a type I had never seen-- and spirits like plum wine.

We were then allowed to eat.

To my surprise, Bo Chen and our Captain conversed in 'broken' Cantonese. Their relationship seemed to be familiar and a friendly one. I was grateful that Mister Lo sat close enough to Harrow and myself to translate if we became interested in any part of the conversation....

Over dinner, I asked Mister Harrow what the history was and here, the story of The Venger actually unfolds. As fate would have it, our Captain had Macau –and this woman-- to thank for his start, for it was here --after the mutiny on The H.M.S. Falcon-- that he took refuge from British authorities. Here, in this part of the world, the British could not come or go as they pleased –not without a serious fight. Empress Chen gave our Captain and the surviving members of the crew safe haven –saving their lives. He sailed under her flag, in the confederacy and made purchase of a sloop called The Ghost and with that sloop, he –along with Harrow and the others-- began their career in privateering. Harrow concluded his history lesson with the words "British Navy be damned."

"The people who invented gun powder can't be all bad!" Rabal said as he put a cooked boar's head on his plate, pulled an apple from its mouth and began his dinner…

"Y-e-s" I said slowly looking at his plate. Not one to enjoy intact boar's head, I felt somewhat distracted. "I suppose you're right."

Suddenly Bo Chen gave a command, "Schoolteacher."

I rose from my seat. "Yes?"

"What does one teach to privateers?"

"We'll most of the men on The Venger are quite educated in mathematics, geography, topography and some science –certainly in gunnery but, I was allowed to set up a school of sorts—"

Bo Chen and the Captain exchanged a quick glance, and I was not sure if she was impressed but I continued, "I often find myself teaching…" I was embarrassed to say, "Poetry and literature, reading and writing."

This created a spark in her eye, and she said something in Cantonese to which all her servants in the room –mostly ladies in waiting-- laughed. Mister Lo looked up at me, "She wants to hear a poem."

"A poem?"

"Please" she suddenly said from her throne.

I remained standing and forced a nervous swallow…

"It better be a good one." Lo-Tan said under his breath as he took a sip of plum wine.

The Captain looked at me as if eager to hear what I was going to say, and my mind raced for the right set of words…

In such a situation as this, I always relied on 'the classics' versus a poem of personal taste so I cleared my throat and said with as much emotional enunciation as possible…

"When in disgrace with fortune and men's eyes
I all alone beweep my outcast state
And the trouble deaf heaven with my bloodless cries,
And look upon myself, and curse my fate,
Wishing me like to one more rich in hope
Featur'd like him, like him with friends possess'd,
Desiring this man's art and that man's hope,
With what I most enjoy contested least,
Yet in these thoughts myself almost despising,
Haply I think on thee, and then my state,
Like to the lark at break of day arising,
From sullen earth, sings hymns at heaven's gate,
For thy sweet love remember'd such wealth brings,
That then I scorn to change my state of kings."

The last line about 'the state of kings' seemed to meet with the approval from our captain and crew but, there was a moment of silence with the rest of the people in the room, who waited to see if Bo Chen approved and once, she smiled, the room was free for applause.

"Wonderful Mister Reed" Harrow said, thoroughly impressed and Newcastle slapped me on the back as if to say, 'good work.'

"I can't take credit for it, it's Shakespeare's Sonnet Twenty-Nine." I confessed in a low tone.

"Well done just the same."

"When you steal, steal from the best." Newcastle smiled.

"I like the part of scorning Kings" said Mister Rabal as he tossed back a glass of wine and moved to refill it. "Scorning kings speaks to me.... I like it.... the wealth part, 'tis good too!"

"I'm glad you approve." I said, unwilling to explain.

At that, Bo Chen spoke another command in her native tongue and a servant brought me a primed, decorated box. I was puzzled by this and ordered to open it. In it were quills of the finest quality, parchment writing books bound with leather and gold elements and fine ink. I looked up, amazed.

"For our schoolteacher." She smiled.

I bowed with gratitude for I was truly grateful to receive this gift.

"Schoolteachers are prized here" Harrow whispered to me.

I was now, quite proud of myself.

After dinner and over casks of plum wine, we had a performance from some Cantonese dancers –and a giant dragon puppet—then we were fortunate enough to have their company as we watched these sumo wrestlers from the islands of Japan battle each other. All the while, Bo Chen sat on her throne smoking her hookah with an almost wicked grin.

As the sky turned orange with the coming dawn, we dismissed ourselves as the party came to an end. We were told to enjoy all that Macau had to offer and given 'a pass' written in the native language and symbols allowing freedom of action as guests of Bo Chen and her confederacy.

At dawn, we arrived back in town, I found Mister Lynch in an inn marked with dragons and gave him one of the books that was given to me by Bo Chen. I did not need all five and I knew he enjoyed illustrating. He smiled and was grateful.

Close by, I saw Merciless and Whitney at a table, Fury was there too, passed out drunk as food arrived in front of them. "Dragon chicken!" Whitney said as he tried to work his chopsticks.

"Nay. Not having it." Merciless said.

"Why not?"

"Because I don't eat dragon." Merciless barked and kicked back a bottle of wine.

Macau, I must admit, was an adventurous and wonderous place and not without its many dangers. But I stayed close to my comrades and –even here-- they were not without a reputation that kept most dangers away.

Streets twisted into dark places with grog shops, saloons, opium dens and gambling houses.

One night, we found a Portuguese theater, the name of which translated to 'The Royal' and there, Harrow, Newcastle, Daws, Kannon, Raeder, Wolfe –who was drunk—Tiberius, Java, Jack-Karr, Sterling and myself and a few others joined the audience. Duncan-Howe and Clairmont sat next to me.

"Do you like the theater, Kristoff?" I asked him…

"I like the arts as much as any man…." Duncan-Howe returned as he took his seat with a pair of Mandarin women who took the seats next to him as his guests….

As the lights were dimmed, we watched a performance of a play titled 'The Pirates of The Seven Seas' —It must have been a comedy for we all roared with laughter at their interpretation of what a privateer was and what a privateer did! There were musicians making music from an orchestra pit and I could see from my seat, through openings at the front of the stage, Chinese stagehands as they worked pedals to make large canvas waves move along the front of the stage while others pulled a rope to pull a 'pirate ship' into position for the audience to see. Other parts of the exaggerated performance led Raeder to say "that would never have happened! Not very real." Followed by "I would never!" And "I'm not buyin' it!" To which members of the audience in front of us, turned and asked him to keep his opinions to himself and be quiet.

--Reader's backhand had to be held back by Newcastle for we were here for entertainment –such as it was—not to fight other audience members.

Next, these characters, the privateers on stage, broke into a song --for this was a musical.

"What's this nonsense?" Wolfe barked, "We don't sing!!!'

"Not well anyway!" Duncan-Howe laughed...

Again, the audience tried to 'discipline us' back into silence and as the song on stage turned into a choreographed dance our ranks exploded in anger...

"They're dancin' now! They're dancin' on deck by thunder!' Jack-Karr motioned to the stage, "They're making us look bad!" He stood and went for one of his guns to shoot a performer, but Newcastle and Howe grabbed him as the round went off into the rafters.

In all, the over-dramatic performance–and an over-dramatic Pirate Captain-- earned some loud, vocal disdain from our audience box and when the pirates lost the battle in the end and the Captain was killed, we almost started a loud riot for this was not the ending we wanted. This was not poetic justice! We wanted the privateers to win and the government special interest –the real pirates-- to lose. This made this show even worse but still, it was a good night and the plum wine helped....

We talked about this play in the streets –complaining about it—until Whitney admitted, that...

"I quite liked it actually."

"Wha—"

"Whit, how could you?"

His comment stirred up some confrontation and for most of the evening, Whitney would be barraged by negative remarks and grunts, until the next distraction came along.

After a two-day drunken celebration in town, we sailed The Venger to a beach just outside of the harbor. There we began work on careening the ship. We were fortunate enough to have local labor help in these efforts and once we ran The Venger aground, we unloaded all the cannon, weapons, cargo –everything, even our birds and monkeys -and made a defensive camp on the beach.

Then using ropes, manpower and pulleys for leverage anchored to several trees we pulled The Venger on its side and formed up to clean and repair the hull. This is hard labor but required, for we were fully aware that this effort affected our speed and performance on the high seas --and the performance of the ship dictated our fortunes. It was also best to do this in a friendly port.

The work would take several days even with a combined labor force of privateers and natives. We'd work in shifts until nightfall, then the work would continue with torch light and another shift in the work force.

Rajiv, Wilder, Tane, Java and the gunners positioned the cannon on the beach in make-shift fortifications to cover the bay and protect us from possible royal visitors and they stood watch like artillery officers for the next ten days. They also shared in the repair work. I even saw Essex and Harrow working on the under carriage during the day.

I also had the 'honor' of scraping the hull clean, so I scraped, scraped, and scraped and when I wasn't working on the hull, I was permitted to explore the town –or I slept in a tent on the beach.

When the job was complete, we sailed The Venger back into the port to resupply.

It rained for some of our time there and one day we forted up in the 'Red Dragon Inn' where I played chess with Duncan-Howe and ate noodles with vegetables and a touch of ginger. The women were friendly, and my mind wondered back to my friend in Port Royal. It had been many months now since I had seen her, and I wondered if she even remembered me. Was I a fool to still have thoughts about this woman still? Was this wrong? I was not so sure –or—very sure of myself in this situation....

News of our raid on Porto Norvo was not far behind us and with repairs done and the ship reloaded, it was to our advantage to pull up anchor and sail on, never staying in one place too long.

I walked through the dock tunnels back to The Venger. Here, men que'd up to find work on different ships. The Venger had a certain reputation. It had sailed through hell and back and despite the ship's track record for victory –or survival, it was the kind of track record that only attracted a certain type of adventurer. We did have need of men but, we needed a certain kind of man.

At the ramp to the ship, Mister Lincoln worked the enrollment desk with Harrow and Mister Daws. Some of the ronin guarded the plank aboard. If a man answered Lincoln's questions to his satisfaction –and was willing to honor our articles-- he was permitted to join the crew.

"Welcome back, Mister Reed." Harrow said from his position at the desk. "Macau seems to have suited you."

"Indeed, it did Mister Harrow. Indeed, it did."

"May I ask, as an educator, wouldn't you rather stay and take in the sights of the Far East?" Harrow had asked me if I wanted to stay ashore at almost every port. I wondered if it was because he didn't like me. After all, I hadn't killed a man yet and although I worked hard, there were far better, stronger crew men onboard who could do my duties twice as fast.

"Do you not want me aboard Mister Harrow?" I asked.

"On the contrary Mister Reed, I've grown to like your little school and I have a great respect for an educated man –prized as it were. I just wouldn't want something to happen to you."

I looked up at The Venger, the sails, masts and guns and this ship now was starting to feel like home in a strange way. "At this point, Mister Harrow, I'm not sure what I would do without you."

He gave just a hint of a smile and said, "Then take your station Mister Reed."

"Yes sir." The samurai let me pass and I went up the ramp just as Rajiv had climbed aboard with some colorful birds on his wrists and shoulders – new mascots for the rafters in the gun deck.

I dropped below deck and loaded in my gear and as I secured everything in my overhead net and in my locker, I shook hands –or—grabbed forearms as was the custom, with the other crew members as they returned, Java, Irons, Dutch, a tip of the hat from Mister Cage, even Baltimore acknowledged me even though he was silent and without words. When I saw Jeddah –after he greeted me with a nod—I stopped him. "Mister Jeddah, I have something for you." I pulled a book from the locker. It was drawings and designs on The Great Wall.

He looked at it, glanced at some of the pages and smiled. He suddenly pulled a massive Arabian scarf from around his neck and handed it to me in trade, before walking forward through the deck. Needless to say, my scarf collection was getting impressive.

Food was being loaded into the galley –the stoves already alive and cooking.

I also saw Mister Merritt sitting quietly at his place, looking out at the sunlight through the cannon door. I realized that I had not seen him once in Macao. I had seen him working on the ship but never in town. In fact, I had never seen him in ANY town. I wondered why that was….

Once in place, I climbed back above. It was hot and damp and the sky was grey. Mazatal and the Aztecs were in a huddle, Mister Thorn at the wheel, Le Clerk and the former Legionnaires were at the armory. I went to the rail where I could see the que of potential volunteers below -- Portuguese from Macau, sailors, a Jesuit –for whatever reason-- and what looked like former Chinese soldiers –some in their battledress and armor-- most likely on the run from their Emperor or now ready to start a war with us, for themselves and for their own financial gain.

Raeder walked the line looking over the potential crew men in a sort of pre-evaluation. Lincoln worked the book, asked the questions, and took the names and blood print and if they made the cut, Daws or Newcastle swore them in.

There was some tension between the Chinese and some of the Japanese in line and the factions seemed about to clash when Tiger, Kai, and some of our ronin took to the planks, pushed them apart and separated them with Kai yelling commands in a deep tone. I never learned much Japanese. The ronin who kept mostly to themselves socially would not share it but, I could understand the message for it was one we all knew-- 'Once you sign on to The Venger, there can be no civil –or cultural—conflicts. No prejudice between ranks.' I could read by his body language, that this was what Kai was explaining in his own, loud way --and it was a lesson some of the new men needed to learn.

We approved a platoon of Chinese soldiers, one named Genghis after the legendary ruler. They were allowed onboard with their weapons and armor. Mister Arson assigned them to bunks and began to line them up for their responsibilities....

--Back on the dock, "This is unlike any ship you've served on in the past" Jack-Karr walked down the line, the wood panels creaking under his feet. "This is not a merchantman or any navy ship. This is The Venger! There is God, then the Captain and if your blood goes into this book," he said as he pointed to the desk, "and you take this oath, I can promise you only one thing –WAR!'

--The blade gashed the thumbs on the applicants as they stamped their prints into the book.

I watched the Jesuit work his way forward. "Is that going to be the replacement for Mister Rush?" I asked...

"Mister Rush was a rare breed indeed," said Foxx, "Both fighting man and preacher. Neither you or I, or that man there, can ever replace him."

"So, do we give the Jesuit a chance?"

"Odds are no." He said, "We need men who can fight first, then, maybe, offer religion second. That man there—" He motioned to the Jesuit with a move of his head, "I'd wager, he can't hold the planks when hell comes knockin'! Give me one of those Chinese mercenaries instead –we'll have a better chance."

I looked to Mister Bishop, as he worked to replace a rail gun. "What about you?"

He stopped and looked at me.

"The men could use a little divine guidance."

He seemed to think on it for a moment, then said. "For that they would need someone divine." And he continued working on the gun.

"But not you?"

"No not me, damn it!" He barked as he suddenly stopped his work, then he tried to collect himself, "See here Reed, of all the men on this ship you have the most promise to make something of yourself outside of our trade and I respect that. So now, don't say anything more to damage your reputation."

"But—"

"No!" He put his hand up. "Do not finish that sentence if you want to remain on your feet."

I wanted to press the issue because I believed Bishop would make a fine minister and what's more, I felt like he needed to get his religion back. But at this time, I remained silent.

Jack-Karr stopped at the Jesuit. "What are you doing here father?"

"It is part of my task to carry the word of God to all places." He looked up at our massive ship as if it was in need of his presence.

"The only preacher we tolerate onboard is a combat chaplain. Savvy?" He had to be a man of dual talents; Karr explained.

"I believe it is my place--"

"--We're not pilgrims Father. This is a warship --can you fight or not?"

"I cannot disobey the Lord's Commandment."

"Then away with ya!'" Karr said and as he waved him off, a light rain began to come down.

On the quarter deck, the Captain turned from the rail towards the commotion below, "How many have we got?"

"Almost a full-compliment sir." Thorn said from the map table as Hallock and Obal pulled the canvas tent roof over it to keep the papers dry and the lantern burning....

"Then let's wrap this up and get underway." He said as a flash of lightning lit up the horizon. "We have business ahead of us."

"Aye sir."

XIX

THE PHANTOM OF DECK TWO

I ended my watch as crewmen stormed the deck to prepare for the bad weather and dark skies. Below deck, men were filing in, for evening meal and out, to take their stations. I moved through the crew, past Laban, Jeddah, and the Moors as they finished their evening prayers. Mister Barack practically growled at me as I passed—

Jeddah put his hands out to Barak as if to ask what the problem was or 'why so angry?'

"I have to get out of the shadow of his debt." Barak explained with his thick accent. "You would think if there is one person on this ship that would need saving it would be him." He motioned in my direction. "But Allah has not been kind –I regret that he has not brought death to this man."

Jeddah nodded and looked at me as I climbed into my hammock and began to drift away to sleep. "Maybe soon someone will try to kill him." Jeddah said.

"God willing."

Jeddah then said in Arabic, "Don't be concerned, all things will happen as God wills it."

The next day, the storm, like a monster on the horizon, moved closer and closer. Maybe it was the sounds of the storm that kept me awake that night –surely, the gun crews had no difficulty sleeping for they were out. I was writing, scratching out thoughts on my parchment by candlelight late that evening when I felt a presence over me. I did not move at first for this business with Standish gave me pause but I did muster my courage to turn and look up where I saw the Captain looking down at me. Rainwater was coming down through the deck panels, and over his hat as he held himself steady with one hand up on the cross beam above his head.

"Writings…is it?" He asked.

I stumbled for my answer. "Yes, I wanted to write, to make note, of some things I have witnessed here."

"Our adventures?" He asked with a look of curiosity in the eyes…

"Yes." I said hoping this would not make him angry…

He looked at me for a few seconds that seemed to take an eternity, then said with a half-smile, "I'd very much like to read it."

"You-you would?" I was surprised.

He smiled, "The world could use a few more thinkers."

I smiled back, "Yes-yes sir." And he moved down the deck into the shadows. I stood up and watched him disappear, then I closed my parchment and walked to the galley lit by lantern light where Hobby was working.

"Coffee lad?"

"Please."

He pointed, "There in the bucket." And he turned back to the stove.

"I just saw someone— "

Hobby shot up straight from the smoking stove as if scared… "Standish?" He asked with a pale white complexion.

"No --the Captain."

"Ah." Hobby smiled in relief, "Much better the Captain."

"I was just surprised, that's all."

"Don't worry lad. He often walks the deck at night checking on the men. It's his way."

"It is?"

"He can't turn in himself for the night until he knows everyone is all right."

"I didn't know."

"Most don't. He's stealth that one. Although he usually finds Therrinfall up but, that man seems to only sleep a few moments at a time in any event."

"Yes...so I've seen."

"It's the years of dirty work he did for that blasted King back in England...and most of the people he lynched weren't even criminals." Hobby continued, "They were debtors or...political rivals or some nonsense." He pulled some bread from the oven and straightened back up again. "Mark my words boy, he'll never find peace so long as a British regular or...British official is left alive."

I dropped my mug into the coffee bucket....

Wolfe came to the galley window, the new stitch work in his face could be seen in the moonlight.

"Hobby, we've got a storm off the port bow –time to batten down."

"Aye Wolfe."

The weather was still working to close in around us....

I had the starboard watch on this night –from the rail--and as per the ritual, used a spyglass to scan the horizon on the banks of the nearby coast, I could see the torches of a remote Buddhist temple as we sailed past...

I heard something nearby and looked towards the bow to see the Aztecs in their huddle but, Upatau was rolling what appeared to be small bones on the deck. I had seen this before on occasion and was aware that this was something they did to get guidance from time to time or insight into their future but this time, the ritual seemed different and on one roll of the bones, they all became still and silent.

Then a cryptic, cautious whisper or two.

Obal stepped next to me as we both looked across to our Aztec brothers, still on the panels, around their small deck fire.

"Anything interesting?" I asked him.

Instead of a quick answer, Obal translated my question into the Aztec language. This must have been out of respect for their ceremony for we all had working knowledge of English.

Mazatal answered.

Obal looked to me, "They say the apocalypse is coming."

"Apocal --the end of the world?"

"The end of their world or...the end of ours." And Obal moved on.

"Is there a third choice?" I asked.

That night, the Captain was keeping watch, in tune with his desire to lead by example. He stepped away from the wheel, leaving it in the hands of Mister Thorn and took a seat at the map table to check his charts. He used the candle to light his long-stemmed pipe, exhaled the smoke and looked down at the chess board next to his maps, and the game he had in play with Mister Jupiter.

Rorry brought coffee from the galley and placed a mug in my hand after the Captain waved the drink off. Rorry then grabbed the empty bucket -- the supply he was replacing-- and asked the Captain if he needed anything. "There's also rum cake below."

"No, thank you lad. Perhaps Mister Reed might like some but, I am fine for now."

"Mister Reed?"

"Rum cake?" I thought with interest --then I quickly thought of my last experience with it in the galley and politely brushed it off. "No. Thank you."

Rorry nodded and left the helm.

"Tis a strong man who can bow to discipline." Essex said getting back to his charts...

I smiled to myself for I had not yet made discipline, my lord and master though, I can attest to the merits of those who possessed it. "Excuse me Captain...pardon my curiosity if you will but, how did you become a privateer? If I may ask...." –and I at once regretted the sudden courage that compelled me to ask this question so, I shifted back into my more natural position of nervousness...

The Captain suddenly turned to me, the flickering candlelight obscuring some of his features in darkness, "You may ask but, you may not find the answer as interesting as you'd like…for I did not turn to privateering because I enjoy brutality. I turned to privateering because the world offered me no other choice." In this regard, he seemed very different from his contemporaries. I thought of the wanted posters all over Bristol and Le Harve that I had seen as a boy. Posters that included detailed accounts of privateering and savagery. Some exaggerated, some true enough but it was interesting to see a Captain –our Captain—seem to stand from something different. "In the Royal Navy, your life has very little meaning to the crown, except, to keep them in that position –on the throne- - beyond that, they don't even know your name. Death and taxes is all you're ever promised back in England."

"Are you a privateer, to revolt?"

"No but, it started with a revolt… a mutiny in fact." He looked up at me and seemed to remember a different life and a different time.

"A mutiny!" I mumbled under my breath…

"I'm not ashamed," he said, "As first officer aboard the H.M.S. Falcon, I believed I had a responsibility to the men. When punishment became unjust and excessive and the risk became too high, I took command…with the help of Mister Harrow and Daws— "

"They were with you?"

"Yes, they were, along with Mister Blair, Sterling, Newcastle --then a midshipman and Merritt who at times seems to regret his decision." He appeared reflective as he spoke, "We cut Sunderland down from the whipping post where he had been left to die after a flogging. He was hardly alive. For getting him medical attention, we were all to be put under arrest. This, along with previous irrational actions propelled me to take command of the ship for the sake and lives of the crew and –without regret-- I did so."

"But wouldn't the Admiralty justify your actions?"

"In the soul, yes! In the court…never. The British navy runs on fear and discipline, they would never justify a mutiny no matter how just and…there is a hierarchy of titles…" He exhaled, "The crown always sides with the title."

NO QUARTER! KILL ALL MASTERS!

"And the Captain?"

"We confined him to quarters and turned him over to the British authorities when we made the coast of Africa and I turned myself in." He paused and appeared to reflect, "There was a trail –however brief—and I was sentenced to the gallows."

"But you're here."

"I am…." He slowly pulled his cravat from around his neck to reveal the scar of the hangman's noose and allowed this mark to make a serious impression on me. "Not everyone wanted to see me hang." He said slowly, "My life was saved by some of these men here –and-- as a result, I owe them the best I have to give."

This explained his conduct. It became clear to me that he still applied some of the art and rules learned in the British navy but also –above all-- valued the lives of those in trusted to him. I deduced that this was his reason to use tactics of civility where they applied –rather than terror. It was –he would say—good business. If one operates with terror, everyone conspires to remove such terror. Make everyone a profiteer and they wish you success and even give aid to your cause. It was best to take ships without a fight – if possible. It was smart to pardon the defenders and, in some cases, even share the profits.

"I have worked hard to keep my rage in check and….revenge is a bad business." He said, "It distracts a man, consumes him, bends him from his mission."

"Do you miss England?"

"I've been back from time to time –quietly—but there isn't much left there for me now."

I wondered if it was the same for me now.

"The world is vast and kind, young man. Far too grand to just remain in England anyhow." He looked into the distance.

Hallock made his way to the helm, "I have the watch," he said ready to take over and I handed him the spyglass. I bid them goodnight and as I started down the deck, Hallock said, "Hobby's made cake. It's like

Christmas around here, you should grab hold of some before it's all gone."
He then looked to the Captain as if confused, "It's not Christmas, is it?"

"No Mister Hallock, it isn't Christmas, not for another few months…"

The next day we rounded the Batswani Islands where bats blocked out the sun. By sunset on the 11th, we were almost upon a whaling ship, but disaster struck --a sudden explosion! Whatever was in the whaler's hold must have ignited and it lit up the horizon. The ocean around the wreckage was on fire. As we moved through the smoke, Essex ordered us to pull the survivors aboard and we did. Some were burned, some covered in whale grease. All terrified.

Rabal, Obal, Sanjuro, Fury and Lau –the most heathen among us— forced them into a line on deck. Irons, Wolfe, Barak, and the rest of the crew parted so the Captain could approach. He remained silent and walked in front of the ranks of survivors. They looked down at their feet, afraid to make eye contact. I must admit we looked like a dangerous bunch. One man, shivering suddenly spit some words out. "I'd like to beg for our lives."

Essex stopped his pacing and turned to him as if he didn't understand what was said.

"I-I'd like to beg for our lives sir?!?"

"What manner of ship do you think this is?" Essex slowly asked as if to enunciate every word.

"A pi-pirate ship my lord."

"I'm sorry...did you say…pirate?"

Wolfe's hand tightened around the handle of his cutlass…

Rabal cracked his knuckles and Kannon just smiled.

The whaler quickly looked from his left to right as if to get help from his crewmen. Essex suddenly closed the distance between them, "Did you use the word pirate?"

"I-I meant no disrespect."

"Yet you call us pirates!" Without breaking eye contact Essex continued in sarcastic fashion, "Are there any pirates here?"

"Nay!" Was the collective shout.

"Nighthorse, educate this man."

Nighthorse suddenly grabbed a clump of the man's hair, pulled his knife, and placed the blade against the skin on his head. The man closed his eyes tight and cried for mercy --at which point Essex gave a slight grin and Nighthorse released his grip.

"We are not pirates! This is an independent operation not bound by crown law or any law for that matter –save our own. You will be allowed to stay on and work until we make the next port."

"Which port sir?" One of them asked.

"It will be a port of our choosing when the time comes."

"I'll not be part of this." A defiant voice at the end of the line cried out. "Call yourselves what you like, I'll have no part of you or this ship –to hell with the lot of ya'"

The Captain gazed at him as if to size him up. "Then it appears we'll have a vacancy." There was a moment of silence. "Rabal--"

Rabal suddenly picked the man up and threw him overboard. There was some screaming –and a change of heart-- from the ocean's surface as the man tried to tread water...

"Anyone else not like our company?" The Captain's eyes darted from man to man all were paralyzed with fright. Then he cut through the silence. "Mister Harrow..."

"Sir?"

"Put these men to work. They're eager to earn passage to the next port."

"Aye Captain" Harrow directed the men down the deck, "With me, all of you." As they moved down the rail they saw their former crew member drift away in the tide –still waving for help—but not getting it. Harrow looked at him for a moment and said, "We only want motivated souls here. Any of you lot get out of line," he continued, "And it's a death sentence."

That night, some of the new men –the whalers—were at the end of their task --swabbing the deck.

Jeddah sparked a deck fire. He added some timber to it, and we gathered around the metal fire bucket to warm up…

Grog and coffee were passed around. Down the deck was some combat training. I looked up to the stars and drifted off. Later that night something—although I'm not sure what—shot me awake. I looked around nervous and confused. On deck as things became quiet, I saw Baako emerge from below deck and for the first and only time --he appeared frightened!

"What is it?" Jeddah asked.

Baako shook his head nervously like a man who wasn't able to breathe and just like that, he left the scene. Gone! Back below deck.

I immediately sat up. I had my suspicions about the situation and got to my feet. This moment stuck with me –and continued to make me nervous-- for I had never seen fear among any of the men, least of all Baako who had always been at the forefront of any danger. I turned and suddenly bumped into to Lo-Tan –who also observed Baako's behavior-- and he raised his glance so he could see under the brim of his bamboo hat…

"It's not man he fears. It's the unknown."

I knew what it was –I think by now, most of us knew but, I had hoped we had left this frightening mystery behind us --but it was back!

The lantern light on deck shifted to reveal Rabal –the giant, Toombs, Jagger, Merciless and Teague emerging from the shadows. Teague looked at us, "No ghost determines my destiny." He quietly said and with a nod, Jagger moved down the deck, then down to the guns where he found Baako packing grenades, hands trembling…

"Bak!" Jagger took a seat on the cannon opposite…

Baako who was clearly trying to keep busy and his mind occupied, looked up for a brief moment, then re-focused his attention on his grenades.

"Remember when we fought those French marines in the swamps around New Orleans?"

"I do –a three-day fight that was." He continued with his deep, African accent…

"Six or eight of those bastards tried to drown you…I killed a few with my blunderbuss, Nighthorse and his Hurons finished the rest and brought you to the surface…"

"They did."

"That was when we first started to respect the tomahawk." Jagger smiled, then his grin grew straight. "We fought for four days in those swamps –destroyed that strange, wicked temple in the bayou—with those catacombs and God-forsaken mummies --burned that blasted French stockade." He laughed. "We almost lost Harrow in quicksand, remember?"

"I do." Baako smiled. "That was a good day."

Jagger paused to frame his words with a touch of sincerity, "There's very little your brothers here would not do for you," Jagger continued, "And there's nothing we can't survive, including the situation we're dealin' with here."

Baako looked up as if to understand the point.

"We don't want to see you troubled."

Baako exhaled, "You survived being buried alive. The Spanish buried you in a coffin and you came back and made them pay for it."

Jagger nodded….

"You are the only 'ghost' I know –and you have earned the reputation."

"Few people still call me that."

"But you are real. In the remote islands on the Spanish Main many of my people practice the old ways mixed with the new. Voodoo. This magic can bring a dead man to life and in some of these remote places, the dead walk…"

"I have heard this."

"There is method to this, sometimes good, sometimes evil but they apply magic, and these men walk and this I understand."

"Aye, so I've heard."

Baako's face was suddenly gripped with a new intensity, "Standish-is-here!" He hissed with a touch of fright though his broken words. "With no voodoo. No reason…. Standish is with us!"

Jagger listened with intent and thought very carefully about his choice of words. "You my friend are not the only man among us who has seen him."

Baako's eyes widened, relieved to hear that he wasn't the only one to witness this –ghost! At least he now knew he was sane.

"No, Blythe, Hallock, Bons….and the schoolteacher, Reed."

"Mister Reed?" This brought a certain credibility to this conversation because of my background in learning and logic.

"Yes –even Takeda thought he saw Standish walk out of the infirmary moments after he dragged him there with the cutlass in his head --while the fighting was still going on."

Baako appeared to think on all this and after a moment, Jagger believed he hit upon the right philosophy for this situation, "Standish was one of us Baako. He was our brother. His spirit may not want to leave The Venger but…. he would never do us harm. On this you can rely."

Again, Baako tried to focus on the words….

"Remember, Standish was with the Captain when he became a privateer. He was family to Harrow and Newcastle…Teague swore by him and…. he saved Addo's life when we raided that money caravan in Cartagena."

"Yes…he did."

"His weapons made us."

"Aye"

"And the Portuguese who brought you to the new world through the slave trade, feared him. He made his living antagonizing your sworn enemies. His presence here is not bad but good and even with one foot in the next world, he is still family."

Baako appeared to breathe easy and accept this logic –for now.

Jagger emerged from the shadows below deck to face Mister Harrow – as the most senior man on this ship, second only to the Captain, he was well aware that he had to address this situation and with one look to size Jagger up, he moved down the deck –through our ranks—towards the Captain's quarters.

Duncan-Howe looked to Mister Baltimore, "So much for burning your damned weeds all through the deck. Much good that did."

Baltimore gave a casual shrug. "One has to try!"

With permission, Harrow took a seat at the Captain's desk. He set down his mug of rum and rubbed his eyes as if the problem on his mind was creating a fierce headache.

Essex looked at him and could read his reluctance to speak, "What is it, George?"

"I'm not sure how to put this Captain but…some of the men claim to have seen Standish between the decks."

There was a pause while the Captain tried to process this, "Standish? Our Standish?"

"Yes, our Standish."

The Captain's eyes slowly glanced at the floor in thought and then he looked back up at Harrow. "Standish is dead."

"Exactly!"

"The crew has seen a dead man on deck?"

"The crew has seen the ghost of a dead man on deck, sir."

The Captain fell back into his seat. "How?"

"That's anyone's guess sir but more than one of our trusted officers have seen it and at different times."

Essex seemed genuinely vexed by this….

"I'm afraid it may be perceived as bad luck or…some sort of curse."

A curse was bad business on a ship, so the Captain took the only possible route he knew "Na, not bad luck --good luck! For it shows a man wants to be part of this crew even in death. The ancient Roman sailors said a phantom of an old shipmate was a sign of protection from the next world."

"Really?" Harrow asked.

"No --but it will sound good to the men so, we'll use it where it applies. If Standish is still onboard, we'll consider it good luck not bad – understand?"

Harrow made a slight smile and said, "I understand, and it will be so." He dismissed himself and crossed paths with Newcastle just outside the door.

Newcastle was waiting for orders on how to handle this...

"We maintain that this phantom's presence is good luck, not bad and that it's a positive omen for all of us."

"What?' Newcastle was ambushed by this.

"Look," Harrow decided to test his explanation, "The ancient Roman sailors said a phantom of an old shipmate was a sign of protection from the next world."

"Did they?"

"No. The Captain made that up, but it sounds good. Savvy?"

"It does." Newcastle admitted.

"Aye."

Newcastle looked as if he was prepared to follow the order but, his expression seemed to convey that he himself did not believe all this so Harrow hammered the point home, "We will make them believe this Newcastle. Our will versus superstition, understand?"

"I do."

"Good. Then see to it."

XX

CYCLONE OF DOOM

"Great Judas ghost!" Screamed Harrow as be barked commands into the wind ordering us to our stations in an effort to keep command of the ship.

The sky was grey –almost black—as this monster of a storm rolled over us. With a wicked scream from the wind, we moved down the lifelines –as waves buried us, flooding the deck—and we moved to ride the rail and help the ship keep its balance.

"All hands-on deck --now!" Arson commanded –and everyone was up. The deck emptied; the gun sections emptied the galley emptied. Waves blasted Hayte, Kannon and Hazzard as they surfaced on the top deck, sweeping them across the planks and hammering them into the base of the quarter deck. Bolt reached out and took a grip of Johnny Kay to keep him from washing overboard --and Madds just started cursing the sky in angry fashion.

Arson directed the crew from station to station to keep control of this ship. We railed up and then I heard the words….

"Good God!"

Ahead was what appeared to be the gateway to hell –massive clouds moving like a giant, dark tunnel rimmed with lightning, off our bow –and we were headed straight for it.

The ship was pulled and surged under my feet. I couldn't understand all the terms the crew exchanged in battling the weather but, I heard the statement "Here comes Lucifer!" And I feared the worst as I gripped the ropes.

The Captain shouted commands, Thorn would spin the wheel and the ship continued to battle for position with the waves....

"So, the ghost of Standish is a good omen?" Harrow barked at the Captain –as water splashed the deck-- in a sorry attempt at sarcasm.

"Now?" Essex barked back as he helped turn the wheel. "You want to discuss this now?"

But the forces of nature were starting to pull the ship away from us and suddenly, we were all thrown onto the deck. This was the one thing I feared most –a storm, something out of our control. The men around me could survive all forms of combat but... this? Nature? This was something no man could challenge.

The darkness on the horizon off our stern seemed to form into a wall of water and closed in on us as if to bury us. Harrow looked back, "My God!" He turned to those of us close by and shouted, "Brace for the locker boys!" His direct tone and the precise enunciation of his words put the fear of God into me...

--My heartbeat pumped through my chest like the hammer in a clock tower. --AND BOOM! There was a strange sound –like bending steel-- and the ship shifted in the water and seemed to slam to a halt. Our whole world seemed to turn on its side as I was picked up in the force of a wave slammed into the rigging and then –I saw a section of the top deck coming right at me as I fell and slammed into it --and blacked out.

I woke up hours—perhaps even days later? I wasn't sure. My head throbbed like I had been hit in the skull with a brick but, I was alive. My vision was blurred but I slowly began to focus, and voices could be heard close by. Strange, there were no signs of the storm, the sun was out, and it was hot. I looked around to see that the ship was miraculously still intact, aground --but we appeared intact.

The Captain, Harrow and most of the others were already up and working, some appeared hurt or moved at a rough pace, but they were alive. A hand was put on my forehead as if to check my temperature, it was Whitney. "We thought you were dead!" He smiled and pulled me to my feet and despite the pain I was in, I could take a survey of the situation around me. The crew was making inventory of supplies –that which survived, and a shore party was preparing to move out to forage.

"Have you concluded your nap Mister Reed?" Harrow barked in passing.

I rubbed my head, still not sure of my condition but, I knew how to reply. "Yes sir."

"Good, report to Mister Newcastle."

"Yes sir."

I located my weapons and found Newcastle and Jupiter near the bow where they were assembling the shore party. "You awake?" Newcastle asked me...

"Yes sir. Where are we?"

"St. Etienne Island, we think." He replied.

St. Etienne was part of a chain possessed by the French government but, this was an island, abandoned after a war. The former French marines in our crew, told us that the French just decided to plant their flag and leave --for some mysterious reason.

There was a sudden warning call from Hallock who had just made it aloft. "Below, in the tide!" And at that moment, as I moved to the rail, we saw a perplexed sight that confused, stunned, and baffled all of us. The ship was stranded –not far from the beach but on what appeared to be the outline of a massive circle in the reef. A perfect circle! This was no sandbar or rock. It was metal of some sort because it reflected the sunlight as the low tide and shallow water washed over it.

"What the hell?"

-Who would forge metal, then drop it into the ocean? And how? Duncan-Howe removed his long stem pipe from his teeth, eyes fixed on this thing.

"Morning Reed." Kannon said, as he took the rail next to me, without looking in my direction, he too, rolled his eyes across the horizon of this strange element under the waves.

I nodded and motioned with my head towards the plate under us. "What do you make of this?"

"I don't know!" He said as he started to get himself and his weapons situated. "I've never seen anything like it."

Some of our men started over the side to make the climb down...

--It was massive in size and scope and from rail to rail, we could see we were stranded near the dead center of it, "Maybe it's some kind of trap." Dos Santos said as I started to move down the wall.

The conversation, as I moved to the stern was the same as at the bow, "Maybe it's religious? An alter or something?" Irons suggested.

"These natives can't forge metal." Jagger confirmed as he waved to the islands nearby. "Not on this scale. Besides...not much of a population to forge it in any event."

"Why make something only to drop it into the sea?" Hayte asked, just as confused as the rest of us.

"That was my question," I said.

"Maybe it was on land once or maybe... this was land once." Johannis wondered aloud...

"--I heard they found pyramids underwater near the Calypso Islands." Jopo added. "A ship, wrecked on them in a low tide."

Newcastle looked over the side, to our iron worker, Reeves who stood in the knee-deep water on the metal platform with Arson, Sunderland and Obal. "What kind of metal is it Mister Reeves?"

"It's not steel, or iron..." Reeves looked up, "It's of a type I'm not familiar with."

"What?" Newcastle was confused, "A metal our iron workers can't even identify?" He then looked to Daws, "How is that possible?"

Arson sloshed around on the surface of this thing, then suddenly stopped, "There be a hatch here!" He pointed as Reeves and Sunderland moved over to it.

There was in fact a hatch, meaning this giant metal disc was hollow! The 'metal' hatch cover had been blown off or removed but whatever was on the deck below –inside this thing-- was flooded in darkness and…sea water.

"Something that's made of metal, that Reeves can't recognize, dropped in the sea and…you can …go inside it?" Howe displayed his confusion that matched all of us.

"Well, whatever's down there, it's trapped in the dark."

Then, Sunderland noticed symbols around the hatch entrance. "There are letters."

"What do they say?" Harrow asked with a shout from the rail.

Sunderland shook his head, "I don't know."

"Send our schoolteacher over." Essex ordered and I began the climb down.

I stepped on to this metal surface as Johannis, Teague and Bons dropped down with me and I made my way over to the hatch entrance. I could see the hand-print sized symbols and, even with the moving tide, I could see they were foreign to me.

"Well?" Sunderland asked.

I studied them and got down in the tide and ran my fingers over them. "It's like some form of Hieroglyphs."

"Hiero what?"

"Egyptian but… it's not," I said.

"Latin maybe?" Reeves asked.

"I speak Latin like all doctors," Said Johannis upon concluding his own investigation, "–That's not Latin or…Roman. Hell, it isn't even Greek." He barked.

"It sure as hell isn't Huron." Arson spit.

Bons shook his head no.

"I have a bad feeling about this." Sunderland said.

"Aye Sunderland, always the pessimist in the face of some mystery—" Arson was unmoved.

"Alright then, when something happens to ya, I'll write your folks." Sunderland returned.

"Maybe we tie a rope around Tiger and drop him down into the debts of the hatch here?"

"Into the darkness?"

"We can light a waterproof fuse; he can have a look 'round?"

As they debated their next move, I stepped away to get a sense of this thing, this mysterious metal plate we were on. It was several hundred meters 'round and it had reef growing over it in some places.

Arson stepped to me, "What is it?"

"Reef." I pointed and motioned to the southern side of the disc, "all over this section."

"So?"

"So, reef takes generations to grow."

Arson peered at me, "What's in your head Reed?"

I looked back at him, "Whatever this is… it's been down here a long time. Hundreds of years, perhaps."

Arson's eyes seemed to widen, and we were both gripped by a sinister, haunting feeling of dread.

Back on deck, Essex turned to Newcastle, "Well, whatever this is, we can't let it stop us. Get your team ashore. We need water and whatever supplies you can find."

"Yes sir."

As Newcastle cleared the area, Jaffar stepped to the rail next to the Captain, and he scratched his chin the way one does when he starts to draw conclusions. It was a look Essex had seen many times.

"Speak your mind Mister Jaffar?"

Jaffar looked at the Captain out of the top corner of his eye. "When I was a boy, some Howeitat riders found something like this…in the sands outside the Farasan Desert." He was pensive as he tried to frame his memories into words, "I did not see it…" He said, as his tone became dark, "But…they said it fell from the sky."

"What?"

Jaffar slowly nodded. "The tribesmen who rode out to see it…did not come back!"

That was all it took. Essex moved down the rail, stopped Tiger from going over the side with some rope and a fuse and called out for our second officer, "Mister Harrow?"

"Sir."

"Break out the weapons, get a strike team on the rail, now."

"Yes sir." Harrow echoed the commands across the deck and the men moved into action. Whatever this was, it was not going to surprise us –or— do something dangerous without paying a price.

We had to wait for the tide to rise before we could go anywhere, and we needed supplies. Water was always in demand but with the ride on the storm, our supplies were down, way down and in addition to water, we could also use any vegetation that we could find –that we could eat--so despite our discovery, the foraging party began to come together…

As repairs on the ship were underway, I was elected for the shore party with Mister Toombs, Jagger, Kon Boar, Baako, Mister Barak, Khan, Irons, Sunderland, Blythe, Akai, Bons, Timbers, Dax-Varrow, Flagg, Calixto, De Leon, Jack-Karr, Kane, Miranda, Favreau and the Legionnaires, Abel, Rajal, Tiberius, Merciless, Fury, Hazzard and Mister Lynch along with Wicks, Gerard, Kipling, Shaddam, Clairmont, Hallock, some of our new Chinese conscripts and a few others. As reported, the tide had us grounded –the water on this high metal object was only a meter high- but the tide was expected, at some point over the next twelve hours to rise again so we had to move now…

We moved across the metal plate, through the water, then, through the waves and up the beach and across a small, shallow lagoon into the jungle. There we formed something of a picket line, moving forward through the trees. The air was damp, the terrain became difficult and obscured by a jungle mist and I could hear wildlife, tropical birds, and such. There was something strange about this island, there was something oddly unsettling here, though the scene was quiet.

We moved forward, through the trees, watching for snakes, jungle spiders and other hazards. Past a set of caves and swamps where, we were surprised by a crocodile --and other obstacles…

As we moved around the base of a cliff, there –within this strange tropical fog--we made a haunting discovery…

-BONES!

-GIANT BONES! Partially absorbed and covered in rocks like they had been there for generations…Bones of a massive skeleton that seemed to stretch for half a league. We stopped in awe. The skull was almost like that of a giant crocodile.

The Chinese in our ranks mumbled to themselves.

"Dragon bones!" Sanjuro said. He then said something in Japanese…

"Dragon…bones?" Blythe repeated.

Lo looked up to see the massive skull from under the brim of his bamboo hat. "I've seen this before. In Manchuria during the war." he said. "Monsters! Buried, in the desert."

"It's been dead for a long time." Newcastle said ready to press forward, "Come on, let's move!"

"But what if there are more of them that ain't dead yet?" Blythe took a nervous look around.

Newcastle turned, "Then we'll have to kill 'em!"

We walked along this giant skeleton, under and through the massive rib cage. I was still dumbstruck by the size and as we moved under the shadows, I got the shivers.

Later, a half a league into our expedition, we found a freshwater lagoon with a waterfall. Mister Newcastle gave orders to mark the spot and Khan shot a flare into the skyline….

ON THE DECK OF THE VENGER…

As the Aztecs, Hobby, and some of our native contingent, were using nets in the tide to fish, Whitney saw the signal flare and lowered the spyglass, "Flare Captain."

Essex looked up from his map table, over the railing to the rocket in the sky. "Good. Have the labor gang stand by."

BACK IN THE JUNGLE...

We maintained our position, Sunderland emerged from under the waterfall where he had doused himself and he caught sight of Kon Boar looking out to the East. There was a circle of vultures on the horizon...

"Mister Newcastle," Sunderland shouted, "Something amiss here!"

We stopped drinking from the lagoon and Newcastle took a survey...

"Something's about to die." Hazzard muttered.

"Wild boar perhaps?" Abel guessed.

Newcastle wanted to investigate but had to frame it up a certain way, "Fancy a brief hunting trip, lads?"

"Aye" Fury replied with some positive rumblings in the background.

And with that, he sent out the Jaguar, Kon to take the lead...

Newcastle refused to split the shore party, so he marked our location and we –as a group—moved due East....

I still had an uneasy feeling and, maybe it was the bones that had me spooked but I felt like we weren't alone, like we were being watched but, even with a constant cautious glance to the north and south, I didn't see anything and the only thing I heard was the occasional tropical bird or bat.

Just as the sun had fixed firmly in the mid-day sky, we made another discovery. It was Calixto who uncovered it with a swing from his cutlass --he spooked a flock of vultures who suddenly took flight to reveal a skeleton –in French military armor and chest plate—and a guard house around it, cut from local timber hidden under the jungle foliage....

Our Legionnaires seemed concerned and started to mumble amongst themselves.

Calixto turned back as Newcastle approached. "French marines." He then looked ahead and ordered us to press forward where we discovered the remains of a military stockade. A French flag, faded and worn, blew in the wind. We moved inside the stockade walls to make a close survey of the situation…

Some of the buildings had been burnt out, same with some of the walls --whole sections burnt away in a sort of combat landscape. 'But who were they fighting?" Our suspicion was advanced when we moved into the stockade square and found the rest of the garrison command –in a pile of human skulls! Flesh not fully decayed.

"Headhunters! "De Leon was appalled, and the rest of the shore party was well aware of the situation, and we pulled our weapons….

"Head what?" I said scared. Natives are one thing, headhunters well, I had my history!

Mister Lynch motioned for me to be silent, "It is clear, we are not alone on this island."

Newcastle gave the command --back to the lagoon. From there, we'd work our way back to the beach until we could rendezvous with reinforcements from the ship.

I, for one, had been on an island with natives that were less than friendly, and I was eager to remove myself from this place before mealtime, so I stepped up my tempo. We began to move –fast--but we were only a few steps clear of the stockade when Bishop and Blair suddenly shot up into the trees, snagged by some sort of jungle snare trap….

Leaves and debris came raining down as they were hoisted up….

Blair let out a startled yell that echoed through the jungle –making birds flock to the sky—and marking our position to any unfriendlies –if they didn't know already.

Just as we moved to cut them down, suddenly hundreds of arrows rained down from the sky, one hit Mister Blair, two hit De Leon, one went through Hallock's hand, and Akai was killed as several arrows zipped into him, hitting him in the temple, ribs, back and through the neck --Some of the Chinese were killed as they raised their weapons.

Bishop cut himself free and dropped to the ground. An arrow struck in the wood of my musket handle –which saved my life—and just as I removed it, another arrow pierced my back shoulder and I dropped to my knees in pain. With adrenaline, I forced myself to my feet and reached around to grab the arrow but when I tried to remove it, it snapped with the arrowhead still in my shoulder. Tiberius grabbed me —arrows, whistling in all around and hitting the ground all around us-- and I grit my teeth in sheer pain as he pushed the arrow forward through my shoulder where I could see it come through my front shoulder muscles, skin and out. The pain was intense, use of my shoulder was gone and I was about to lose consciousness. Just then, Tiberius helped me to my feet and started to haul me forward...

Just when I thought it couldn't get any worse, painted natives stormed out of the jungle and jumped from the trees to attack us –some even swung in on vines! We pulled our weapons and fired into the tree line dropping several –one with a musket ball to the head! Then we followed up with pistol shot and blades but, our position was quickly overwhelmed. They swarmed all over us.

"To the lagoon!" Newcastle shouted, ordering a fighting retreat as he cleared the way –killing several natives at once with his blunderbuss -six or so bodies hit the ground in the blast.

Takeda dragged his katana across two natives as they attacked, killing them both. Bons planted his tomahawk into a skull, he, Able, Toombs and Jagger were reluctant to retreat and by their actions, it was clear that they wanted to fight it out here and now, without being forced from the high-ground but Newcastle insisted "BONS—WE—ARE--LEAVING!"

As we continued to move out, our rear guard, Mister Gerard and Mister Kipling were overwhelmed and swallowed up by sheer numbers and killed. Tiberius had several arrows in him but still made his way forward. Our ranks started to get scattered and suddenly the terrain under Mister Flagg's feet collapsed as he disappeared into a pit. Bons reached for him, but Flagg had already been impaled on the spears below. Others in our party also fell victim to various traps....

We made it to the lagoon but there was no sign of reinforcements, so we splashed through it on our way to the beach –with more arrows coming in! Clairmont lit and threw a grenade, the concussion of the blast echoed across the island and got everyone's attention on the deck of The Venger. Men on board turned and moved to the rail...

Tiberius took more arrows –in the back, shoulder and through the arm—but he kept moving. I collapsed, exhausted, and dazed and just when I was sure that this would be my end, I was hoisted aloft and thrown over the shoulder of Tiberius as Mister Toombs covered us, pulling reserve pistol after reserve pistol, and firing until all six and been cleared. Tiberius must have had fifteen arrows in him at this point but, he still moved quick...

Favreau –the Legionnaire—killed one of the natives just as he was overwhelmed, with spears coming in –and slamming through him-- from every direction. Before he was killed, he managed to light a grenade and intentionally held it close --the grenade exploded, ending it for himself and three headhunters...

Our party made it to the beach where we were met by Mister Harrow, Thorn, Teague, Rabal and more of our shipmates just as they stormed ashore, firing as they moved up –clearing the sand of angry natives. Mister Jeddah helped the wounded De Leon and others helped to move and carry our wounded through the low tide.

Several more natives were killed by musket fire but more –and more-- appeared from the jungle in waves. I looked up and saw what appeared to be hundreds –HUNDREDS--of natives who suddenly emerged from the tree line...

"They're not makin' this easy!" Dax-Varrow reloaded.

We were about to be overwhelmed --an arrow bounced off Shaddam's curved sword as he used it to take the arm off a native, then his head...

Suddenly, there was a strange sound like a horn echoing in the distance but not from our ship, --from the island! I looked up as hundreds of arrows darkened the sky. We moved for cover but several of them struck the side and deck of The Venger, ripping through the sails...

As the natives closed in for what I thought was my last few moments on earth, the cannons across deck two lit up and a bombardment hit the beach, killing a large contingent of headhunters –blowing some apart and cutting down trees! Deck three then opened up and the explosions started to drive the rest of the surviving headhunters back into the jungle...

I was dropped in the shallow tide, bleeding and breathing but, barely. I looked up and saw the shadow of Tiberius' as it rolled over me, blocking out the sun –his breathing was heavy, his eyes appeared distant –no doubt exhausted from carrying me to safety. Then, under the weight of about two dozen arrows, he suddenly dropped face first into the water.

I reached out to him –as if to help save him-- as I was picked up by Dutch and Killing Bear who started to haul me back to the ship, "Please don't leave him!" I begged and as I was taken away from his body, it started to drift in the surf, turning the tide red...

Calixto, Sunderland, Sterling and Baltimore ran past me, splashed though the tide and picked up Tiberius and started carrying his body towards the ship. It wasn't my request they had honored it was our practice to bring our shipmates back aboard –whenever possible –dead or alive.

I was put in the cargo net with the wounded. and raised to the deck where I was handed across the rail and lowered to the planks. I rolled on my back, in fierce pain, looking up at the sky, wondering if this was where I might meet my end...

--Strange, I thought of being a young man again, running through the streets of Bristol before I had even learned to read. I thought of the seaside by my home and of holding my mother's hand. I don't know why my mind flashed back to these things but, it did. Kind memories. Now....so distant. So far away.

The sound of cannon blasts, from the deck beneath me, shaking the planks and a sudden slap from Merciless brought me back. My eyes focused and I saw Merciless looking at me. "Now that you're back from the dead, care to help us Mister Reed?"

I couldn't speak but I knew my answer and I nodded yes when Doctor Jopo pulled me to my feet. "Not at this time, let me cauterize his wounds!" Jopo said, as I was helped to a section of the top deck where the wounded were assembled and worked on...

Our physicians started removing arrows –usually by pushing them through the body--and started patching up the wounded. I was advised that you never pull an arrow out –you push it through as was the case with my wound. If you pull it out, it rips twice as much muscle tissue. 'What a kind invention' I thought sarcastically, looking at all this medical work being done. Bloody arrows now littering our deck.

By midday, our makeshift on deck infirmary was full. Doctor Jopo put a piece of wood in my mouth and told me to 'bite down' as Abel and Obal held me in place, so he could cauterize the wound with a red-hot knife blade --I screamed through this God-damned stick until I lost my strength. Pain was going to keep me on the brink of death –or life—for this entire day if not longer.

When all the exhausting medical work was done, Doctor Johannis rubbed his chin, unaware that he had marked himself with the blood of the previous patient, since it was all over his hands, as he reached for a glass of wine and took a seat, exhausted. The Captain moved through our ranks to check on the wounded –as he always did after an engagement—and seek a report.

"Sixteen wounded and, as of now, one dead.... Locksley." Johannis then exhaled and he offered up more bad news, "I've been advised that Favreau, Gerard, Kipling, Akai and Flagg met their death ashore…"

The Captain gave a slow and regrettable nod. He was angry, "For water supplies! Damn it all!"

"Most of these men will be back in action within a few days except for De Leon, I'm watching his wounds for infection and… Tiberius." He took a moment, "I don't expect him to make it."

-Harrow stopped his pacing on deck when he heard this, with a look of concern. Then after a moment, he continued to his duties.

The Captain looked around at this mess.

"There are a number of men missing sir…."

The Captain seemed to give way to thought for a moment then, with a thank you to the Doctor, he dismissed himself. He emerged on the quarter deck where Harrow, Thorn and Mister Newcastle awaited his presence at the helm. Thorn lowered his pipe, "How is it sir?"

"Well, thank God the arrows that plagued us weren't poisonous, however, as you no doubt know, some of us are missing. We're running a head count now."

"Dead? Like the others?"

"Or alive waiting to be sacrificed and…eaten."

"I saw Gerard and Kipling overwhelmed by numbers…I doubt they could have survived it." Newcastle reported.

"Alive or dead…we need to make sure." Harrow said, "We can't leave them sir."

The Captain looked to Harrow, "No-we-cannot." He seemed angry about the situation getting progressively worse. He looked around at our setting. "Can't leave until the tide comes up in any event."

"Aye --another six hours at least." Harrow gave pause then said, "I shall call for volunteers and lead a search party ashore?"

"With respect, sir" Newcastle interrupted, "It was my shore party, I feel it my place to go."

Essex took a sharp look at him, "Very well, you will accompany me - and I want the toughest we got."

"Yes sir."

This was a command decision that I doubt would have been the same had our stations been in the Royal Navy. The risk of going back ashore, I believe, would have been too great for a navy captain and he would have removed himself from the island to save his majority. But Essex, however, knew that decisions like this –however hard—eared the respect of the crew. The thought that if it had been Wicks, Blythe, myself or any one of us stranded in the presence of hostiles and our men would come back for us, gave us a renewed sense of loyalty to each other.

The command was for the toughest we had –Teague, Baako, Jaffar, Rabal, Toombs, Jagger, Nighthorse, Bons, Hatano and all the remaining ronin –who wanted payback for Akai-- Lo, Jack-Karr, Bear Killer, Merciless, Fury, Strange, Cage, Mister Foxx, Tiger, Silence, Baltimore Kon

Boar and the Aztecs, Lau, Wolfe, Obal, Raeder, Sharp, Tane, Barak, Shaddam and some of the Moors, Abel, Bastien, Cyril, Roux, Jupiter and another thirty in number loaded up with weapons and this time, the shore party was under the command of Captain Essex....

I struggled but brought myself to my feet. "I should like to go ashore sir."

Johannis stopped his work. "You're not going anywhere."

I persisted trying to maintain my balance, "Please sir."

"You walk to that beach you'll die." Johannis continued.

Essex looked at me "I appreciate your honor Mister Reed..." he looked over my wounds "But a man in your condition will be more of a hindrance I fear, than an asset."

These words perhaps hurt me most of all. I was not going to be allowed to remedy the situation. I wasn't wanted...

Suddenly, there was another echo from the horn ashore. We all turned towards the island as a blizzard of flaming arrows rose into the sky and zipped in on us—

"Damn it to hell!" Arson barked.

The smoke turned the sky black.

"What the—" Harrow ducked as the sail above him caught fire. Cyril and Lau hit the flames with a water bucket and Cyril took a flaming arrow to the chest, then five of six more upping our death count.

Strange, Bolt, Flynn and Rift were all hit. Wiley was hit and fell back against a loaded cargo net, and could not grab hold of it so he dropped into the cargo bay and down several decks below...

Johnny Kay dropped into the cargo hold and managed to grab hold of the top deck as he fell, keeping his grasp until an arrow went into his hand forcing him to let go but, just as he was about to drop to his death, Jeddah grabbed him by the wrist and pulled him back up to the top deck –under fire with flaming arrows zipping in all around them...

As more of us were hit, Daws raised the red flag--

--No quarter!

The natives may have not understood it --but we did!

"Well damn it all to hell! That's it!" Teague shouted and he stood straight up in the face of all the oncoming arrows. "You see the flag?" He pointed to it as arrows and streaks of smoke darted past him on both sides. Some hit the rail where he stood. "You know the command." He yelled. "It's time to do what we do best and punish these bastards! Now!" And with that, our shore party was galvanized to attack, and they stormed over the rail, down into the shallow tide, across the steel plate and started moving forward as oncoming arrows zipped by...

The party made the beach, the men formed a combat line, cannons firing over their heads, clearing the jungle with explosion after explosion.

Even though it was not quite dusk, Abel, Rabal and several others lit torches. "Scooooorched earth!" Rabal shouted --for they were to set fire to anything and everything in their path that posed a threat.

I watched from the top deck, my arm and shoulder bandaged and in a sling with the wound still smoldering. The other wounded took a stance at the rail with me. No more arrows were coming in, which meant to us that the beach and the immediate jungle had been cleared of opposition.

By night fall, there were fires blazing on several parts of the island and in the distance, we could hear the havoc...

At dawn, the island was hidden by a dense wall of smoke. I continued to watch as Rorry handed me a cup of coffee. I didn't realize the tide was back up –and the ship had been lifted off our ancient metal platform-- until I saw our long boats dispatched and our pilots row them back to our hull. Essex, his face covered in blood, had brought the bodies of our men back and destroyed the island in his wake.

We helped the men onboard, and the dead were prepared for burial. Nighthorse, Bons and Baltimore all had fresh scalps –in the dozens. The others had their trophies as well and all were marked with blood.

Jeddah reported to Mister Harrow for a quiet conversation, not too far from me at the helm. "I do not know the Christian prayers but, I would be willing to give them…" he motioned to the dead men, "A blessing in our Islamic tradition if you wish it."

"I appreciate your civility Mister Jeddah and lo, at times like these we do miss the presence of Mister Rush." He looked at him, "I'll take your prayers and I hope you don't find offense if I stand in for Mister Rush and offer what words of comfort I can, from The Bible as well."

"That is to be expected." Jeddah said. He put one hand over his heart and with a bow, dismissed himself.

I was raised under the King's Bible. It was what I always imagined an audience would hear at my funeral. However, in the absence of our minster, Mister Rush, I thought it quite kind that Jeddah made an offer to do what he could –even though his faith differed from mine. I also wondered, when I looked at the dead, does any of it matter? Do the words matter? Does it change anything? Is there anything beyond this?

I looked to our Captain and he gave orders to get us underway. Essex would not speak about what happened on the island but, I privately questioned if any of the natives were left alive. This was not something our Captain wanted to do. It was something he felt compelled to do. It was an ugly business at times, this code --this law-- we were compelled to live by. But we could never be men again if we did not do this awful thing.

For a schoolteacher, I really lacked broad perspective until this moment advanced my education. We used the term savages because we lacked the intellect to come up with something proper, because we didn't respect anything different from ourselves and as I looked around at our ranks –and our men, covered in blood—I realized what I must have always known deep down about this crew –that we were the real savages!

--And the steel altar in the sea? It was now, after all this killing, of small consequence. Just another mystery on a trajectory of mysterious events that now made up the backbone of my existence…

XXI

THE LORD OF TWO WORLDS

DAYS LATER....

We sailed through the fog, past the San Fernando Islands, a volcanic archipelago further south. The Volcano was still active, and I could see the red glow in the mist through the infirmary window...

I battled infection but was allowed to pull myself together and clear the hospital. Tiberius, Miranda, and the others were still in the sick bay...

"Twenty-six arrows!" Johannis turned away from the hammock that held Tiberius to Jopo. "Must be some kind of record."

"Aye" Jopo said with his thick African accent. "He is a tough bastard; I'll give him that."

"That he is."

I went back topside, over the next few days, I was given light duty, until I healed up, spending most of the time on deck in the tropical heat. I took coffee there, kept watch –saw my first whale and slowly got the use of my shoulder back.

In time, I thought less and less about the combat on the island against the natives and more about what lie ahead, South America, around the horn and back to Jamaica a place I was now quite fond of but what actually happened next was something I could not have foreseen for we entered an area of the Pacific known as 'Iles Fantomes' –Dutch for The Ghost Islands. Past these islands were smaller ones, marked on the charts as 'colonies' once settled with an influx of Europeans, but now, if one was to look around, through the fog, they appeared almost abandoned.

Old brick buildings lined the coast, staged as if this was any other port but not much in the way of life. In fact, the only life I could see from the rail was a young man who stood still on a dock looking at us like a zombie. I had to focus on him because he appeared to be blind –his eyes were solid white.

We also saw a wicked looking plague doctor standing –perfectly still— in the mist.

"Curious sight" I said.

Duncan-Howe was working the ropes close to me with Blythe, Addo and Johnny Kay and his bandaged hand. Howe stood tall, watching the world pass by as we sailed, pipe clinched in his teeth….

"A land abandoned." Blythe said.

"War. Pestilence maybe." Duncan added.

To this theory, I had no answer but, I continued to look at this mysterious place. Buildings looked damaged from what may have been tropical rains or a monsoon and there was very little light –lanterns or candlelight—anywhere. Unusual for this time in the afternoon….

EDITOR'S NOTE.
RE: THE LORD OF TWO WORLDS

{The following is a chapter from Donovan Reed's Combat Record with The Venger. His editor (London based Giles and Hatchett Limited) made the decision to edit the following passage out of his overall combat narrative because they felt it was not to be believed. That the average reader could not retain the darker elements in it. It was more of an 'All Hallow's Eve' story than the notes of a notorious privateer. None the less. It is here. The first of several of the 'missing' chapters as it were….}

THE LORD OF TWO WORLDS CONTINUED…

We slowly sailed through the 'Fantomes Islands' with its abandoned townships, and that evening, there was a warning flare fired off the port bow. We moved to the railing to see a long boat in the distance, drifting through the fog....

"Curious?" Harrow put down his spyglass. He looked to Mister Thorn, "Bring us alongside. We'll check for survivors."

As we rolled up, we got a closer look of an image that was more suited for a dream –or nightmare—than our own reality. We could see people onboard, looking pale and lying in an almost peaceful looking manner as if asleep. Everyone on the longboat was in their Sunday finest clothes but --they were all dead! The women and the children.

--One woman was still clutching her parasol.

Mister Jopo and Doctor Johannis dropped onboard the launch and began checking the passengers to see if anyone was alive. They all had violent neck wounds, blood stained their collars and garments. "Damn curious!" Johannis said. He stood up from his examination and turned to look back up at Essex at the rail.

"What is it doctor?"

"It is as it appears sir. All dead." He looked over the bodies of the young children, "Regrettably." He added.

"What killed them?" Harrow asked, "Plague?"

Johannis remained silent for a moment as if to place his words carefully. 'Dehydration and...blood loss." There was more to his report, but he held his tongue so as to not alarm the crew.

Essex nodded. He'd take the report in confidence later and just as we started to bring our medical staff back aboard, there was another warning from the crow's nest. Hallock pointed forward to the northeast and Lynch called out, "Ahead...in the fog!"

In the mist, a shape began to slowly emerge --a ship! Run aground on some rocks. It was a suspicious sight. The Captain applied caution, checked our depth, and ordered the men to weapons as we pulled close.

Therrinfall handed me a gun, then pulled the hammer back on his. Thorn, Bishop, Mister Toombs, Bons and the rest of the Hurons took to the railing next to me ready to fire...

Newcastle lowered his spyglass and looked to Essex. "It's the Marauder!"

"Out of Yorktown?" Harrow asked with a touch of curiosity, making sure the identification was correct.

"Van Guardian's ship!" Essex knew the boat and the Captain.

"All the way out here?"

As we pulled closer, we took sight of something, something quite horrific. The body of a man was fastened across the wheel as if it was a whipping post.

"Good God!" Harrow exhaled.

"Raeder. Wolfe. Take your men aboard!'

"Yes sir." Raeder gave the signal and his men swung across the water and crashed down on the deck. They began to spread out to secure their surroundings, weapons at the ready. De Leon and Lau moved to the quarter deck and slowly approached the poor soul, harnessed to the steering, crucified to the wheel, eyes open and rolled over white, mouth locked open –as if he died screaming.

Upon closer examination, De Leon found the wound that killed him, a viscous wound on the neck. Like a beast had taken a bite of him. Missing throat, voice box and jugular –and some of his jawbone was exposed.

Lau's blade cut through the air with a whistle as he revealed it, then swung it down to cut the man clear of the steering. His body dropped to the deck.

Wolfe kicked the doors open to the officer's quarters and moved in for a search. Maps, documents, a pistol, and a lantern on the last of its wick but still aglow....

Essex watched from his position on The Venger as Rabal and his men dropped below deck to continue the search. There, on the gun deck, there was a strange –almost eerie—silence and very little light. Obal began to open the gun port doors to let in some daylight and a little fog but other than the guns, there was nothing there. Not a soul. No gunners. No crewmen.

Nothing.

The cannons locked in place. Weapons still in their racks. Powder and ball still secured.

Even further down, the hull had been breached but the water had only risen to the level of the tide on these rocks --waist high. Kannon slowly stepped into the dark water, using his hands to feel around for anything relevant.

What was also odd was that the ship was provisioned. There were barrels of molasses, salt, rum, fresh water. Obal checked the supplies and with a taste, found that they were good. None of it seemed tainted. Kai, Town, our Zulu, Kannon, and others began to offload the cargo.

Raeder climbed back on top deck and called out his report to the Captain.

-Full cargo.

-One -dead- man aboard.

"Doesn't make much sense." Harrow said as his eyes darted to the Captain. He looked back with a look that seemed to suggest there might be reason to be concerned....

A party, myself included, moved to the phantom ship to assist in the removal of her cargo. The decks of The Marauder seemed cold, and our boarding party was very cautious.

Below deck, the hull was creaking as we continued the process of unloading their cargo, loading it in the massive nets and using ropes and pulleys to pull it up through the decks then over the water, across to The Venger. As always, we took everything, food, silks, tools, weapons, rope, canvass, spare lumber, nails, dates, sacks of coconuts, candles, lanterns and barrels of water, sugar, wine and spices....

I was about to head topside when I noticed some damage to the woodwork by the bilge bay hatch. Something that looked like -massive, deep claw marks. I ran my fingers over them. "What the hell did that?"

"Never mind that" Kannon got my attention, "Let's clear out, before the hull collapses!"

"Right," and we started the climb back up....

Back on The Venger, the sun was beginning to set...

"It seems damn peculiar." Harrow said he turned to see the Captain and Mister Thorn going over the maps to plot a course out of the area...

"Of that I am aware." Essex didn't look up from this work. "I know how your mind works Harrow. You must fact and figure until there is no mystery left."

"Tis true. I hate the odd fact and I do despise mystery but, I heard the report and I dare say that this situation here should bother you too Captain." He paused, "Should it not?"

The more Harrow talked the more Essex felt inclined to reach for the bottle of rum holding the maps down but, he withstood the temptation...

Harrow slowly continued, "One man...strapped to the wheel!'
Suddenly, Jaffer stepped on the quarter deck –and though I had never seen Jaffar show fear, he did appear concerned. "Captain?"

Essex looked up....

"Off the starboard side sir....in the fog."

Essex stepped to the rail, took the spyglass from Daws, and focused on the area off the starboard bow. There in the mist, a beach could be seen but it was not the beach that was the concern, on the beach, hanging from posts were -body cages! Each one seemed to imprison a skeleton. This is how they punished privateers back in England. They imprisoned them in a body cage and left them to die there.

Essex slowly lowered his glass. "Bastards!" And without taking his eyes off the coastline he said, "Mister Jaffar, put a combat party together. Prepare to go ashore and fire the town."

Out came the weapons and torches as Jaffar moved to assemble some men.

Teague, Addo, Kai, Jagger, Lo-Tan and Toombs along with Miranda, Nighthorse, Bons, Sanjuro, Kan Bor and a few of the Aztecs, Rabal, Irons, Duncan-Howe, Giroux, the former French Legionnaire, Tane and myself joined Jaffar, Mandagan the V (fifth) and Barak as he emerged from the infirmary and a few of the other Moors appeared --fully armed.

I had long since become aware of a common pattern here. If Teague, Jaffar and Nighthorse were going ashore in an unknown land, then there was going to be violence or --a small war-- and that night, we went ashore…for vengeance! The sight of the body cages, on the beach and in the tide --lined with bones, made us angry. Mob justice against those of us from the sea was not to be tolerated. Our fate was not for townspeople to decide --and I for one, feared the cage. Pirates had been known to survive them, immobilized for several weeks—unable to prevent being picked apart by vultures-- before death set in.

Once ashore and out of the tide, the Aztecs –superstitious as they were known to be—became nervous and formed up into tight ranks, like a defensive position, clicking their small words and sounds together in a nervous fashion, weapons ready….

"What's gotten into you?" Teague asked.

Kon Boar mumbled a few broken words and clicks in his high-pitched voice as he continued to look towards the sky in a fearful fashion. I looked up, other than a few bats and a full moon there was nothing to be afraid of but, it was obvious they were scared and would not advance.

Teague surveyed Kon Boar and calculated his disposition. He then looked to Jaffar, then to Nighthorse in his war paint, Rebal and the rest of us and asked, "Anyone else?"

There was silence. Though, I must admit, I wanted to raise my hand and volunteer to stay behind on the beach–and Teague looked at me as if he suspected that I was about to do just that, but I was well-aware that I would never live it down, so my hand remained a clinched fist around the handle of my cutlass.

He then ordered our platoon forward, leaving the Aztecs on the shoreline to protect the long boats. Teague thought not to press them, perhaps because a scared, superstitious man is more dangerous than the enemy and Teague only wanted willing men in combat.

As we moved through the darkness, I quickened pace to get alongside Duncan-Howe, again, a confidant who would not rob me of my self-esteem when I asked a question, others would think foolish. "Why are the Aztecs staying on the beach?'

"Superstition." He confirmed as he stopped to ignite his pipe which lit up his face for a moment. He then said with clarification. "They're scared!" He exhaled the smoke and looked me in the eye to see if his words had any effect as if to see if I was sacred too.

--And indeed, I was.

The unknown had always scared me most of all and although, I had some confidence from the men around me, the darkness that lay ahead had me on edge. What was up there on the dark road to town? I was even more alarmed by the fact that Duncan-Howe did not tell me 'not to worry' or that there was 'nothing to be afraid of' but his silence seemed to imply that, indeed…. There was something to fear.

We pressed forward, through the fog, the mountains up ahead, against the moon, speared out of the ground like claws. An unsettling sight. We used torches to cut through the darkness and moved up the beach, under the trees and over the old gothic stone bridge that bricked its way over a lagoon. From there, we moved forward through a low-lying fog to an old Christian cemetery, and we moved through the jagged stone markings, crude in their shape, chiseled with a certain imperfection.

Beyond that, we came upon the first signpost….

Under a lantern we could see a proclamation. 'Beware' and what appeared to be orders for the populace to move indoors and off the streets before dark. Mind the warning bell and bolt your doors.

"It's as if they were expecting us!"

Indeed, the warning was much like the ones posted throughout the colonies about us—it had a similar ring to it. Perhaps that's why Addo put his torch to it and as the flames lit up the area, I looked around. "This feels bad," I said with caution, "This is dangerous."

"Good." Barak said, standing over my shoulder a meter or two back, "Let us hope so --for you." He grinned rubbing his chin as is he was waiting for something to try to kill me.

We moved forward, into the township proper. Lit by the full moon, the buildings, however, appeared dark. Abandoned. There was a little lantern light in a window, here or there, but very little life. We made a survey of the area then continued to move up....

A slamming sound suddenly got our attention and we looked to our right at a building that had its front doors banging away in the wind. Teague tilted his head in that direction and Rabal and Irons kicked the doors open and stormed the dark building. It was dead inside. Empty. They made an exit, eased their weapons and we continued into town....

We moved up to an inn and decided to enter. Giroux remained on watch outside. The inn was lit by candlelight, there was an innkeeper behind the bar though he appeared almost motionless and had a still, nervous expression. He was clearly surprised to see us enter.

Teague surveyed his surroundings and Irons moved forward to the bar. "Rum!" He commanded.

"I have none, sir." The rattled innkeeper returned, "But-but I do have wine."

Irons waved it forward. The innkeeper's hand trembled as he reached for the bottle, he filled a mug which Irons made vanish in one swallow.

Teague leaned against the bar, close to the innkeeper. He picked up a coin off the bar and passed it through his fingers like a magic trick and keeping his eyes locked on the coin he began to speak to the landlord, "Tell me the truth and you may live. Lie to me..." his eyes looked up at this nervous man, "And I'll kill you!" He shifted his posture. "Who planted those cages on the beach?"

Mandagan The V put both hands on his swords, waiting to pounce if he did not like the answer.

"The Magistrate."

Jaffar grit his teeth.

"And where-is-this-magistrate?"

"Gone sir."

I did not like to see a man threatened and although I knew my place, my conscious fired off an impulse that made me step forward to say something --but Duncan-Howe put his hand out to stop me.

Teague either didn't notice or didn't care at any rate, he slowly continued his interrogation. "Gone where?"

"He...he was taken." Something seemed to prevent this man from speaking but he did manage to hiss an answer, "The devil took him!"

"That, my friend is impossible!" Teague slowly looked up; his eyes looked dark in the dim candlelight. "For I am the Devil!"

--And out came the weapons!

"NO WAIT!!!!" The innkeeper panicked as Teague cracked his knuckles then threw his grip around the man's throat. "Please don't kill me!"

Suddenly the building shook like an earthquake.

"What the hell--"

We froze and looked up. Something had slammed into the roof like a powerful concussion blast. Dust fell from the rafters and shingles fell from the ceiling. The innkeeper couldn't breathe! He just trembled, gripped by a violent panic attack.

Just then, there was a gunshot. Giroux suddenly stumbled through the doors from outside –pistol smoking--and he collapsed inside the tavern, clutching his neck, which had a hole ripped into it –he was bleeding heavily. He tried to raise himself off the floor while clutching his wound....

Toombs took a defensive position and pulled two fresh pistols. Addo and Kai tried to help Giroux to his feet, but he was already dead. They checked the wound --most of his neck was missing. Miranda was in shock over the damage, "What manner of weapon did that?"

The tavern keeper was beside himself "It's the shadow!" He looked up at the ceiling as if a monster was on his roof, almost bouncing up and down in terror. "It's here! It's here!"

Teague released his grip and pulled a pistol. We formed a defensive circle, weapons out, eyes locked on the ceiling. We could hear a creaking sound like footsteps on the panels above....

-Then silence.

-A strange silence.

I felt the danger had passed and just as I lowered my weapon, suddenly, the floor exploded --Irons was pulled through the floorboards as they turned into splinters, and he disappeared under the building.

Pistols went off blasting into the darkness. Sanjuro, Mandagan and Jagger jumped in the new hole in the floor –weapons ready-- and lit the foundations up with a torch but Irons was gone! The sub-structure was vacant --there was nothing there!

They climbed back though the shattered floorboards when something that felt like a hurricane blew past the building almost shaking it apart, rattling shutters, doors, walls, and the foundations with violence.

Teague and the men stormed outside for a fight --but there was none to be had. The streets were empty. He turned to look at the rooftops but there was nothing directly above either.

But then, down the street at the edge of town there was something, a dark figure of sorts standing on the edge of a rooftop and—it appeared to be facing us—almost as if it was looking at us.

There was a loud craaaaack as Teague fired a round at it. "Jaffar...Kill that thing!"

Jaffar pulled his scimitar and closed in on this shadow –followed by the rest of us but the shadow seemed to just step back into the darkness, and it disappeared into the black landscape.

Lightning lit up the area. I confess my instincts were to flee but the rest of the war party was not having it. These men had never run from anything in their lives, and they weren't about to start now. I stood shoulder to shoulder –such as it was—with Tane, though the tattooed islander was much larger than I was and, he too was frustrated by all this....

Back behind the bar, the innkeeper was shivering in a ball–cowering in fear. Tane's massive hand reached over the bar and gripped the man by his hair and pulled the coward to his feet.

"What is that thing?" Jagger asked as we stormed back inside…

"The devil! He's been praying on the village since last Autumn. Most of us were made to flee."

"But not you."

"No…."

"Why?"

"It-it has left a few of us alive for some reason. It prefers to stalk women and children."

"Women huh!" Jagger scoffed. "Where can we find it?"

The innkeeper became even more alarmed. "It can't be killed!"

"Did I ask you that?" Jagger shouted.

"We can kill anything!" Teague added as he walked back inside, "And if you don't tell us what we need to know --we're gonna kill you first!"

"It's at the fortress," said a small voice from the corner of the room. We turned as the innkeeper's daughter –maybe eight years old-- stepped into the candlelight.

"You can't go there!" There was even more of a shiver in the innkeeper's voice "No one goes there!"

Teague was point blank in his tone, "Why?"

"Because it is an evil place --the kingdom of the shadow!" He continued through his chattering teeth, "The monster descends in darkness. He has cannibalized this town. No one who has ever gone to the fortress has ever returned since the creature made it his domain!"

"Tell me about this…. shadow!"

"It takes the form of a man or sometimes a wolf or jackal --and it lives on the blood of its victims."

Teague's eyes darted over to Jagger as if to size up what his thoughts were.

"It's gone! Back to its fortress…ha-having won for the night!" The innkeeper exhaled.

"Won?" Jagger questioned, blade still in hand. "The hell it has!"

"I will not be taunted!" Teague said and Jaffar smiled in almost evil agreement, a grin that said, 'Let's kill this thing, be done with it so we can get on with our evening."

"Where is this…. fortress?"

Only the outline of the castle could be seen against the moon. We got a better look at it when the lightning flashed.

A black carriage rested alone, inside the main gate --abandoned. There were no guards for us to murder. The fortress itself appeared vacant but, there was something there. My instinct, paranoid as I was, was not often wrong when danger was around.

We passed the gate and moved up the steps. I was hoping for a more subtle approach in our assault, but V and Toombs decided to just kick the front doors in and once cracked open, they relied on the great strength of Addo to push them clear the rest of the way….

"What manner of fortress doesn't bar its doors?"

"One that isn't afraid of unwanted visitors." I answered, checking out my surroundings.

Inside was a great hall but from the looks of it, it had not been occupied for years. It had gothic ceilings like that of an old Roman cathedral, tall windows and cobwebs covered everything….

"Spread out and find this bastard."

"Spread out?" I asked with a swallow.

"Aye. Spread out now."

We did as commanded and we were rough about it, flipping over a banquet table and bashing furniture apart until the first floor was reported clear. Then we took to the massive staircase, moved up and stormed room after room…

Finally, orders came down to torch the place. "Light it up!" Teague said and we did. We used our torches to light curtains, ignite tapestries and anything else we could light and destroy…

Suddenly, Nighthorse called out. He had found a hidden staircase heading down into the shadows like a tunnel, below the castle. We gathered around the entrance and looked down into the pit of darkness. Blythe pulled a grenade from his pack, sparked the fuse, and bounced it down the steps and it exploded below. There was a flash and an echo from the blast.

Just when I was about to question our next move, Nighthorse pulled his tomahawk and Teague did not hesitate to lead the way down. The descent seemed to take us down several levels, through cobwebs and into overwhelming blackness --I can now admit that I tried to stay behind Tane using his size as a shield for cover and peering over his shoulder from time to time....

Once we hit the base of the stairs we fanned out. The air was damp. Here was a vast underground chamber as if the mountain side was hallowed out. We could hear water dripping but could not see much even with our torches....

There was a strange breeze, and I could hear waves like we were close to the tide or under the rocks near the beach...

"How far underground were we going to advance?" I asked.

"All the way to hell if needs be!"

I swallowed, "To hell? Like down to Satan and such?"

"Move." Jagger ordered me forward.

But before we could take another step forward, I suddenly heard a—

"Pisssssssssst!"

--And I froze in my place. Then, I could hear a quiet voice above me in the dark. It hissed my name. I looked up and raised my torch into the shadows above to see the floor of a massive cage hanging by a chain, from the unseen chamber ceiling with --Irons locked in it!

"What the—" As I illuminated my surroundings, I could see several other cages above, slowly moving in the breeze. Some with townspeople locked inside --pale and barely alive—the others were lined with skeletons....

"My God!" We all looked up to take notice...

This thing was keeping people in cages and feeding off them.

"Get me the hell out of here!" Irons said in the appropriate tone of terror.

"Tane, give me a hand." I said and Tane boosted me up to the cage, I climbed up –making the cage swing-- and heaved myself up to the lock. I pulled my knife and tried leverage to break it but, no luck. "It's no use."

"What about a grenade? Can we blow it open?" Duncan-Howe asked looking up from the ground.

"Not without killing him."

"Reed!" Jagger said in a defiant tone. "Take a grenade, open it up and pour the powder into the lock and ignite it." Jagger then looked to Teague, "How many places does he have to raid with us before he knows how to blow a lock?"

Without waiting for an order, Duncan-Howe pitched me a grenade and I dropped my torch for Addo to catch. I screwed the grenade open and tapped the powder into the keyhole then asked for my torch back. We had seen enough combat to know what to do at this point –if this was to even work—I'd drop to the ground as I hit the lock with my torch, Irons would turn around and get down to protect himself and from there we'd just hope that my calculation on the amount of power was enough to blow the lock without killing all of us.

I looked down and Addo threw me the torch back and as I gripped it, I mustered my courage but just as I was about to press the torch to the lock, something dripped on my head. Water? Or….?

I slowly looked up, using the torch to light the darkness above me and-- "AHHHHHHHHHHHHHH!"

--There it was! Right above me!

The shadow standing on top of the cage. Looking down at me with black eyes that reflected my torch light. I panicked and fell to the ground, screaming! Musket and pistol fire erupted, and the blasts illuminated the room with a series of flashes like lightning.

The shadow moved from cage top to cage top drawing fire --making a horrifying, high-octave scream like that of a banshee only ten times louder.

"Kill this damn thing!"

Howe threw a lit grenade skyward, and it exploded, lighting up the cavern and blowing shrapnel in every direction as the shadow disappeared.

"Howe, watch that!" Teague shouted, "You're going to blow us all to hell!"

"I think we're already in hell!" Duncan-Howe's teeth clamped down on his pipe as he gripped another grenade. "I've fought the Dutch, the Crown even God damned cannibals but I'll be damned if I let some evil shadow be the end of me."

"Just don't kill us all in the process!"

"I'm not dying in no damn cage!" Irons dropped to the cage floor and shouted down to us, "Rabal, pitch me your torch."

Rabal stood in a defensive stance -cutlass in hand-- not sure from what part of the darkness this beast would strike, and he threw the torch up to Irons and pulled a second blade.

Without concern, Irons placed the torch against the outside of the lock and ---BOOOOOOOOOOOOOOOOOOM! The explosion blew the lock apart, rocked the cage on its chain and sucked all the air out of the immediate atmosphere around him leaving him wounded and gasping....

The cage was blown across the chamber like it was on a pendulum.

Suddenly, my clothes ignited –there was powder on them—I slapped out the flames, rolled to my feet and looked into the darkness above. Where was this damn thing?

It then began to quiet down again for a moment…

Suddenly the cage that housed Irons dropped to the floor --the blast must have displaced it from its mount. I jumped when it made an impact on the ground, then let out a sharp exhale to pull my wits about me.

"Now may be a good time to reassess our situation!" Blythe said in a calm manner though his eyes remained fixed on the chamber above him.

"Were not leaving until we kill that thing!" Teague said through his teeth. "Understand?"

"Aye" Jagger agreed as he regripped his sword. "No damn shadow will command my destiny. We kill this bastard now!"

Just as Miranda nodded in agreement, he was suddenly gripped and pulled up into the darkness, kicking and screaming --again we unloaded our guns until his body was dropped back to the floor. Eyes open. Claw marks on his shoulders and rip in his neck! Dead!

"Time to balance the odds!" Suddenly Howe pitched a grenade to Sanjuro. They unscrewed the two grenades and poured the powder into a wide circle around us, then they used a torch to ignite it and light up the room with a ring of fire. "Now we can at least see this bastard!"

Jagger pointed his sword "There it is!" Just beyond the flames the Shadow was walking towards us getting larger and larger as it got closer. This beast must have been three meters tall.

We braced ourselves for attack –or in my case, defense as the shadow slowly walked through the flames, it caught fire but did not flinch until it picked up speed and started to come at me --fast "Oh damn!" I started to backpedal…

It charged me full force, gripped my neck, and blew me backwards until I wheeled back and fell into the cage –Iron's cage—on the ground behind me! The cell door slammed shut on us with this beast on top of me. We were trapped! I found myself locked in close quarters fighting –screaming--for my life but I managed to get the blade of my knife in between its sharp –fang like-- teeth so it could not clamp down on me.

The shore party stormed the cage and jammed their swords through the bars to kill this shadow and a few even fired muskets with total disregard for me and my safety…

"Get me out! Get me out of here!!!" I screamed as blades came in from all sides. I kicked and punched for my life as this thing ripped my flesh and cut my face.

Suddenly it stood up with such force that he threw the cage open. Then Sanjuro stepped up, gripped his blade, grit his teeth, and took the villain's head clean off with a power-swing!

Its body remained in place, standing upright. Still on fire but…headless! Until it slowly fell back, –dead!

I was singed, cut, exhausted…but alive. "I feel you may have used me as bait?"

Teague began to give me a hand up, "They said this thing attacks woman and children and –well-- you're the closest thing to a woman we could find!" He smiled. Jagger and the others laughed at my expense. Lo and Duncan-Howe dusted me off and helped me clear of the cell.

I looked at this burning body in front of me with morbid curiosity. What was this thing? What was this place? And, as my eyes canvassed the ceiling --was it alone? As the fire burned this beast down to a skeleton, I saw the large key ring in his smoking ashes. I picked it up with a scarf and showed it to the others and we opened the cages of the surviving townspeople so they could seek their freedom.

Dawn was starting to break, as we stepped clear of this fortress and as we moved back through town. We picked up the bodies of our fallen comrades, Grioux and Miranda and carried them with us for they would be buried at sea. Teague, without breaking stride, slammed what was left of this beast's severed head on the signpost, a new warning for any more of its kind who may want to descend upon this town.

Back on board The Venger, we climbed over the rail, Hatano pitched Teague a bottle of rum which he up ended until it was half empty, then he passed it around to the shore party and made his way to report to the Captain….

Harrow and Doctor Johannis were in Essex's cabin. They backed up as Teague entered so he could have the floor.

"Teague."

"Captain." He coughed up a little rum from exhaustion and began his report.

--Back on the top deck, Hobby had brought a bucket of coffee around with some biscuits. Although he could not imagine what had happened, he could tell by the look of us that we had been through hell. He stopped and looked closely at me, "Are you alright…Mister Reed?"

I nodded though my hand trembled when I took the biscuit. I looked down the deck towards our Captain's quarters straining to hear how Teague framed our action up….

"And the Aztecs remained on the beach?" Essex asked.

"Aye."

"In defiance of your order to advance."

Teague remained silent.

"That offense carries a death sentence." Harrow added.

"Not this time." Teague said, he quickly looked to the Captain. "Beggin' the Captain's pardon!"

Essex thought about it for a split second. "I've never known the Aztecs to be cowards."

"Nor I," Johannis backed him up. "We've been through many a scrape with them as you well know. I've patched them up, cauterized their wounds. They don't take battle damage like a damn coward."

"Still, we can't have our scouts holding the tide when a raid is underway. It'll sow descension."

"It would, aye." Teague said, leaning against the Captain's bookshelf, a fresh bottle of rum in hand. He took another sip of the Captain's hospitality and said, "I'd be the first to shoot a man dead who disobeyed the articles. Of that we're well aware…. but, in this case, Captain." He locked eyes with Essex. "I believe pardon is in order."

"And Kon Boar? If we don't make an example of him, what will he and his men do next time we're in action?" Harrow asked. "Do we kill him then?"

"Mister Harrow," Teague said, "There are few I respect as high as you…but I've bled with the Aztecs. I've fought on four continents with them. We all have- "

With a knock, Newcastle entered….

"And…?" Essex asked.

"I've talked with Mazatal and Kon Boar." Newcastle got comfortable against the wall. He put up his hand and declined Teague's offer for a drink from the rum bottle...

"And what were his words?" Harrow asked.

"First, he said he and the rest of the Aztecs will respect our decision on punishment whatever it may be...."

"Even a death penalty?" Harrow questioned.

"Yes...even a death penalty."

"And?" Essex pressed him to continue.

"And that his presence would have been of no benefit in that town in any event." Then Newcastle slowed his speech down, "Not against the devil!" His eyes rolled up to Teague as he finished his sentence.

"Aye, it's true...we encountered something wicked ashore. The Aztecs sensed it."

"What do you mean?" Harrow asked.

"There was a beast there, the likes of which I've never fought or encountered. Three meters tall with enough satanic power to wreck a building." He paused, "It held the town citizens in cages in a dungeon to, ah, feed, off them ya might say."

"Good God!"

"No." Teague stood tall, "God was not ashore with us."

"Can't hold a man to blame against the Devil." Essex said as he repositioned himself in his chair. "Tis a forgivable offense given their combat record."

Teague nodded with gratitude, and he left the cabin.

Harrow waited for him to leave. "Are you sure about that sir?"

"Harrow if we kill them, it'll sow descension in their ranks. Besides, they fought well in the past."

"Dare I say sir...you're getting soft."

Essex curled his lip into a slight grin, "Perhaps I am."

BELOW DECK-

"On the earth yes…we fight everything." Kon Boar made a motion with his hands representing a globe. "But a gateway to the next world had opened. We do not fight in the world of the Gods."

Teague dropped below deck on his way to his bunk and as he passed the Aztecs, they became silent –as did the rest of the deck. Those of us at meals froze, mid-bite as Teague slowly walked past. He stopped, stood close and looked to Kon Boar.

I looked back to the Moors by a fire on one end of the deck -- motionless. Jaffar holding his sword as if he was about to sharpen it, but he stopped to watch Teague, as did the samurai, the Hurons, the Africans and the rest of us. Even Lo-Tan raised his head to peer at the upcoming events from under his bamboo triangle type hat.

After a long look, Teague pointed to Kon Boar. "You ever fail me again I'll kill you…you understand?"

Kon Boar slowly nodded.

"For now," Teague started walking down the deck again, "Let's just forget this ever happened." And he collapsed in his bunk, in his small, narrow cabin and immediately passed out.

I was not aware at the time, that Teague had asked for the Aztecs to be spared given their foreshadowing and perception of what we were about to go through when we landed ashore, and Teague didn't want any of us to know. What he wanted was an example in front of the crew of what would happen to any of us if we entertained the same notion. Therefore, his death threat was real and very much directed at all of us.

XXII

BREAK THE BOLT THAT LOCKS ME IN

I climbed down the rigging and dropped on the deck as Hallock and Mister Hayte, with a nod made the climb aloft. I was handed some sake from Kai who stood with the ronin surrounding a deck fire and by now, I had actually become accustomed to the drink and even knew a few words of their language though they only really spoke it amongst themselves and conversed in English the rest of the time and on this occasion, they were talking about a legend –or debating the truth of it—about a monster that rose out of the sea every few decades to sack Odo Island and stomp on the beachside huts there. Go-Kujira or some nonsense. The Sake seemed to help with the stories.

There was a section of the deck that stood above the open windows of the galley below and depending on what Mister Hobby might be cooking that night, it could be quite a pleasant place to stand during our watch....

I was there –at the rail—with Daws, Bishop, Baltimore –the Huron witch hunter—Duncan-Howe, Briggs and Java who had climbed on deck to clear his lungs of all the smoke from the gunnery practice earlier.

Lynch was working with his drawings under a lantern not far off and Merciless was asleep –or close to it—by the longboats, his new scar was causing him some pain in his face even though the stitches would be removed in a few days....

Tabor had just made it down the rigging to our position as Sterling began to take his place and make the climb aloft for his watch...

"Heavy fog on the horizon." Tabor reported as he went for the coffee bucket and dropped a mug in, "It may burn off by morning."

"I'll tell the helm" Briggs dismissed himself and went towards the wheel....

"We fought the Brigantine for six hours in a fog once." Duncan-Howe said, packing tobacco into his pipe. "Damn bastards scuddled their own ship rather than let us sack it. Went down with all hands, a real tragedy that..."

"It was." Java agreed exhaling smoke from his own pipe, "The Brigantine was bad magic."

"You and your brothers are too superstitious. It was the Captain that was bad, no devil on the deck that day..."

"Says you."

"Aye, says me, for if there's only one Lucifer then.... how can Teague be in two places at once?"

We all laughed for we respected Teague but, he did have the look of the devil in him...

Suddenly Harrow emerged out of the shadows and worked his way down the deck, "Snap too lads, get this squared away...."

"Yes sir." The men moved to complete their work detail...

"Where to Mister Harrow? Rio de Janeiro?"

"No boys...Port Royal." And just like that, Harrow disappeared into the darkness of the deck towards the bow....

"It will be nice to get back to Port Royal." I said with a sense of excitement I could not hide.

"And this time with some money in your pocket. You can move into town for a few weeks or hell –even buy a coconut plantation and pretend to be a Lord."

"Yes," I smiled. "It'll be good to get back." Although I had respect for these men, I still did not have the confidence to speak too openly between the decks about anything outside my duty and, I was quite fearful of what my reputation would become if I was to speak in honest fashion about my fears or my thoughts so for the most part, I remained quiet on matters too personal.

As reported, I was somewhat afraid of certain members of the crew…I was certainly fearful of Teague and 'the ghost' Jagger. I might muster the courage to speak to Blythe, at times, or Daws but, I couldn't speak open and honestly with the Moors, the Africans, or the ronin -never the ronin! For they seemed to outlaw emotion in their ranks except for excitement in the art of killing or when drunk…

"Yes, it will be good to get back." I repeated.

"Fancy yourself a coconut farmer Mister Reed?"

"No, I- I…." I went silent at a loss for words….

"You what?" Daws continued, working a knot with his hands. "Have a score to settle or something?"

"No, I-ah- I have a friend there…" And with sudden surprise and courage I said, "A woman."

This did not stop the men from their work. They continued, uninterrupted as if I had said nothing at all. I almost wondered if they had even heard me. Maybe they had all gone deaf, like Java --all our gunners were almost deaf.

"I said a woman." I repeated to make sure I was heard.

"And that's what? Some kind of secret or something?" Daws asked picking the ropes up from the planks and placing them on his shoulder….

"No, it's not that…it's just…well—" I seemed to clinch up in pain and discomfort as I tried to find the words…

Daws made a concentrated look, then his eyes shot up at me, "Is she… a leper or something, then?"

"No" I smiled, and I looked back, for I did sense a level of compassion in Daws that was absent in most of the others. So, with some effort, I slowly worked up more courage, "She-ah-she…works in a house of ill repute."

Baltimore looked confused. Lynch yawned like my conversation was boring him...

Tabor looked up from his coffee cup, bewildered. "A house of what?"

Duncan-Howe shifted his position on deck with a step or two, "He means...she's in entertainment business." He said with near perfect enunciation as he started to repack the tobacco in his pipe with his index finger....

"So, what's the problem?" Tabor clearly didn't understand what my trouble was. "I like entertainment. Of all sorts really."

"Well, polite society being what it is— "

"--Polite what?"

"So-ci-e-ty!" I emphasized the word for him...

"What's that?" Tabor didn't understand the word.

Daws had to think for a moment, "What the hell does society have to do with it?"

"Good question!" Duncan-Howe said through his teeth, clinched around his pipe stem.

"Why the hell are we talking about this?" Daws asked and Duncan-Howe shrugged as if he didn't know...

My shipmates seemed genuinely vexed. "Well, it's just that—" My apprehension was still getting the better of me. "Well, I--"

Daws peered at me as if he was fighting off a headache. "Stop there." He raised his hand. "You have feelings for this woman?"

I paused before my confession, "Ye-yes...I--I do."

"And the problem is?"

"I suppose, I'm slightly apprehensive of the fact that she's of a different culture than I."

Again, more confusion and I was beginning to think I should not continue to speak.

"Damn idiotic if you ask me" Duncan-Howe inhaled as his pipe flared up with a glow....

"Damn right, it's idiotic." Daws said, heaving the rope, "Now I want the last three minutes of my life back for they've been robbed of me by this conversation."

Tabor continued watching this exchange from the coffee bucket as my shame seemed to mount....

"Do you let society govern your happiness?" Daws asked.

I searched for my answer...

"Take her! Make her your own --society be damned!"

"That's what I say!" Duncan-Howe added, "I fail to see the problem in this. Mark my words Reed..." he belted out, "It is a tragic man that allows his life and his happiness to be dictated to by some ass with a title and a nice wardrobe in your so-called society..."

Back home, I could lose all standing over such a relationship, interracial as it were. My career as a teacher would be forced to end, I would be ousted, fined, or even imprisoned but, here --in this world-- that social order didn't apply. These men had no fear of social repercussions and there was no shame in the company they would keep. They loved –and lived— as they pleased and would answer to no one for it.

Tabor smiled at all this. "I should be so lucky," he said. Tabor had been at sea since the age of six when he set sail from Europe with his family. Their ship was attacked and raided by a pirate named El Rojo who captained the 'War Hammer' and killed his family and pressed Tabor into service as a cabin boy. That would be his station for many years, working –first under the constant threat of death—then his way up the ranks, until the 'War Hammer' was attacked by The Venger, and Tabor joined this crew. So, he knew little of society outside this ship and this world...

--But what did any of us know outside of our own violent tendencies.

XXIII

SABOTAGE

There was a sudden, massive explosion somewhere below deck –and some of our men went flying. The entire ship shifted in the tide. Some of our crew even tumbled on the top deck. The port side power storage exploded. The thickness of the gun walls –one of the ships engineering advantages in a fire-fight-- stifled the explosion but this blast still blew a massive hole up, through the deck. scattering planks out all over the ocean.

"What the hell was that?"

Below deck there was a secondary explosion killing Mister Temple, blowing Pharaoh across the deck, and seriously burning Rajiv…

"What the devil!" Just as Doctor Johannis stepped clear of the hospital, another explosion blew through the planks from below, dropping him to the floor and spilling several of the wounded from their bunks. Several of the Chinese soldiers we picked up in Macau were wounded –some had their decorative uniforms catch fire….

"What the damnation?" All hands dropped below deck.

There was a fire in gunnery section two.

"Get the fire buckets." Newcastle shouted, "Move!" We scrambled through this stifling smoke to the walls and pulled our fire buckets, passing them down, hand-to-hand, man-to-man in a combat line to throw the sand on the blaze and begin to put the fire out. Mister Foxx, Tiger and Java carried the wounded Rajiv to the sickbay –even his turban was smoking. They had to move around the hole blown in the floor, but they got him there –the left side of his body was melting flesh and muscle.

Essex suddenly emerged below deck, and he made his way forward moving past the flames to the far end of the deck where Flynn, Merritt, Khan, Mister Silence, some of the Masai killers and a few of the Moors dropped down. They continued to descend through the decks below, past the blaze to secure the other powder holds before they too ignited. This was a very dangerous job but, if the holds weren't secure, everything on the ship would be blown sky high.

We continued to work through the gun decks ---the flames turned the deck into an oven. The heat murderous. Tane, Jeddah, Blythe, Hallock and a few others used ropes and dropped buckets out the gun port doors, to haul sea water in.

We started to get the situation under control and the blaze started to calm down.

On deck, as we battled the fire, two men from Macau tried to move through the empty space to lower a long boat away but, before it could hit the water, Harrow stepped into view, "Hold there!"

They froze and looked over at him. Harrow stood on deck, in the wind, his fists a hair away from his pistols...

These men suddenly released the rope –dropped the boat -- and went for their weapons. Harrow pulled his guns, blasted one –who was blown over the side-- and made the other freeze in his tracks. "Don't move!"

We climbed on deck, black faces, and hands, covered in soot, to see what the gunfire was about. Lynch, Sunderland, Madds and Jagger closed in around Harrow to see what the trouble was --their eyes turned to the one remaining man at the jolly boat who had his hands up.

"What's all this then?" Sunderland asked.

"This gentleman here and his friend tried to lower a long boat without orders."

Essex and some of the fire party made it topside. The Captain stepped to Harrow. He could size the situation up and he directed his words carefully to the man in front of him, "You have exactly ten seconds to explain yourself."

Dakar lowered a blunderbuss, Jagger pulled his knife and stepped forward. He grabbed the man's hand and put his index finger against the blade ready to cut it off. "Every ten seconds, I cut off a finger." He said as the blade drew blood, "Here, let me show you that I'm serious." And he suddenly made a swift cut removing the finger from the man's hand.

He screamed and gripped his own hand in pain.

"Here goes another one" Jagger said as he re-gripped both the blade and the man's hand.

"I was offered ten-thousand pounds to sink The Venger." He suddenly confessed.

Essex raised his chin to the sun, "By who?"

"The order came from a Lord Roberts of Ashboro, through the Macau Embassy."

"I suspected the Portuguese." Essex said quietly.

"A Lord would never engage in this kind of terror campaign." Harrow barked in disbelief.

"There's a price on the head of every man here!" The suspect said, "They passed orders on every trade ship through The Caribbean and Indian Ocean."

"Sabotage! As if dealing with descension wasn't enough, now we have an outright trader here!"

"How many men did we take onboard at Macau?"

"Thirty-six sir. Not including the Chinese military veterans"

"Thirty-six." He repeated disappointed.

"Should we kill 'em all?" Harrow asked.

Essex looked at him as if to say, 'Not just yet' then, "Bring them up…." He ordered.

We did as commanded but some of the Macau recruits, like the Chinese soldiers --like Genghis-- were wounded in the blast—others risked their lives to help us fight the fire so, they became exempt from our suspect list and when we lined these men up on the top deck, we separated those recruits, pushing them down the deck, reducing the numbers to about sixteen. Harrow ordered the others to "Stand to!"

At the same time, Toombs, Bolt and Foxx fashioned the suspect with a section of ropes around his ankles and another harness around his wrists that was attached to a pully and rigging system.

--I got a bad feeling when I saw this. Bishop shook his head and cleared off the deck, whatever was about to happen, he didn't want to see it.

Essex slowly turned away from our suspect and looked at the men in line, "Men," he started, "We have a saboteur here! He came aboard in Macao along with the rest of you." He spaced his words out carefully, "You men swore an oath to The Venger. Your thumb print –in blood—is in our book." He raised his voice to a loud level, "That oath has been betrayed!"

The men in line looked very nervous. Essex began to rein in his temper. "Now, as I see it, you have two choices. If you are an associate of this man and come forth and confess now, then I give you my word that you will live. If you remain silent and we reveal your true cause here, then you-will-die!" He paused and then said "Now, let me show you that I'm serious in my intent" He turned, "Mister Foxx, a demonstration if you please." Foxx suddenly pushed our saboteur off the front of the ship screaming….

As he dropped in the ocean, I watched as Lau, Bons and Blythe grabbed hold of a rope threaded through a pully to this man's wrists as Rabal, Towne and Sunderland, on the port side, pulled another section of rope through a pulley that attached to the man's ankles and when they pulled on the ropes, the suspect was suddenly pulled under the water…

The punishment I was about to witness was called keel hauling. The pully system dragged the suspect under and along the hull of the ship. His body --his skin and muscles—were ripped open by barnacles, like razor blades. The ripping and tearing of this man's skin was so deep and severe that the men in our lowest deck, still putting out embers from the fire, could hear the slow sound of dragging and cutting through the hull at the bottom of the ship.

As this practice took place –which seemed to take forever—Essex eyed the other suspects to see which one flinched or gave sign that they were involved in this vicious plot --they all looked nervous.

Having made a complete pass under the ship, Lau, Blythe, and the others heaved the ropes and pulled the saboteur from the water and hoisted him up over the stern for everyone to see –heavy streams of dark blood greased our deck. He was cut to ribbons –whole sections of his flesh removed—as if he was victimized by a butcher and had been to the chopping block.

Johannis checked him and nodded 'no' to the Captain. This man was dead. We cut his body down and threw him overboard.

"Mister Fury prepare the next man for the haul!"

At that, a man reluctantly took one solid step forward, and raised his hand slightly, giving himself up. Takeda put the blade of his samurai sword against his neck as a warning for him not to move. "Yo-you promised I would live." He shivered.

"That I did, "Essex said, "And so you shall."

The traitor was kicked into a jolly boat head first. Mister Newcastle skippered the launch with a loaded gun, keeping a weathered eye on the prisoner as Mister Hazzard, Calixto, Hawkquez and Foxx worked the oars. I watched from our deck, as they reached the small sandbar at low tide. This criminal was pushed off the long boat and he fell into the tide as Newcastle dismounted, pulled him to his feet and marched him onto the sandbar. There was one palm tree on this small 'island.' –just one.

Newcastle gave this man a cask of water, a small packet of food --his Bible-- and a pistol with one round –to take his own life before madness set in.

The man tried to come back towards the boat as Newcastle stepped back aboard but, Warrick stopped him with a crack from the butt of his musket. This criminal then dropped to his knees, hands clasped as if in prayer and he started crying, begging not to be left behind....

"God be with you." Newcastle waved.

I watched as our men started to row away. I could see this man run into the water after them, begging to be taken back. He then tried to swim towards the ship....

"Make sail" The Captain ordered; his eyes fixed on this man swimming towards us.

Deck hands gathered around the capstan and started to push in a circle, to raise anchor and then, we began to pull away...

We brought our brothers back aboard. The Captain looked to the other fifteen replacements. "If another act of sabotage is committed on this ship or against our crew, all of you will be put to the knife. No exceptions! Understand? So, keep an eye on each other."

--They understood.

The crew was dismissed. I looked towards the sand bar with the saboteur in the water a few meters off, and I could hear this man screaming in the distance. Duncan-Howe and Merciless pushed me away from the rail and back to my work...

We plotted a course southeast leaving the traitor to his new kingdom, a small sand bar in the middle of The Pacific Ocean with the tide slowly rising....

Below deck, I walked past the infirmary. It was loaded with patients. Rajiv, Sterling, De Leon –all wounded, along with some of the Masai killers –burned and scarred-- who remained absolutely silent despite the pain and a few of the Chinese regulars. Mister Silence had his hands burned and they would be of little use to him in the weeks to come. Johannis and Jopo were using a small opium ration for the pain, raided during our work in the Far East but, only for the most severe and only for the first day in an effort to prevent addiction.

What captured my attention was Mister Strange who was hurt and shivering but through his teeth he kept saying over and over, "Pain is my friend, pain is penance. Pain is my friend. It tells me I'm alive. Pain is my pennant."

I watched this for a moment, until Whitney, Jack-Karr and a few others pushed past me to move into the infirmary to help. "Could you use another hand doctor?" I asked Jopo.

Jopo turned, just as they cleared a wounded man from his working table and pointed. "That man there,"

I turned, looked, and saw Pharaoh –the young man, not more than fourteen--on the panels burned.

"Pick him up, bring him here."

"Come on," Jack-Karr helped me raise him and we placed him on the operating table in front of the doctor.

Jopo checked his eyes and then the wounds, he then pulled a bowl with an ointment in it that looked like honey. "Here, help me apply this."

I took the bowl and Jack, and I used our hands to cover his wounds but every move we made, every point of contact forced pain on this young man as he winced. Some of his skin came off as we worked, and I paused before forcing myself back into the work. "Sorry" I said, "You'll be ok in a moment…"

Then, Pharaoh's eyes opened up and he looked at me, "Teach" he almost tried to smile.

"I'm here."

"Teach," his eyes closed again, "Will I see my mother again when I'm in heaven?"

I stopped my work --stunned by the question.

Karr looked at me as if to see what my answer would be. "Reed" he whispered and motioned me to continue working the wounds –and I did.

"You will see your mother again, Master Pharaoh, that I promise."

And with that came a smile. A real, genuine, smile with emotion that transcended the pain he was in, for now, no burns could stop the joy he was feeling, the joy of what was a long-awaited reunion between a young boy and his mother. A reunion he wanted more than anything, "Thank you Mister Reed-" He said, "Thank you." Then he followed it up with words that for some reason caught me off balance. "--For everything."

Jopo stepped up to us, "Alright, he needs rest, clear out."

I stepped out of the hospital and stopped. I slowly collapsed against the door panel, just outside stunned. 'What am I a part of? Who am I?' I then heard Jack-Karr's voice.

"That was a kind thing you did Reed."

I slowly turned and looked at him.

Karr, who always appeared so wicked with the scars of a tiger claw cut into his face, suddenly appeared much more soft and compassionate in a way. "It was a kind thing to do," he looked to me, "I thank you for that." And he held out his hand for me to shake...

Later at the galley window, Hobby covered my square plate with bacon, gravy, and grease. I took a biscuit and then a seat. I sat quietly in the place where my small school would normally be held --not too far from Tabor, Mister Lynch, Rajal, just back from his prayers and Clairmont who was humming something, poetry words or a song of some sort, to himself.

I looked up as the Moors walked by. Other men, Cage, Foxx, Hatano, Baltimore and the like, piled through the galley and found their way to the tables for food and conversation without even mentioning the incident. My mind kept repeating the events of the afternoon, and for the first time, I was afraid I was losing my humanity for I believed the Captain's actions were correct –and that scared me. The other men didn't seem to think much of it, like it was business as usual. This also scared me. It was becoming easier for me to embrace horrific deeds -or- make excuses for them –and—on the other hand, I was still very much compelled to shepherd a sense of compassion and love to those who need it. I feared that against the politics of my environment, that my sense of compassion --that had always been with me to a degree-- was now becoming my mission. I had to --despite the world around me—bring compassion into it. I had to bring more compassion into this place.

The spirit of Mister Rush –or something more-- was still very much with me.

The next morning was Sunday morning. I made a decision. I turned my back from the early morning mist at the helm and took a place at the mast

–where Mister Rush once stood—alone. I opened my weathered Bible and there, I began reading out loud…

Mister Fury and Wolfe turned from their work at the rail and looked at me with a touch of curiosity. "What the hell do you suppose he's doing?" Wolfe asked.

Fury shook his head, as if he didn't know.

Duncan-Howe stopped and removed his pipe from his teeth as I read…

I continued with a mix of a Bible verse I loved and my word words, "I may walk, unsure of my step" I said, "I may walk through a world of fire and pain…."

As I stuttered through most of it, Harrow turned from wheel on the quarter deck as Essex looked up from his map table.

"—But, but through this pain, I may ha-have heart" I continued as the foot traffic around me seemed to slow down and stop, "I may have heart for I know the shield of the Lord protects me…." As I pushed through the words, some of the Moors turned from the rail. Jeddah smiled –though he didn't care much for my book-- he had a smile that basically said he was impressed with my drive to embrace this moment and get my religion out.

"And the Lord said unto me, fear not for I-I have plans for you. Plans to prosper you and not-not harm you." I continued to struggle, not with the words but with trying to convey an emotional connection with their meaning to my audience –and as more men stopped to watch me read, my nerves took hold, and the flow of words became even more difficult. I continued to stutter and as I looked down at the text --a hand suddenly gripped the book and stopped me…

I looked up to see Mister Bishop standing there. His expression was one of understanding for what I was trying to attempt and, in a calm, understanding voice he quietly said, "I'll take it from here if you don't mind Mister Reed."

I smiled and released the book.

Bishop took The Bible and stood tall "I have plans for you…" he said, "Plans to help you, prosper you and not harm you," his voice gained power like an opera singer with the message, and I watched as if witness to a man who suddenly transformed to fit back into his natural place in the world. "I have plans to give you hope and a future. For my plans honor you for the men that you are and the honor you bring to others through your actions…." He had perfect voice, diction and tenor, the words seemed to flow from him like fine music or poetry and there was great comfort in them.

Men started to gather around.

Daws looked up, holding a deck rope, and smiled at the sounds of this, and at that moment, Barak tapped him on the arm, gave him a nod and motioned to take the rope from him and take over his work --as was the custom between cultures onboard-- while Daws embraced his church….

"One must, where one can, make the world around him a better place. For this invention, that is the Lord's must be made whole for all of us." Bishop closed with some words from Proverbs "Seek His will in all you do…and He will show you which path to take." He closed the book and looked up with a touch of pride and optimism like he had found himself again and then his eyes bolted over to me.

I smiled and he gave me a nod of approval. If a man could say thank you with a look, this was it --and on this day, I began to feel whole again.

XXIV

THE ROYAL TREATMENT

Dolphins escorted us towards our destination. We stood at the rail with the island before us. Some of our crew just jumped in the ocean and started to swim for the beach.

"The lads can't wait." Harrow said as he moved past us, "Glad you lot have some sense."

I stood next to Mister Wicks and realized that he had his footlocker box with him.

"Are you taking all your possessions ashore?"

"I am."

It seemed a lot to be concerned with so, I asked why…

"Because I'm not coming back."

"What's that?"

"This was my last voyage; I just spoke to the Captain and asked for permission to take my leave." He looked at me, "I'm going to catch a sloop to Saint Croix." He paused and let out a deep exhale that seemed to extinguish stress. "It's time I go home and….be the father I was meant to be. I'm going to put my profits to work and start a farm. Get away from the killing, for a little while at least."

I smiled and held out my hand, "I'm sorry to see you go but, I wish you well."

"And I you Reed. You've been a good man onboard –not the best fighter but, a good man and, you proved yourself worthy to be here."

These words did have an effect and I did feel proud of myself, more so, because it was my help with his letters to his wife that made this his course and destination.

Wicks looked ashore, "One last night in town then?" He asked, "I owe you a debt actually, it was you teaching me to write letters that kept my mind focused on what was important and the family I was missing."

We jumped from the long boats into the tide, Blythe, Rabal and the others could not move into town fast enough. Duncan-Howe dismounted from the boat next to me, "A drink lad?"

"Yes," I replied "But...I have an errand I must execute first."

"Fine. I'll save you a place at the table. I heard The Sparrow raided a shipment of scotch whiskey and sold it to the King's Arms. Should make for a nice evening." He watched some of the ronin march through the tide from our boats towards town, "Maybe I can get some of these killers to trade some barrels of sake for something more sophisticated." He started off, "We'll make room for ya' lad." He said with a wave.

"Thank you. See you shortly," and I moved into the marketplace which seemed loaded with fireflies this particular evening. I walked past the street merchants and the people, past other privateers, wagons, and men on horseback to...the tailor. I bought dresses in every color, describing the size and height of Uralan –as I remembered it to be--and also made purchase of a few hats made in the current European style. I also bought myself a new tunic.

I picked up my boxes, stepped out of the shop, under the sign and into the street and as I started walking, I realized the fear that possessed me on my first visit here no longer owned me. It was gone. Replaced, not so much by my weapons or the idea that I now belonged to a crew that was not far off but by months of training and surviving on the high seas. The set of skills that were hammered into my spirit made me return to this place with a new outlook and the belief that I could take care of myself and the township itself was made to feel more like home.

At sunset, I made it past the torches that lit the entrance to The Witches Den. The place was quite lively some of our men like Therrinfall, Ward, Lo-Tan, Doctor Jopo, Johnny Kay, Bolt, Kane, Sterling and Obal were in the crowd, but I managed to make it to a table by the open-air window facing the beach....

I put my boxes down and looked around with a sense of excitement at the tavern surroundings for sight of my friend. I admit, nerves were getting the best of me and that was made worse when through the door walked Newcastle and Teague --like they owned the place along with The Ghost, Jagger, Addo, Jack-Karr, Lau, Bliss, and they had some of my samurai comrades with them. They had been celebrating and I let out a nervous exhale. 'What were they to make of this?' I asked myself as I sat with my boxes, like a nervous schoolboy on the first day...

They made their way to the bar and the crowd moved to reveal my friend behind it –that's where she was, armed with a smile and as beautiful as I remember. She greeted the privateers and casks were passed all around. I stood up and by chance she caught sight of me as I put my hand up in a 'hello.' There was a look in the eye—a look I had hoped for—a look that not only remembered me but...remembered me with approval as she smiled. She picked up a tray of rum filled mugs and came towards me, "Well...if it's not my favorite schoolteacher."

I stood up...

"It has been a very long time."

Her accent, the rhythm in which she talked was music to me. I remained standing out of respect, still schooled in the old ways of being a gentleman. "Yes, it has been too long. Ah- how-how are you?"

She put a mug –from her tray—down on my table, "Things are always good here," she said with a keen smile, "As you well know...it has been ages for you and I." She suddenly ran her fingers through my hair as if to clear my face so she could re-examine my features. I had changed in my time away –weathered and darkened by the elements with added strength, size, and scars-- and I could see she realized it but, then she smiled again and did not seem to mind...

"I've been to Asia…and Africa but, I've thought of you often."

When she locked her green eyes on me, it made me nervous yet again…

"It is good to have you back."

I was at a loss for words until I remembered the boxes, "Oh, I-I picked up a few things for you…."

She smiled and offered up a surprised look, "Presents?"

"Yes, I hope you don't think it too forward of me…but it seemed like…the right thing to do." And I opened a box to reveal a red dress.

She appeared to be genuinely surprised, pulled the dress out and held it up against herself….

I was taken by the very look of the red against her dark skin, "I- I was hoping I could ask for your company this evening…."

She smiled but just as she moved to speak, a big, giant beast of a man bellowed into our space like an earthquake, "The very nerve!!!" He shouted as he took her by the arm, pulled her from the table and then faced off with me. "You!" He barked, "You think you can move in on my woman here? Offer her gifts of finery – you think that qualifies you to be in her company?"

I was stunned and fumbled for my words as I tried to make sense of the situation, "I-I-I'm sorry I didn't realize— "

"Yes, you are sorry --and she'd prefer a real man's company so pack up and get out and take your blasted trinkets with ya!" Just as he moved to drag her away, he turned into Teague and Newcastle who had closed in on this disturbance….

"You overstep." Newcastle said through his teeth, his sword –on his back—with the handle reflecting the lantern and candlelight.

"I overstep?" He said with disdain, "Do you know who you are talking to?"

Both Newcastle and Teague looked at each other, vexed….

"Bartholomew Saint Ives!" He belted out with pride.

Newcastle and Teague still looked vexed --Who?

"Bart Ives!" He waited for them to get it.

Newcastle shook his head, "I'm sorry?"

"Bartholomew Saint Ives!" He repeated with mounting frustration...

They were still confused...

"--Of the Black Eagle! I've sailed with Lord Swan and fought with Vincenze down the coast of Argentina."

Teague suddenly looked at this man though his dark eyes, "And what? Is that supposed to make you dangerous...or something?" He asked with a slight reaction from the crowd around us, who were well in tune to the tension....

Ives threw my friend into the bar with some force to make way for a stand-off and so Teague and Newcastle could have his full attention....

I moved to help my friend off the tavern floor. She was hurt in the ribs but not bad...

"What's mine is mine!" Ives bellowed.

"You forget yourself sir! The woman was in the company of this man!" Newcastle nodded in my direction as I helped my friend make it back to her feet...

"Fine!" Ives threw his mug to the floor and gripped the handle on his saber, "I'll kill him...then take her. How'd that be?"

"Not good ----for you!" Newcastle said.

"Look here, no one wants to kill ya' tonight," Duncan-Howe said as he stepped in between this crowd, "We just want you to recognize your bad manners. Apologize to this lady and our friend here and we'll be off to more important social business tonight."

"Kill me? Apologize? Not today and certainly not to this coward!!" Ives motioned to me, then turned to the men in his corner with a half laugh, "Never thought I'd come across a coward in this place."

Newcastle's eyes darted over to me then back to Ives, "This man is many things, but a coward is not one of them."

"I say he is!"

"Fine!" Teague agreed with a sudden sense of directness, "Since you won't willingly apologize...we'll beat it outa ya!" Teague cracked his knuckles...

A man next to Ives quickly leaned into his ear, "That's a Combat Captain from The Venger –Teague of Gibraltar!"

Ives suddenly looked uncertain, almost nervous.

'Gibraltar?' I thought Teague was from The Americas.

Upon learning Teague's identity, Ives seemed to change his posture. "I-I didn't realize you were 'Calypse Teague when I called out your friend."

"Now you know." Teague said slowly.

"Calypse --short for Apocalypse!" Duncan-Howe tipped me off, "We may have some of that havoc now—because of this man here!"

Ives tried to find the right words –and tone-- in an effort to put this situation right, "My fight's not with you Teague."

"It is now!"

"Maybe if you just apologize--" Howe suggested.

There was a moment of silence, then, Ives looked to the floor in shame and spoke, "Very well, I apologize--"

"Not to the floor, to him." Newcastle said as he motioned to me.

He then brought himself to look in my direction, "I apologize."

"It's too late for that!" Teague said.

Newcastle rolled his eyes with a move that signaled his frustration at not being able to solve the situation.

"Am I not allowed satisfaction for being wronged?" Ives pleaded.

"And you're about to get it." Teague started to remove his guns so he could have a clear hand to grab this cutlass….

"But Mister Teague--" Ives continued his protest…

I had just about heard enough, "Damn-it-all!" I shouted as my temper got the best of me. I could not believe the words came up through my teeth –it was as if I had no control of what I was saying but I realized that I would never be worth this woman's attention if I didn't stand up for her --and myself—now! And after she was thrown into the bar. I had to make a stand. It had to be me and no one else.

The room went silent. Both Teague and Newcastle looked over at me. The rest of our crew was also silent. I looked to Uralan, then back to Ives and mustered up-- "This fight is mine!"

Jaffar suddenly smiled at these words –as if I had finally come into my own. The rest of our crew also seemed to approve.

"Well then," Teague gave a nod in my direction then looked to Ives, "If we're gonna fight it out, then we're gonna use the 'Lord Carol's Rules' and that way, when he kills ya'--" He motioned to me but spoke to my opponent, "--It's gonna be legal!" He raised his hand and the crowd stepped back to form a near perfect fighting circle, "Choose your weapons. Knives? Blades? Or guns?"

Ives moved to speak but Teague stopped him— "Not you. You drew offense on this man" He motioned to me, "The choice is his…"

I was speechless and tried to stammer out an answer but there was none, so Teague quickly made my choice for me, "He picks knives!"

"Fair enough!" And Ives pulled a blade that was more like a machete….

Newcastle stepped up to me, "Ready Reed?"

I tried to muster a 'NO' as if I had a change of heart but, it was no use, this situation was going forward…

Newcastle pulled my knife from my sash and with a disapproving look he said, "This is no good for a fight like this."

He speared it into the bar top, blade first and pulled his own blade, "Here, use this," and he planted it in my hand.

Teague stepped towards me "I picked knives, so you'd have half a chance." He said, "You showed some promise with it in training."

"Half a chance?"

"Any other weapon and we'd bet on your death, but with this--" he motioned to Newcastle's dagger, "You may surprise us."

"Any advice?" I managed to ask….

"Yeah, next time I offer to kill a man for ya' stay out of my way and let me do it –ya' damn idiot!" Teague barked.

He had me there. "Any other advice?" I asked slightly dejected.

"When he moves --kill him!" Teague moved back into the circle next to Ives….

Newcastle pulled me close "You've been in combat before. Remember what we taught you." He turned me towards my rival who was getting primed for this event and Newcastle marched me forward, "He's big so make him move about and he'll lose his wind -get him tired. Once he's tired --strike! And go for the neck –or joints-- if ya' can."

"I-I ah, I--"

"--And dare I say" Newcastle added with smile and a look to Uralan, "Your friend here is very much worth fighting for! You have good taste in women Reed!" And with that, he pushed me forward into the combat circle….

Suddenly a shackle was slapped on my wrist with the other shackle slapped on Ives, like we were prisoners chained together, "What the—"

--Lord Carol's Rules meant you fight shackled to your opponent!

"Oh God!" Was the only reaction I could muster.

I gripped Newcastle's knife and looked around at my settings, one side of the circle was made up of men from The Venger, Baltimore, Baako, Rabal, Reader, Wolfe, Hatano, Hallock, Kannon, Merciless, Ward, Jagger --Duncan-Howe taking bets-- along with Jack-Karr, Tiger, Sterling, Mister Cage, Jupiter, Jeddah, Tane and several others…

The other half of the circle was energetic strangers probably from the Black Eagle since they clearly seemed to have an interest in seeing Ives win….

We were brought face to face for a few pre-fight words from Teague. "Now, this is to be a fair fight. Are we clear on that? Gouging, choking, and biting…are all legal but no insults towards a man's mother or his God –understood?"

"Understood!" Ives growled with confidence.

I gave an affirmative nod.

"Now here…" On Teague's instruction, a bar maid stepped away from Doctor Jopo, Java and Lynch at the bar and in between the two of us with two mugs of rum. Teague handed one to my opponent and one to me. "Drink up and let's fight and die with honor!"

"Ready to die lad?" Ives asked me as he kicked his drink back…

"Actually, I'd rather put death off a bit if possible…."

Ives smiled and took his fighting stance, his blade cut through the air with a 'zip' sound.

Teague raised his black hat above the action as if to say 'ready' and then he swung it down and the fight started. I took an immediate punch to the chest that sent me back only to be pulled forward by the chain and shackles, to be hit again and I saw flashing stars! The crowd erupted….as I was thrown around the room, into furniture, into spectators, everything….

Teague watched, arms crossed –Jaffar had a similar stance at the far end of the circle --as others like Baako shouted simple combat advice like, "Killllllllll him!'

I took another blow to the head as Ives threw me against a post, I ducked as he dragged his blade against it –making a gash in the wood— I stood back up, swung my blade up and happened to catch Ives on the chin with the upswing.

My crew cheered….

Ives put his hand to his chin bone as if in shock that I drew blood and that shock tuned to anger as he slammed me against a table, and I fell to the floor where I rolled just in time to avoid his boot as he tried to stomp it down on my head…

Duncan-Howe continued to work the crowd for bets, making what accounting he could with a quill and a little book. With my strike to the chin, Hallock, Wilder, Bear Killer and Bishop were all now in the betting. Duncan-Howe turned to Mister Silence watching the action like a statue "You?" Duncan-Howe asked, "Are you interested in a bet?"

He remained stoic and still with no response.

"No? Thought not." And Duncan-Howe went back to working the crowd…

I rolled, swung, and cut Ives across the shin, then rolled back to my feet as he grabbed me by the shirt, and I saw him try to re-fix his eyes as if he was dizzy and confused. My blow to the chin must have caused more damage than I realized…

--Teague looked back to the bar maid who gave him a cryptic nod and a wink. What was between them? The barmaid looked to Mister Jopo next to her and he nodded back.

I swung again with my confidence building -slightly. Sparks flew as our blades clashed, then clashed again. I swung at his mid-section, and he jumped back looking even more misplaced and confused. He swapped the blade in his hands, left to right and back again as if to distract me from where the strike was coming from --and then he took another jab at me.

I jumped to the outside of the thrust and cut the outside of his arm and ducked as he swung his arm back and I quickly brought my knife up cutting his chest...

He suddenly froze and looked at me. He then dropped his knife and put his hand over the gash. Again, he fostered a look of shock and distance in the eyes.

I stepped on his knife and raised my blade. "Yield?"

He exhaled, exhausted and more so, confused that he had been bested and slowly, he gave a nod...

I lowered my blade, Mister Hallock removed my shackle, and I turned just as Ives fell to the floor behind me like a tree trunk. Everyone cheered –LOUD--except the men of the Black Eagle who reached for their coin in order to settle up with Duncan-Howe...

I took my congratulations from my shipmates as I moved to the bar. Jaffar -who stood at the forefront of the other Moors, nodded his approval to me. Others gathered around me in celebration, even Sanjuro slapped me on the back to congratulate me. We, as a crowd, moved up to the bar where Newcastle ordered drinks all around...

"But" Jopo said with his thick accent, "This round is on me for I won ten doubloons on your action...."

"You Mister Jopo?" I said surprised, "I was unaware you had such faith in me."

"I admit my confidence in you was in question but...." He clutched a sort of tree root in his fist and looked to Teague -and then the barmaid-- as if they had a secret between them, then he cleared his throat and continued, "It's bad form to bet against a shipmate…"

I pointed to the tree root, "What's that?" I asked.

He quickly hid it, "Never mind about that, time to celebrate….You did us all proud!"

"Yes, you did us proud, lad." Teague smiled.

"I-I don't know how I did it" I admitted, "It was just like a miracle."

"Yes" Newcastle said with a touch of suspicion, "It clearly was God's will." Then he changed his tone, "Well, let's not ask too many questions and have another drink, shall we."

My friend, Uralan was welcomed in our circle for drinks and celebration and there were smiles all around until a loud holler from the tavern entrance silenced the room….

We all turned—

There stood Vincenze, Captain of the Black Eagle --a man well known in these parts --with some of his men.

We turned and stood in silence, sizing up his intentions and allowed him the floor…

"I understand there was a display of violence here this evening."

Duncan-Howe removed the pipe from between his teeth and slowly nodded….

"My men tell me that our man –Ives—was bested by a schoolteacher." He continued to speak in a very loud tone…

The room still remained silent….

"Nay" Vincenze continued "This cannot be true for Ives is one of the best among us and a simple schoolteacher hasn't a chance against him……unless he cheated."

"No cheating on this day Captain Vincenze." Duncan-Howe remarked, "Our man beat yours fair and square –though I do say that the whole conflict might have been avoided if your man had better manners...."

One of Vincenze' men gripped the handle of his sword though he didn't draw it….

"Manners?" Vincenze's anger rose, and he asked. "You speak to me of manners?"

"I do –as you damn well heard!" Duncan-How continued, lowering his pipe hand to where his pistol was.

"Perhaps I should teach you some myself?"

"That my friend would be... ill-advised." Duncan-Howe gave a piercing look. Behind him, Bons's hand dropped to the tomahawk in his sash, and he tapped on the blade, waiting, watching....

"Come now..." The tavern keeper spoke up, in an effort to keep the peace, "There has been enough violence for one night and the affair has been settled, let's have some rum and forget---"

"--The affair has not been settled to my satisfaction and the reputation of the Black Eagle is at stake here."

"Your satisfaction is not our concern." Teague shouted, "Now, be off!"

"I don't take my orders from you Teague!"

"Aye, to be sure, for if you did --you'd live longer!"

"You may be a terror on the continent Teague but here, I make my own law."

The tension in the room seemed to grow even more intense. I saw Jaffar's eyes shift from Teague back to Vincenze as if he was anticipating some action and sure enough, men began to clear out of the way...

Newcastle also appeared focused and Sanjuro's hand dropped to his katana. Other crewmen got close to their weapons. I slowly moved in front of my friend as if to shield her from any possible danger, the tension in the room could be cut with a cutlass...

"Then let's decided this here and now!" Teague said.

Vincenze suddenly pulled his saber as a que for his men to follow suit—

As they reached for their weapons, we did the same, Jagger flipped a table towards these men as Sanjuro and the ronin rifled several throwing stars that zipped through the air and struck down several 'Eagle' combatants in the head, chest, and shoulders, killing several...

And just like that, both sides ran into each other in the center of the room, Blades, axes, and hammers brought down on all of us. Lo using his three-section staff with a swing to the heads of several --and then a low swing to another man's knees dropping him to the floor in pain....

Addo threw his knife into a man and tackled another...

Jaffar made a swing of his curved sword cutting a man across the middle as all the Moors charged forward into the action....

Duncan-Howe tried to rise above it, pipe back in his teeth as he asked for new bets on the new fight.

Jagger emptied his pistols and then pulled a knife in each hand, Bons threw his tomahawk and hit a man as his pistol went off, the bullet pierced the rum barrel next to the tavern keeper's head and the sight of the rum escaping was more than the man could take, "Now that's just plain sacrilegious!" He cried....

Newcastle and Vincenze locked up and Vincenze, a man of great size, lifted him off the floor by the neck, Newcastle countered with a quick sweep of his knife across the man's stomach. Newcastle was dropped and he made a swift kick to the knee dropping Vincenze to the floor before two other privateers tackled him and they all rolled back into the crowd....

"Stop this madness, stop this at once," the tavern keeper ordered as he shattered a bottle of rum over one assailant's head.

Suddenly there was a massive explosion!

The street outside was lit up and the concussion of the blast belted through the tavern like a hurricane –even removing some shutters. Then there was another explosion that lit up the night sky. The whole island seemed to shake under the pressure of a bombardment. The fighting between us seemed to ease up as we all tried to get our bearings...

More explosions ripped into the street and town square and the church tower was hit when a cannon ball bounced off the iron of the church bell --ringing it-- as the bricks and mortar came tumbling down...

"What the hell?!?" Ward looked up as parts of the ceiling fell down.

More cannon fire ripped through the tavern. An explosion blew one privateer airborne, and he came down to be impaled on a hanging iron chandelier –extinguishing some of its candles.

I along with Duncan-Howe, Wolfe and Reader climbed under a table for protection from the falling bricks. "Damn bastards!" Wolfe shouted clutching a rum cask and trying to protect it from the dust…

Another blast brought down a giant support beam, "This is going to affect business" Duncan-Howe shouted, "These heathens will try to flee this site without payin' up on their bets!"

I was more concerned about the town being smashed by cannon and the night continued to light up under rapid explosions and blasts…

"IT'S THE BRITISH!!!" shouted a man from second floor of the customs house as he pointed to British frigates entering the harbor….

In the harbor, with some of the ships at anchor, sinking or on fire, The Venger with only a skeleton crew onboard—and most of our men ashore-- fired a round from the cannon on deck three, the only guns she had men to man and as she left the harbor, she fired up a yellow flare.

"God damn Brits!" Shouted an angry Hallock as he moved some broken, shattered furniture off himself, "I'll kill every one of them" and just as he stood up, a cannon ball punched a hole in the tavern wall, took his head clean off and smashed through the other wall and exploded on the street --his headless body dropped to the floor…

--Just like that Hallock was gone!

Vincenze and Newcastle had gone back to trying to kill each other and a blast brought them to their feet -still gripping each other by the throat, knives ready to cut each other apart—and with another round of explosions and they both let each other go "Once this is settled…." Vincenze hissed, "We'll resume this."

"Until then, consider yourself lucky!" Newcastle barked as more explosions hit the street –one cannon ball smashing though the top floor of The Witch's Den…

Vincenze caught his breath, and he ran off to join his crew.

My friend Uralan, and the tavern staff dropped down through a trap door in the floor –to a wine cellar/shelter-- behind the bar of The Witch's Den. She did not want to be separated but I forced her down the ladder. "I'll come back for you."

"I'll take care of her lad! She'll be safe here." The keeper said to me as he closed the hatch door behind him with dust coming down from the rafters…

Inside, they jumped to the floor of the wine cellar where Uralan kicked open a box with guns in it and pulled two pistols –island justice!

"Maybe you should go save him?" The Tavern keeper said as he caught sight of the pistols.

The tavern keeper also picked up a weapon, ready to defend his staff and cellar if it came down to violence. Uralan then went to the wall, turned her back against some shelves loaded with rum barrels and began to backpedal forcing the shelves to slide to the left to reveal a secret passage –an old smuggler's tunnel.

"What are you doing?" The tavernkeeper asked alarmed.

"Our people are out there we have to open up the tunnel and get as many civilians inside as possible –for protection!"

He looked at her, then he looked to the other women present –the look on their faces seemed to suggest that they agreed with this idea, and he slowly nodded his approval. He didn't want to do it, but he had to do it and they re-gripped their weapons, grabbed some lanterns and started down the dark, secret tunnel...

Teague and Newcastle –with cannon blasts all around—rallied the few men close by as if the blasts, fire, and flying debris had no effect on them. Nighthorse, Baltimore, Roux, Toombs, Le Clerk, Takeda, Blix, Lo-Tan, Sunderland, Jagger, a few of the Moors, Lau, Silence, Foxx, Cage, Tiger, Wolfe, myself, and a few others. With everyone else running in panic to escape the bombardment, we moved towards the action, to the beach. We moved and jumped over obstacles, walls, and part of the bell tower as it crashed down into the street in front of us…

Several buildings were now on fire and the docks were hit, blown apart and a blaze. We got to the beach under cannon fire and there we saw several warships in the bay, rolling cannon in our direction with British long boats, loaded with marines being rowed through the smoke towards our position…

--Where was The Venger? Our ship was not in the tide.

Newcastle made a bold decision, the British bombardment was rolling deeper into town, the beach where their troops would land and was now exempt from artillery attack --so as to not to shell their own men-- therefor, the beach was now the safest place for us to make a stand and Newcastle – as the ranking officer among us—ordered us to make ready for a fight. We took cover at the top of the beach between the sand, the palm trees, and the edge of the town. Some of us took cover in the tree line. Some trees had been blasted from their roots, on fire and cut in half and provided a perfect shield for an entire rank of privateers….

--Some of us took cover, ready to fight from the damaged beach front buildings.

We passed around shot for our pistols. Those, heavy in rounds gave to those without. We primed everything and there, in the darkness we waited, weapons ready….

I looked around to see several men from the Black Eagle in our ranks – fighting these British invaders was a priority over fighting each other at this time. "We'll kill each other later!"

The British –God bless them—made the predictable effort to form up into ranks in the shallow tide, then move on the town in an orderly fashion. Their near perfect formations and picket lines made for quality target practice…

In their ranks, giving commands, on a purchased military commission was Lord Blakely, well known as a man who pretended to represent the cause of government while being owned by the special interests such as the

Royal African Slave Company, this dandy had his men unload his mount and wait until he was comfortable and ready to order them forward....

"Well, look at this now!" Newcastle turned to Teague, "Blakely."

"I see him!" Teague said through his teeth. The sight of this man betrayed British intentions. He was here to pacify The Caribbean for the slave trade. "He'll die by the end of this."

Kannon peered at him, "The rapist of Africa." Then he planted his blade in the sand where he could reach it quickly after the guns emptied.

"Rapist of The Canadas" Karr said double checking his pistols.

"And the rapist of Albany!" Teague added.

"Albany too? This tyrant gets around." Newcastle said. "It may be best to kill this bastard here before he rapes something else."

"Or kill him here for the hell of it—one less corrupt official for the world to deal with."

"Aye," Newcastle looked to Teague, "But which one of us gets the honor of killin' him?"

"Me!" Teague said.

"No. I do." Newcastle countered.

"Care to wager on it?" Teague said, oblivious to the burning palm tree that crashed down behind us.

"Ten Spanish dollars says, I get the privilege."

"Make it twenty!" Another burning tree collapsed.

"Why stop there if you got so much confidence?" Newcastle said, "How 'bout a hundred?"

"Would you two focus on the action at hand, please." Karr asked.

"Aye, we'll settle this matter soon enough. Besides if this bastard hit the beach, you can bet that war criminal Roberts is close behind!"

"Well, why don't we bet on his death too then?"

True to our fashion, we held our position and kept silent until the marines marched up close and into range --and still...even closer! We waited until they were almost right on top of us, closer, and closer, sweat dripped from my trigger finger as it twitched.

Newcastle suddenly shouted the command to fire, and we opened up --a snap of the hammer-- and lead started to rip through the air cutting the marines down with rounds ripping into ribs, faceplates, knees --and dropping several red coats in the sand dead including several officers -- always a prime target.

We unloaded a second volley that cut into them, Then, we fell back into town, and formed up on the edge of the township between the church cemetery and town square. Again, we took position and waited for the regulars to walk in it. IT –being a storm of more lead....

They came up from the beach and into town with more caution, still, the burning palm trees lit them up for us to see --and we could watch their approach as we reloaded our weapons...

They fixed bayonets, adjusted their battle flags, and re-formed their ranks just as we opened up and cut into them again. At close range, a lead shot cracked bones and could punch a good size hole into the man or even rip...through them!

Blood now covered the beach and the path into town.

The Brits returned fire in our direction. Bullets hit the grave markers around us. A regular peered over the cemetery wall at us and Jack-Karr fired his pistol, putting a round through the soldier's hat and into his skull. Suddenly, more regulars came over the cemetery wall and charged us as we engaged in close quarter combat. Swords and pistols against their bayonets. Blades banged off headstones –with sparks--and skulls. We emptied guns just a meter or two apart. Tiberius cleaned several regulars off the top wall with one swing of his morning star, then pulled it back for another swing, smashing headstones along its path. The chain then wrapped around a man's neck and Tiberius pulled him to his knees and started choking him.

More British stormed over the west wall, weapons out, Hazzard took a musket ball in the chest, and he collapsed near me. I moved over to his position, men firing and reloading all around. "I have you Mister Hazzard" I put my hand on his wounds. He tried to speak, he was trying to apologize in his final moments to the almighty, for everything but, he died before he could completely repent.

Under a new hail of gunfire, Newcastle shouted commands for a fighting retreat out of the cemetery –but we would contest every tombstone.

I looked to the dead Mister Hazzard, closed his eyes, and retreated with the others. Towne, Flynn, and several others had been killed. Rajal's body was draped over a tombstone with his blood dripping down to its base.

Another palm tree crashed down, ablaze and cut the battlefield in two and bought us a momentary respite to fall back a few meters….

We moved back into the darkness, stepping over bodies --several civilians had been killed in the bombardment, some of them women. A very harsh reality to this kind of warfare. We helped who we could and tried to direct survivors to safety as we moved….

Suddenly, Mister Lynch ran out of the darkness from the south with Hayte, Dakar, Kato, Dax-Varrow and a few others….

"Where the hell have you been?" Newcastle snapped.

"Fighting the British. They've landed at Point Fear. They're all around us!" Lynch explained.

"That's why there was no resistance from the fort guns!" Cage added, musket fire hitting all around him. "The fort is in British hands --damn pirates!!!"

"Can we take it back?" Newcastle asked.

"What about The Venger?"

"The ship's gone?" Kannon yelled as he fired a reserve pistol.

"What?"

"That can't be?"

"No point in arguing about it now!" Wolfe spit the taste of gunpowder out of his mouth.

Mister Foxx put the equation together in his head, "Damn it all! We're trapped here!"

"The ship sent up a yellow flare on her way out of the harbor." Fury reported. "She'll make for the south side of the island."

"LOOK!" Jack-Karr pointed as the British started to put the town to the torch. "They've lit the town!"

We all turned to look –and in fact, British marines were using torches to light all the buildings on fire. "BASTARDS! They've condemned everyone on the island to death."

"There are families here." I shouted and everyone around me stopped for a moment and looked at me –some in slight shock.

Kannon stopped loading his gun for a moment, tuned to me, and said, "You've picked a hell of a time to become a hero, Mister Reed."

I tried to muster a response that I directed to the whole platoon, "I-I just thought that, if we have to fight, maybe we could save some of them in the process."

"Enough politics!" Karr shouted. "Why don't we just kill 'em all?" He said referring to the British invaders, "Then we'll have nothing to worry about."

"Aye, let's get to the business of doing that!"

Teague got everyone's attention. "Listen here! We're gonna form up and fight our way across the island –any way we can. Rendezvous at the old Spanish fort at Thunder Point. We'll make our last stand there among the ramparts! Right?"

"Aye." Sterling spit out his support and others in the ranks voiced their agreement. "Let's settle this!"

"The damn Brits are behind us, so we'll fight our way west."

"Through the town?" I asked looking at the buildings on fire….

"Aye, through the town! Spread the word and let's move."

"What the hell," Jagger said, "Today is as good a day to die as any, I suppose."

We called to the rest of our battle group, fighting to the left, to the right –fighting everywhere-- and we moved out of the cemetery into the cyclone of fire! Buildings, palm trees, dead bodies --all on fire. Some civilians were trying to save some of the buildings with buckets of sand and water and as the timbers came down on us, we'd duck or jump over burning hazards as walls collapsed around us in flames…

We moved towards the canal, the fish market and the lagoon that marked the old smuggler's cove. Suddenly, we came around the corner and collided right into a battalion of British regulars. There was a moment of shock, then both sides went for their weapons. First pistols and muskets, then blades.

Several British bodies fell into the dirt dead. Raeder had kicked two regulars back into the flames of a burning tavern. Jack-Karr swung his cutlass, the blade was on fire, and he would wield it at the heads and necks of our challengers as it dragged smoke across his body.

--Uralan, kicked open the tunnel entrance, she caught sight of British regular preparing to put a building's thatch roof to the torch and she fired. The musket round slammed him against the building, she raised her second pistol and fired again to make sure he was dead. Then she motioned for some of the civilians to run towards her to take cover in the tunnel…

I turned in the fighting and caught sight of her. "Uralan!" I quickly ran to her as Teague, Karr, Saint James, and some of the others formed a defensive square around me, shooting and killing who they could, then reloading or drawing their blades. "Come on." I said, motioning her to come with us…

"I can't!" She shouted, "There are people here, civilians. I must help them." She waved some women and children into the old smuggler's tunnel behind her and frantically, I looked around to see what I could do, where I could help but, the scene became a melee of steel and chaos…

We all quickly came to the same conclusion –defend this space and get as many civilians into the tunnel as possible so, without command, all of us formed a defensive perimeter, backs to the tunnel and guns out, shooting and killing who we could. Civilians could pass through our lines on the run –the British invaders got shot.

--The British eventually closed in and engaged and the scene got fierce fast. As we were stormed, our lines started to break. I was tackled and went to the ground, with a British marine and Kannon –the marine was killed instantly upon impact with the ground and as I started to get to my feet, I saw the doors of the smuggler's tunnel close –and with the lantern light behind them, I could see the heavy enforcement bar drop into place, the civilians --some of them at least-- had made it inside to safety but just as I smiled at this little victory, our world descended into another lever of hell as redcoats closed in from all directions…

Dos Santos took a cutlass across his metal chest plate and a sudden musket ball slammed into his head and killed him. Sterling and Cage were killed immediately by gunfire –though Cage gripped a red coat's tunic and pulled him to the ground as he fell.

--Wolfe was blinded by gunfire but swung his cutlass with vengeance trying to cut anything close to him until several rounds went into him, dropping him in the dust –dead!

A musket ball went through Kane's hat and missed his skull and as he stood there amazed, a second shot went through his neck. Gunfire also took Calderon, Hawkquez and Mister Foxx, killing all of them with multiple rounds. Foxx lived long enough to spark a grenade when the British descended on him –and with a wicked laugh, it blew a squad of marines apart.

Bons pulled his tomahawk out of a regular's skull as a bullet zipped by and grazed his shoulder. There was another heavy exchange of gunfire as the tide-of-the-fighting rolled the action past some burning shops and into the canal. A boat in the canal exploded, –bullets killed some privateers on the floating bridge fashioned out of barrels and they dropped into the lagoon. I was clipped by some lead that zipped across my temple and I tumbled across the sand into the water, damaged. My vision was blurred but I could see the images and shapes of the fighting all around. I crawled forward when I got bashed on the back of the skull by a sergeant who pushed my head into the canal lagoon to drown me. I took water into my lungs, and he pulled my head up by the scalp, in a sinister manner as if to add a torture element to my murder—and just before he was about to force me back under water, I suddenly, heard a slicing sound as steel cut through the air and his body and head hit the water in two parts.

--I cleared his grip, coughing and saw the top of his head in the red water next to me. I quickly picked myself up from the lagoon, stumbling to get my balance as Arson and another platoon of Venger survivors moved into the area.

"That's two ya owe me." Arson shouted. He paused his fighting to hold up two fingers to make sure I understood my debt, then he went back to killing.

Chaos continued to turn the situation into more of a nightmare. Some of our men peeled off to make a last stand in the flames and burning buildings. I looked around, and in the madness, our battalion was now only a fraction of our original fighting force. Bons, Tiger and the others ran past me in top-flight, "Come on!" I picked up my weapons and moved after them as a rocket zipped in and exploded behind me forcing me to pick up the tempo but, we stopped suddenly as a burning building collapsed in front of us, cutting off our escape route. I looked to move to my left but British regulars came from that direction, and as we turned, they emerged from the east and a moment later they also arrived from the south....

--We were trapped!

Bayonets came down all around us –one even cut the side of my face to mark me. "It's the hangman's knot for you...pirate.!" A scarred British sergeant sneered as I slowly put my hands up.

The others who were still alive also surrendered --for this was the end.

XXV

PRISONERS

As the sun rose over the palm trees and smoke covered the landscape, our men were shackled, beaten, and wounded as we stood there –prisoners- -in front of Lord Blakely. We were shamed and angry as we awaited our fate…

Many of us were missing and presumed dead but somewhere, out there, a few survivors were still fighting –since we could hear the occasional gun shot or the echo of a grenade…

As luck would have it, I was in line next to Ives who had somehow survived the attack. What we fought about earlier seemed silly standing here now. Also, in this prison train was Raeder, Bishop, Fury, Bons, Jack-Karr, The Dutchman, Ward, Therrinfall, Watson, Sampson-Rift, Baako, Shaddam, Merciless, some of the Aztecs, Dax-Varrow and a few others. The nearby iron worker was hammering shackles on Whitney before he was pushed into line with us….

--Our weapons were confiscated, racked, and piled up on the parade ground and as I looked around my smoldering, burnt out surroundings I was gripped by a strange sense of calm. The end seemed present, the fighting –months and months of it-- now seemed over and for some unknown reason I was at peace.

"Brave men of The Venger," Blakely started with a touch of sarcasm added to his upper-class accent. "Real-live-pirates!" He moved in front of our ranks and had the look of a man who sought merit and accolades, but his actions seemed to lack real courage. His men apparently did the fighting for him. Only in the presence of men in shackles did he display any real courage.

Some of us grumbled at the use of the word –pirate-- but we appeared to have larger problems at this time. He started walking down the prison line with some directives, "The British defectors among you will be sent back to England in shackles and tried for your crimes against the King." He continued to walk, "There is a body cage waiting for each of you back in London –a touch more civilized than the ones you left for our men in the tide of New Haven." He stopped at Raeder who grumbled his disdain like an animal.

"Charming," Blakey sneered.

He continued down the line, "We intend to make a public example of you. An effort to dissuade any of our fine sailors from following your – rather poor-- example. Hence, we will crush the illusion that piracy is a good thing for any man."

--His grand sense eloquence was starting to make me sick to my stomach and rob me of my earlier sense of peace.

He suddenly stopped at Baako, "Take this one away," he ordered, "We'll turn him over to our emissary and sell him to the Portuguese. We wouldn't want to be implicated in the slave trade directly, now, would we?" He smiled at Baako as they pulled him out of the line and pushed him over to the corner of the parade ground and cracked him on the head with the butt of a musket to collapse him into the dirt. Then, they started beating him in the corner…

Shaddam, Raeder and Bishop took a step forward, wanting to stop it but, the marines dropped their bayonets to keep us in place.

Undisturbed by this beating, Blakely continued his walk down our line and then stopped in front of some of the Aztecs. "These belong to the Spanish. Pull them aside we'll trade them back." He then looked to Shaddam, "You see Gerald," Blakely said to an officer not too far off, "-- Even in this part of the world there are heathens." He then stepped close to look at Shaddam in detail. "You –and all of your kind—will be put to death…"

Shaddam's English was poor but, he understood.

He then stepped back and addressed us like a politician –which made this even more revolting. "These colonies exist for the benefit of the crown, not the benefit of men who take the law into their own hands. However, I sense that if you gravel correctly, some of you may be pardoned to a life of hard labor and you may skip the hangman's knot."

This thought caused Ward to spit in the dust.

Blakely saw this and stopped. "Captain Lively?"

"My Lord?" A British captain replied.

"Do you have a count on these men here?"

"Thirty-six my Lord."

"Wrong," he answered, "Thirty-five." And Blakely pulled a pistol from the officer next to him, aimed and shot Ward dead at almost point-blank range.

"Bastard!" Bishop barked as he was slammed back, stock of a musket against his skull.

It was at that moment, that a British officer appeared and spoke to this bastard, Blakely privately and after a few words, Blakely turned to our ranks, "Who is the ranking officer among you cutthroats...?"

We remained silent. Some of us straightened up with a touch of defiance –as if he dared to even ask.

Blakely walked down the line, taking a close look at each of us. He said 'no' to Whitney, 'no' to Merciless then he stopped and peered at me as if trying figure out my position here. There was something about me that got his attention. "No" He finally said, more to himself than to me, "You're different from the rest of these killers but you're not in command." He walked past, Therrinfall, Sampson-Rift –with a frown, Tiger and Bons, then stopped at Dax-Varrow and after a moment to size him up, pointed, "You." He nodded to his marines, "Take him!"

Despite protest, Dax-Varrow was pulled from our ranks....

"HOLD!"

The British froze in place and looked down the line to...

Newcastle.

"I'm in the ranking officer here, Newcastle of the warship Venger."

Blakley smiled and slowly said, "Take him instead."

Moments later, a 2nd lieutenant led the way as Newcastle was marched back into the smoke of the battle zone. Past damaged buildings and homes, where wounded civilians tried to dig out the remains of their lives and possessions, past stacks of dead bodies in canvass bags being hauled to a mass grave, past a medical tent loaded with British wounded, the field armory, past several operational tents with officers issuing orders to different dispatch runners and finally, to a command tent on the edge of Royal proper.

--There, British regimental battle flags blew in the wind.

This temporary headquarters was set up amongst the ruins that was once our town. What was left of this district of Port Royal was still on fire – devastated. The entire place had a haunting effect.

Smoke rolled over the gallows that had been built in the early morning hours of the dawn by carpenters of the British Navy and…they already had tenants –privateers from The Revenge and The Tempest- who had survived the fighting the night before only to be rounded up, captured, and stamped with death at the end of a rope. Their bodies were left to drift in the wind.

Newcastle looked around and surveyed his surroundings…some civilians were being rounded up and marked as collaborators. Supplies were being impounded from private businesses and households. The Pastor who had given Reed a Bible once upon a time, was dragged down the steps of his own church –the roof of his church was smoking and on fire-- and there, directing the action, across a landscape of flames like Mammon himself stood Lord Roberts. His back was to his present company and his officers –along with members of the Royal African Company, presented township maps to pinpoint areas that required their special attention. Officers took their orders then moved to stamp out the last pockets of resistance on the island.

Newcastle was held in place for a moment at the edge of the command tent. He watched the gallows floor give way under the feet of a platoon of privateers as they dropped to their deaths.

"Take a good look, you're next." The 2nd Lieutenant said with a slight smile.

"Come now," A regal voice echoed across this killing ground, and Newcastle looked up to see Lord Robert walking towards him "Politics and peace cannot commence until we move past this hostility." He slowly stepped out from the shadows of the canvass into the sunlight, "Welcome Mister Newcastle. It's been a long time."

Newcastle peered at him. "It has been."

Roberts looked at his shackles, "Those won't be necessary."

"He's dangerous sir."

Lord Roberts smiled, "I know."

The shackles were removed. Newcastle recognized Roberts from his earlier days when Newcastle was the property of the Royal Navy. They had fought together, off the coast of Africa against the Spanish, when Roberts was in command of a joint military expedition –before he bought his seat in the House of Lords. A seat he had since resigned, in an effort to find fame and fortune abroad. They had also --fought against each other and clashed in the north Atlantic and on the beaches of Iceland in the battle for Hades Gap when the British eradicated the privateer base there.

"I see the rank of midshipman didn't hold you for long."

"Neither the rank, nor the imprisonment of the Royal Navy."

"Imprisonment, a harsh term from one who showed such promise as a young man. Too bad your skills have been misguided."

"Liberation has its price." Newcastle added.

"Quite." Roberts then motioned over to a command table, covered with maps, military documents, a tea kit and some captured weapons, handguns, swords and what appeared to be other confiscated weapons from earlier 'guests.' "May I offer you something?" He motioned to a tea kit with some bread and cheese.

Newcastle looked and wondered how a man could enjoy tea a few meters from the gallows and shook his head. No.

Roberts did have an evil charm about him. He moved in a calm, relaxed manner, and spoke with a diction that was precise, clear, and direct and he quickly got down to business. "I'm looking for these men." He pointed to some wanted posters out in front of him, with crude illustrations of Essex, Sanjuro and some of the other men from The Venger. "–This one in particular," he pulled out an arrest warrant for Teague. "We believe this one was a former royal marine –Spartacus Division possibly-- who took the head of a judge. Judge Thatcher of Innsbrook-Fullam." Roberts tried to read Newcastle's expression to see if there was some recognition with the warrant illustration. "We suspect he is still on the island with a platoon of rebels and sense that he is the type of man to make our lives a living hell."

"Tis true…" Newcastle said, then he added as an insulting afterthought, "…you are right once in a while."

Roberts cracked a slight smile. "Then you know the man?"

"I do."

"Then we'll outfit you with a white flag. Find him and convince him to surrender."

"You'd have a better chance of bringing Jesus back from the dead a second time –besides, he's more likely to demand all of you to surrender to him in any event."

"Is that so?" Robert sneered. Beyond him, more privateers were marched to the gallows to be executed and this grim sight put Newcastle on edge. This was read by Roberts, "Tis a dark thing for a man to see his future, isn't it?"

Newcastle looked to Roberts before both men refocused on the executions at hand….

"Though….it need not be your future Warrick." Roberts slowly turned. "I cannot sanction your past, and I have no real stomach for desertion, however, if you can give me The Venger's heading and destination, an exception can be made."

Newcastle looked at him trying to calculate how much his soul was worth to this man. "You want me to betray my crew?"

Roberts paused, "I want you to do what is right."

At that point, Newcastle stood up straight, "That I cannot do."

"Think twice on that Newcastle. The gate to hell opens only once to release a sinner." And just as he closed out his sentence, more bodies dropped through the floor of the gallows as if to foreshadow Newcastle's fate.

Still, he remained silent and defiant.

"The Royal Navy has launched a blockade from Spanish Florida to the coast of Brazil and our squadrons are cruising these waters in an effort to round up every rogue privateer, rebel and slate criminal in existence. Every secret pirate base and outpost will be put to the torch. The damages will be large and the crown unforgiving. Unless, of course, you can arrange a meeting with your commander."

"And if I do, what then?"

"Leave the rest to me. Tell me the ship's heading or, location and you'll be on your way to London to start life-a-new –on parole of course." Roberts looked back to the gallows as a new set of privateers were marched up to the noose. "We will run that ship down Warrick," Roberts continued keeping his eyes on the executions, "With your help or without it."

Newcastle knew crown policies well and the crown was not to be trusted so rather than get involved in some Shakespearean subterfuge, he remained silent.

Roberts took this as his answer and in disappointed fashion, gave a reluctant nod to march Newcastle off to rejoin his condemned colleagues.

Newcastle was thrown into the dust.

"Welcome back." Blakely said with a touch of sarcasm as Newcastle slowly took to his feet.

"Nice visit with the commadore." Bishop whispered through the side of his mouth.

"Yeah," Newcastle dusted himself off and spit out some blood. "If you hadn't guessed, he means to kill all of us."

"What a surprise." Bishop returned under his breath as he looked to Blakeley out of the corner of his eye. "Got to hand it to the British, what they lack in imagination, they make up for in arrogance."

"Silence there!" Blakely barked and he then stood back as if proud of himself and gave us one last look, "I want to thank you all for the promotion I will undoubtedly receive for your arrest and execution but, this affair is over." His smile then faded, "Slaves to the prison barge! The rest of this scum…to the gallows."

The British marines closed in on us, bayonets down. I focused on the blade, on the marine's gun in front of me and its reflection in the sun as it was marched towards me. The words 'This is it!' echoed in my skull to signal the end of my existence as I closed my eyes tight, when SUDDENLY-

---KAA--BOOOOOOOOOOOOOOOM!

Suddenly, there was a massive explosion –the armory blew apart and turned into timber. Everyone around it was picked up, thrown through the air and back to the ground by the blast as shingles of wood and splinters cut into all of us. Signal flares started shooting into the sky with a flash – in every direction-- ripping across the jungle!

"Teague!" Karr surmised as he was buried in dust and wood fragments. Newcastle didn't wait. "Kill 'em! Kill 'em all!" He screamed…

This was it! We all jumped and blitzed forward for the fight of our lives was right here, right now! Some of us were shot immediately as we rushed forward –despite being shackled—and we collided into their ranks. Grab! Claw! Bash! Rockets –that had been ignited in the armory explosion were shooting everywhere –over us and across the skyline, some coming into the parade ground. One flare went through two marines as they closed in on me, killing them both….

Raeder jumped forward and charged a terrified Blakely, dropped him to his knees as he quickly got behind him, wrapped the chain of his shackles around his neck and pulled --squeezing the life out of him! Blakely started to turn blue. The regulars started firing at Raeder and lead rounds hit him in the shoulder, arm, and hip but he kept his grip and squeezed –laughing in pain-- even as regulars continued to fire musket rounds into him, blowing him apart, blast after blast, he just grit his teeth, held on and laughed as he choked –and choked—and choked!

The British focused on saving their commander and there was less opposition to us. We killed who we could, then stumbled to the iron station –Laurent and Dutch were shot in the back as we got there, a bullet meant for me, hit Clairmont and killed him! We clamored to bust off our shackles using the tools and taking casualties to the left and right. The bodies were piling up! A rocket came in and caught the roof of this blacksmith station on fire and smoke filled the parade ground. Therrinfall, Rift and Bishop were liberated, then Bons. Before saving himself, Ives busted my shackles off with the hammer and was suddenly shot in the face. His head rocked back, and he fell back into the dirt, dead....

"Let's move!" Therrinfall shouted and we stormed towards the weapons.

--Shaddam still chained, was fighting hand to hand, picking up a British regular and throwing him head-first into an anvil, then into the blacksmith fire, then picking up another marine and slamming him against two others. Baako gripped his attackers with the last of his strength, he grabbed one around the throat and pulled a chunk of his voice box out when bayonets and bullets started to bring him down. More of us were killed as we picked up our weapons. Bons reclaimed his tomahawk and rifled into the back of one of the regulars beating on Baako, then quickly closed in, removed it, and slammed it into the skull of the soldier on the left, then killed the one on the right in rapid, quick order. He dropped to his knee to check Baako, but Baako was gone --dead! There was a quick two- or three-words worth of a Native American prayer then Bons was back in the fight....

Raeder continued to draw fire taking round after round as British regulars closed in. Blakely, now dark blue, pleaded for his life and gasped out a "Pleeeease" when he started coughing up some blood only to have Reader grit his teeth and squeeze even tighter—

"We...intend...to make a public example of you!" Raeder said through his teeth using Blakely's own words against him. "To...dissuade any of our fine sa-sailors from...following your rather poor bastard-like example you pompous AAASSSSSSSSSSS!" Blakely's left eye popped out of his skull from the pressure, and he was dead. Raeder dropped him, let out a laugh as if proud of himself and then fell forward to his death.

"Get to the coast and kill every soldier you can!" Newcastle shouted as our survivors seemed to scatter in every direction or, in some cases stay and fight in last stand fashion…

Bons, Tiger and a few others ran past me in top-flight, "Come on!" I picked up my weapons and mustered after them. We ran into the jungle as musket fire cut up the area around us.

"Move! Move! Move!" Bishop shouted. We killed who we could and moved into the jungle…

We were in full-flight, Therrinfall, Bons, Bishop, Jack-Karr, Rift, Toombs, Shaddam, Tiger, Kai, Lo-Tan and myself --the rest of our group Newcastle and the others were either dead or scattered.

Parts of the jungle were on fire from the rockets. Tree trunks, palm trees, some under growth –all a light but, most of the green just smoldered into a dense smoke…

There were a few scattered civilians –families-- making a run for it, away from the fighting here and there, or just scared, trying to lay low until it was all over. We bolted past them, through the wilderness and then we slowed down and got quiet as we reached the edge of the jungle by the Saint Rains Road. Bishop motioned for us to stop in place. There was a British engineering platoon working its way down the road moving towards us.

We quickly moved for cover, made ourselves invisible and I slid behind some giant banana leaves. We got down as low to the ground as possible. There, we waited in silence, sweat dripping into my eyes, when there was a sudden –SNAP! We looked up as some former slaves suddenly ran past us and out onto the road --there was musket fire and some of the people hit the ground dead. Suddenly a scared, young boy rolled under the giant leaves to our position --he was eight or nine years old maybe. Bishop quickly slapped his hand over the boy's mouth, hissed him to be silent and held him still. I put my index finger to my lips to make sure he understood.

Then, I turned my eyes to the jungle road where I could see redcoats –and some grenadiers run past on the heels of the surviving, liberated slaves on the run. Others stopped and speared any possible survivors lying on the road with their bayonets. They took a survey into the jungle towards us --- one seemed to look right at me but, he didn't advance.

-They owned the road, but once they moved off the road, we had the advantage. We could ambush them from any tree or from the undergrowth. They knew this which, is why the search effort didn't extend into the trees too far....

"Any more of them?" I heard a corporal call out as the regulars continued to explore the edge of the road. Bons pulled his tomahawk, ready to swing into this man's forehead. Bishop and Karr readied their weapons with a quiet hand. It was clear we may have to fight our way out of this...

"There's nothing more here!" The British regular suddenly said as he reset his position and pressed forward on the road.

I had thought for sure he had seen us. I thought he was looking right at me—and maybe he was and maybe, he just didn't want to die this day.

Once clear, we picked up –crossed the road--and continued to make our way 'cross country through the jungle –we could hear the battle in the background and there was a trace of smoke in the air from the fire which must have been burning its way across the island. After we moved about a league, I happened to turn and saw the boy was following us. I stopped and waved him off "Go away –go back!"

He didn't move. He didn't run. He just looked at me.

My ship mates were by now moving far ahead of me into the jungle and I was certain I would get lost or be left behind so with more urgency, I waved the boy off again, "Go a-w-a-y!" Conflicted, I started running again.

Another rocket zipped into the tree line with a trail of smoke. I ducked –and the boy was still following me. He stopped when I saw him as if he was caught doing something wrong and I don't know why it didn't occur to me earlier but, I realized at that moment, that he was scared –and scared to be alone and with this notion, my tone changed, "All right, come on." I waved him forward and he ran to catch up --I had no idea what would come of this, my only thought was that it was quite possible that it was his parents killed on the road and that I should get him out of here and through this day. Beyond that, we'd have to figure it out.

XXVI

INFERNO

We cleared the jungle and made it to the beach, clear of the fight. The sounds of war were still not too far off. Some of us collapsed in the tide, exhausted and wanting for relief from the heat.

--But there was no ship here. No rescue. The Venger was nowhere to be seen.

"Now what should we do?"

"I don't understand. The ship should be here." Karr splashed up from the surf, thinking...

"We can't go back." Therrinfall stated.

I turned around, behind us was a giant wall of fire slowly rolling forward, destroying everything in its path, huts, trees --people! The island –and what seemed to be the world entire—was a blaze. Dense smoke covered the jungle and the beach, choking us as it bellowed into the sky....

There was still some faint screaming in the distance --women! Bishop, Karr, Bons and the others looked back towards the flames and intense heat, a hundred meters behind us as some people emerged from the wall of fire –screaming—they were torched and collapsed on the sand –dead.

"My God!" It was like we were on the edge of hell. We had to help any possible survivors, and just as I took a step forward towards this wall of fire, a figure suddenly emerged from the flames like a dark shadow! It stood there for a moment at the edge of this hazard then it slowly started moving towards us....

I focused for a sharp look. "What the---"

--It was Teague!

--His clothes were on fire and his skin was black from soot. Despite this, he planted his cutlass in the sand and just stood there for a moment trying to catch his breath. He was holding something in his left arm –a bundle wrapped in cloth, the size of a human head. With his right hand, he slowly slapped the flames out on his burning tunic and then pulled his blade from the sand and started to march towards us, clothes –and skin-- smoldering.

We took a few steps towards him and as we got close, I focused on what he was carrying wrapped in this blanket with a sense of doom –fearful of what I might see-- and I shuttered at the idea that it was Blakely's head!

--Teague –after all—was a man who kept his promises and he had taken the head of a judge or two.

His clothes were still smoking, and he was covered in black ash that rained down from the sky and even though his footing betrayed him as a wounded man, he still moved with strength and determination. Just as he got in front of us, he suddenly planted his sword back in the sand and collapsed down on one knee –bleeding from his temple and mouth.   Then he leaned forward slightly as if trying to protect what he was carrying and keep his balance at the same time –and the bundle in his left arm rolled out onto the sand and across the beach...

--I looked and swallowed back my fear as my eyes followed this bundle as it rolled and unwrapped itself and then ---shock!

--It was a baby!

Teague had saved a baby in this madness! I lunged forward to pick her up. Bishop and Toombs helped Teague to his feet, and I looked to him amazed. This man –who struck a chord of fear in all of us—had just saved this newborn from the flames somehow and I couldn't help but smile and release a fractured, relieved laugh.

"What?" He said, direct and calm. "Never seen a baby before?" And with that –we all smiled.

"Nice to have you back Teague!" Bishop lowered his cutlass.

Indeed, we all felt a little better about our situation now. I held the baby, Tiger picked up the blanket and pitched it to me and we wrapped her back up.

Teague looked to the young lad who had followed us out of the jungle. "It appears we're running an orphanage now." He stepped into the tide and looked from east to west.

"There's no ship Teague." Bishop reported although Teague could clearly see that for himself. "What should we do?"

Bons, Rift and Karr who stood in the tide, looked over to Teague for his answer. Teague appeared to look up into the sun on the horizon but, he was actually looking at the point where the old Spanish fort stood. An old place, since replaced by a modernized fort --after the island's earthquake-- on the southeast side of the island. "We do as planned and move into the ramparts of Cuidad De Fantasmas."

"And hold up there!" Bishop said, "As good a place to die as any I suppose."

"We're not gonna die there." Teague said. "They are! Now move."

"What about this baby?" I asked, clutching it.

"I didn't run through that inferno to abandon her now." Teague said already several paces ahead in the direction of the fort.

"But-but?" I stammered for the right words, was I supposed to take care of her?

As we started out, Bishop pointed to the baby in my arms. "Hold on to that. That's your responsibility."

"Why me?"

"Because you have compassion." Bishop said, then he smiled, "Plus, you're no good in a fight Reed so, let's put the skills you do have to good use."

I had to admit, he was right.

We made it to the old Spanish fort. Or what was left of it. This place was rumored to be haunted at one point, decades earlier, the graves of the Spanish soldiers who died here were dug up and left empty and open --the bodies gone! And the island gave way to rumors of ghosts and hauntings in these parts. Most of the local populace would not even go into this part of the jungle at night for fear that 'the dead' walked on this part of the island. It would be the perfect cover for highwaymen.

We moved through a massive hole in the wall, made by a cannon blast a generation before and surveyed the ramparts. The fort had not been maintained at all. There were no cannons. No weapons or supplies. Holes had been punched in the walls at different points and there appeared to be old fire damage.

I climbed up to the top of the wall, from there, I could see most of the island in chaos. The town and most of the countryside appeared a blaze. Flares still lighting up the sky from the armory explosion. There were warships –and a prison ship-- in the bay. It was a devastating site and somewhere, out there, the rest of our crew were fighting for their lives.

Karr kicked an old barrel across the parade ground. "Killed by the English would be my fate but...I never thought I'd die in a Spanish fort."

Bishop took a survey, "Not much left to defend."

"And not much time to repair it."

"Then we better get to work." Teague commanded, "Rift, Tiger, weapons. Kai, Tan, with me on the ramparts." He stepped into the parade ground and shouted up at me, "Keep your eye out for the men we mean to kill."

I nodded.

"And Reed..."

I looked back down.

"We could use the ideas and opinion of an educated man right about now. Savvy?"

"I'll put my mind to work sir."

On the ground, Therrinfall, Rift and Bons were using old, rusted tools to expand the graves into limited trench works.

"Nine grenades between us" Therrinfall reported.

"Pass 'em 'round and make sure we have an equal allotment of lead, for I mean to mark these Brits and if we die --they die by thunder!'

There was not much in the way of weapons and ammunition. We grabbed what we could in a panic before we took flight, a satchel of about thirty-two rounds, a slight amount of powder and a few blades. Not much of an armory.

The crew went out into the surrounding jungle and created what traps and barriers we could. Sharpening sticks into spears and hiding them under the foliage.

As the sun was starting to set, I jumped, startled, from the watch tower --I could see red coats, what seemed like hundreds of them moving through a jungle towards us....

"Here they come!" I couldn't prime my weapon fast enough.

Just as we started to scramble for our positions, this baby started crying. I picked her up in her blanket from the floor of the watchtower and looked around for something to pacify her with, but I had nothing.

"Hold up" Tiger used his hand to hold me in place, then moved out and moved through a hole in the wall in the fort and worked his way up a palm tree trunk like a wild animal to a couple of coconuts. Bons moved underneath him and waved and as Tiger knocked them down, Bons caught them and quickly used the pike end of his tomahawk to puncture them, and he got them to me.

"Where'd ya learn to do that?" I asked Tiger as I poured the milk --a little at a time – in the newborn's mouth.

He slid back into his combat position. "I have nine brothers and sisters –we were very poor."

As the sun continued to descend, the shadows began to stretch across the jungle until it was gripped by the evening darkness. We moved out, beyond our traps, into the shadows and the trees and we took our combat positions. Out came the weapons....

The British reconnaissance scouts came forward, to get an eye on the situation. They used caution, focusing their attention on their main target, the fort, and that was when we came out of the darkness and dropped them! Kai, Therrinfall and Tiger with the blade, Bons with his tomahawk, Rift with his hands and Lo using the chain that attached his three-section staff to choke a soldier of his air. Jack-Karr actually came out of the shadows behind a marine and got his cutlass in front of his neck, covered his mouth, and pulled, opening his throat up.

We reduced their numbers by about ten. Then repositioned ourselves in new hiding spots, having bought a few more moments…

Toombs, Bishop, Rift and Jack-Karr climbed into the empty graves for cover and prepared for the next fight. –Kai, Lo and Bons hid against the trees, in with the traps. Therrinfall, Tiger and myself took to the wall, weapons ready…

--But we were without Teague. He had disappeared.

The British marines discovered that they're scouts weren't coming back. There would be no report. At an informal field meeting, under some torches, the noncommissioned officers had their concerns about following up, in the darkness. The officer in charge who most-likely bought his commission did not. He did not have to fight, and he did not care about his men who did. He only wanted the victory –however small—that he could embellish in the officer's tent back at headquarters, so he ordered his men to press forward despite the darkness –and they reluctantly moved out for round two….

The full moon lit the jungle but where we were-- between the shadows and trees--was anyone's guess.

Moments later, there was sudden screaming –the traps! A man had been speared--two actually--one had been killed, the second had a wooden spear shoot through his foot and took another spear through the palm of his hand as he fell forward. Other men tried to pull him from the trap –bloody and screaming. They pulled the stakes from his body and started to carry him back as other marines tried to cautiously work their way forward and round other defense obstacles. All of them became cautious.

A sergeant looked up as something was thrown his way, through the moonlight, smoking— "Grenade!" He called out but, it exploded in the ranks before the men could scatter. Rift, Karr, and Toombs unloading more grenades. The blasts started to light up the terrain –and blew a couple marines apart, wounding several others. The jungle was now filled with screaming –maybe underscored by Bishop's laugher.

"Hold!" The sergeant ordered.

The British seemed to be in conflict. The captain made his way forward. "I didn't order this advance to halt?"

"No sir. I did."

"You?"

"Yes sir, they're tearing us apart and we can't even see them. They've got damn savages in their ranks, fighting like heathen rebels."

The captain was rattled, "I cannot allow a few savages and pirates to halt this advance."

"Sir, they own the wilderness and have undoubtedly fortified the fort. We already have nineteen casualties. If we press up this hill, we could have a hundred more by morning."

--Psychology can work against you –or for you, in battle.

The captain turned his pistol on his sergeant. "I'll not hear it. I have a reputation! Take this hill right now. That is-an-order!"

The Sergeant appeared surprised and angry about looking down the barrel of a gun but, he reluctantly brought himself to obey this order....

Again, the marines pressed towards the fort. Each step meant possible hazard or death.

Karr was low, as the marines approached –and began to pass--his position, he raised his pistols in the darkness and suddenly fired a round to the right –hitting a man-- and a shot to the left, killing another and then he dropped for cover. In a panic, the marines turned and started firing on each other –unaware of what they were shooting at. After a few minutes of chaos, the sergeant ordered his men to stop. "Hold now!" He shouted, "You're killing each other!" He looked around at all the wounded, "Bloody pirates have no damn civility. Damn barbarians!" He called a pause to the advance.

From my position on the wall, I could see the graves and our men in position below and the occasional flash in the jungle. Some panicked shooting seemed to continue, although it gradually began to fade away.

Rockets were still lighting up the island in the distance with flashes of red and white, like fireworks and as I watched this, I could not help but wonder…if this would be the last beautiful sight I would see. My last night on earth? Did I, a simple school teacher, travel around the globe only to die in an old, haunted fort in The Caribbean? It would seem so.

Therrinfall and Tiger were close by. Tiger sharpening his knife on a stone. Therrinfall in quiet thought, looking up at the stars. Shaddam was praying. He appeared calm and at peace.

"How is it you are so relaxed with the British outside?"

"All is as Allah wills it." He smiled.

Tiger stopped sharpening his weapon for a moment, as he heard this, then went back to it.

"I wish I had your confidence." I confessed.

"All is written."

"Is it?" I had to ask. Was all this the divine plan?

--What were the people of Bristol doing tonight? Walking the streets? Was life going on as it always had? I looked over the lad who traveled with us, the orphan. Was this what God had planned for him? Parents killed, in the presence of privateers defending a fortress --I had no answers.

"Here they come again." Therrinfall whispered and we all got set. "When they come at us, fire and then move, then fire again. Keep them confused."

"Right."

"Where the hell is Teague?"

"Maybe he was killed."

"Ha. Impossible." Therrinfall snapped. "Can't kill the Devil."

We saw their shadows in the moonlight close in and we fired, moved, reloaded, sometimes on the run, reset and fired again –bleeding them every step of the way. But the shot was running out. There were maybe twelve rounds left between us....

Back at the officer's informal command post, more torches were lit and without the courage to move forward himself, the captain waited, almost with a sense of excitement for news that we had been killed. No matter how many lives it would take, the final result was all he wanted and as this officer looked to the fort, Teague suddenly emerged from the shadows behind him. He quietly killed a picket guard by putting his hand over his mouth and using his blade to open up his throat. Then, he moved up, covered the mouth of the valet, and gashed him.

"What is the hold up?" The captain couldn't contain his frustration, "Incompetent Sergeant, damn ignorant---'

"You're right." Teague surprised him and lowered his gun.

The officer suddenly turned around, startled. The two junior officers with him were unsure of how to react. If they moved, they were sure to be killed.

"--It is damn ignorant." Teague finished his sentence for him.

The commander stuttered to find his words as Teague got the attention of the other two men with him. "You men, there, listen to what I say...carefully." A tense pause gripped the situation, with the occasional gunshot in the distance. "I'm going to kill this officer here, at which time, you'll pause your advance and return to your command back in town – alive."

The captain tried to talk through his fear, "Don't be-be rid-rid-iculous-"

Teague ignored him and continued to talk to the other two officers. "He's dead either way. You can still leave the field in peace. Stay...and I'll kill all of you. Your choice!"

There was a tense pause, then one of them suddenly straightened up and said, "Very good sir." And with that, a deal appeared to be struck.

"WHAT?" The captain shouted as his exec started to call ahead for the marines in the field to retire –and then he turned back to Teague as his blade cut right through him –between the ribs--killing him.

At the fort, from our graves and fortifications, we watched the British, as they pulled up their weapons, picked up their wounded and began to leave the area. Sampson-Rift looked down at the last ball of shot in his hand. One single round. Not a moment too soon.

A few moments later, Teague emerged from the darkness at the fort. "We're all right for now."

We were puzzled about what happened. "What did you do?" I asked as another flare lit up the sky.

He looked at me then started to clean his weapons, "I politely asked them to leave, and they agreed."

Something told me that wasn't the whole story but who was I to question what I was told.

XXVII

A KIND ACT

A dawn, just as the darkness became light, The Venger appeared, coming up the coast.

Damaged and tired, we rowed back to the ship and as we arrived alongside, Bishop said, "Give the baby to Toombs."

"Why?"

"The men will respect this more if it's in the arms of someone tough."

So, I handed her off for the climb up. Back on the ship, different combat parties climbed over the rail, exhausted and damaged –from fighting all over the island. The Venger had been picking up combatants and survivors down the entire coast throughout the night. I was among the last to climb out of the long boat, up the rope net, back aboard –almost the last, once I made it onboard with a hand from Dakar, the deck crowd parted as the young boy climbed onboard behind me….

There was silence. Some might suggest stunned silence.

"What's this?" Harrow asked.

"His family was killed, on the Crown Highway. I tried to turn him away. but--"

"So, you brought him here?"

"Aye" I replied in a tone that might suggest an apology. "As I said, I tried to wave him off, but he was…rather determined."

"The damn boy looks eight years old –and a baby? This isn't a place for children."

"I know but…I think one of the slaves that was bayonetted on the road was his father and I-I couldn't bring myself to leave him in the jungle….to the British." Which meant death or sold into slavery. Needless to say, if I had a hand in either one, it would haunt me.

Harrow's eyes softened. "Blythe...."

"Sir."

"Get this baby below to Doctor Johannis. He'll care for it until we can find a suitable solution to this dilemma. Maybe the nuns on Saint Marcos can take her...."

"Aye, sir." Blythe took the baby and worked his way through our ranks and started below deck...

He then looked to the boy and called for Mister Arson.

"Aye, Mister Harrow?"

Then Harrow said, "Teach this man the trade if you please."

And Arson made the next move and pushed a bucket into the boy's chest almost knocking him over but, he regained his footing and grabbed hold of the bucket and looked up to the deck officer. "Every man works, and every man gets an equal share onboard The Venger." he said, "What's your name?"

The boy couldn't answer or –wouldn't answer.

"He hasn't said a word since we ran from the British."

"Defiant hey," Arson said, "Very well, that is what we'll call you...Mister Defiant --until you tell us to change it." Arson then, motioned to the deck, "Start with the decks and when you've mastered it, we'll teach you something else."

I smiled remembering where I had made my start.

"Alright, back to work you lot!" Harrow commanded and the crew started to move back to their stations.

I caught up to Harrow, "Sir, I'm sorry I brought the young man aboard."

"No matter," he dismissed it. "You did what you thought was right – there's still an element of humanitarianism in our trade."

"What will happen to him?"

"He's too young to fight! He'll learn the ship, then we'll turn him over to Hobby I suppose, for galley work. Until we can put him ashore somewhere."

I moved to apologize again, for I felt that I brought additional burden on to the men, "I---"

"Stow it!" Harrow said and he took a few steps down the deck, leaving me at the rail, then Harrow turned. "Don't be hard on yourself Reed," he said, "Many of us would have done the same thing!" He then smiled, "We're not all heartless criminals."

The baby was brought below deck, past the cannon teams as they worked, down to the infirmary which was loaded with rescued wounded from the island. Dax, Fury, Jagger –Kannon who was complaining through the stick in his mouth, as Jopo used his pliers to pull the lead bullet out of his forearm-- and Newcastle, who sat in the corner, next to the infirmary window, exhausted, bandage around his head. Newcastle took to his feet – though he displayed some pain and discomfort—and moved to dismiss himself.

"Where the hell do you think you're goin'?" Johannis asked.

"To the deck, where I'm needed."

"No, you don't. Your wounds, require further inspection."

"I'm fit and ready for action."

"I command the hospital, Newcastle." Johannis said with a strict tone.

"Yes, you do doctor." Newcastle straightened up. "Have I your permission to return to my duties?"

Johannis peered at him for a long moment, then said, "If your wounds start to flush, be sure to report back here immediately."

At sunset, we came across the smoking, crippled remains of The Black Eagle…

"Vincenze." Harrow looked to Essex.

The Eagle, famous in the North Atlantic and the terror of the Eastern seaboard and home –as we all knew, to one Captain Vincenze.

The fire was out, but the decks still smoldered, billowing smoke into the sky. A deck officer, covered in ash, held up his hand and signaled us to come along side.

"What happened?" Harrow shouted across the water to their rail.

"The British happened." The officer replied.

Essex looked to Harrow, to assess what his thoughts might be, then back across the water. "Where's the Captain?" Essex asked.

He gave the hand signal for…wounded. "In the sickbay."

"How many hands do you have?"

"One hundred and seventy-one, remain. Including twenty-one walking wounded."

"We're gonna bring you aboard." Essex said and the officer nodded, hopped back from the rail, and started getting his men moving….

Essex looked to Johannis as he made it to the top deck as he always did when we encountered another ship, in case his services were required and indeed they were in this case. "Doctor, if you please."

Johannis gave a wave and asked us to pass the word to our carpenters for assistance.

"Rajiv." Essex stopped our top gunner, "Unload all their cannon."

"But sir, we already have a full complement of cannon. None are damaged."

"Take their guns apart for now and lower them in the hold."

Rajiv was confused as to the why but didn't question it, "Yes sir."

"And Mister Rajiv, all of the cannon and every round."

Rajiv nodded and started barking commands to the Bengals to get aboard The Warlock and start the work…

"Rations will be tight." Harrow reported, "The additional cannon will slow us down."

"I know it will." Essex said, "We'll argue about it later, for now, just get these men onboard."

We used planks to march the men across to our decks, some staggering, wounded and with assistance. One, burned and loaded with shrapnel was Vincenze and he happened to take to our deck with some assistance from Mister Newcastle.

"Newcastle."

Newcastle looked him over.

"I suppose, you're happy to see me, loaded with death and metal. The work, in my killing is all but done for ya."

Newcastle looked at his wounds, "I take no joy in seeing a man on the edge of death. Especially one who, despite a character flaw or two, values the concept of freedom. You take some time to heal up properly, then we'll see about killin' each other."

Vincenze gave a slight smile, followed by a nod, "Aye, I'll do that and...thanks Newcastle."

The survivors continued to move aboard as we swung above them, overhead into their rigging and dropped to the panels. We started working our way below deck where our 'gun tigers' started to dismantle the cannon and heave them out of place. We opened up their armory –and although this resembled a sacking, there seemed to be some reverence about this as we took everything of use.

Our men jumped on the ropes, and we pulled the cargo nets loaded with cannon and cannon parts over the water, across to our deck and we lowered them several decks below into our hold where our crew unloaded them.

Back on our quarter deck our officers were in mid-discussion, "We've got fifty-five men still unaccounted for, either dead or fighting somewhere on Jamaica" Lincoln reported "and the infirmary's loaded."

"Who else made it off the island?" Harrow asked as Essex moved to the quarter deck rail to look out over the ocean.

"Maybe, The Exeter. The Wraith and The Charlemange were sunk in the bay." Duncan-Howe said, standing in front of a line of the Venger's rogue samurai as he exhaled some tobacco smoke.

Toombs used some hand signals to say, 'The Shadow was seen off Smuggler's Cove before the action started.'

"Do we know their heading?" Jupiter asked.

Toombs shook his head no.

The surviving first officer of The Eagle reported to Essex and introduced himself, "Hastings, sir."

"Well, Hastings, you're the captain of this lot now." Essex said, "Until Vincenze is back on his feet."

He was exhausted but managed a response, "Aye sir."

"Care to tell us what happened?"

"We got off the island well, some of us did anyway and we ran into a squadron off the point and with a skeleton crew onboard well…they thrashed us. It was all over very quickly, sad to say."

"The point?" Essex asked.

"A blockade sir."

"The damn Brits are going to move west and destroy everything in their path." Harrow realized.

Essex nodded as if he could appreciate the situation, then looked to Hastings. "Get your men below, we'll get them something to eat until we can figure out our next move."

IN THE GALLEY…

Hobby loaded a coffee bucket and heaved it to the wooden countertop. "For Johannis," he said.

"I'll take it." I said and I put the bread I was eating down on my plate. Just as I was prepared to move, I stopped. "Hobby," I asked, "Do you have any rum cake by any chance?"

He looked at me as he worked his hand clean in his apron.

"I thought, for the baby."

"Aye. I do." He said and Rorry slid a plate of it across to me to pick up.

"Thank you."

I made it down the deck to the infirmary, knocked –as one always did-- even though there was no door, just an open entryway and I was given permission to enter.

Johannis was cleaning his instruments.

"Coffee, sirs."

"Ah, thank you Reed, put it there will you." He motioned to his small table.

I put the coffee down and handed him the plate. "For the baby."

"Always the humanitarian." He smiled.

"I thought she could use it."

"Teague brought something earlier but no matter, we'll put it to good use."

"Teague?" I was surprised.

"Aye." Johannis said. "He brought food down, he had mashed up, all soft like so the baby could eat it." he went back to cleaning his tools, "As if we doctors didn't know how to care for a newborn."

Jopo chuckled.

As I made my exit, I looked at the baby in the hammock by the door. She appeared wide-eyed and curious –and of course, innocent of all this.

Two days later, I looked up from the galley and heard the commands echo across the top deck. We had arrived at our destination. I looked to Mister Defiant, who was working the stoves with Rorry. "This is your last chance, Defiant. Stay, or go?" He looked to Rorry. The galley crew froze in place and awaited his answer.

"You should go lad." Hobby finally said in a compassionate tone. "This is no place for a boy to grow up."

He looked out the window to the island on our port side and looked back to me. "I- I's" he said adding a 's' as if to make I plural. "I's like to stay aboard…sir."

"You could be killed here boy." Hobby warned. "The business on this ship is none too pleasant."

The young man swallowed back his nerves, looked to Hobby then back to me. I lowered my coffee mug…. "Once you make the decision son, you must own it."

He seemed to give it an additional split second of thought then repeated his answer. "I want to stay."

Hobby nodded, Rorry smiled and continued to help him with his work, and I took to the top deck.

I stepped out into the wind with a hand-out of the hatch from Jagger. "The boy?" he asked.

I shook my head, "He doesn't want to go." I replied. "Believe it or not, I think he likes us."

"Aye, that is hard to believe."

"It's his decision" Harrow barked cutting through the chatter, taking charge of the moment as he so often did, "--And he's made it. Now, onto the business at hand." He threw me a bag of coins "The Captain pulled this from the general treasury. Take it with you to help with the cost."

I looked ashore, on the edge of the island, under the palm trees, was the mission that housed the Protestant missionaries Saint Lo. A refuge.

Harrow fixed his eyes on the simple buildings. "Be quick about it," he said.

As we moved to the rail, Johannis brought the baby forward wrapped in heavy canvas. He handed her off to me and joined us as our landing party began the climb over the side. I looked at Mister Teague and summoned my courage to speak. "Sir...wouldn't you like to be the one to deliver her to the mission?" I lifted the bundle slightly.

Teague's dark eyes looked at her for a moment then shifted from her to me. "No" he finally said, wanting no attachment. "Let someone with merit deliver her. Besides...." He said, "If I step foot on holy ground, I may get struck by lightning."

"Ain't that the truth of it!" Johannis said under his breath nearby...

I nodded, not wanting to challenge his decision and I began to climb down to the long boat where Jupiter helped me take a bench and we rowed away from the ship. At the oars, Whitney, Fury, Karr, Rift, Mako and Lo quietly pulled....

On the way over, Lo-Tan used his bamboo hat to shield her from the sun and he hummed something, some old Buddhist prayer type song that made the rowing easier...

We got to the shoreline and the missionaries came out to meet us. At first, they were unaware of our mission and appeared cautious and concerned. I imagined they hid their provisions and gold candle sticks when they sighted our ship --and they became relieved when they realized that we came there in peace and our weapons would remain housed.

"This is holy ground ya heathens," an old monk said, "And I won't have the Lord's house tainted by bloodshed or the presence of disrespectful killers like yourselves."

"Rest easy Father." I said as I raised my hand, "We're men of The Venger. We come in peace and on an errand of some merit." and with that, they seemed somewhat relieved.

"Very well, how can I be of service?"

Johannis stepped forward, bundle in his arms….

I motioned to it, "We rescued this baby from the fighting on Jamaica."

"Fighting inspired by you and your kind no doubt."

"Actually, it was the crown that burned it to the ground. It seems they value their slave trade more than civilian life."

His eyes drifted to the ground as if to confess that he had spoken too soon and with assumptions that a man removed from a situation should not make.

"Will you take this child in, and protect it?" I asked and as I did, the canvass was pulled back on the second jolly boat revealing provisions, for we had intended to pay our way with this request.

He breathed in, "Of course." One of his monks moved forward to take possession of the young child. "Does it have a name?"

I paused to think. "Her name is…" --what name was appropriate? "Her name is, Teague-Ann."

Our landing party stopped their motions for a moment and became still. Whitney smiled….

"Very well."

"If our ship is in the area, as long as we are able, we will deliver supplies here on occasion, for your effort and Father, if there is any mistreatment, then---"

"--Have no fear, we will care for young Teague-Ann here. She will be safe and not because of the supplies you give us but because…it is our way."

I nodded and accepted this, "Thank you." I left him the coins and we started to leave and as we parted, he stopped with one more sentence to say…

"I shall pray for you, my son."

Without thinking, as a matter of enforced habit, I raised my open hand up, almost as the Hurons would and I put it over my heart like the Moors would --and with that move, that now seemed so natural, I realized that I had become a product of several different worlds.

Johannis leaned up from behind me, "Teague-Ann?"

"It seemed fitting." I said with confidence….

"Aye," He agreed as he rocked back into his place. "It does that."

And again, there was balance to my soul. Some good had now overtaken the recent bad like a weight lifted off my heart and I could breathe again and smile –slightly.

We worked the oars and rowed back towards the ship…

"Ya know Reed," Fury suddenly broke the silence as I looked at him, still smiling, "All those years I was grave robbin', I could do it with a clear conscious." He suddenly looked vexed, "Damn-it-all if you have me thinking about some of my life's decisions."

I quietly laughed and again I realized that this kind of thing may have been my mission all along.

We climbed up towards the deck, with a hand up from Jupiter, "Why are you smiling?" He asked as he pulled me over the rail back aboard.

"The man revels in a kind act." Duncan packed his pipe close by, as he read the situation and with that, Jupiter looked back to me and nodded his approval.

Arson and other deck officers pushed past, "Look alive and get to your stations." He commanded, "Move! This isn't a Christian charity," he stopped and looked at me, "Except when Reed's aboard apparently." then he continued down the deck barking commands….

XXVIII

THE PHANTOM FROM THE GRAVE

Suddenly, there was a call off the port bow. "Ready for action! All stations!" Echoed through the decks. On the horizon was the shadow of a ship. It was as if it had just suddenly appeared there in the fog. Some of our crew thought it might have been the Flying Dutchman --a ghost ship-- rumored to haunt these parts.

Most of the ships we had run into in the past days were destroyed by the British fleet, left to rock hull-up in the water or beached smoking wrecks with their crews either dead or hauled off to a prison barge someplace but, this ship appeared intact....

Without fear, our Captain ordered us to close in...

The atmosphere became still as we moved closer to our target. "Should we fire a warning across her bow Captain?" Asked Merritt, from the helm, as if he was ready to shout the command down the hatch to the gun crews....

Essex looked up at our black flag blowing in the wind, then back to the target. "No. Hold course and wait for the word..."

Merritt nodded. Thorn maintained a tight grip on the wheel. Other men –somewhat curious—made their way to the rail to see this specter slowly rocking towards us and murmurs of 'The Dutchman' could be heard in the ranks.

Rajiv looked up from the hatch. His crews ready for havoc.

Then, when we were about two leagues out, the specter shot up a red flare. The Captain's eyes followed it as it arched in the sky and he smiled, "It's the Phantom!

Daws...answer them." He did just that and launched a green flare from the deck. The signal for parley and conversation.

The command went through the ranks to stand easy, and we relaxed on the weapons....

The Punisher --also known as The Phantom-- was a fully loaded frigate, built on the French coast but, since then, it had been outfitted with Spanish cannon captured in a raid on Cadiz....

We pulled alongside and positioned ourselves almost rail to rail with this 'Phantom', we dropped anchor and their boarding party –scarred, burned, and heavily armed-- crossed the plank to reach our deck as our Captain stood ready to talk.

Captain Faulkner, the man in command of this ship was the last to touch down on our planks. "Well, The Venger! The terror of the high seas!"

Essex smiled and gave a nod. "Still trying to escape the Devil?"

"The Devil will get us all in the end I'm afraid."

"Indeed, he will." And with that they gripped each other's forearm in a handshake.

I had seen him before for a quick moment in Port Royal, but this was the first time I got a close look at him. I noticed that Faulkner had scars on both wrists –from iron shackles-- and he appeared to have a lot of stitch work done down from his temple, his neck and on his forearms. The man had seen quite a bit of action. I was surprised by both his presence and attitude.

Perhaps it was his Yankee accent --I would be told later that he was from Virginia by way of Albany and wanted by the colonial government there, because of his work as a 'highwayman' with a certain devotion to robbing local politicians –this, of course, before he took to the high seas.

Faulkner's Quarter Master –De Gaff—who took the deck right behind him was a former military engineer who kept his mind occupied by quietly counting things, including men and weapons that surrounded him. Even if one tried to engage him in conversation, you could still see his mind working, numbers, facts and figures. The rest of his men that came aboard, seemed our sort --brass, guns, and blades. Scars, strength, an edge for killing and the presence of possible evil.

Essex looked over his crew –many of which were hardened criminals from different criminal colonies –and it was clear they had been in a fight. "What happened?"

"The British hammed us, caught between the frigate Reliant and the fort guns, right at the thirty-three. They sank Oberon and traded cannon rounds with us for six hours. Damn savages."

Essex looked to the Phantom then back to Faulkner "Should we send over our physicians?"

"No, our carpenters did a beautiful job in saving what they could but, I could use a drink."

A few minutes later, on the quarter deck, as the sun began to rise, Faulkner lowered a brandy bottle and turned away from the sea to see Essex and a few of our officers taking a relaxed position around the map table for a conversation. "What happened out there?"

Faulkner's eyes shifted from officer to officer, "I see you've been in a fight –but the real news hasn't reached you yet."

"All I know is that all hell's breaking loose and that Royal got smashed."

"Right." He said, "The whole Caribbean is at war." He exhaled, "Bloody inferno it is."

"Who is it now? And what do they want?" Harrow asked, well aware that war was the common stock and trade of politicians.

"It's everyone." Faulkner said in a direct manner. "The English are blasting their way from island to island. Every privateer on the Spanish Main is under threat of extermination --we took to the coast of Brazil, ran into a squadron heading to the horn, fought it out and sailed back here."

"What brought this on?" Harrow asked.

"You!" Faulkner said.

Harrow looked confused and was trying to make sense of what he just heard...

"You killed the Governor of New Haven."

"That's what this is about?" Harrow seemed almost surprised.

"Now wait just a moment, "Essex interrupted, "That Governor was unjust –and our men were killed on a peace keeping mission to New Haven."

"—Including our vicar." Harrow barked.

"Right." Essex added with a touch of anger." They crucified one of our Moors, exterminated the rest making their last resting place a mass grave."

"Those that survived were tortured. We found them at the hands of sadists, in a Spanish dungeon repurposed to keep the population at bay!"

"We did no wrong that day." Essex stated in defiance. "And I stand by Harrow and the men."

"Be that as it may, they are now –as we speak—using that crime to redefine all their imperial boundaries."

"Bastards!"

"Bastards aye--" Faulkner agreed, "You'll get no argument from me on that point. But ah, killing the entire garrison Essex? All the state officials...they say that some of them were found in cages, dropped in the tide. The ironwork was stamped the mark of The Venger."

"Damn right it was!"

Essex looked to Harrow. They could not deny their handy work –not that that was even a consideration.

"Every respectable citizen in the islands and on the continent is terrified of you –the crown has to take action. Even the Governor's valet had a tomahawk mark on his skull." Faulkner's eyes darted over to Nighthorse who stood, arms crossed at the wheel. When he was called out for this action, he actually pointed to Bons as if to say, 'he did it' and Bons shrugged it off.

"As I said, I stand by the actions of my crew –no peace keeping mission should ever be met with torture and death, regardless of politics."

Faulkner nodded –he had to agree with this code of ethics. Though never the architect of any peace keeping effort of his own, he knew no man should be tortured under a white flag. "They've been rollin' over on privateers for more than twelve months now. Killing 'em where they can. New Haven, I sense is just an excuse."

"Maybe we take a letter of marque from Spain." Harrow suggested, "Drift in with the Spanish fleet a while, until things settle down."

"I doubt you'd get one now." Faulkner said and as he continued, he put his words together carefully as to not offend any of us, "There are those who say you're running weapons to Aztec revolutionaries in New Spain -- and Panama? Well…Panama has captured the imagination of the world." He smiled, "I've heard of it in every port, and I admit, I swelled with pride in the knowledge of knowing –first-hand—the men who made such a daring raid. The Spanish didn't appreciate it though! And letters of marque are revoked at moment's notice in any event. It would hardly do you any good. Once one side makes peace with the other, all the privateers get sold out as part of the treaty and reprimand."

"That's true." Essex said, "We raided a ship off New Holland and found a box with letters stating that very fact. They employ and then kill when it suits them."

"More good news --you should also know that the Portuguese have put a price on your head."

"What?" Harrow was angry, "I thought you said good news."

"That was my attempt of sarcasm, feeble I know but, with all this talk of war I wanted to try to lighten the mood."

"How much?"

"Ten thousand escudos."

"Ten thousan-" Essex asked, "Is that all?" Essex looked disappointed in the amount. "I highwayman is worth more than ten thousand escudos."

"I know" Faulkner chuckled.

"Cheap bastards!" They both suddenly said together.

"That confirms the reasoning behind the criminal action to blow out our hull." Harrow said.

"What?" Faulkner asked.

"Some bastard terrorists tried to sabotage us off South America, just before The Horn."

"Still, I value my head at a lot more than ten thousand escudos." Harrow continued.

"Well, I'm not sure what the Dutch are offering but I think if you add the ransom from every government you've offended, it ought to resemble a respectable amount." Faulkner added, "If that makes you feel better."

The Porto Norvo sacking weakened the commerce of the Portuguese Empire and as Faulkner stated, all of our crew was now wanted in Lisbon where declarations for our arrest were stamped with the word 'priority.' And although this raid was celebrated in the dark corners of every seaside tavern, there were those who –despite their admiration and the daring aspects of this attack—could not understand our move to liberate the slaves instead of taking them to sell in the marketplace --for this was the common practice with many other privateers.

--But not us. Too many of us were slaves of some sort –or—owed a debt to a former slave in our ranks and as reported, we could never profit on the ownership of another human being.

"Damn-it-all" Essex said as if ready to spit. "The real villain here is The Royal African Company slavers. They own every politician in parliament. We've been destroying their business." He then looked to Faulkner, "Tell me everything you know about this situation…."

"Well, before we fled—ah—that is, left in a hurry, the British were moving from island to island starting with Queen Lota Island to New London, they blasted Port Royal—"

"Yeah, we know about that."

"Then you know that they're moving towards Pitchtag, Clivetown, and the islands west of Satan's Square---"

Harrow looked to Essex with growing concern.

"—They're rounding up every ex-slave and native they can sell, killing every privateer and burning every base we've ever used, to the ground."

"Any resistance?"

"Some from the Spanish –but I'm sure England will work out a compromise --if they haven't already."

"What about the privateers?"

"Most have fled –a few –like Stannis, Harker, Wilson-Fixx and The Black Death stayed in the theater to fight it out --Rafer-Davies tried to stop them in the Atlantic and been blastin' them from island to island."

"We need to go back and put a stop to that!" Harrow said.

The Captain needed to think it over.

"If our actions caused this, we have to put it right."

There was a sudden warning from the lookout that brought our conversation to a close. We all looked up and Bolt pointed ahead off the bow. "Warship off the bow!"

The men jumped to their combat stations as Essex raised his spyglass. Through it, he could see the Union Jack and squadron flags flying. "British. They must have followed us from Royal." But just before he could order us into firing position a series of flares went up.

Faulkner moved his shoulder. "They want a conversation."

"Daws answer them." He lowered his spyglass. "Let's hear what they have to say."

PEACE MEETING.

This was strange sight, backed up against the morning skyline, the British stood in a picket line at the top of the beach of this small sand bar –battle and regimental flags blowing in the wind. The infamous Lord Roberts sat under a quickly erected canvas tent, without walls, before them. A small staff of officers, valets –and R.A.C. officers-- accompanied him and he had tea with all the trimmings waiting....

On the corner of this tent, a corporal held a staff fixed with a white flag that reflected the sun...

As we rowed towards the sands, Obal used his spyglass to size up the situation. He checked the battle flags for unit identification then scanned the troops. "Sixty-second Royal Marine detachment, Captain, company strength at least."

Essex stepped out of the boat and into the tide.

Roberts waited in his chair, teacup in hand and watched Essex walk through the tide towards him,

"And there he is...the devil himself!" Karr said in a low tone as he spotted Roberts, hands not too far from his guns.

Essex marched up, slowly with only Jupiter at his side. The rest of the shore party waited at the water's edge where we slowly fanned out into a line that matched their own at the top of the beach, the tide rolling over our boots with the morning sun at our shoulders and our hands on –or very close to our weapons. Nighthorse, Khan, Mazatal, Sanjuro, Mako, Calixto, Jack-Karr, Watson, Lynch, Barak, Laban, Sunderland, Therrinfall, Tiberius and his wrecking ball-- and myself, waiting for the moment when all hell would break loose.

The tension was stifling. The heat, coming off the sands in waves, blurred the Governor's vision he could not make the image of the Captain out until it became clear just a few meters away at the edge of the tent...

"Welcome Captain Essex. May I offer you some tea or, something stronger perhaps?"

"No...thank you."

The Captain appeared cautious, and this was read by Roberts, "You may stand easy Captain, I bring you good news..."

"Really?" Essex asked with a suspicious tone, "Why do I find that hard to believe?"

Roberts smiled and continued in the same friendly tone, "Please sit." He motioned to a waiting chair and Essex took his place equal and opposite this infamous man, "I represent Lord Drax and The Earl of Carfax in this matter who, I'm sure you're aware have authority in New World matters and I'm here to offer you a pardon on behalf of the crown."

"A pardon?"

"Yes...a pardon. Though it goes against my better judgement..."

"Does it now?" The tone which was struck by these words was one of a sinister nature, making the situation seem to be teetering on possible violence.

Roberts suddenly looked like a man agitated by the need to offer an explanation but, he did so, "Your crimes are well known Captain. Your mutiny and the disgrace of Lord Hall, your commanding officer, your raid on British commerce throughout the Empire and not least of all, your massacre of the New Haven Township and it's Governor."

"Massacre, was it? I seem to remember crown sanctioned genocide on the island!"

"Now Captain—"

"--Former Spanish subjects tortured, famine....and a peacekeeping mission of our own accord met with murder and imprisonment and torture!"

"I cannot speak to the details or policies of the Magistrate based there but, I can say, that it was hardly cause for you to storm ashore and kill everyone."

"Ah but we didn't kill everyone."

Lord Roberts corrected himself, "Everyone-of-note" he said with disdain. "As I see it, you have caused great grief sir not to mention financial ruin to the African Trading Company," He motioned to the R.A.C. officers standing with obvious disdain nearby, "And the East Indian Trading Company both of which carry considerable weight with parliament back home…"

"Soooo, that's it, is it? An errand for your special interests? They crack the whip, and you jump."

"Not entirely." Roberts remained calm. "But you would be wise to hear our terms."

"Very well. Let's have it."

"As you no doubt know, your offer for a letter of marque from the Spanish was revoked, thanks to your work on Panama, even still, the Spanish King wants you and others like you to be brought to justice as part of the peace process— "

"Meaning?" Essex knew what it meant but he wanted to hear this politician explain it.

"Meaning, in an effort to avoid a new war, you and all the so-called privateers are to be...eradicated or, turned over to his Majesty the King of Spain to stand trial for your crimes --and you, dear Captain, are a top name on the butcher's list..."

Essex listened....

"The man who sacked Panama, raided or destroyed six other Spanish ships and ran weapons to Aztec rebels is a very wanted man indeed." Roberts put his teacup down and a valet re-filled it, "Though it is also said that you helped the Jesuit order in the town and that they –the brotherhood of God-- have made a statement on your behalf...."

"Have they now?"

"They have but...as a protestant, I can say, a statement by Catholics won't save you!"

Essex smiled "Of course not. Why have understanding when another religious based civil war..." He peered at the R.A.C. officers with an edge of disgust, "...could-be-so-profitable."

Roberts smiled as if surprised Essex understood the situation. "Now is not the time to speak truth to power."

"When is the time exactly?"

"You insolent bastard!" A R.A.C. officer stepped forward in anger...

Roberts stopped him and put him back in his place by raising his hand. "As you see Captain, passion behind matters like this sometimes get the better of us."

"Yes, it does."

"I can however make amends and, all you need do is --surrender."

"Surrender?"

"Um-hum." He nodded and rolled the top of his black cane in his fingers continuing to size the Captain up. "You've spent a lifetime warring on the high seas, one must grow tired of a life on the run. Don't you think it time to put that all a side?"

Essex looked up for a moment and his eyes did in fact appear tired and seemed to signal that he agreed. He had been at war and on the run a long time now.

"It's time to shed your responsibility to all these men around you, heathen and otherwise. No need for you to continue to be their savior. Time to lay that burden down. All one needs to do is say 'enough' and…. surrender." Roberts added.

"And if I do. What then?"

"For you--should you accept this offer and surrender—you will take a return trip to England and once there, you'll present yourself for a series of engagements where newspapers and the British press will be allowed to write your exploits in graphic detail –and of your capture as a deterrent for other pirates and sailors who may have –shall we say—similar thoughts and ideas."

"And then?"

"And then you will finish your tour with the British navy that you so rudely disrespected and your debt will then be paid in full…"

"And my crew?"

"Ah, that is another matter. Your ship will once again become the property of the Royal Navy –to be surrendered immediately-"

"And the men?"

"The crown –as you know-- doesn't recognize the natives of America to be anything more than the savages they are so, your Aztec crew members are to be turned over to the Spanish –as a show of good faith-- and executed as traitors since they are the property of New Spain and have fought against their masters…

"All former slaves are to be returned to the economy. Information and the location of all outposts and townships that harbor your kind is to be reported to the authorities immediately. Any former political prisoners in your ranks are to be turned over to the law to complete sentence and face new charges for piracy. Any--"

"--Always making money off the prison system!"

"Any" Roberts continued an octave louder, "Any member of your crew who fled military service in his majesty's armed forces –with the exception of yourself-- is to be turned over to us for immediate court martial and execution. And all remaining heathens are to be turned over to us for immediate conversion from their heathen ways."

"Conversion? What's that?"

"They will convert to Christianity or be put to death. There is no place for the rogue Hindu or the rogue Muslim in the new Empire."

"How very Christian of you."

Roberts smiled again, though he cared not for these men or for the opinion of Essex on the matter. Anyone of a different religious practice was just an obstacle to this man. "I believe I have been quite charitable with these terms Captain. We will have order here and you --and the scum you represent-- have been a thorn in our side long enough. The millions of pounds you've cost British industry, combined with this notion that you and your friends are above the law and free to form some sort of democracy with savages is quite revolting and, in my opinion —unforgivable." He took a breath as if to relax "But the crown is much more gracious than I. For if I had my way, you'd spend the rest of your days toiling away in the salt mines of The Mediterranean.

On this note, the Captain took notice but remained in place...

"A new world is to emerge here. Forces loyal to his Majesty have flooded into this area with the idea that we must pacify it. We will raze pirate bases and harbors to the ground. A new world and a more civilized world will take its place. There will be no refuge for you or your type here...anymore. So," Roberts motioned to the parchment before him, "If you'd be good enough to sign your name to the document before you, these men will take you into custody and you'll be on your way... "

"Allow me, if I may, to recite this offer so that there is no misunderstanding between us."

Lord Roberts nodded as if to say- go ahead...

"My ship is to become the property of the British Navy."

"Correction. Our ship –stolen by you—is to be returned to us."

Essex nodded as if to agree "And any former naval officer will be turned over to the armed forces for execution."

"Charged for desertion and dereliction of duty –then executed,' he said as if he wanted to make the record clear. "And –incidentally--any other men under your command who may have seen fit to desert their own government to join your service will be offered the opportunity to join the Royal Navy or they will be returned to their perspective crowns for sentencing."

"And the former slaves— "

"Former slaves will go back into the economy....to be sold immediately, the profits of which will be put towards your restitution. How many do you have onboard? Please tally them up so we can make the calculations."

"Your-calculations," Essex wanted to make sure he heard him correctly, "Meaning, the value they hold to you and these criminals here?!?" He motioned to his R.A.C. audience.

"Yes, and please supply a count on any political prisoners you are harboring, the same goes for them."

"And the Moors, Hindus and Jews in the crew will be put to death."

"The Jews we can forgive, after all, Jesus…was…a carpenter." He almost smiled at this touch of wit.

"And our native contingent?"

"Must we go through it all again Captain." His temperament was becoming strained. "Yes. Your natives –savages that they are—will either be returned to the Dutch authorities in New Amsterdam, The British Colonial Government in North America, or the Spanish …. if they are native to New Spain." He stated with emphasis "And on that point, there is no negotiation. The Spanish want to make an example of your Aztec compatriots by burning them at the stake in a public square and I plan to give them that satisfaction in the name of peace."

The Captain's expression suddenly betrayed a look of disgust….

"They want to quell rebellion in that part of the world. Seems you –and others like you—have convinced the natives that they may seek a better life elsewhere without their Spanish masters…."

"They're not wrong."

"That's enough!" Roberts barked. "I've spent more time than I care to on this matter. You know the terms. Sign this document and yield to your King."

"Sir, I owe my life to these men you speak of…"

"Good God man! Do you hear yourself? You sound like one of them. We owe these pirates nothing sir. Do you hear me? Nothing."

"They were your men when you needed help to fight the Spanish years ago." Essex shouted. "They were good enough for you then."

"And now that the war is done, and times have changed! They've served their political purpose, it's time to be done with them, once and for all. We cannot ever forgive those who trespass against the crown. That ship out there," he pointed to The Venger "Is full of men, who escaped military service –their duty! They're nothing more than deserters, a rabble --and in the company of slaves? Good God man! It's unholy!"

A R.A.C. officer continued, "Think of the effect these men could have on the economy in the future, the idea that slaves can turn pirate –the whole community of these bastards will revolt. Our colonies will be lost to these savages and on another note, we will not have natives of the Americas believe that they are our equal -- never! No heathen is my equal before God and we shall put them all in their rightful place. This territory belongs to the crown and the Royal African Company, and I'll be damned sir if we'll allow these natives to corrupt it."

"Many of the men you speak of were born here sir. They were here before us— "

"It makes no difference. We are here now, and they must abide by our law. To think that these men can build their own society. My God! The very thought of men sharing a table with these Africans, natives, or heathens, I doubt their souls can ever be recovered! We shall see who is right --and under God, I swear, we will enforce the rightful law of the land.

Be it known, Essex, the slave crop and the slave economy will once again be a source of pride for all of us to share in. Better days are coming."

The Captain remained still; eyes fixed on Lord Roberts. He remained that way for a long moment, until Lord Roberts started to become nervous, a feeling he tried to mask with agitation but the R.A.C. officer continued, "Do you believe this man?" He looked to those around him, "This man sits here in silence. In the face of his Majesty's gracious offer and this, this common criminal has the nerve to just sit there and think he is better than us."

"On the contrary." Essex slowly said, as his eyes shifted up to the R.A.C. officer. "I have your answer!"

A sudden feeling of impending doom came over Roberts as the Captain slowly stood up,

"This is my answer, right here!" He suddenly pulled a pistol –and took aim at the R.A.C. officer's face as the British jumped for their weapons and we reached for ours and picked out targets.

"No!" Roberts ordered his men to hold hoping the situation would not erupt in total violence. "This isn't the time or place for a fight." – And he hadn't the men, or ship's guns, for it in any event.

Essex remained in place, a battery of muskets aimed at him from every direction but, he remained there, holding his gun in place an inch from the R.A.C. officer's eye, almost as if to add more terror to the situation.

--Was this the moment that would cost him his life? We waited; weapons ready to open up.

Roberts then spoke in a slow and even tone. "Perhaps the Captain needs time to think about it?" He paused for a split second, "Settle any outstanding business you may have, then, sail The Venger into Port Royal for a public display of surrender in ten days' time, sign this surrender document there and we'll consider the matter settled."

Essex lowered the gun an inch or two and the R.A.C. officer suddenly spit, "Sign it now ya pig!"

And with that, Essex pulled the trigger and fired at point blank range –
BAM--hitting the R.A.C. officer in the neck. He fell back in the sand,
clutching his throat and gasping for help---

---It would take several moments for him to die.

Again, the marines went for their weapons.

"HOLD!" Roberts shook his head and in calm fashion stood up,
unconcerned with the R.A.C. officer bleeding to death on the sand next to
him. His men based on his command held their weapons in check as he
turned back to Essex and said through his teeth. "Let it be said that it was
the infamous Captain Essex who violated the rules of war here today and
violated the white flag. Not the Crown!

Essex just stood there as the gun smoke cleared.

"I'll expect your real answer in ten days. It's time for you to save what
you can of yourself and your crew for if you do not, we'll run you down,
kill every member of your crew and then eradicate every island in the
Caribbean."

Essex walked back towards us –smoking pistol in hand-- as we slowly
lowered our weapons.

"Ten days Essex!" Roberts vocally enforced upon the Captain's exit
from the scene.

"Well?" Newcastle asked, standing in the tide...

Essex climbed aboard the long boat, "We surrender in ten days!"

"Wait, we what?" Confused, Warrick and the rest of us climbed into our
boats, grabbed the oars, and muscled our way through the tide towards The
Venger.

XXIX

STEEL, GUNPOWDER…
AND A GOOD SUPPLY OF BODY BAGS.

DAWN, TEN DAYS LATER…

Port Royal was still a smoking wreck and certain collaborators had been put to the noose and lynched in the town square where their bodies remained, blowing in the wind, as an exhibit to the new authority. A reminder to what happens to those who had an independent idea or two against the Imperialists…

The residents had, despite their pain, started to rebuild their lives and begun to reconstruct what they could, using damaged parts mostly.

At dawn on that Sunday, a watchman called out from the fort tower and pointed to the west as Lord Roberts emerged from his command tent on the beach and stepped out to see The Venger on the horizon, with a massive white flag flying…

"They surrender sir." His executive officer reported with a touch of excitement in his voice.

"At last." Roberts smiled, almost eager with anticipation and pride that Essex had taken him up on his offer and had arrived in Port Royal to give himself up. "You see Jenkins, the rebel grows tried of rebellion and all one need do is offer him a way out…"

This was indeed his moment of triumph, one that might even get Roberts elected to Parliament.

The residents of the island, Uralan among them, stopped their salvage work to watch The Venger sail in, stunned by its arrival and --the white flag!

Many of them appeared sad to see this, for this was much more than a surrender. This was the end of an era. The end of a concept. The end of freedom and they felt that their freedom was being surrendered with it – and-- to add insult to injury, the ship was about to surrender to the very imperial criminals who had leveled their homes...

"Call out the guards, have your blacksmiths ready with shackles." Roberts ordered as the ship seemed to slow down on its arrival. "Send a message to Karakas, the slave trader and our Spanish emissary ---his Aztec rebels are here for their punishment."

"Sir." An aid dismissed himself to carry out the message.

"And prepare our executioners." Roberts stepped forward and as he did, he lowered his tone, "–Their heathens I'm sure will prefer death to losing their own way of life."

"Yes sir." A second officer dismissed himself...

Roberts took a few more steps forward, "This will be a day long remembered. We have seen the end of The Venger and the end of a rebellion."

The R.A.C. officers in the command tent behind Roberts smiled and raised their glasses to celebrate the ship's surrender. "To a bright future and a world where nothing stands in the way of a thriving slave trade." They kicked their glasses back, then stepped out of the tent and lined up with Roberts to witness this historical moment up close...

"Get an accurate scalp count," a voice shouted, "Native scalps still fetch a good price back in Albany."

One R.A.C. Officer leaned towards Roberts, "Remember our agreement, I am to take possession of all the Africans on board."

"Yes, yes Bellows, you'll be able to make your example and torture them all you like AFTER the work at hand is complete." The British regulars lined up behind them at attention and assembled to take custody of the ship and everyone on it...

"I already have the whipping post ready." He started to laugh, "I'm going to brutalize every one of those bastards into submission, until...there...is.... nothing...left," His laughter slowed down until...it eventually stopped...

--Something was wrong.

--An insecure feeling began to surface...

--Suddenly, the white flag was cut loose...

The two men looked up and watched as it blew away in the wind, "What the—"

Lord Robert's smile slowly faded, and pressure started to mount into a sinking feeling in his gut as he watched the massive skull and bones rise above the quarter deck into the sky --and all the gun port doors suddenly slammed open, and the cannon rolled out.

"My God!"

"Cover!" The British tried to scatter as The Venger opened up, deck after deck, smashing the British camp, steel exploding into their ranks. One cannon ball ripped through Robert's tent and punched through a R.A.C. officer, ripping him in half as it exploded on the other side of the canvass.

The civilians cheered --fists in the air.

Roberts just stood there --in place—his blood pressure gripped him and paralyzed him, and his anger rose from his gut to his head as explosions hit his camp, blasted the fort, and smashed the area all around him. Finally, he collected his wits and ordered his men to their action stations. "After it! No one rests until that ship is destroyed!"

--They had already started to move. No order required! The cannon at the fort started to return fire and cannon rounds hit the water next to The Venger's quarter deck. Essex looked up as one shot ripped through the main sail.

The British ships in the port fired back as The Venger passed opening up a quick pounding match and their crews started to mobilize to sail out and hunt them down...

Everywhere the British scrambled into the fight --on the beach –and on the decks of their ships, they jumped into action. Roberts, under fire, climbed on board a long boat and ordered it rowed to the decks of his frigate The Albatross as blasts hit the water around him. When he was helped over the rail, he was in full tantrum. "Run them down! MOVE! I want that ship in the locker!"

On our quarter deck, Newcastle watched with his spyglass as we left Port Royal's shipyard smoking behind us …and the British fleet was beginning to move.

The Captain stepped to his shoulder, "Do they follow…?"

"Oh yes Captain" Newcastle lowered the glass with a smile. "They follow. They-all-follow.

TEN DAYS EARLIER…

At that very moment in time when Essex ended his parley with Roberts with a gunshot and returned to the deck of The Venger to face Harrow and Faulkner….

"Well? What did that bastard have to say?" Harrow asked.

"He wants us in chains but, he doesn't have the firepower here and now to do it."

"In chains?"

"Some of us anyway. He thinks we'll settle for our own freedom and sell the others out. Like that bastard Hornigold."

--Hornigold, a privateer who took a pardon from the crown, then ran other privateers down as he lobbied to become the Governor of The Bahamas.

"Too hell with Hornigold and others like him. Damn Judas! They'll get no such treachery here." Harrow barked.

Essex ignored his second officer for a moment and stepped to Faulkner. "If we go back, does The Phantom back us up?"

Faulkner let out a deep breath. "It's a possibility. But it has to be a plan my men would agree to and damn it, the rewards would have to be high."

"Isn't smashing the British reward enough?"

Faulkner shrugged as if to confess, 'maybe.'

"Where is Stannis and The Black Death?" Essex asked.

"With Armitage, off June Point at last reports." He said, "Rafer may be in the area too if he hasn't returned to his native Haiti."

"Armitage." Harrow almost spit, "Damn fool almost got himself killed in a duel in Africa."

"You know the weather this time of year brings us all home." Faulkner confessed, "You have Vincenze, and Flannigan and his blockade runners may even be here."

"Captain." Harrow finally said, "Regardless of what commanders are in the area, if we caused this, we have to go back. We must go back — I...must go back."

Faulkner paused, he had something on his mind and finally, he put his thought forward, "Ya know, if word got out, we could put together something of our own squadron and--" Faulkner stopped himself.

"What?"

"There's one other option."

"And that is?"

"Vasquez is in Cuba."

"Bring a Spaniard into this?" Harrow hissed.

"Aye," Faulkner laughed, "He's a tough one to be sure but, let him settle the score in Jamacia and it might ease the pain of Panama."

"What's to keep him from taking the island?"

"He doesn't have the men." Faulkner preached, "He's got the ships and the crews for a fight at sea but, not the men to take an island against our presence."

"So, you're saying he would support our attack out of the kindness in his heart?"

"They're at war and Spain is taking a beating, like they did in the last one. He may do it just to become a Vice Admiral or something and he respects you Essex."

Essex stopped, "I'm not sure that counts in a situation like this. We'll be asking his men to lay their lives on the line for this."

"We may only have this one shot at freedom. If not now, when?"

Essex looked at him, then stood up, "I'll put this to the men. It'll be their decision."

From a visual, I could tell our officers were split. Essex and Harrow seemed to be genuine about revenge. Newcastle seemed neutral, Arson seemed un-enthusiastic and Teague, Howe, Sanjuro and Jaffar just listened to the war-council-exchange.

Arson, who was not afraid of a fight but also not much interested in a fight we could not win stopped the Captain before he could take to the wheel, "Captain, we have less than nine hundred hands onboard and some of them are walking wounded. We can't man all the guns and raid. Are you sure you want to run right into the teeth of the tiger?" He looked to Jack-Karr and his infamous tiger claw scar on his face, "No offense, Jack."

"We also have the survivors from The Eagle." Newcastle added.

Essex looked down at the planks then back to Arson, "I've been running my whole life and I'm tired of it." He paused and looked to Faulkner, "If it's as you say, the British will be at The Horn and The Cape, waiting for us if we make a run. So, if we're to go down then…it has to happen here."

A few moments later, Essex stood at the helm and addressed the men on deck. "Attention everyone, please…"

The men started to gather around and became quiet…

Essex tried to find the right words but, true to his way, he just cut right to the point. "The Caribbean is in flames. the English are trying to inflict a genocide on the population. There is no defense against their tyranny. We are outgunned and outmanned but the only way this ends, is with a fight." He paused, looked down at the planks then back up at us, "My place is on this ship –it is my home and…I will die here. But I will die, quite content to be free of their oppression." Again, he paused as if the gravity of the moment required an extra thought or two. "I know some of you have families on these islands and, like myself, would like to settle it. I know some of you have your own interests which should be respected also. So, take tonight and think on this. We vote in the morning."

At sunset, Newcastle along with Jaffar, Addo, Sanjuro and Lincoln along with two of Faulkner's officers sat down for dinner on the deck. It was a low-spirited affair for there was much on everyone's mind. But Hobby did what he could to offer comfort with sea turtle soup, a slab of boar and mangos. Several bottles of wine were opened and Sanjuro offered up some sake –which Faulkner seemed to like best. I stayed with rum and carved a piece of coconut to sweeten the taste. I couldn't help but feel that this was a last supper of sorts and the conversation seemed to be a device to distract and it turned to matters of industry --stockades, treasure ships, imperial objectives and possibilities, even assassination of public officials --something Faulkner seemed very at ease with…

As the conversation drifted in different directions, Faulkner turned to me, "Tell me about this peace keeping mission?"

"Well, I wasn't on it. I was on the trip that settled it."

"Were you now?" He said surprised.

"I was. I found our man crucified, a few imprisoned and a marker for a mass grave."

"Bad business –and no comfortable place for a schoolteacher I'd wager."

"No sir but," as I tried to find the right words, I realized that I had a confession to make in order to feel right about what I had witnessed. "I wanted to be there. When I saw what they did to my friend, I wanted to put it right…."

"To kill them?"

I could not say I was comfortable with that idea but, I could say, that. "I was angry, and that anger was in full command of my faculties."

"Happens to us all."

"It was not right what they did. It's not right to do that to any man -- much less one who lived his life by the Bible."

"Well, The Bible is more like guidelines than actual rules." He said, "I know the clergy around the time of King James made editorial work on the good book –and—included some of their own ideas but, the book itself is more like helpful ideas –if you like."

I owned a Bible and even though I believed its teachings, I tended to agree with Faulkner's statement that it was a set of guidelines--although many of the men around me had broken all the commandments and replaced them with their own.

"A man knows through intuition what is right and what is wrong. He needs no book."

"Doesn't he though?"

"No. Not if he is in tune with himself...." He said kicking his glass back, "You'll know what to do when the time comes Mister Reed!"

'Will I?' I wondered.

"And that time is going to be very soon."

LATER THAT NIGHT

Down in the galley, under the lantern light, the debate was under way...

"Go back?" Blythe said, "Just to start a war? It makes no damn sense."

"Wars can be profitable!" Jagger said.

"So are the trade routes of the South Pacific." Watson argued. "And we don't have to fight English conscripts.... often!"

"Harrow says the British are at The Cape and The Horn, it'll be hell moving out of The Atlantic."

"We caused this." Jack-Karr said, "We can't run."

"So, what, we've done a lot of wrong, we can't start putting it all right."

"Can't we now?" Duncan-Howe suddenly said, cutting into the conversation as he sat by a candle, not looking in our direction but looking into the flame but very much aware of what was being said.   "Can't we start putting things, right? Can't we put THIS right?"

I looked to Jeddah who sat alone in this debate without offering any input.

"I've got family there! I'm for going back." Whitney barked.

"So, do I." Said Kannon, "They could be killed by these bastards if we don't do something."

"I've done a lot of wrong." Merritt suddenly spoke up and the crowd became silent. "Most of you don't know but --I killed a man. Over petty circumstances. To many of you, that's not much to bark at but, to me it's always been big. He didn't deserve it and I've never been comfortable with it. Since running from that, I've stacked up a lot of wickedness and I've lived with the wrong, day in and day out for a lot of years. Just for once, I'd like to do something that I can be really proud of and maybe take some of this pain away." He slowly looked around at us, "Going back and saving those families, those women and children, well...I can die proud of that."

That was an inspired statement, and my conscious took hold of me, thinking I could put some things right too. "I'm for that!" I suddenly barked. I surprised myself and quickly became silent as everyone turned and looked at me. "I'm sorry, I didn't mean—"

"It's alright Reed." Jagger said, "Every man gets a say and if you're for a fight, you have every right to preach it."

"It's no secret, I owe the men on this deck my life--"

Barak looked away annoyed. "Except me!" He hissed in barely audible fashion.

"--I've been saved from cannibals, the Dutch and other privateers. To think that my passage through this life has caused more pain for those in my wake," I continued, "Well...like Merritt, I'd like to correct that."

Bishop agreed, "Aye." He nodded, "I'm in."

"Me too." Whitney piped up, "Think about it, we could change the world's perception of us, with one crushing victory. Maybe even force them out and build our own privateer state."

"History won't remember any peace keeping mission," Merciless said, "They'll call us pirate and use other bad, shiny words to convince the public that their corrupt war machine was right to kill us. They'll tell them they're safe and scare them into thinking so –and our cause, however just, will never be mentioned."

"I think it would be nice to put a few more bodies in the ground." Fury said.

"--Rather than dig 'em up like you use to" Karr laughed citing Fury's past as a grave robber.

"We've only got about nine hundred reliable hands-on board. Even if we empty the sick bay." Bolt reported.

"And a lot of the men we picked up in Macau haven't seen any real action yet –aside from those Chinese soldiers." Madds added as he looked around to some of the Chinese –in their Imperial armor—close by, he gave them a nod of confidence.

"I'd still take our nine hundred against any the Royal Navy's got!" Jagger said.

"Because you've defied death –I'm not sure where we would stand in an all-out fight against Royal marines of two nations."

"Wolfe is dead. Reader is dead. So is Hallock, Hazzard and Clairmont." Teague suddenly emerged from the shadows, bottle in hand. "No more poetry! We left a lot of men on that beach and in Royal and Freedom Town and I'll be damned if I'm going to let that stand." He looked around at each of us, "We know if we run, the English will read it as weak. They'll be motivated to run us down and our reputation will never keep anyone in check again! However…." He grinned, "If we go back, terrorize them and settle it, then no one will ever feel confident in challenging us again…."

The eyes of the crew fixed on his every word like gospel. Merciless nodded like he had just heard the word of God and the message was in tune to his violent religion.

"Now…who are we? Are we men who bring havoc? Or are we the cowards who run?

And in came the votes…. "Havoc."

"Havoc."

"Havoc," I nodded as most of the men around me agreed.

"Then let's let the killing begin!" Teague finished.

"Any man not up for this conflict can sit this out…." Jagger said, "There will be no reprisals and no man will think ill of ya' so each man makes his own decision."

"Well, I reckon whether it's a fight I want or not," Blythe said, "That it's my place to blade up with the rest of ya so let's do this."

Faulkner was surviving a hangover, in the early morning fog of the next day with an empty rum bottle in his fist when Essex found him.

"Can you get word to Rafer and the others?"

"I think so. If they're still alive." He said, "Though I may have to hijack a few courier ships to canvas the area."

"Do it, hijack whatever you need and get a message to Vasquez."

Faulkner nodded, "What do I tell 'em?"

"Tell them all to make sail for Raven's Island, we'll be there."

"Aye" Faulkner said with a touch of encouragement. "But…what's at Raven's Island?"

"Death!"

Three days later, Rafer-Davies came aboard and as the other privateering commanders crossed our deck, Rafer's ship, The Revolution, circled The Venger in a defensive position. Essex and Rafer shook hands and Rafer appeared to crack a slight smile. "It's been a long time."

"Too long. How was Haiti?"

"Hell. Every port is a battleground. The French are turning over all the privateers to the British if the price is right."

"And British always make sure the price is right --whatever it needs to be."

"I'll not be encased in a body cage. As I see it," Rafer looked around, "It's better die on my feet with my freedom, then live on my knees."

Hobby stepped up on the quarter deck and dropped a coffee bucket. Daws put the lantern down on the map table as the men, the different Captains and their officers gathered around.

"This isn't going to be easy." Essex looked to his own warrant officers --Teague, Jupiter, Jaffar, Newcastle, Harrow, Rajiv, Nighthorse, Mazatal, several other key commanders and then to Faulkner and his brass, Vincenze, Armitage and at the far end of the table, partially concealed in darkness, Rafer-Davies.

"Twelve British warships occupy the waters around Jamaica," The markers loaded down the map, "Along with eighteen troop transports and a prison ship sitting off the beach here." He marked the spot. "Their base of command for their current campaign is here. Port Royal." He tapped the position on the map, "Which as I understand it, is still burning…"

"Aye in another three days time, it'll be gone."

"In order to have any chance at winning this, we need to split them up --to wreck them. Therefore, I suggest we go on the offensive…" He dragged his index finger along the map as he talked so everyone could follow the plan and certain officers could even visualize the locations that applied. "We'll wait in darkness and at dawn, we're going to sail past Royal, under a white flag so they think we're about to surrender. Instead, we'll get close and open up with the guns, smash and shatter the vanguard ship here, protecting Royal, the rest of the fleet and the beach base command, doing as much damage as we can, then, sail right past…"

Teague looked up, Harrow was clearly confused, 'Sail past?'

"They will get to their stations and come after us." Essex looked to read the expressions of his men, making sure everyone had a grasp on what he was saying. "By sunset, we will sail through the Channel Islands off Raven's Point, here to this bay, drop anchor off of Vulcan Island and wait for them."

"Beggin' the Captain's pardon sir," Jack-Karr asked, "Ah, wait for 'em?"

"May I remind the Captain," Rajiv added, "Many of the gun tigers are wounded. We don't have complete gun crews."

"And you'll have even less when the action starts."

Rajiv looked even more confused.

"When they descend on the ship, your gunners will have to shift from port to starboard as the action demands, but before that happens…" He pointed back to the map again, "The British fleet will have to sail through this narrow channel here and come at us, one ship at a time—or they'll run aground." He focused our attention on a narrow channel, "Once they come through here, we'll open up on them from shore batteries hidden on the islands on both sides of the channel…"

Teague smiled; Faulkner almost laughed.

"We'll turn every channel island and sand bar into a fortress. Make them fight through, island after island…..

"We'll offload twenty of our one-hundred guns and the guns from The Eagle. These guns will be manned by Vincenze and his survivors along with what men we can spare."

Vincenze nodded.

"They'll rain down whatever hell they can. The British will try bombardment, then they may try to land a shore party to clear each island's gun station, one at a time, before they can move on and get to us here in the bay." He looked to everyone again, making sure the next set of details were understood, "Once the situation becomes untenable, our crews, will retreat, to the next island in waiting long boats or through, the shallows and reefs and move island to island, in a fighting retreat, staying just one step ahead of their slow, lumbering maneuvers. We'll bleed the British to death…..

"Rafer will hold the far side of the channel here." He marked the position, "If the British try to sail around, which will take several hours." He looked to Rafer, "You engage them and then begin a fighting retreat back to our position with Armitage."

Rafer-Daves gave a slow nod.

"Fight your way back here." He pointed again to Vulcan Island, "And when the British advance into the bay, we'll have batteries on the shoreline" he motioned to the half-moon shape of the beach "And make our last stand on our decks here. We'll try to get as many of you –the gunners and shore party-- on board before British set on us. Once the fighting on our ship starts, we hold, fighting everything that comes our way, and once all the surviving British ships force their way into this bay, we'll send a runner through the jungle here, two leagues to this Cay --Faulkner's position—You," he looked to Faulkner, "Will sail in behind, close the bay and trap whatever's left here and hammer them. Understand?"

We all understood. Some of us almost smiled.

"To your stations and let's get to work."

Armitage didn't move, he looked up at the Captain and suddenly said, "I can't fight against my King."

"Not again." Harrow vented in a disappointed tone.

"He's not your King, not any longer." Faulkner barked.

"How many men on your decks are out of Africa, or, liberated from different colonial wars?" Essex asked.

"See this?" Faulkner put up his wrist where the shackles he had worn for years had scarred his skin into bracelets, "He's got a body cage waiting for you back home Armitage. He'll hang you up at the port and laugh doin' it. Just like he did to Captain Kidd!"

"Innocent civilians, women and children were put under the guns at Port Royal. Their homes burned. Sacked by the crown." Essex added. "Now, we don't have time for you to come to your senses."

Armitage suddenly nodded, "Alright, this time I'm with ya, but ya better have a vicar nearby 'cause I'm gonna have some repentin' to do when this is all over. God help me."

On deck, the Moors raised their heads off the deck and rose from their prayers.

We opened up the holds, pulled the cannon from The Eagle, loaded them to-the-ropes and heaved them up to our decks. Crates of cannon rounds were also heaved up, then moved onto the long boats and rowed to positions on the shore....

Our metal workers along with Bolt, Bliss, Sampson-Rift, and a few others made grenades by the hundreds. Every scrap of metal that wasn't already a weapon, ammunition or some valuable part of the ship was melted down and recast on deck into grenades and gun rounds.

Blix and Sunderland worked under the sparks as they wheeled the sharpening stones on every available blade…

On shore, on the different islands, on both sides of the ship, the combined crews, built gun emplacements, fortifications and even a trench network in the tree lines. Every small island, even the islands as small as a quarter league or so had some sort of defense work installed on it.

Armitage was on the beach explaining the plan to his officers as his men worked all around him, "Once the British move into this channel, we'll fire on them from both sides, and move down from island to island, killin' as many of The King's men as possible along the way," He crossed his heart as if asking for divine forgiveness, then continued, "We'll be anchored off the last island there," he pointed to a point about six leagues away. "We'll keep jolly boats in the water and row like hell to get back to our decks, from there we'll fight ship to ship --if any of 'em are left."

"Sounds damn risky." One of his men barked…

"It is but, it gives us half a chance to live so, look sharp."

"Why don't we just evacuate the area?"

"There's no place to go!" Armitage shouted. "They're rollin' the whole damn place and there's a blockade damn it!"

Our men were unloading hundreds of rifles, muskets, and pistols –along with powder and grenades and placing them into our combat trenches. Newcastle and Whitney watched as some of our Chinese soldiers cut down a few trees and fabricated catapults designed to launch an 'ignitor round' onto the decks of the British ships –a round that was designed to start a fire –and this is where the old world met the new.

"Damn ancient, isn't it?" Whitney asked.

"My feeling is, old or not, if they know how to fight with it, then…let 'em use it."

Jack-Karr and I marked barrels of Byzantine fire with a white stripe so we could see them better in the dark, then we raised barrels by net, into some of the palm trees above --as Bons, Kato, Blythe, and I, tied a barrel off, I saw Harrow look up and smile…

"Sir," I asked, "How do we know the British will land here?"

"They can't help themselves." He said, well aware of the English drive to convince us –and the rest of the world, that they were superior –a frame of mind that made them almost predictable in action. "They can't allow us, or these islands --such as they are-- to be free from their tyranny." He looked at me, "They are compelled to get in a fight and take them by force, no matter what it takes. They have to demonstrate their will." Then as an afterthought he added, "It's what they do."

Just then some of our ronin moved in between us, "But," I said, "Can't they just go around the channel?"

He shook his head no. "Eventually. It would take six hours or more, depending on the tide and wind. they'd rather force us off, than move around. They can't stand the idea of their moves being dictated. Have no fear Reed, these islands will be covered in British dead before you know it."

Our natives cut trees into spears and lined some of the trenches with them and created some other traps. On the first small island we refit an old stockade --built by the Spanish during what appeared to be the dawn of time—and cleared a few old abandoned, colonial buildings and turned them into fighting bunkers. What few civilians there were—runaway slaves most of them, were warned and many cleared out to hide.

Hell was going to be the new name of this place. At the first island in the channel chain where the action would start, Jack Karr had the peace of mind to make the British a welcome sign for what we predicted was the beach landing site. He took what was left of the white paint and went to work....

"Welcome isn't spelled with a V, it's a W." I said as he applied some paint.

"That is a W."

"No" I said, as I walked over to help him, "A W is two Vs." I did it for him and said, "Ya should have come to my school more often."

The sign was hammered into place. "Welcome to Hell."

XXX

KILL 'EM ALL

AT MIDNIGHT ON THE NINTH DAY--

I prepped my weapons with Tiger, Bolt and Jack-Karr, "This is the day…" Arson barked, walking through the ranks below deck as men picked up their weapons and moved to their war stations, "This is the day you get immortalized in history or…you enter Valhalla. Either way, by the end of this, you'll be in a better place." With his closing words, he seemed to look directly at me, as if I was the one he was speaking to, specifically, when referring to 'a better place' –that being dead! Arson then nodded to us as if to say, 'let's get to it' and then he continued through the decks….

Khan and the Moors –all in a line-- collectively rose from the prayers –the final prayers for some-- and then began sharpening their blades. The samurai were tying on their black and red armor, adding chest plates and armor to their forearms and shins. Mako pulled his smoking needles out of his skin, then got equipped.

Everyone loaded up on grenades, muskets and extra pistols and rounds. Nothing was left in our armory.

War paint was applied by our native contingent and skulls to Jupiter and his men. The Masai applied their black and dark red across their eyes and Jone --one of the toughest--requested permission to eat his enemies when the fighting was done and who were we to object? ---Less men to bury!

There was a sense that this was it. This was going to be the end –for many of us. The odds were stacked high against us, and we accepted this situation –or at least I did. I was past the point of fear or concern. You get to a point where you're defiant against the feeling of fear and want to fight ---literally—through it. I don't think Jack-Karr or Jaffar and the others cared about the odds. I think they felt that this was just another day and there was some killing to do. No one in our ranks –not even the youngest among us—seemed to betray a hint of fear or even apprehension, in fact there was more of a sense of vengeance between us, like this was payback.

--More anger than fear! The system had exploited us, used us, demeaned us and many of us saw this as a chance to finally bring that system down or die trying --and death was the way out for many of us. I suppose it always had been our path to freedom.

The ronin were lining up at their prayer box. One at a time, they took a moment to themselves then clapped and moved on with their business –as they started marching past me, Takeda stopped and looked at me, "Die well." He smiled, fastened his 'death mask' and moved towards the top deck.

"Die well?"

"Make it hard for them to kill ya' Reed." Bolt said, loading his baldric and sash up with every possible pistol it would fit, "Make them remember you. Be the tough bastard that haunts their nightmares for decades."

This was not my lifelong goal. I was not destined to be a ghost in someone's head but, for the sake of the men around me, I was going to do my best to get all of them –and myself-- through this somehow and I took a knee and for the first time in a long time, I prayed. In this prayer, I made a promise, the kind of promise one often makes when they have their backs against the wall but, I actually intended to keep mine. My promise –if I survived--was to continue to do my best and to do what was right. Not what was right based on a King's law or that of any church but what was right based on my conscious. If I lived through this, I was going to live better and do better for the society around me.

--Barak gave me a hand up from my knee.

"You may get your chance to settle your debt today?"

"Yes." He smiled, "God willing."

Johnny Kay asked to go ashore and fight in the trenches. Newcastle pushed him away, "Not today, you're too young."

"Damn it, Newcastle. let me fight."

"You'll fight from here, with the gun crews. Odds are better you'll survive."

At that Johnny Kay kicked a nearby cannon in anger and almost broke his foot.

"Ah see, there you go, that'll teach you."

I looked at these men closely, wondering which ones I may never see alive again. Then, Mister Lynch interrupted me. "Reed."

I looked at him as my concentration was broken, "Yes."

"I want to give you this." He handed me his book of illustrations. "In case I don't make it out of this today…see to it that this serves as some sort of marker—or sign—that I had lived."

I took the book but was reluctant. "I think it's bad luck to-"

"You and I both know there's no such thing as luck but, as a teacher, there is no one I'd trust more, to make some value out of this." He gave a slight smile…

I nodded and he moved down the deck to join his war party. I put his book in my footlocker and stood up, face to face with Jack-Karr "Let's go, Reed. We got killing before us this day and we don't want to be late to Valhalla." He slapped me on the back to push me along and up to the top deck we went, different nationalities, different cultures and different men with one –unionized—cause.

On deck we were met by our Captain who turned to us as we circled around. After a moment of silence, he found his words, "This is the day we've all been waiting for. As young men, you no doubt wondered if you'd amount to something special. If you'd be the hero, to be immortalized in the history books, well…." He looked out to the horizon for a moment then back to us, "I don't know about books but, I do know about history and our work here is just. It may be the most 'just' thing we've ever attempted. In recent months, we've saved men, women, children from shackles and certain death and God has repaid us by allowing us to live well on the frontiers of the world and if it ends here, today, well--then you may smile with pride as you walk through the gates of the afterlife. For it was you who stood up against tyranny. It was you, they had to kill and it's the idea of men like you…that they will always fear."

--This was the truth and these words hit home with a touch of emotion and all the subtlety of a hammer.

"Now," he continued, "with respect, let's kill every one of these bastards."

We approached in darkness, so this assault would be timed with the dawn. We wanted them to see us and follow us so, just after midnight, we moved towards the target. We blew out the lanterns, extinguished the pipes and deck fires --no sparks, just the lights of Port Royal in the distance.

There was not a word spoken on deck as we closed in on the town, just dead silence and as the sun started to ascend, the British lookouts saw us and reported our arrival with a warning from the fort watchtower.

--There was no going back now.

The marines scrambled on the beach and picked up their weapons. We watched Lord Roberts emerge from his command tent, with members of the Royal African Company.

I looked back; our Captain remained silent.

I then looked to Daws who stood by the white flag of surrender, and I watched him pull his machete…

I could feel our floor panels move with a rumble as our gun tigers quietly moved into position around the cannons below deck. Rajiv looked up at the mid-morning sun coming through the deck hatch, waiting for the order to slam open the gun doors and light up the town.

Roberts and his men began to assemble in formation for our formal surrender and as we got closer, I could read the expression –of arrogance and self-satisfaction on his face. He looked like a man who had won. A man, who had beat us, a man who thought himself…better than us.

This, made my temper pulse through my body in a rage and just when I was ready to explode, I heard the command—

"LET IT FLY!!!" Essex yelled.

Daws cut the white flag of surrender away and Irons, Bons and Kannon dragged on the rope that raised the 'skull and bones' into the sky with anger and defiance.

Roberts smiled faded as we jumped to our stations and opened fire! The British went running as the steel cut them apart...

After the initial attack, on the run, we worked our stations...

Essex gave the order to drop our speed and slow down, giving them time to come after us and we ignited two barrels of whale oil on our deck –to make us look wounded-- and let the smoke billow into the sky. It was a sight they could not miss.

The British appeared on the edge of the horizon behind us --one ship after another—until it looked like the entire Atlantic fleet was closing in on us.

Essex looked to Thorn who marked our position on the map, then to Bishop at the wheel as Arson stomped on to the quarter deck, weapons ready, "This is a fine day to unleash hell," he said in his low, grumbling voice as he appreciated the beautiful weather. "A fine day to end it all."

I looked back, beyond Arson, beyond the stern rail to the fleet of British warships as they continued after us. If they caught us, out in the open ocean there'd be hell to pay so, the pressure inside my skull was building. I walked down the deck, between the weapons and the men to the ronin where I collected some throwing stars for my satchel and found myself next to Duncan-Howe who stood with six guns in his belt as he lit his pipe. "Rest easy Reed. The killin' hasn't even started yet."

I looked over his shoulder, over our bow, to see the Channel Islands up ahead. We couldn't get there fast enough. I then looked to the Hurons nearby –two, Ten Bear Killer and Sky were just out of the infirmary –just in time for this party, and they were adding to their war paint. They seemed to be gaining confidence because of this act, as usual and I said, "I could use some of their spirit magic today."

Howe turned to look, just as Bear Killer heard me and stood up. He stepped up to me and looked me directly in the eyes in a way that made me somewhat nervous, then he dragged two fingers marked with black war paint, down the left section of my forehead, over my left eye and down my cheek and he mumbled something in his native language.

"He says, you now have the strength to kill ten bears." Howe translated, "So you can quit your senseless jabberin'"

"Yes, quit your jabberin' the lot of ya." Harrow barked as he barged past us, "Stand to --pay attention and above all, remember the plan."

I felt like we were running, just ahead of the teeth of some massive beast and I exhaled with relief when we made it into the channel –now all we had to do was kill all these Brits.

It was time to get down to business. Essex ordered us to drop what was left of the 'Byzantine death' into the tide and we started to lower rope nets loaded with what was left of this explosive 'fire' into the water to drift towards the entrance of the channel. Two or three barrels to a net, eight nets total, leaving them to float there. Daws and Rajiv had marked each net with a target flag so the Bengals and our gunners hidden ashore could see them better from the gun placements.

Without slowing down, all available hands started to clear the deck and as The Venger continued to sail, we dropped into the long boats, men, weapons and all --and we rowed ashore and moved towards the different battle stations as The Venger sailed into the cove, slowly turned, dropped anchor, rolled out the guns and…waited.

Our long boats were put into the planned positions so we could retreat and evacuate from island to island as the battle progressed and once this was done, our crews moved into the trenches and fortifications for the fight…

I ran, with Bons, Mako, Hayte, Irons and some of the Chinese soldiers, down the beach and over the inlet as privateers everywhere jumped into position and prepared for the final fight. We moved down the sandbar –in knee deep water--as the tide lowered and over the two small islands to our positions where Newcastle, Jupiter, Teague, and some of the others were already stationed, waiting for the action to start.

The British fleet was on the horizon and just moving into the area when we arrived.

"Nice warpaint Reed!" Merciless took note of my face as he made his final wartime adjustments.

"Thank you."

"Let's hope it helps you rise up to actually kill somebody."

The afternoon sun began to turn the sky orange --a look that seemed to give the pending battle zone a sinister touch. As the men around me made their final adjustments for war, I check and rechecked my weapons and for some strange reason, I straightened my Arabian scarf and tunic in nervous fashion, because the thought shot through my head that when I died, I ought to be presentable.

Suddenly there were some signal flares between the British ships and the first British warship sailed towards us to run the channel…this was it!

"Here they come. Right into the teeth of the tiger." Jupiter smiled, "Pre-dic-table."

--Everyone took their combat positions.

We moved into our fortifications, hidden in the tree line. Fury pulled his cutlass and threw away the scabbard. "I'm not gonna need this any time soon, if ever again." And with that, others threw away their scabbards and planted their blades in the sand next to their stations where they could quickly draw them-- as if to demonstrate that they would never house their blades again.

"Less to carry into the afterlife."

"Here we go!" Madds slapped me on the shoulder and gripped his gun as a massive frigate, H.M.S. Enron, sailed into the channel first, the only sound it seemed to make was the sound of the crashing waves it created as the bow pushed forward through the tide. It slowly moved up on our position as we waited –and waited—hidden by our camouflaged gun positions, and as it began to slowly pass us, it cast a giant, ominous shadow on our side of the beach as I looked up at it. Our guns remained silent as everything became dark. We could hear the sailors on their decks, unaware that we had them targeted.

A second frigate sailed into the channel –The Concord, and then a third prepared to advance, still unaware of our positions. Now the wait was becoming painful, 'What's the hold up?' --who was going to start his fight? And when?'

"Do you think Armitage lost his nerve?" I asked in a whisper.

Newcastle looked to the islands across from our position. "No. We wait, until the channel is loaded."

Then, suddenly, it happened… BOOOOOOOOOOOM –the first cannon opened up, then quickly a second, third and fourth gun fired and rocked back to be reloaded. Explosions lit up the sky as the cannon on the opposite island started to fire. I could see the British on deck jump and reposition themselves for a fight as some of them were blown overboard – on fire. One shot went right through a cannon door and exploded inside on their gun deck sending their gun crews running.

Now, all the gun positions opened up, one after another ---like an earthquake! We fired and reloaded, fired, and reloaded as quick as we could. Blast after blast! They fired back but their guns were positioned too high at first, and they cleared trees behind us as cannonballs zipped over our heads.

"Bring the havoc!" screamed Newcastle, fist in the air.

Their gun crews were getting killed and cut up by splinters as our cannon rounds smashed into their woodwork. I watched as one frigate had its mast snapped which came down on our beach –and another ship's deck started smoking as one of its sails caught fire…

The hammering continued as a fourth war ship started its channel run. Their gunners got their calculations right and their cannon rounds started to hit our positions and explode all around us opening up a pounding match…

Through the smoke and against the late afternoon sun, Newcastle could see the silhouettes of the troop ships change their position and prepare to put their combat battalions ashore. "War party to the beach!" He ordered.

By sunset most of our combat team had moved from the guns –facing north--and repositioned ourselves in the tree line on the beach –facing west-- where we expected the British landing. Toombs passed grenades out to the ranks near him. Jagger pulled the hammers back on his double-barrel pistols.

I looked, as Duncan-Howe had trouble sparking the tobacco in his pipe and I sparked a fuse and lit it for him.

"You're a kind one Reed, I'll give ya that." He said, "Shame you'll probably die today."

I struggled for the right words in response. "Thanks…I suppose?" Was all I could muster.

The enemy closed in with an almost relaxed pace as we took to our weapons and waited for this to become a close-range fight. Their long boats rowed towards the beach --closer and closer—and once in range, we suddenly opened up with a crack of gunfire and threw grenades which streaked a trail of smoke through the air, before they crashed down and exploded, in the water, on the sandbar, overhead –and—sometimes, in mid-air, above marines, or in between them, blowing them apart.

--Their boats were hit and blown into pieces. It became chaos.

--Typically, a grenade with a five second fuse was thrown up, in an arc, to come down and explode, but these grenades had real malice behind them, and some were thrown direct and straight like a speedball or rocks, across the battlefield right at our adversaries. One grenade even hit a marine in the head and jarred him just before it exploded.

"Take that, ya Satanic bastards!!!" Merciless rifled one grenade, turned and was pitched another grenade with the fuse already lit, and across the tide it went, to blow a man's arms off, before he was tossed another lit grenade to unload, then another and another!!!

As the British forced their way forward, we continued to fire, killing more and blowing some upright and out of the boats and into the water. Their bodies now loaded the tide and then the beach, there were so many bodies that it was as if a man would walk from his boat to the beach without getting his boots wet.

I aimed my weapon with intent to kill as a dark, spiritual shadow seemed to roll over me as if my conscious paused my action, but I regripped the trigger determined to do my part in this fight. Jupiter fired next to me and as I continued to aim my gun for the perfect target, he ripped it from my hands, aimed and fired it, blowing a marine back into the tide, then tossed my gun back to me, "Reload it."

When they tried to carry the wounded back and load them onto their medical long boats some of those valets were targeted and hit. Officers too were targeted to take the head off the command structure and cause chaos. In all, everyone in a British uniform was blasted with complete malice – even the drummer boys had to duck a run for cover in a panic.

There were more flag signals between the ships –to the west, we saw a large detachment of soldiers in dark blue uniforms, unload from another troop ship and they began to row towards us. Jupiter focused on their regimental and battle flags. "It's a language and symbols I have not seen before." He said, "Madds?" He handed Madds the spyglass.

Madds looked for a moment at the men as they closed in, then at their flags in the wind. "Damn bastards have brought Hessian killers with them."

--Hessians, Prussian mercenaries raised from a young age to be cultivated for total war. War was their career. War was their life. War was all they knew and now—war was exactly what they would get!

He closed the spyglass and tossed it back to Jupiter, "Fancy that! I sail three thousand leagues to escape the bastards and here they are, right here in front of me! Well, you have to admire their commitment to destroying us." He laughed. "They're serious about it if they brought these bastards!"

"More to kill!" Jagger shouted in a wicked tone as he fired, "Now, let's get back to business!"

We fired another volley, reloaded, and fired again, killing, and wounding men in what seemed to be in the hundreds, metal rounds smashed into them and cut through them! When they tried to form up in the tide, we fired again. Bolt even threw a grenade that bounced off a captain and exploded at his feet, killing him and everyone around him – soldiers were launched through the air—and a wounded man tried to crawl through the tide holding his own blown off leg in shock --as if it could be reattached.

Like a monster who wants to display its strength, the British kept coming and tried to use numbers –and ignorance-- to wear us down.

Eventually as bullets and grenades started to run light, they managed to assemble. When there seemed to be two full regiments formed up on the beach, in knee deep water –and under continuous fire, they started to advance under the sound of drums, to our tree line. One of the drummers was hit, a round went right through his drum and clipped him in the hip, ending his musical career.

We held, allowing them to come in close, very close range, just a few meters away --and CRAAAACK—the blizzard of lead and bullets continued.

Breathing became difficult, the air stifled by smoke and gunpowder. Wounded and dead privateers began to pile up! Under fire and with heavy casualties, the British managed to get three battalions ashore with more rowing towards the beach…

They marched over their dead, stepping right on the bodies, and eventually closed in on our trench. Jupiter gave the order to retreat, and we fell back from our first position, and gave up the beach. We moved back into the jungle, avoiding what traps we had made, back to the cannons.

When we made it to our gun placements—which were still firing at the war ships in the channel, Jagger shouted, "Clear the island," waving everyone back, "They're ashore! Clear the island. Move to the next."

Dax-Varrow fired up a blue flare –seen through the spyglass of Essex on the deck of The Venger back in the bay. He knew what it meant –the first island stronghold had been lost. Evacuated.

Merciless and his crew, blew the guns in place and destroyed them so they couldn't be captured, turned and used against us as we made our retreat...

We continued to evacuate, picking up weapons, powder and any wounded and we moved towards the next island but, as we started running, Teague walked past us, back into this deathtrap. I stopped, turned, and watched him as he walked back towards our empty gun positions and stood there –with our gun positions on fire all around him. I then looked ahead, past him, where I could see British Marines and Hessians advancing off the beach and through the trees towards him.   Just before I could call out to him, he pulled his pistol, aimed it up and into the trees and fired. There was a sudden snap and a popping sound, then --an explosion! He fired a round into a barrel of Byzantine fire above in the palm trees and it rained down an ocean of flames that turned the island into an inferno. Flames covered the detachment of screaming British marines as they closed in and what was left of the gun powder we left behind, exploded as Teague walked away from it.   "We're here to kill these men." Teague shouted to us, flames burning the countryside behind him making him awash in a sinister orange light, "Let's get serious about this!"

"Now we can leave." Merciless shouted seeing the tiny island engulfed in an inferno, and we ran across the sandbar –in knee deep water--to the next island to defend. We had crews already on it, exchanging fire with the British frigates that had passed us. We got to the fortifications and here some of the Chinese soldiers and ronin were manning the cannon, still loading, and reloading in this cyclone of shrapnel...

Some of these Chinese soldiers were firing their catapults and launched 'ignitor rounds' --on fire-- across the sky and onto the decks of the British warships to light them up. We could see smoke and even sailors –clothes on fire--battling the flames.

There was another massive explosion and the first warship in the channel –The Enron--started taking on water and the bow started to go down in the tide. The channel was suddenly blocked by this wreck, close to the position of Armitage and his gunners. I saw Sanjuro's fist go into the air and the men in our ranks roared –because with that ship, wrecked in the tide, there was now a sense that we might actually win this fight.

The crew of the sinking warship moved over the rail and swung down on ropes towards Armitage and his command --to fight on land-- and we could see muskets and pistols flare up as the fighting quickly became hand to hand there.

Another series of flag signals and other British warships maneuvered north, to sail around our defense points and storm the channel from the far side, several leagues to the East –where Rafer-Davies was waiting. But here, now, at our position, the British navy was trying to clear Armitage from the island across from us and they were trying to blow their own ship apart to clear the channel for the rest of their squadron to move forward! They had taken the first island, now in flames to the west of us, and their marines were marching towards us on this second island that we were now fighting to hold.

We had our hands full. The British marines and some of their Hessian allies waited for the fire to die down, then they fought their way forward from palm tree to palm tree, trench to trench but every step cost them in blood—even the traps we made were taking a serious, painful toll with a sharpened stake through the gut, boot or hand--and the bodies continued to stack up.

The British carried their wounded back to the beach to a casualty clearing station where their doctors worked on hundreds of wounded. Amputations, cauterizations, and some, just bled to death waiting by the tide, moaning for their mothers and fathers.

As the sun went down, the cannon fire –and the burning islands, lit everything up. We prepared for the next round of this fight and as flares lit up the sky and our surroundings, we could suddenly see, the British advancing on us out of the darkness –much closer than we thought --and we quickly engaged with small arms.

"Let 'em have it!" Newcastle shouted as the gunfire continued and bodies dropped all around him.

Again, we held out as long as we could, making the British pay for this island with body bags and waiting until the British were only meters away from us to fall back and retreat.

--Again, another round went through a barrel of Byzantine, up in a palm tree and it exploded, covering our exit with flames.

Redcoats-on-fire! Everywhere!

We stumbled, tackled, and fell into our long boats. Fury pushed me ahead of him, into one jolly boat and he and Hayte climbed into another under fire...

Whitney, Rift, and I, jumped on the oars and rowed like hell through the thirty --or so--meters to the next fortified island with Merciless, Kannon and Dax firing back at the British –Kannon with a pistol in each hand. As we rowed, the longboat next to us was hit and exploded blowing Hayte into the air and killing Ono, Fury, Fixx, everyone on board.

I stopped rowing in shock, as parts of the destroyed long boat plastered us –and I realized that Fury was dead because he pushed me to escape ahead of him. Screaming from Kannon Saint James snapped me out of my moment--

"Come on Reed!" Kannon shouted as he fired, "ROW!!!"

I worked past my shock and cranked on the oar. Pull! Swing! Drop! Pull –then again and as I worked, I looked up, to see a Hessian platoon, step out of the jungle and into the water behind us having cleared the island, and they started firing on us, Foxx was killed, a bullet clipped Bliss and another round, smashed into the wood rail right outside of my seat in the boat.

"That one had your name on it." Whitney shouted...

We got to the beach and we moved through the tide and took to our new defensive positions, The British had to move their long boats over each island behind us as they cleared it –our boats were already stationed where they needed to be for us to move and retreat fast – but for the Brits, they had to wait for the flames to die down, then use eight or ten man teams to haul their boats over the jungle wilderness so they could then row to the next island –and all under sniper fire from us. This errand took time and worked some of their ranks into exhaustion. When they began to load into the boats to take the next island, we would use grenades and guns and continued to kill them –rounds would snap into bones and cut through muscles, one marine even took a shot to the eye and stumbled around, actually dead for several steps before he finally dropped into the tide.

Again, we moved back into the tree line of the next island....

--Blood covered every inch of ground.

I moved quick, Teague was the only one who directed the battle in a calm, orderly fashion like a school master telling students where to move and what to do. He even stopped to roll some tobacco and lit it with the fuse of Jagger's grenade then tossed the lit grenade back to Jagger for him to throw it, while still giving orders –fire and explosions destroying everything around him!

When the weapons were emptied, the ronin used throwing stars –since they had fashioned extra--to clear the area and rip into these marines – blades to the neck, skull, face and back...

Duncan-Howe, Toombs, Rabal, some ronin and a platoon of our Chinese soldiers, led a counterattack and charged the marines as they first got ashore on this island. I had never seen the Chinese in collective action before that and it was like a wave of kicking, punching, and breaking!

British exhaustion also worked to our favor, and we racked up some serious casualties before the order was given, to quickly fall back into the jungle...

As the pounding between the ships and our guns continued, more British warships tried to clear the channel by firing on their own wrecked cruiser until she was damaged enough so they could sail past.

"Firing on their own ships." Sunderland said, "They're all in this now!"

Again, we held as long as possible, then blew the guns in place and moved just before the mass of British marines and Hessians could storm us.

We made it to the next beach and stumbled ashore, just as one of our cannon emplacements was hit and exploded. Lead cut right through Bolt next to me and I stumbled forward and collapsed with a loud ringing in my ears. I tried to get myself up off the ground and got to my hands and knees and turned, to see some of the gun crews firing. There were wounded and dead next to me but, I could not hear them –or anything, Shaken, I tried to regain my focus….

Suddenly, I was picked up by Upatau and Sampson-Rift who started dragging me out the fighting. Upatau was suddenly shot and collapsed. Bear Killer replaced him, and he picked me up, under fire and we stumbled into the tide where they threw me onto a long boat with some other wounded…

I looked up to see a flare rocket across the sky and gradually, I could hear my own breathing, then distant voices and commands and I moved, to see Bliss Monroe, damaged –bad--and bleeding along with Stamp, Volkan and a few others too wounded to move. I looked back to the battle to see Lo-Tan, Jagger, Addo and others in our ranks still fighting with everything they had and I did the one thing that I knew I had to do….I grit my teeth, crawled out of the boat and dropped into the tide, from there, I pulled myself onto the beach, wounded and hurt, then I struggled to pull myself up, first one knee, then the next, and then to my feet and with a deep, determined breath, I stood tall. Damaged but standing --if this day was going to end, it would not end with me wounded in a boat. I was going out on my feet.

I turned back to the long boat for a moment and there, breathing heavy and gurgling up blood and gunpowder was Bliss and after a moment, he looked at me and managed to raise the handle of his cutlass towards me as if to say, 'take my sword and go get 'em!' I took it, turned, and moved back towards the action.

Explosions to the left and right tried to throw me from my march back to the fight, the concussion from one blast after another dropped me back or blew me into trees or obstacles and on to the ground again, against dead bodies --but every time, I got back up until I finally got back into the combat line.

Duncan-Howe was barking orders as things exploded all around, and he had to look at me twice when I arrived at his shoulder, as if amazed that

I was standing there. "What the hell are you doing here Reed? You were put on the casualty boat with the wounded."

"I know" I said still trying to muscle up and collect myself, very much determined.

"Well, what the hell ya doin' here?" He shouted as some more musket rounds came in and cut up the area around us.

I looked at him, out of breath, blood coming from my temple, and mouth and my warpaint smudged "Stoppin' the British." I said, "Any problem with that --sir?"

Duncan stopped, slowly removed his pipe from his teeth as if stunned and then smiled. "No," he calmly said, "No problem at all."

"Very well then."

He then said in calm fashion with explosions nearby, "Have at it, Mister Reed."

By now, the dead were everywhere but the British kept coming with determination. We tried to hold the island –the LAST island before the lagoon where The Venger waited. I saw tomahawks and samurai blades swing in every direction as the melee rose an octave in intensity. Then, I saw pistols firing and then our survivors ran towards me. "We're moving out!" Newcastle shouted as Bons and Lo ran past "That's it! Time for the last stand!"

We were at the end of our tether. The British were now on every island and moving into the channel from both east and west. There was no telling how bad the fighting was at the other end of this channel where Rafer-Davis was. Was it all on fire? Were they holding out? Were the British closing in on us from both directions now?

And across? Armitage? What was left of his crew? I could see the occasional flash of gunfire but who was killing who? And who was left alive?

The only area that I could see that was still held by us was the lagoon with The Venger, the crescent moon shaped island around the lagoon and part of the island to the east where Faulkner was fighting. The rest was on fire or surrendered.

"Back to the last position," came the order. We moved to the final beachhead. The Venger already had its guns blazing at the oncoming British.

Blythe was suddenly shot next to me –blood from the wound sprayed me as he dropped. He tried to get to his feet, coughing up blood and as I grabbed hold of him he looked at me. "Damn Reed. You of all people." He tried to smile and collapsed...

I started dragging his body. "Yes me, damn it! Now, watch me save your life."

He laughed up some blood as his laugh turned into a painful groan. "I always liked you Reed," He hissed, "Ya can't kill a damn thing but, you're a missionary, I'll give-give ya th-that!" Again, his laughter turned to a painful cough...

Some of our men tried to retreat down the beach, Sanjuro started to push one of our long boats off the sand as our men stumbled onboard, Kai wounded, Dax-Varrow who also had a musket round –or two--in him and Lynch who was suddenly shot as he climbed into the boat –and he fell back into the privateers as they rowed.

Our men were now dying everywhere...

All the long boats pulled off the beach with explosions hitting the water next to them as they rowed back to The Venger. Our crews returned to her decks and her cannon was firing at a high tempo, again and again.

I dragged Blythe's body back to the medical tent on the beach —a tent without walls, which was lit by torches. This area was being held and hadn't been evacuated yet but, there was still fighting all around.

"Stop holding me back Johannis!" Merciless was getting his head bandaged and asking the doctor to speed the process up so he could get back into the action.

"Believe me, with your temperament, I don't want ya here one minute longer than you need to be Merciless but, you'll not advance until I'm done with ya. Understand?'

"Damn task master!"

"Quiet! I have rank here." Johannis kept working…

"Yes sir." Merciless said back as if ashamed.

I dropped my weapons, was quickly checked for my injuries, then put outside by Jopo and told to wait. The area around me was covered with wounded. Those that were a higher priority were worked on ahead of me and I watched island natives carrying wounded and helping where they could.

Suddenly Newcastle and some of his war party arrived.

"Get me an Aztec runner." Newcastle yelled.

"Most of them are dead sir –or engaged!"

Newcastle stood among the wounded. "I need any man who can stand or walk."

"Sir?"

Kojo, the orderly stopped him. "Mister Newcastle, sir…none of these men can fight. Surely you can call on someone else?"

"Then get me someone we can spare, that we don't need in a fight…" He said as more explosions lit up the beach near us…

"Mister Reed?" Kojo called out for me.

--Of course.

Again, if I was going to die here, I was going to go out remembered so I forced myself to stand up and I reported. When I did, Newcastle looked at me for a moment, then nodded. It was a look of pride in my actions to volunteer, mixed with gratitude as if he knew he could count on me –at least for something like this-- and it was the first time I had seen a silent reaction from him that was genuine in this regard. "Wipe the blood from your eyes, grab your weapons, it's time to go back to work." Newcastle said.

"Yes sir."

"I need you to make it to the far side of the island with a message for Captain Faulkner."

"Sir?"

"There's heavy fighting there but, he needs to disengage. We have Lord Roberts closing in on us. He needs to launch a fighting retreat, move up his attack and strike the point to close the bay." He handed me a letter scribed by Essex, with The Venger's seal on it –the grim reaper--so there would be no doubting the authenticity of the command. "A fighting retreat back to this point. Understand? Be quick."

I took the letter and as I moved out, I stopped by the medical tent to pick up my weapons. My hands were trembling. Johannis saw this and looked up to me, "What in God's name are you doing?"

"I need to cross the island with a letter, orders for Captain Faulkner."

"Good God," Johannis snapped "The British are all over the place!"

"It's all right. I can make it." I threw my baldric over my shoulder, grabbed my cutlass and pistols and as I did, I looked out at some explosions and fire that rose above the trees in the distance where I was to advance. "I just wish I wasn't going alone."

"You won't be alone!"

I turned to look over my shoulder and there, ready for war, was Mister Barak. "I will go with you." He was wounded, waiting for Jopo to pull some shrapnel out of his shoulder but he got to his feet and stood there with a surprisingly calm attitude. One hand, across his body on the handle of his curved sword, the other, slowly rubbing his chin as if to size me up as he wondered how much work he might have to do to protect me....

I smiled. "All right."

He motioned as if to say, 'after you' and we moved out....

"You're going to have to hurry the hell up, we'll be evacuating back to the ship soon." Johannis shouted as explosions hit the tide next to his medical tent.

--We made a fast exit.

We moved though the wounded coming in –dragged, carried, or crawling towards the medical tent. We moved past some artillery positions, with men making a last stand, digging in, loading rounds and firing, then into the trenches that led to the far side of the island, where the last of our men were fighting. We stepped over some of the dead, and we kept moving forward, keeping low as bullet rounds cut into the area around us.

We passed Tiger and Kato, carrying a wounded Dutch – like half his body had been blown apart by a cannon ball…

We made it to the edge of the line where Arson was in command as more explosions hit the area. This was a dangerous place. Even more dangerous than the rest of the place, but this was the edge of no man's land.

"Reed" Arson shouted, "What the hell are you doing here?" He seemed to resent my presence.

I pointed ahead, "I need to get through there." And just as I said it, some explosions forced the fighting crowd around me to move for cover…

Arson looked at the terrain, then to me, "No one is going through there…the British own that side of the island and the bastards are dangerous."

"Sir, I must." Another blast hit the edge of the trench and we all moved for cover.

"We're about to retreat back to the ship--"

"--I have a message for Captain Faulkner beyond that place, to attack the point—"

"--He knows to attack the point!"

"No sir, we need him to move his attack up, we can't hold." I held up the letter, "This is the order to move up and attack now --and I have to get it to him…"

There was a pause as the men around me seemed to calculate the reality of the situation.

"Want to wait until the moon moves behind the clouds?" Mako asked from his combat position.

"I can't." I said, "I need every moment for my—" I stopped and motioned to Barak behind me "--Our mission."

Jack-Karr looked back to Barak. "You're going with him?"

Barak nodded.

"Some sort of life debt still?" Karr guessed.

Barak gave a slight smile.

Karr looked back towards the action, "That's a dumb rule. You know that don't you?"

"It is my code, though today, I may come to regret it." He said as another explosion lit up the sky.

I looked to him, and suddenly for some strange reason, I was possessed by a divine confidence, "No." I said, "We'll make it."

Arson accepted our decision, "All right then, we'll hold the boats as long as possible."

"Wait for our volley to cover you, then go," Karr said as he looked to the men around us, "Come on lads, let's bring some hellfire."

They moved to reload and position their weapons. Arson stepped to my shoulder, "On my signal Reed."

"Yes sir."

He turned "Light them up!" He arched a grenade in the air, with a streak of smoke behind it and the moment it exploded, they opened up with the guns –Arson slapped my back, and we started running for the tree line....

--Running for our lives really, as musket fire tore up our surroundings....

We moved through the jungle to the edge of a road. The sounds of fighting were all around us. I looked left and right, then to the left and then to the right again.

"What are we waiting for?" Barack asked.

"I'm, I'm just being cautious there are men out there that will try to kill us."

"Yes!" Barack suddenly smiled and said, "God be praised!"

I looked to him....

"The sooner they try to kill you...." He was compelled to explain again, "The sooner I can be relieved of my burden—"

"Yeah, yeah, I know."

"--So, let's hope they try to kill you. Very soon."

We moved inside the tree line along the road, passed a burning military carriage and bodies --British marines, one with a saber blade in his back. There were some dead privateers too. Men from The Black Eagle.

We ducked down as a military carriage and a team of horses, with riders carrying torches, moved past us. "Damn, they've moved cavalry on to the island."

We picked up, moved past some trees on fire and used the thick smoke as cover to cross the road...

On the dark side of the road, we climbed into a trench built by The Eagle's crew, but it was abandoned –cleared in the fighting so we moved down it, cautious at every twist and turn in the trench line so we would not be surprised by the enemy and finally we came to a gun position manned by a few wounded survivors that had been cut off.

--They turned ready to fight, but I quickly held out my hand to identify us. "Venger!" I shouted.

They eased up on their weapons, "Where the hell did you come from?"

"The west side of the island, through there." I motioned behind us.

They looked over my shoulder and seemed to be impressed that we had crossed that section of the island and made it here alive.

"Where can I find Captain Faulkner?"

He shook his head like he didn't know, "Somewhere up the line, the fury is all around us and we're the last one's holding out here but...I think Faulkner's holding the beach."

"—Fighting off a British landing!" Another member of the crew said.

Suddenly, we were attacked as Hessian soldiers collapsed around us and stormed our position.

Sparks flew as blades banged into bayonets and I was gashed across the cheek but, we managed to push, punch and break through the Hessians who piled into our trench and tackled us. Just as we seemed clear of that obstruction, Barak –with blood splattered on his face and robes-- emerged from the fight as a bomb with a lit fuse zipped into the trench and landed close by. It exploded, blowing him back and out of the trench and me back against the rampart wall, gasping for air as the sand rained down.

--Everyone else was killed.

Once I could collect myself, I climbed out of the trench, spit the dirt out of my mouth and moved towards Barack who was lying out in the sand, his robes on fire. "Damn it!" I slapped the flames out of his clothes but, he was gone, motionless. This was a hard, tragic moment for me, to see a man sworn to protect me, dead. I straightened out his body, waved away the smoke from his burning robes and leaned in close to his ear, "Go with God my friend."

Then came the moment where I had to work through my pain –I had to leave him behind and get this message through so I grit my teeth and forced myself to advance and as I moved away from Barak, I moved quicker and quicker, each step becoming more determined and deliberate as if to stamp out the pain of this situation as fast as I could --so I ran and ran, through defense works, over the wounded, through pockets of men, fighting and even shooting at each other at close range. With a desperate sense of determination and dread, I advanced; even a streak of smoke from a grenade zipped across my path –but I kept moving.

I was a target as more grenades started coming towards me --exploding here and there. Then a sudden explosion rocked the terrain and sucked the wind out of my lungs –again—as it lifted me up off the ground and slammed me back down! I just looked up at the sky, motionless as flares shot overhead and I tried to pull myself together, coughing, feeling like my ribs had been broken but before I managed to collect myself, I could sense and hear a reconnaissance platoon, come out of the jungle, and close in around me.

--I had failed at my mission. Right now, the men on The Venger were fighting for their lives with the British closing in on them from all sides – and I failed them! And that failure was what was actually going to kill me, not the blast from the grenade or the busted ribs, but my failure to do the one thing I was asked to do ---get the message to Faulkner and save the ship. As I lay broken on the ground, that thought was what inflicted the most pain- worse than anything these tyrants could do to me.

A marine dropped a bayonet on me. "This one is still alive," he reported as the platoon kept moving. I was pulled to my knees, battered, and resigned to my fate.

"Kill him," said the officer in charge, "And let's be done with it."

"Right."

I was ready to take a bayonet through the back.

"Any last words, pirate?"

"Yeah," I said, "Don't call me that."

The marine paused, as if confused, "What?" he asked, "Pirate?"

Suddenly, I was surprised as words came from me that I had not designed, words that were organic, genuine, and angry but very sincere and frightening –even for me! "I'm not a pirate. That's you ya bastard! --I'm a privateer!"

"A what?" He knew the word but didn't seem to believe I spit it out.

"I'm what your whore-masters in London fear the most --a free man! A privateer and master of my own fate!"

"Wrong!" The marine said, "You were a privateer!" He pulled his weapon back to slam the bayonet through my spine and I grit my teeth and I clamped my eyes shut, hoping it would just be quick when suddenly, I heard something, like a slice through the air –then another...

A moment later, I opened my eyes. There were two bodies dead on the ground and a head rolled next to me. The Brit who had my collar seemed paralyzed. I tried to slowly turn my head and looked up to see Barak's massive saber --like a crescent moon in late afternoon moonlight—up against the man's neck and with just a touch of the blade, blood started to drip from the voice box of this Brit as Barak cut his jugular "It is written that you are to die here today." Barak said with a scratch in his voice as he slowly eased the blade forward expanding the cut in this man's neck and then he pulled the blade back separating his head which dropped to the ground in front of me.

The body dropped in the dust.

I looked away from the horror of the severed head and when I turned, Barak's hand was in front me, to give me a hand up. His robes were still smoking, and he was bleeding from his wounds but stood tough and made a rhythmic, Arabic move with his hand and cocked a half smile. "Allah be praised." He said, "We-are-even-Don-oh-van."

I smiled. "Yes -we are!" Then the magnitude of the situation seeped in, "Damn it!" I realized, "My mission!" I started to move with renewed urgency, "Will you still come with me?" I asked not sure if his work ended with saving my life.

"I will see you get the message through." Barak said and with that, we went back to the action...

We moved from this clearing to Faulkner's fortifications --there was fighting all around. This was the thick of it. The British were already here. Faulkner's men were fighting on land and from his ship. There was a smoking British warship in the tide --destroyed--and his frigate --The Phantom--- was rolling and firing all their guns. In the distance, I could see Rafer's ship also engaged in a pounding match with two British cruisers as a third passed him, moving down the channel towards our position back where The Venger was...

"Captain Faulkner? Where is Captain Faulkner?"

An officer pointed to Faulkner on the beach, his men trying to hold the jungle around us.

We moved towards him at his command table where he was barking orders and sending out messengers and reinforcements...

"Sir?"

He turned towards us, "Well, if it isn't schoolteacher Reed." He said as explosions hit the sand.

"Captain, I need a word--"

"No offense Master Reed but we're a little busy at the moment, as you've no doubt noticed, these British bastards surprised us."

"Sir, I have a message from Captain Essex."

"Well, what is it?" He stopped and looked at Barak, robes still smoking, "You look hurt. See our doctor."

Barak raised his hand as if to say he was alright.

"Sir, the Captain requests that you move up your attack on the point and advance to his position at Skull Rock and the bay, now."

"He what? No offense Reed but the party is right here."

"Sir, he has the main British fleet on him, including Lord Robert's flagship—"

With that Faulkner paused, "Lord Roberts?"

Faulkner's executive officer suddenly looked like a child that was about to have Christmas and he smiled.

"Well," Faulkner straightened up, "I suppose we can kill these second -class Brits later, after we put an end to Lord Roberts, hey De Gaff?"

"It would be better." De Gaff said in his French accent.

"Right. Give the order to disengage. We move at once." Faulkner looked at us, "Well lads, you're welcome to sail back with us."

"Sir, with respect, it will be quicker for us to cut back across the island."

"Suit yourselves but mind ya, these jungles are crawling with Imperialists that don't like us much, so keep a weathered eye out."

"I will sir and sir—" I stopped him as he started to move towards his ship just to verify, "I'll see you at Skull Point sir?"

"Aye, "He smiled, "That you will Reed."

And with that we parted....

We ran through the jungle at breakneck speed, sounds of the fighting all around us. We ran right past British scouts, then past some wounded, then into the next set of trees --we even surprised and ran past a set of officers having their tea but all we got was a confused "Hello?" And they didn't seem interested in running after us.

We made it back to our beach. The hospital was being evacuated, all the survivors and walking wounded were rushing back to The Venger for the final stand. The ship itself was firing and firing as British warships entered the lagoon with explosions hitting the water all around it. One cannon round was sent through a floating barrel of Byzantine, and it exploded, the ocean and the bow of the British warship caught fire. Two more barrels went up, lighting up the sky and catching the side of the other British frigate on fire.

"Damn." I said, "Two warships are already here."

"Here!" Jack-Karr shouted, and he waved us forward from the last departing jolly boat. "Over here! Come on…"

Barak and I ran through the tide towards the boat just off the beach and were helped aboard by Mako, Arson and Johannis as Obal, Kojo, Merciless and a few other survivors rowed….

"Just in time Reed." Arson smiled.

"And here, I thought you could walk on water," Karr joked as he cleaned the blood off his cutlass.

It seemed that the whole of The Caribbean was on fire around us. Cannon fire continued to light up the night sky as we rowed and pulled alongside The Venger. With an almost strange sense of excitement, we almost panicked to get aboard for the final showdown. We got everyone on deck we could from our boat and the other long boats as they pulled up, -- wounded Chinese, some of the fighters from The Eagle, everyone who could make it…

When I made it over the rail –it was like I was home. Our cannons were firing, some of our men were moving from position to position or giving orders. Others like Teague just stood on deck, facing the enemy with his arms crossed waiting for the moment that this engagement would go from a cannon match to a fight he could get back into….

"Welcome back." Jupiter hit me on the back as I crossed the deck.

Bishop fired and reloaded a rail gun, "Ah Reed, you made it." He then turned, to Daws, "Pay up, he made it." --They had bet on my survival.

I smiled, proud of myself and for the first time –when death seemed to be guaranteed, I was not afraid. In fact, I was gripped by a strange sense of calm and a divine, reassuring feeling that I was exactly where I was supposed to be at this moment in time. Shipwrecks and cannibals, slavers, storms and imperialists, this time and place, here, was always where I was supposed to be, and I would not change places with anyone.

Essex heard Bishop call my name and he turned from the map table to see me—

--I nodded. Message delivered! Mission accomplished!

Essex nodded back and his expression was one that said, "Good work."

"I knew I could count on ya Reed." Newcastle said as he passed me at the weapons rack.

"Yes sir." I said with pride.

"Now it's time to choose our fate!"

I got to the rail, and I could see one British ship on fire, running a ground on the beach, another closing in on us, despite the exchange of cannon fire...

"Ah Reed." Duncan-Howe smiled. "You survived your errand."

"I did."

"Good," He looked back at the burning British warships closing in on us.

Just then, Sanjuro moved past and handed me two samurai blades from the armory to replace my missing cutlass. Spare weapons were being handed out to anyone who needed them and with no time to argue about the style, I jammed the two blades into my sash and looked out as a third British cruiser –The Albatross, under the command of Lord Roberts--made it past the inlet, into the bay and started moving towards us....

"This is going to be interesting."

"Yeah." Karr responded. "Maybe you can bore them to death with one of your school lessons."

I had to smile at the wit of his insult. It was the perfect time for it.

I slowly moved down the rail, looking out at the fire and flames as the British warships got closer and I took position next to Teague, Nighthorse and Jaffar.

--I felt I was living in my final few minutes. That 'this' was 'it' and in a moment or two, it would all be over for all of us, and I wanted to go out next to a few heroes.

"Remember when you die today, Reed," Teague looked at me out of the corner of his eye, "It's only 'cause they couldn't' tell you how to live!"

"Get ready!" Newcastle called out as first two ships –on fire— overcame the cannon exchange and closed in.

I looked down, checked my weapons, and saw Nighthorse as he ran his thumb over the blade of his tomahawk, he cleaned some skin and human hair off the sharp end and he caught me watching this and smiled as if to say, 'Here we go.'

Suddenly, the samurai went into a collective yell, swords in the air -- one last battle cry for morale.

The sun started to rise, then out of the smoke came the British warship Boris –wounded, fumbling and clumsy like a dumb animal. There was another exchange of cannon fire, water splashing up on our decks. A smoking cannon ball smashed and stuck into our side, just below me at the rail. I looked down at the smoke, stunned, that it didn't explode.

"Ha. You might survive today after all." Jagger said with a smile.

Suddenly Rajiv hit another net of the Byzantine and it exploded, lighting up half the world. We cheered, fists in the air but this British ship rolled through the flames, taking more cannon fire and it smashed right into us....

We held on, kept our balance, and stayed on our feet as we opened up with muskets just as they tried to storm our decks, blowing them off the ropes and killing some marines, mid-jump. I slammed my samurai sword down on a grappling hook and watched a sailor drop into the water below.

Below deck, Rajiv was pounding at close range, our gunners were right on top of theirs, face to face, firing, exchange after exchange until – BOOM! A hole was ripped into them, just above the water line and in an instant, Java, picked up a half-sized powder barrel and tossed it into the hole that had been blasted into the other ship and it triggered an explosion blowing iron and timber in every direction. Flames crawled up our side to our position at the rail and splinters and smoke blew towards Java below deck as he was blown backwards --Locke, Fallon and Steed were killed.

Rajiv looked into the ripped opening of the enemy ship as water flooded in and their crew began to panic to escape. Their hull began to give way and the ship began to collapse below the waterline. As it shifted, several boarders up top, on the top deck, dropped into the ocean or tumbled onto our planks to be set upon with axes and blades…

Just as we seemed to gain an advantage, with bodies landing all over the deck or getting cut down and kicked into the ocean, the other frigate emerged from the smoke of cannon fire on our opposite/port side....

"Sir!" Whitney pointed and yelled to the Captain just as Essex turned.

Essex dropped to the deck hatch and screamed below "Raaaaaaaajiv!!!!"

Rajiv turned, stepped out of the smoke, and looked up.

"Port side now!!!"

Without even a survey, Rajiv ordered the surviving gunners to shift to the port side cannon and they scrambled across the deck and took up their firing positions, by the time they were ready this warship was just about on top of us...

"FIRE! FIRE! FIRE!" Rajiv screamed and the crews opened up at close range. The damage was high, a good section of the ship was dismantled but that didn't stop it from colliding into us, rocking our decks and throwing some of our crew into the wood.

--We were now in between two ships...

Teague kept his feet, killing men to his left and right. "Mako, Jaffar, port side now!" And with that command, whatever men we could spare from the fighting on the starboard side, turned and charged into the oncoming marines storming the port side rail...

More gunfire, a lantern shattered and somehow Arson ignited and caught fire, he tumbled on to their decks a blaze but, he continued to kill men all around him, flames riding everything into smoke. Tiberius cleaned the deck with this cannonball smashing men in the skull and breaking bones –he even removed the head of a midshipman, separating it from his shoulders as he was hit by musket rounds and was checked by a royal navy lieutenant. Then, Tiberius wrapped the chain of his weapon around the neck of this officer and they both went over the side and into the ocean --the weight of this iron ball pulled this man under the tide --drowning him!

Laban picked a marine up and threw him overboard. He grabbed another to snap his neck and as the marine reached out for help, he lost his fingers and right hand to a samurai sword.

Khan was killed.

The cannon fire --from only a few meters away—continued, deck to deck, our third deck shooting and exchanging fire with their third deck, our second deck with their second deck and so on....

With an exchange of grenades, their top deck seemed to ignite. Many of the crew were on fire. Some jumped overboard or fell below deck as the flames cannibalized their planks and made it collapse.

The gap closed between the ships and the cannon continued to pound each other. Whitney managed to throw a grenade through a gun port door. It exploded and erupted 'something' as there was a chain of additional explosions –the hull was blasted apart, and a hole was blown through the top deck! Splinters pierced the crew –one sailor was caught in the eye with sharp stake of wood as some of their officers were blown overboard.

--All hands on all the decks were thrown forward by the blast. My sword went flying…

I hit the deck and was suddenly grabbed from behind, gripped by the scalp and a blade dropped down to the front of my neck but just as it made contact, crunch –a steel rod smashed into this man's skull, crushing it. Lo swung the rod back up and brought it back down--- boom, splitting this man's skull as blood rained across the deck.

Mister Silence pulled me to my feet, swinging his tomahawk to the left, then to the right, sweeping the deck with it as he took one bullet round after another....

--The dead continued to pile up.

I looked forward to see several marines pile on to Newcastle and without even thinking about it, I rifled a throwing star into the back of one of his attackers. I froze! Amazed at what I had done. The Brit released Newcastle and rocked back as he tried to pull the throwing star out of his back but, he couldn't. He twisted and turned in pain but could not reach the blade. As Newcastle fought his way clear, I stepped forward to close in on this marine but, he was suddenly picked up by Jeddah and thrown over the side.

Suddenly. The Venger was rocked again, like an earthquake and we turned as another ship slammed into us aft. I kept my balance and looked back, the ship that collided with us was low, below our steering deck but, I could see her masts –and suddenly, a series of grappling hooks shot up and gripped The Venger's back rail. Their crew was going to climb up and board us so, I jumped to the back part of the ship, made it to the rail and as I looked down, over the side, I saw a platoon of armed marines starting to climb up towards me....

'What do I do?' Then it clicked. At first, I reached for my knife, then, I turned and looked to the wounded Mister Silence crawling across the planks and held out my hand, he grit his teeth, fought through the pain, raised up and threw his tomahawk into the rail next to me and in a split-second, I pulled it out and slammed it down the on the ropes, cutting all the climbing hooks in place –pound! Pound! Pound --one after another, I looked over the side to see the marines fall and drop below, some landed on top of each other, others landed on the deck, and some hit the railing and tumbled into the ocean.

I moved as a volley of cover fire, ripped up my position. Just as they prepared to make another attempt to climb up, our ship was rocked AGAIN! I turned as the destroyer Albatross had slammed into the sinking British ship Boris and then into us on the port side as it rode the current to smash against our stern.

We now had four enemy ships slammed against us on essentially our four sides with boarders storming our decks at all points –we were trapped!

At my position, the British marines were preparing to make another climb up the back of our ship, covered by constant musket fire which turned the railing around me into splinters. Shaddam arrived to help me hold off the invaders just as a bloody and critically wounded Kato, pierced with several broken cutlass blades, sparked a grenade, and jumped over aft side, dropping through the smoke below with a suicide yell and lighting up their decks with an explosion killing all the climbers and blowing a few other sailors overboard.

Suddenly there were more explosions on this ship pinned to our aft section, but not from grenades –from artillery. I looked ahead, across through the smoke, and I saw The Phantom, firing on this British cruiser as she entered the lagoon.

Faulkner had made it!

--And just as I yelled to celebrate the rescue, The Phantom started to trail smoke and explosions started to drag it below the waterline. British frigates met it at the mouth of the bay and blasted it. Some of Faulkner's men were blown overboard –clothes on fire as the ship started to go down. The British had just smashed our rescue…

I watched --as rockets shot over my head—and The Phantom continued to take a pounding. Faulkner's guns erupted in what seemed like a last stand but the British continued to hammer and hammer and hammer until there wasn't much life left in this ship.

--Through the smoke I could see that The Phantom refused to strike her colors despite explosions lighting up the sky –and the deck-- like lightning all around her. There was the flash of gun fire and grenades exploding in the mist, desperate combat actions meant to scar the British in those last, final moments before the bitter end and just before The Phantom was about to become a massive grave marker in Vulcan Bay the horizon suddenly erupted in a wave of fire!?! Massive explosions on an apocalyptic scale that sent shockwaves forward and rocked our ship, slamming me against the rail.

"What the---?"

As I got back to my feet, I looked and through the smoke and fire I saw…

–Spanish warships!

They fired on the British at the mouth of the bay just in time to save what was left of Faulkner's ship and crew, then they started firing on the ships we were engaged with as they moved into the lagoon. Blasts hit the ship pinned to our aft as I continued to try to repel boarders.

"The Spanish are here!" I screamed so loud as they closed in, that I scratched out my voice and just when I thought we might actually survive this, a British grenade came up over the railing and landed at my feet, "Holy---"

–Shaddam dived on it as it exploded, blowing me off the steering deck and onto the planks of our main deck where I landed with a thud. I couldn't move --I was stunned, gasping! My hearing was gone, replaced by a familiar, loud ringing in my head. I was dizzy, my vision a blur and I was sure I was hurt! I was slow to get my movement back as I tried to turn over to pick myself up off the panels. I looked up and tried to focus as all the action around me seemed to slow down…

--I saw our men in the fight, Newcastle waving his cutlass to direct any survivors into a last desperate action. I saw Irons slowly crawling towards me on the deck, in a heavy trail of dark red blood –it all slowed down! Then I saw Teague. He had just killed a man, then another, then two more, planting his cutlass into the skull of a marine as the British seemed to pile on top of him. He suddenly took a saber through the shoulder and was speared against the mast behind him. I looked on, horrified, broken and in shock as he kicked his attackers back, snapped the blade that had pierced him to the mast and pulled himself off that remaining part of the blade that had stapled him to the wood. He then grabbed a lantern hanging on the spike nearby and looked to his left as a platoon of redcoats came over the rail, then to his right as British marines stormed through the flames, "Time to blow you all to hell!" He hissed and he turned and slammed the lantern into the on-deck powder storage. I watched, helpless as the barrels caught fire and then….

BOOOOOOOOOOOOOOOOOOOOOOOOMMMMMM!

The deck was blown apart and my world went dark.

RESSURECTION.

I woke up on the beach having been blown off the deck and into the water. I was pulled ashore but, not sure by who. Later, I sat up and tried to take my first look at the world around me. I'm not aware how long I had been out but, it was a day at least, maybe two.

Smoke rolled across the landscape. There were bodies in the tide which was red with blood. There were bodies on the sand, one close by, with a cutlass through the back staking him into the beach. More dead were silently floating underwater –like ghosts locked in place-- caught in the rigging or weighed down by lead, equipment, and shrapnel, slow to rise back to the surface….

There, in the lagoon, surrounded by four crippled British warships, The Venger sat in shallow water, damaged with thick black smoke billowing into the sky from her burning deck. A massive shadow on the horizon. I looked at it with the setting sun behind it. The ship had been my home for so many months and seeing this was like the same sense of sadness one would suffer while watching your home on fire. It was a tragic sight and as I looked in silence, tears rolled down my face. Yes, I was relieved I was alive but also shaken by a great sense of loss. Gone was the world around me.

Part of the jungle was on fire, pumping smoke out over the ocean.

The H.M.S. Albatross was half under water and smoke rose silently from her decks as bodies floated all around it. The other three warships were also crippled or destroyed.

The Phantom was a smoking wreck in the distance.

Suddenly a water bucket was in front of me, Mister Defiant was making his way from survivor to survivor under the direction of Hobby, with water, making sure the wounded could drink.

"Thank you." I took some water, and my senses began to improve.

I noticed that he had Wilder's monkey on his shoulder. "I see you've found a friend."

He smiled and nodded before Hobby directed him to move off and get water to the other survivors who littered the beach…

There were light sounds of fighting in the distance, survivors still trying to kill each other on some corner of the island. I just sat on the beach, exhausted, my hand still clamped and locked around the tomahawk, Silence had pitched to me.

Nearby, a young British officer was slowly crawling towards me in pain –a broken Chinese sword stuck in his back but, he was somehow still alive. "Father" he said through the blood and sand in his mouth, "Father, please don't be ashamed of me. I-I tri-tried." He coughed, "I di-did try -to make you proud." He looked up and suddenly seemed to catch sight of me --and the tomahawk. He must have wondered if this was how his life was supposed to end, --thinking of the road he traveled through his youth, joining the navy, proud of himself as an upstanding member of his church, town, and community –now broken and exhausted on a beach, as he undoubtedly waited to see if I was going to plant the tomahawk into his skull…

After a moment, I watched him as he slowly reached out for my hand and by some strange force, I was compelled to reach back out to him and grab hold. Once, I locked hands with him, he seemed to smile slightly –as if relieved he would not die alone. "Tell my father, I'm sorry." He said and I held his hand for what seemed like forever --but what was actually only a few kind moments-- until he faded away.

The tide around him was red. Not blue or white but red with blood.

The wounded and dead being pushed up on the beach. There were so many dead that this small island chain in the Caribbean would be renamed Grave Site, --later Grave Town—Jamaica.

Lord Roberts was bloody and wounded, his ship, long since destroyed in the chaos. Now, all that was left was the shell of a man as he crawled through the tide, leaving a trail of blood as he slowly pulled himself onto the sand, broken, bleeding and exhausted from the fight. His only goal at the time, was to make it to the beach and survive –and just as he did, he stopped and looked up, Teague stood not too far off –cutlass blade still stuck through is shoulder and clothes charred, sending smoke into the air. Behind him a few meters back, Nighthorse and Kon Boar silently stood, splashed with blood from all the fighting, and as Roberts looked up, Newcastle came into view…

He tried to cough out a few words. "I-I am Lord- Lord Roberts. I represent Count Drax. I am Lo-lord Rob-Roberts…."

Newcastle looked at him, "A man who has to remind everyone who he is…is no man at all" and with that, Nighthorse threw Newcastle his rifle and without any ceremony Newcastle aimed, fired, and put a bullet round through his head, killing him –and making Roberts the last casualty of the battle.

Newcastle lowered the smoking gun and though fatigued, near motionless and stoic he said… "That's one hundred you owe me."

Teague's eyes slowly bolted up to him, "Nay," he slowly replied, exhausted, "I let you kill him, the bet is void."

As Robert's body rolled dead in the tide, a Spanish flag came into focus behind him as it was raised on the beach. Newcastle and the others looked over as Vasquez walked forward from the massive flag blowing in the wind --and his officers who raised it-- exhaling tobacco smoke with one hand draped casually over the handle of his cutlass.

Teague raised his glance. Nighthorse remained silent.

"Men of The Venger…I welcome you to what is now… Spanish Jamaica. Please enjoy your stay as our guests." He smiled as Spanish doctors came ashore in long boats. "Mister Teague, you should have that cutlass removed from your shoulder…It could cause an infection." and he motioned to the Spanish medical tent being set up on the beach behind him. "This way if you please."

Teague gave him a nod and stumbled towards the tent for the Spanish doctors to look at him. Newcastle and Vasquez looked at each other, there was a slight smile, the kind of smile one gives when one understands, accepts and is alright with a situation. The debt of Panama had been paid with the islands off Jamaica. So be it, we were even…for now! Newcastle walked towards the medical tent, followed by Nighthorse and when Vasquez's eyes rolled over to Kon Boar --a man he undoubtedly knew had Spanish blood on his hands—he nodded to the Aztec revolutionary as if to say in a casual manner, 'it's alright, you too can get medical care --we'll settle with you at another time,' and Kon Boar was allowed to report to the beach infirmary as well, without any animosity.

In the distance, some doctors and holy men worked through the bodies on the beach. Most were beyond saving but they did what they could. It was Whitney that helped carry me out of the tide and I was eventually taken to a medial tent, surrounded with more wounded and as I was put on a plank in the shade, it was actually a surviving doctor from a British warship that was the first to check on me…

"How do you feel?" he asked with the accent of a gentleman.

I tried to answer but could only shake my head no, like I was unaware of how I felt.

"Well, you're damn lucky to be alive. Rest easy son. I'm going to patch you up."

Here I was, after a fight with the British, being saved by a British doctor –I had come full circle.

In the day and days that followed, Hobby cooked from the beach, the wounded started to get their wits about them, and the Spanish paroled the British survivors with a conventional promise that they leave the Caribbean theater of operations. A common request I was told –since neither side could really accommodate prisoners-- and a common promise that was most likely never kept by any imperialists but, it did keep the peace during the recovery in the days that followed and there was even a strange sense of 'survivor's camaraderie' among most of us. We had the fight –and now it was over.

Construction crews hammered away all day, saving –if they could save –The Venger. Fortunately, the powder storage just blew the deck off and that could be replaced.

I moved slow and breathing was painful but still I wanted to help dig the graves, so I worked with Bishop, Whitney and even some British survivors and Spanish officers to dig grave after grave, through the sunset and under torches throughout the night into the next morning. The British helped without malice. They were respectful when they helped lower our dead into a grave and we acted in kind when we helped them bury their friends.

We made crosses where appropriate, marked some with the star of David and we made funeral pyres when called for and no one said a word about it that was negative.

This was the right thing to do.

I looked down at the crosses and thought of the 'no quarter' order issued on New Haven Island. The actions that led to it and the actions that followed because of it. All the death, destruction, and sadness. A cycle of disaster. A world out of control at times. I don't know what it was but, this battle was an experience that changed me more than any other. Not just surviving it but, the graves. As always, it could have been my lifeless body they covered in sand. A lonely cross on some unknown beach to mark the fact that I even had lived --that I had been a man in this world with a heart and actions. Only a sad cross in this distant place no one would ever visit.

--Was this how it all ended for men like me? Buried and forgotten? Would anyone even know that these men even lived at all? That they had done anything worthwhile?

Lynch was lowered into a grave as was Bliss Monroe, Locke and Bolt –though half his body was missing from shrapnel—there wasn't much left of Fury who saved my life when he pushed me into the jolly boat ahead of himself or Hayte or Shaddam who dove on a grenade to save the quarter deck --and. some of us were still missing, presumed to be housed under the sea someplace so, we made up the distance with prayers and there was no religious conflict.

The battle zone was treated like holy ground. Bishop and the Protestants were allowed their say –as were our Moors with no disdain from the

Spanish Catholics. I thought this bit of tolerance may have been under orders by Vasquez but, in truth, after what all of us had been through, no one cared what another man's religion was any more.

The smoke from the battle could be seen for hundreds of leagues and as a result, ships sailed into the area to see what service they could provide. For the most part, they helped with the wounded and removed British casualties to travel to a nearby outpost or hospital.

I sat on the beach after the funerals and a British marine sat down next to me. There was no division, just two survivors. He had a small amount of tobacco and he offered to share it. "Would you like some?"
I nodded.

"It's sour from the salt water." He said, as if embarrassed, "Terribly sorry."

"No matter," I said.

He lit a pipe then handed it to me. The tide rolled up towards us and he said, "It seems strange how quiet it is here now but, this is actually a very pretty place."

I took notice of his words and looked around, it was as if I had seen this world around me for the first time and in fact --it was beautiful! Amazing what you miss when you're preoccupied with the art of killing everyone around you...

He suddenly spoke up again, as if looking for the right words to start a small conversation, "My mother back home has a garden... with roses in it." He said this with a touch of child-like innocence. "Some other flowers too. Tulips and such. It's a peaceful place, not like this but, in its own beautiful way."

I could almost imagine it, "I'm sure it is." I said, still somewhat exhausted but I smiled at the thought of this...

"Aye, it is. I used to take tea there." Then, in an almost apologetic tone he said, "I'm sure that sounds quaint to an adventurer like yourself. You have no use for gardens," he said, "But I will say, there is no place more beautiful than your mother's garden." He smiled, "I had hoped to finish my enlistment and return to take care of her ya see, since my father died of typhoid, and she has no one else." He laughed, "Good thing I wasn't killed in this fight for then she'd be alone."

I thought of this possibility for a moment and the thought made me sad for him.

He paused, smoked then said, "Do-do you have a garden at your home?"

I pointed to The Venger, smoking in the bay "That was my home."

He looked and his tone changed with a touch of regret, "Ah, I am sorry. Still glad to have survived. I have only minor injuries myself. My friend was hit in the back with a Japanese blade of all things" He chuckled, "Then he was thrown overboard and had to swim to shore and wait for the doctors to stitch him up."

I heard this and a sense of relief washed over me –since I was the one who threw the blade into his friend's back.

Suddenly a bosun called him and others around to the long boats to board a visiting frigate for a trip to some unknown place –a hospital or an outpost of some sort.

"Well," he said as he picked himself up and dusted off the sand, "Good luck to ya." He held out his hand...

I looked at him, "And to you." I smiled and we shook hands and as I watched him walk off the words 'A garden is the most beautiful place in the world' was repeated in my head. A garden? Who were we really fighting? They certainly seemed innocent enough when they stood on their own –away from the political Shakespearian machine. I wondered if they even knew what the killing was about.

Later, I worked with Mister Crowe and the carpenters to salvage parts off the dead British frigates and use them in our work to rebuild our own ship and I was beginning to sense that The Venger would sail again but, whether you believe your future is written or not, what happened next seemed so unexpected --yet so fitting for my soul-- that it felt like an act of fate and as I was hammering deck planks on to the Venger's superstructure, my name was called…

"Mister Reed." Essex barked from his command tent on the quarterdeck, stopping me in my work.

I stood up, turned, and ran over to where the Captain stood with Mister Harrow, Vasquez, Newcastle, Thorn –and his charts-- Lincoln and a few British officers, unaware of what he wanted.   "Yes Captain?"

He looked at me, then pointed to a ship in the lagoon, that had come to offer assistance in the aftermath of the fight. "That ship is The Endeavor."

I looked at the ship towards the sun, then glanced back to Essex for more details. "Yes Captain?"

He smiled then slowly said, "She's about to set sail for New York."

"Yes." I turned again, blocked out the sun with my hand to see the ship again, then turned back to the Captain not sure if I understood…

Then, after a long pause, Essex finally added, "There's room for one more."

"Sir?" I stopped, still unaware what he meant, then suddenly, it clicked, and I became overwhelmed with the emotion of this bittersweet possibility --but I was afraid I may have mis-heard or misunderstood so I remained in place gripped by a building sense of enthusiasm, until The Captain confirmed that I had the right idea.

"Your passage has been paid, compliments of Mister Harrow here as a thank you for your service."

"Mister Harrow?" I looked to him…

Harrow nodded, "The world needs men like you to help build a future. You'll do more good there, than with us."

"And if I may say," The Captain added, "You're long overdue."

Harrow smiled, "The classrooms await."

"But?"

"—This is your chance to tell the world what you really know and…be of real service."

"Gather your things Reed," Newcastle smiled and decided it best to cut through this sentimental moment with an order, "Their waiting…."

Speechless, I reflected on the prayer I made before the fighting –where I promised that if I survived the battle, that I would make the world around me a better place –and with a sense of divine guidance and excitement, I did as I was ordered. With help from Whitney, I picked up my locker and bag below deck...

"I don't really make friends often..." Whitney said as he tried to work the rest of his feelings into words, "I'll miss ya Reed. Thanks for...teachin' me how to read and, being kind to me."

I looked at him, realizing that I had made some small positive contribution to this young man's life, "Use it, will you." And we shook hands.

I collected my pay with a nod from Mister Lincoln, and as I came back on deck, I paused, compelled to say something, but ...I just couldn't muster the right words. The three officers just looked at me, like proud parents sending a son out into the world for the first time so I gave a thankful nod and a wave, and I made for the rail, where Teague, Nighthorse and Watson were working....

"On your way back to the world Mister Reed?" Watson asked as he watched me approach...

"Aye." I smiled....

"Well, the world needs a few more thinkers." He said as he put his hook to his hat to salute a goodbye.

I looked to Teague who was salvaging weapons, "Mister Teague..." again, I was compelled to say something even if I wasn't sure what exactly....

Teague paused, looked at me and true to his character he cut right to it, "I'm working here, Reed."

"I-I...I'm leaving and I...I just wanted to say thank you...for everything."

"Back to the classroom?" He peered at me.

I gave a look that said anything was possible....

He suddenly pointed at me, "Finally...you're going to a place where you actually could be dangerous." And I could swear there was a slight – almost wicked—grin from this legend.

In any event, I smiled back, and at the launch, Mister Jaffar stopped me. "You go back to your world now?" He said in his deep, scratchy voice.

I answered with a touch of excitement. "I do."

"All is as God wills it." He said, he then placed his hand over his heart and said, "I will pray for you, schoolteacher."

I smiled and put out my hand, "And I, for you."

He nodded and just like that, the Moors walked off, back to their duties as if I never existed.

I looked around the ship one last time, though under re-construction, I knew, that the world of The Venger would continue with new destinations and adventures and I climbed down into the long boat with one last wave to Duncan-Howe, Whitney, Java, and others who stood at the rail to see me off. I then took my seat and as we rowed away, I could not bring myself to look back from that point, for my emotions had taken hold, fate had taken grip and tears were now running down my face.

--For I knew that I would never see these men again.

AFTERMATH

With snow landing on the edge of the windowsill, I turned to watch Mister Dearden –Editor N' Chief of H.N.C Brands and Literature—looking through the last of Lynch's colorful illustrations. He then read the final paragraphs of my writings and looked up at me, eyes fixed above his spectacles as he smiled…

"It is an interesting story to be sure. Adventurous to say the least."

I gave a half-hearted nod in agreement and reached for the glass of red wine that had been offered, Dearden taking notice of the scars on my knuckles, wrists, and hands…and again he smiled as if impressed by this unlikely --and favorable-- situation….

"I can offer you six hundred pounds…. plus, ten percent of any profits derived from this text and eight percent of any rights sold regarding such…"

"Such as?"

"A play, opera, Sunday serial in The Weekly Londoner, items like that."

"No operas please." I said, remembering how my shipmates had reacted when we saw one together in the Far East.

"No?"

"Best not." I smiled. I then stood and looked out the window in thought for a moment thinking of my friends –my family of The Venger—their faces, their voices, the sound of their laughter --some of them now gone.

Dearden misread this as disappointment in his offer. "I can make it fifteen hundred pounds for a first edition and twenty percent of any profits."

I turned to him, "Agreed."

He quickly wrote with his quill in a manner that conveyed excitement, "Here, sign here…" He handed me the quill and opened up a cash box where he removed two bags of coins "You may count it but, have no fear for I would be afraid to shortchange such a dangerous man as yourself."

I stopped writing when he said this --was this what people would think? It was an uncomfortable thought to be sure but, one I would have to live with. I then continued to finish my signature and took the payment…

"You must promise," he pointed as an after-thought, "To allow me a first look at anything else you write…."

"I will."

Moments later, we stood at his office entrance, I looked around at the New York streets --covered in snow—civilization –or society like this-- now seemed very foreign to me. "And what will you do now, Mister Reed, return to school and instruction?"

I thought to myself, about how little I actually knew of the world when I was a teacher and how much I seemed to know now and that the profession –that of a teacher-- no longer seemed right for me. "No," I confessed. "My future is…for now…uncharted."

"Uncharted!" He repeated with a smile and a touch of excitement, "Such a pirate term!"

"As you now know Mister Dearden, I was never a pirate…just a humble privateer."

"Well," Dearden said as he extended his hand, "I'm sure adventure will find you…."

I walked the cold, snow covered streets, but I could not stay. Civilization wasn't my place anymore. I no longer felt at home among big brick buildings, commerce, and a class system so I booked transit on a merchantman and headed south. A new man, with a new outlook, I rode the deck and returned to that part world of wide-open spaces. I found the woman who had made such a powerful impression on me, once upon a time, when I first went ashore in The Caribbean and without fear of what society would think, I asked her to be part of my life.

--For I now, lived by a new set of 'learned' principals that a man's past was his past and that was not to be held against him –and woman's past was her own as well and when a new chapter begins, she should not be judged by it.

I bought a small coconut plantation where social standards of the day had no hold over me for, I had learned to love what was important, to live by my own rules, not the ones society had framed around us…

---And I was a better man for it.

THE END

ABOUT THE AUTHOR

Ethan Dettenmaier started as a courier at Warner Bros. Studios before working in Feature Development where he worked with Writer/Director John Milius (Apocalypse Now, Conan The Barbarian, Red Dawn) Producer Steven Ruether (Pretty Woman, Under Siege) and later did some script work for Steven Seagal, Producer Jon Divens (Blade, Blade 2) and Dark Horse Comics. (writing scripts for Voodoo Man and King Tiger).

He is currently based at Universal Studios and is the Producer of Combat Radio/Brigade-Radio-One and is an advocate for children battling NMO/NMOSD and pediatric cancer and runs a charity with his wife Lota and daughter Shawn (More at: www.make-the-world-a-better-place.org)

www.ingramcontent.com/pod-product-compliance
Lightning Source LLC
Chambersburg PA
CBHW060948280326
41935CB00009B/655